沖縄文化への招待

Sketches of Okinawa World

宮城　信夫

MIYAGI Nobuo

聞得大君の簪（儀礼の際に使われた大簪）
（口絵 1-23、P50 参照）
Kikoe Okimi's large hairpin used for ceremonies
(Frontispiece 1-23, See page 50)

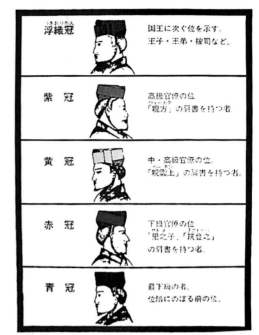

冠（口絵 1-27、P60 参照）
Crowns (Frontispiece 1-27, See page 60)

組踊り
玉城朝薫の代表作「二童敵討」
の一場面（国立劇場おきなわ）
（口絵 3-16、P116 参照）

Kumi-odori, a scene from
Tamagusuku Chokun's
masterpiece Nidou-tekiuchi
(National Theater Okinawa)
(Frontispiece 3-16,See page 116)

琉舞
「四つ竹」。四つ竹の清らかに済ん
だ響きに合わせ、華やかな衣装と
大輪の花笠を被って演じられる祝
儀舞踊（口絵 3-18、P117 参照）

Ryubu "Yotsudake," a celebration
dance performed to the pure and
clean sound of yutsudake (four
pieces of bamboo), wearing gorgeous
costumes and large hanagasa (hats
with flower-shaped hats)
(Frontispiece 3-18, See page 118)

琉装（口絵 3-19、P118 参照）
Ryusou (Frontispiece 3-19,See page 118)

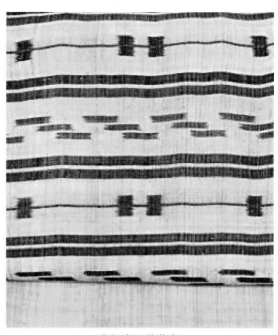

喜如嘉の芭蕉布
（口絵 3-20、P119 参照）
Bashou-fu in Kijoka
(Frontispiece 3-20,See page 119)

南風原町の琉球絣 (第 32 代、ミセス
ブーゲンビレア絣の女王・具志堅萌
子さん）（口絵 3-21、P120 参照）
Ryukyu-*kasuri*:The 32nd, Mrs. Bougainvillea
Kasuri Queen, Moeko Gushiken
(Frontispiece 3-21,See page 120)

紅型（琉球王朝時代には、その着用すべき生地の地色、紋様は身分ごとに明確に区分さ
れていた。黄色は、王族のみが着用を認められた尊い色とされていた。これは、中国の
皇帝が使用する色が黄色だったことに由来するといわれる）（口絵 3-22、P121 参照）
Bingata(During the Ryukyu Dynasty, the ground colors and patterns of the fabrics to be
worn were clearly classified according to status. Yellow was considered a noble color
that only royalty was allowed to wear. This is said to have originated from the fact that
the color used by Chinese emperors was yellow) (Frontispiece 3-22,See page 121)

東道盆（とぅんだーぶん）。琉球王国の宮廷料理の一つ、又はそれを盛り付ける漆塗りの蓋付きの盆のこと（口絵 4-24、P167 参照）

Tundaa-Bun(One of the court dishes of the Ryukyu Kingdom, or a tray with a lacquered lid on which to serve food (Frontispiece 4-24, See page 168)

沖縄そば（口絵 4-24-1、P168 参照）
Okinawa-*soba*(Frontispiece 4-24-1, See page 168)

ゴーヤーチャンプルー（口絵 4-24-2、P169 参照）
Gouyaa-Champuruu(Frontispiece 4-24-2, See page 169)

イナムドゥチ（口絵 4-24-3、P170 参照）
Ina-muduchi(Frontispiece 4-24-3, See page 170)

ジューシー（口絵 4-24-4、P170 参照）。赤と黄色の箸は「うめーし」と呼ばれる沖縄の伝統的な箸。赤は漆（うるし）で滑り止めの役割、黄色はウコンで着色することで殺菌、抗菌効果があるといわれる
Juushii(Frontispiece 4-24-4, See page 170).Red and yellow chopsticks are traditional Okinawan chopsticks called *umeeshi*.Red is lacquer, which prevents slipping, and yellow is colored with turmeric, which is said to have sterilizing and antibacterial effects

中味汁（口絵 4-24-5、P171 参照）
Nakami-jiru(Frontispiece 4-24-5, See page 171)

山羊汁（口絵 4-24-6、P171 参照）
Yagi-jiru(Frontispiece 4-24-6,See page 171)

豆腐餻（口絵 4-24-7、P172 参照）
Toufu-yoh(Frontispiece 4-24-7, See page 172)

ゴーヤー（口絵 4-24-8、P172 参照）
Gouyaa(Bitter melon),(Frontispiece 4-24-8, See page 172)

島豆腐（口絵 4-24-9、P173 参照）
Shima-doufu(Frontispiece 4-24-9, See page 173)

タコライス（口絵 4-24-11、P174 参照）
Taco-rice(Frontispiece 4-24-11, See page 174)

クーブイリチー (口絵 4-24-10、P173 参照）
Kuubu-irichii(Frontispiece 4-24-10, See page 174)

タンナファクルー（口絵 4-27-2、P177 参照）
Tan'nafa-*kuruu*(Frontispiece 4-27-2, See page 177)

ちんすこう（口絵 4-27-3、P178 参照）
Chinsukou(Frontispiece 4-27-3, See page 178)

サーターアンダギー（口絵 4-27-4、P178 参照）
Saataa-andagii(Frontispiece 4-27-4, See page 179)

山城まんじゅう（口絵 4-27-5、P179 参照）
Yamagusuku-*manjuu*
(Frontispiece 4-27-5, See page 179)

天妃前まんじゅう（口絵 4-27-5、P179 参照）
Tempinumee-*manjuu*(Frontispiece 4-27-5, See page 179)

のまんじゅう（口絵 4-27-5、P179 参照）
Noh-manjuu(Frontispiece 4-27-5, See page 179)

きっぱん（口絵 4-27-6、P180 参照）
Kippan(Frontispiece 4-27-6, See page 180)

チンビン（口絵 4-27-7、P180 参照）
Chimbin(Frontispiece 4-27-7, See page 181)

ポーポー。中に油味噌が入っている（口絵4-27-8、P181参照）
Poh-poh, there is oil *miso* inside(Frontispiece 4-27-8, See page 181)

ハブ（口絵5-1-1、P186参照）
Habu(Frontispiece 5-1-1, See page 186)

マングース（環境省やんばる自然保護官事務所）
（口絵5-1-2、P186参照）
Mongoose(Frontispiece 5-1-2, See page 187)

カンムリワシ
タカ目タカ科の鳥で、全長は 55 ～ 76 ㎝。ヒマラヤ、インド、南アジア、台湾、中国南部に分布するが、日本では主に石垣島と西表島に生息する。全身の羽毛は褐色で、翼や腹面には白い斑点が入る。頭上は白と黒のまだらで後頭の羽毛が冠状になることからこの名が付いている。食性は動物食で、両生類、爬虫類、甲殻類、昆虫等を捕まえるが特にヘビを好む。1977 年に国の特別天然記念物、1993 年には国内希少野生動植物に指定された。
Kanmuri-washi (Crested serpent eagle)
A bird of the hawk family, 55-76 cm in length. It is distributed in the Himalayas, India, South Asia, Taiwan, and southern China, but in Japan it is found mainly on Ishigaki and Iriomote Islands. Plumage is all brown, with white spots on the wings and abdomen. It is so named because its head is speckled with black and white and its occipital feathers are crowned. They are zoophagous, feeding on amphibians, reptiles, crustaceans, insects, etc., with a particular preference for snakes. It was designated a national special natural monument in 1977 and a domestic rare wild animal in 1993.

イリオモテヤマネコ(口絵5-1-3、P187参照)
Iriomote *yamaneko*(Frontispiece 5-1-3, See page 188)

ヤンバルクイナ(口絵5-1-4、P188参照)
Yambaru-*kuina*(Frontispiece 5-1-4, See page 188)

ノグチゲラ
(口絵5-2-3、P191参照)
Noguchi-*gera*
(Frontispiece 5-2-3, See
page 191)

デイゴ(口絵5-2-1、P190参照)
Deigo (Frontispiece 5-2-1, See page 190)

久米の五枝の松(口絵5-2-2、P190参照)
Kume'no-Goeda'no-Matsu(Kumejima Town)
(Frontispiece 5-2-2, See page 190)

グルクン(口絵5-2-4、P192参照)
Gurukun(Frontispiece 5-2-4, See page 192)

オオゴマダラ(口絵5-2-5、P192参照)
Ohgomadara(Frontispiece 5-2-5, See page 192)

はじめに

　沖縄県はユーラシア大陸の東端、太平洋に浮かぶ東西約1,000km、南北約400kmの広大な海域にまたがり、大小約160の島々（有人島は約40）からなる小さな島国である。東シナ海をはさんだ西側には台湾や中国大陸、北側には日本列島の九州、南側にはフィリピン、そして東に接する太平洋を遠く隔てると北アメリカ大陸がある。県都・那覇市を中心とする半径2,000km～2,500kmの圏内には東アジア諸国・諸地域の主要都市が位置している。この地理的位置は、各地からこの小さな島々に様々な恵みをもたらす一方で、中国、日本、アメリカなどの大国による政治的・軍事的利用の口実とされ、その歴史に深い影を落としてきたのも又、事実である。

　アジアの交差点と言われるこの地には、かつて「琉球王国」という独立国が存在した。琉球人は中国皇帝から王国として承認され、その権威を背景に東アジアの中継貿易国として発展した。14世紀末から16世紀にかけて繰り広げられ、大交易時代と呼ばれる約150年間

那覇港に入港した進貢船（沖縄県立博物館・美術館所蔵）
A Tribute Ship in Naha Port

がその時代である。日本が南方貿易を始めたのが16世紀後半。琉球王国はそれより1世紀以上も前から東南アジアで盛大な交易を展開していたのである。

　明治政府による廃藩置県後の琉球王国滅亡（1879年）や1945年の悲惨な地上戦、その後の27年間におよぶ米国による統治、今なお続く米軍基地の過重負担を強いられている沖縄県は、他府県とは大きく異なる歴史や文化に加え、独自の県民性を持っている。周りの大国に翻弄されながらウチナーンチュは、「ウチナータイム」や「テーゲー」、「ナンクルナイサ」などのキーワードに代表されるような狭い島社会における良好な人間関係を維持する方法を生み出した。長い歴史の中で、物事に対して万事おおらかな精神で臨んできたのである。

　コバルトブルーの海や抜けるような青空のほか、トロピカルな自然や温暖な気候、観光客をもてなすホスピタリティ。沖縄にはこれらの観光地としての必要な資源が十分にある。それらに魅了されて来沖する国内外からの観光客数は着実に増加を続け、今や世界有数の観光地・ハワイをも凌駕している。観光地としての沖縄を紹介する出版物も数多く発行されている。

　他方で、沖縄には前述したような暗い過去を併せ持つ別の顔がある。特に外国から訪れる観光客には別の面を持つ沖縄の素顔も知って欲しいのだが、沖縄県など行政側からのその観点でのアプローチは十分とは感じられない。今日でも沖縄関連の書籍発行は絶えることがないが、歴史や文化など本土と大きすぎる差異が理由なのか、「難解過ぎる」という多くの読者からの声を耳にする。県内における学校教育の現場でも十分な指導がなされているとは言い難く、沖縄の独特な歴史や文化、民俗について県民でさえも間違って理解しているケースが散見される。

　本書は、他府県民のみならず沖縄県民や、琉球王国にルーツを持つ世界のウチナーンチュたちの沖縄への理解を深めるため、独断で選んだ幾つかのキーワードの概説を試みたものである。本書では日常生活の中で県民が話題にする項目を取り上げており、沖縄に興味を持つ読者の手引き書として学習に役立ててほしい。

Preface

Okinawa Prefecture is a small island nation consisting of about 160 islands of various sizes (about 40 inhabited), spanning a wide area of about 1,000 km from east to west and 400 km from north to south in the Pacific Ocean, at the eastern tip of the Eurasian continent. To the west across the East China Sea are Taiwan and mainland China, to the north is Kyushu in the Japanese archipelago, to the south is the Philippines, and far across the Pacific Ocean bordering the east is the continent of North America. Major cities in East Asian countries and regions are located within a radius of 2,000 km to 2,500 km from Naha, the prefectural capital. While this geographical location has brought various blessings to these small islands from various parts of the world, it has also cast a deep shadow over their history as a pretext for political and military use by major powers such as China, Japan, and the United States.

This land, known as the crossroads of Asia, was once home to an independent country called the Ryukyu Kingdom. The Ryukyuans were recognized as a kingdom by the Chinese emperor and developed as a transit trading nation in East Asia on the back of their authority. The period that unfolded from the end of the 14th century to the 16th century was about 150 years, known as the Great Trading Age. Japan began its southern trade in the late 16th century. The Kingdom of Ryukyu was engaged in grand trade in Southeast Asia more than a century earlier.

After the Meiji government abolished the Ryukyu Kingdom in 1879, followed by the disastrous ground war in 1945, the subsequent 27 years of U.S. rule, and the continuing overburden of U.S. military bases, Okinawa Prefecture has a history and culture that differs greatly from other prefectures, as well as a unique prefectural character. *Uchinanchu*, despite being at the mercy of the larger nations around us, has developed ways to maintain good human relations in our small island society, as represented by such key words as *uchina*-time, *tee-gee*, and *nankuru-naisa*. Throughout our long history, we have always approached everything with a generous spirit.

In addition to the cobalt blue sea and clear blue sky, Okinawa has all the necessary resources for a tourist destination: tropical nature, mild climate, and hospitality that welcomes tourists. The number of domestic and foreign tourists attracted to Okinawa has been steadily increasing, and now surpasses even Hawaii, one the world's leading tourist destination. Many publications have been published to introduce Okinawa as a tourist destination.

On the other hand, Okinawa has another face with a dark past as mentioned above. I would like tourists, especially those from overseas, to get to know the other face of Okinawa, but I don't think the prefectural authorities have taken enough approaches from that perspective. Even today, there is no end to the number of books published on Okinawa, but many readers say that they are too difficult to understand, perhaps because of the huge differences in history and culture between Okinawa and the mainland. Even in the field of school education in the Okinawa prefecture, it is difficult to say that sufficient guidance is being given, and there are cases where even prefectural residents have a wrong understanding of the unique history, culture, and folklore of Okinawa.

This book is an attempt to present an overview of a few key words that I have chosen at my own discretion to help not only people from other prefectures, but also Okinawans and *uchinanchu* around the world who have roots in the Ryukyu Kingdom to better understand Okinawa. This book covers topics that Okinawans talk about in their daily lives, and should be used as a guide for readers who are interested in learning about Okinawa.

目　次

第1章　歴史 ‥‥‥‥‥‥‥‥‥‥‥‥ 18

1.琉球・沖縄史の時代区分 ‥‥‥‥ 19

2.先史時代 ‥‥‥‥‥‥‥‥‥‥‥‥ 20

3.山下洞人 ‥‥‥‥‥‥‥‥‥‥‥‥ 21

4.港川人 ‥‥‥‥‥‥‥‥‥‥‥‥‥ 21

5.サキタリ洞遺跡、世界最古の貝製釣り針 ‥‥‥‥ 22

6.貝塚時代 ‥‥‥‥‥‥‥‥‥‥‥‥ 23

7.マキヨ ‥‥‥‥‥‥‥‥‥‥‥‥‥ 24

8.間切り ‥‥‥‥‥‥‥‥‥‥‥‥‥ 25

9.按司 ‥‥‥‥‥‥‥‥‥‥‥‥‥‥ 26

10.グスク時代 ‥‥‥‥‥‥‥‥‥‥ 26

11.グスク・石積み技法・城跡 ‥‥‥‥ 27

　①グスク　②石積み技法　③今帰仁城跡　④座喜味城跡
　⑤勝連城跡　⑥中城城跡　⑦浦添城跡　⑧首里城
　⑨知念城跡　⑩ミントン城跡　⑪玉城城跡　⑫島添大里城跡
　⑬豊見城城跡　⑭島尻大里城跡

12. 英祖王統以前の王統 ‥‥‥‥‥ 39

　①天帝氏王統　②天孫氏王統　③舜天王統

13. 南走平家 ‥‥‥‥‥‥‥‥‥‥‥ 41

14. 久米(閩人)三十六姓 ‥‥‥‥‥ 42

15. 三山時代 ‥‥‥‥‥‥‥‥‥‥‥ 43

16. 冊封体制と進貢貿易 ‥‥‥‥‥ 44

　①冊封体制　②進貢（朝貢）貿易　③冊封使

17.天使館 ‥‥‥‥‥‥‥‥‥‥‥‥ 46

18.天妃宮 ‥‥‥‥‥‥‥‥‥‥‥‥ 46

19.大交易時代 ‥‥‥‥‥‥‥‥‥‥ 47

20.長虹堤 ‥‥‥‥‥‥‥‥‥‥‥‥ 48

21.三司官 ‥‥‥‥‥‥‥‥‥‥‥‥ 49

22.ノロ（ヌル、ヌール） ‥‥‥‥‥‥ 50

23.聞得大君、三阿母志良礼 ‥‥‥ 50

24.聞得大君の「御新下り」儀式 ‥‥ 51

25.位階制度 ‥‥‥‥‥‥‥‥‥‥‥ 52

　①位階　②王族　③王子　④按司　⑤上級士族　⑥親方
　⑦親雲上　⑧一般士族　⑨里主　⑩筑登之　⑪子、仁屋

26.平民 ‥‥‥‥‥‥‥‥‥‥‥‥‥ 58

　①百姓と地方役人　②地頭代　③夫地頭　④捌理　⑤文子

27.帕(冠) ‥‥‥‥‥‥‥‥‥‥‥‥ 60

28.ジーファー(簪) ‥‥‥‥‥‥‥‥ 61

29.カタカシラ ‥‥‥‥‥‥‥‥‥‥‥ 62

30.日琉同祖論 ‥‥‥‥‥‥‥‥‥‥ 62

31.薩摩藩島津氏による琉球侵攻 ‥ 63

32.喜安日記 ‥‥‥‥‥‥‥‥‥‥‥ 64

33.首里王府の編纂書 ‥‥‥‥‥‥ 65

　①おもろさうし　②歴代宝案　③中山世鑑　④中山世譜
　⑤琉球国由来記　⑥球陽

34.琉球王国の英傑たち ‥‥‥‥‥ 69

　①舜天王②英祖王　③察度王　④尚巴志王　⑤尚円王

35.沖縄の五偉人 ‥‥‥‥‥‥‥‥‥ 74

　①儀間親方真常　②羽地朝秀　③名護親方寵文
　④具志頭親方文若　⑤宜湾親方朝保

36.野国総管 ‥‥‥‥‥‥‥‥‥‥‥ 77

37.琉球王国の有名な武将 ‥‥‥‥ 78

　①護佐丸　②阿麻和利　③鬼大城　④オヤケアカハチ
　⑤謝名親方利山

38.琉球王国の著名な女性たち ‥‥ 82

　①百度踏揚　②宇喜也嘉(オギヤカ)　③真壁按司加那志
　④サンアイイソバ

琉球王国の歴代王統‥‥‥‥‥‥‥ 86

第２章　琉球から沖縄へ ‥‥‥‥ 87

1.琉球と沖縄 ‥‥‥‥‥‥‥‥‥‥‥ 87

2.人頭税 ‥‥‥‥‥‥‥‥‥‥‥‥‥ 88

　①人頭税　②人頭税廃止運動

3.廃藩置県 ‥‥‥‥‥‥‥‥‥‥‥‥ 89

4.頑固党と開化党 ‥‥‥‥‥‥‥‥‥ 90

5.琉球処分 ‥‥‥‥‥‥‥‥‥‥‥‥ 91

6.番所 ‥‥‥‥‥‥‥‥‥‥‥‥‥‥ 92

7.バジル・ホール ‥‥‥‥‥‥‥‥‥ 93

8.ベッテルハイム ‥‥‥‥‥‥‥‥‥ 93

9.ペリー艦隊の来琉 ‥‥‥‥‥‥‥ 94

　①背景　②ペリー提督
　③ウィリアム・ボード事件、泊外人墓地

10.ジョン万次郎 ‥‥‥‥‥‥‥‥‥ 97

11.村屋 ……………………………………… 98

12.謝花昇 …………………………………… 99

13.方言札 …………………………………… 100

14.軽便鉄道 ………………………………… 101

第3章　文化・史跡 ………………… 102

1.ニライカナイ …………………………… 102

2.アマミキヨ・シネリキヨ、アマミキヨ族 ………… 103

　①伝説 ②南方から北上した海洋民族説

　③本島北部上陸説　④大陸からの渡来集団説

3.ガマ(洞窟) ……………………………… 105

4.御嶽、イベ(イビ) ……………………… 106

5.神アシャギ ……………………………… 107

6.根屋(ニーヤー)、根人(ニーンチュ) ………… 108

7.根神(ニーガン) ………………………… 108

8.火の神 …………………………………… 109

9.オナリ神、オナリ神信仰 ……………… 110

10.斎場御嶽 ………………………………… 110

11.久高島 …………………………………… 112

12.東御廻り ………………………………… 113

13.今帰仁上り(今帰仁御廻り) ………… 113

14.キジムナー ……………………………… 114

15.空手・古武術 …………………………… 115

16.組踊り …………………………………… 116

17.琉歌 ……………………………………… 116

18.琉舞 ……………………………………… 117

19.琉装 ……………………………………… 118

20.芭蕉布 …………………………………… 119

21.琉球絣 …………………………………… 120

22.紅型 ……………………………………… 121

23.シーサー ………………………………… 121

　①石獅子 ②獅子舞

24.ウェーキ(ウェーキー) ……………… 123

25.毛遊び …………………………………… 124

26.針突き …………………………………… 124

27.石敢當 …………………………………… 125

28.土帝君 …………………………………… 126

29.ビジュル信仰 …………………………… 127

30.首里城周辺の史跡 ……………………… 127

　①龍潭 ②円鑑池 ③弁財天堂 ④円覚寺跡 ⑤園比屋武

　御嶽、園比屋武御嶽石門 ⑥弁ヶ嶽 ⑦御茶屋御殿跡

　⑧万国津梁の鐘 ⑨天山陵跡 ⑩玉陵 ⑪守礼門

31.識名園 …………………………………… 136

32.崇元寺跡 ………………………………… 137

33.屋良座森城跡 …………………………… 137

34.三重城跡 ………………………………… 138

35.御物城跡 ………………………………… 139

36.浦添ようどれ …………………………… 140

37.佐敷ようどれ …………………………… 140

38.命どぅ宝 ………………………………… 141

39.しまくとぅば(島言葉) ……………… 142

第4章　沖縄県民の日常生活 ……… 143

1.ウチナーンチュ気質 …………………… 144

　①ウチナータイム ②ナンクルナイサ

　③テーゲーとテーゲー主義 ④イチャリバチョーデー

2.チャンプルー文化 ……………………… 147

3.旧正月 …………………………………… 148

4.初起し …………………………………… 148

5.十六日 …………………………………… 149

6.二十日正月 ……………………………… 150

7.ウマチー ………………………………… 150

8.浜下り …………………………………… 151

9.ユタ ……………………………………… 152

10.門中・門中墓 …………………………… 153

　①門中 ②門中墓

11.屋号 ……………………………………… 154

12.清明祭(シーミー) …………………… 156

13.トートーメー(位牌) ………………… 156

14.ハーリー ………………………………… 157

　①那覇ハーリー ②糸満ハーレー

15.トゥシビー(生年祝い) ……………… 160

16.旧盆行事 ………………………………… 161

17.エイサー ………………………………… 162

18.綱引き …………………………………… 163

19.ユイマールとモアイ …………………… 164

20.泡盛、古酒、ハブ酒 ……………… 164

21.オリオンビール ………………… 165

22.三線 ……………………………… 166

23.カチャーシー …………………… 167

24.琉球料理 ………………………… 167

　①沖縄そば ②チャンプルー料理 ③イナムドゥチ

　（イナムルチ）④ジューシー（硬・柔）⑤中味汁

　⑥山羊汁 ⑦豆腐餻 ⑧ゴーヤー ⑨島豆腐 ⑩昆布、

　クーブイリチー ⑪タコライス

25.ポークランチョンミート(ポークの缶詰) ……… 175

26.カメーカメー攻撃 ……………… 175

27.代表的な沖縄の菓子 …………… 176

　①ムーチー ②タンナファクルー ③チンスコウ

　④サーターアンダギー ⑤沖縄の三大饅頭（山城ま

　んじゅう・天妃前饅頭・ぎぼまんじゅう）⑥桔餅

　⑦チンビン ⑧ポーポー

28.沖縄の墓 ………………………… 181

　①歴史と特徴 ②掘り込み墓（横穴墓）③破風墓

　④亀甲墓

第5章　沖縄の貴重生物 ………… 185

1.沖縄の貴重動物、東洋のガラパゴス …………… 185

　①ハブ ②マングース ③イリオモテヤマネコ

　④ヤンバルクイナ

2.沖縄県の植物、県花・県木・県鳥・県魚・県蝶 ……… 189

　①県花（デイゴ）②県木（琉球松）③ハイビスカス

　④県鳥（ノグチゲラ）⑤県魚（タカサゴ）⑥県蝶（オ

　オゴマダラ）

第6章　沖縄戦 ………………… 193

1.沖縄戦の特徴 …………………… 193

2.対馬丸遭難事件 ………………… 194

3.十・十空襲 ……………………… 195

4.第32軍司令部壕跡 ……………… 195

5.旧海軍司令部壕 ………………… 196

6.地上戦 …………………………… 197

7.鉄の暴風 ………………………… 198

8.集団自決 ………………………… 199

9.ひめゆりの塔 …………………… 200

10.健児之塔 ……………………… 201

11.魂魄の塔 ……………………… 202

12. 南北の塔 ……………………… 203

13.カンカラサンシン ……………… 203

14. 艦砲ぬ喰ぇー残さー …………… 204

15. 慰霊の日 ……………………… 205

16. 平和の礎 ……………………… 206

第7章　米軍統治時代 ………… 207

1.アメリカ世 ……………………… 207

2.サンフランシスコ講和条約 …………………… 208

3.高等弁務官 ……………………… 209

4.米軍関連の主な事件・事故 ………………… 210

　①由美子ちゃん事件 ②宮森小学校ジェット機墜落事故

　③国場君轢殺事件 ④B52墜落事故 ⑤主婦轢殺事件

5.島ぐるみ闘争 …………………… 214

6.祖国復帰運動 …………………… 215

7.コザ反米暴動 …………………… 216

8.屋良朝苗 ………………………… 217

9.瀬長亀次郎 ……………………… 218

10.阿波根昌鴻 …………………… 220

11.アメラジアン ………………… 221

第8章　日本（祖国）復帰 ……… 223

1.復帰後の米軍関連事件・事故 ………………… 224

　①米兵による少女暴行事件 ②沖国大米軍ヘリ墜落事件

2.ナナサンマル（7・30交通方法変更）…………… 227

3.沖縄国際海洋博覧会 …………… 228

4.SACO合意 ……………………… 228

5.辺野古新基地建設 ……………… 229

第9章　沖縄から世界へ ………… 231

1.ソテツ地獄 ……………………… 231

2.海外移民 ………………………… 232

　①日本の海外移民 ②元年者 ③沖縄県の海外移民

3.県民のハワイ移住 ……………… 234

4.海から豚がやってきた ………… 235

5.世界のウチナーンチュ大会 …… 236

6.世界のウチナーンチュの日 …… 238

Contents

Chapter 1 History 18

1. Period Classification of Ryukyu/Okinawa History ...19

2. Senshi-*jidai* (The Prehistoric period) 20

3. Yamashitadou-*jin* 21

4. Minatogawa-*jin* 22

5. World's oldest shell fish hook at Sakitari Cave site ...23

6. *Kaizuka-jidai* (The Shell Mound Age)....................24

7. *Makiyo* 25

8. *Magiri* 25

9. *Aji (Anji)* 26

10. *Gusuku-jidai* (*Gusuku* period) 26

11. *Gusuku and* Stone masonry technique 27
　① *Gusuku*　② Stone masonry technique　③ Nakijin Castle Ruins　④ Zakimi Castle Ruins ⑤ Katsuren Castle Ruins　⑥ Nakagusuku Castle Ruins　⑦ Urasoe Castle Ruins　⑧ Shuri Castle　⑨ Chinen-*gusuku* Ruins　⑩ Minton-*gusuku* Ruins　⑪ Tamagusuku Castle Ruins　⑫ Shimasoe-Ozato Castle Ruins ⑬ Tomigusuku Castle Ruins ⑭ Shimajiri-Ozato Castle Ruins

12. Dynasties before the Eiso Dynasty 40
　① The Tentei Dynasty ② The Tenson Dynasty
　③ The Shunten Dynasty

13. Nansou-Heike(Fallen Heike warriors fleeing to the south) 42

14. Kume-*sanjuroku-sei* (Bin-*jin-sanjuroku-sei*) 43

15. Sanzan period 43

16. *Sappuu-taisei* (The tribute system with the Chinese emperor), Tribute trade 44
　① *Sappuu-taisei* ② Tribute trade ③ *Sappuu-shi*

17. Tenshi-*kan* 46

18. Tempiguu temple (Tempi temple) 47

19. *Daikoeki-jidai* (The Great Trade Period) 48

20. *Chokou-tei* 49

21. Sanshikan (Three prime ministers) 49

22. *Noro (Nuru, Nuuru)* 50

23. Kikoe-Okimi (*Chifujin*) and *San-amushirare* 50

24. *Uara-uri* of Kikoe Okimi (the inauguration ceremony of Kikoe Okimi) 51

25. *Ikai* (rank) system 52
　① *Ikai* ② Royalty ③ *Ouji* (Prince) ④ *Aji (Anji)*
　⑤ *Joukyu-shizoku* (Senior samurai) ⑥ *Oyakata (Uweekata)*
　⑦ *Peechin (Peekumii)*　⑧ General-*shizoku* (General samurai) ⑨ *Satunushi* ⑩ *Chikudun* ⑪ *Shii, Niiyaa*

26. *Heimin* (commoners).................................58
　① *Hyakusyo*(Peasants) and local officials ② *Jitudee*

　③ *Bu-jitou (Buu-jitou)* ④ *Sabakuri(Sabakui)* ⑤ *Tikugu*

27. *Hachimachi* (Crown) 60

28. *Jiifaa* (hairpin) 61

29. *Katakashira* 62

30. *Nichiryu-douso-ron* 63

31. Invasion of the Ryukyu Islands by Shimazu clan, the Satsuma Domain 63

32. Kian-*nikki* (Kian diary) 64

33. Compiled books by the Shuri Royal Government ...65
　① *Omoro-saushi (Omoro-soushi)* ② Rekidai-houan
　③ Chuzan-seikan ④ Chuzan-seihu
　⑤ Ryukyu-koku-*yuraiki*(Ryukyu Kingdom Origin Story)
　⑥ Kyuyou

34. Heroes of the Ryukyu Kingdom 69
　① King Syunten(1166〜1237) ② King Eiso(1229 ? 〜1299)
　③ King Satto(1321〜1396) ④ King Sho Hashi(1372〜1439)
　⑤ King Sho En(1415 〜 1476)

35. Five Great People of Okinawa (Five politicians representing Okinawa) 74
　① Gima-*oyakata* Shinjo (Chinese name: Ma Heikou)
　② Haneji Choshu (Chinese name: Sho Shoken)
　③ Nago-*oyakata* Chobun (Chinese name: Tei Junsoku)
　④ Gushichan-*oyakata* Bunjaku (Chinese name: Sai On)
　⑤ Giwan-*oyakata* Choho (Chinese name: Sho Yuukou)

36. Noguni-*soukan* (General Officer of Noguni Village) ...78

37. Famous Warlords of the Ryukyu Kingdom 79
　① Gosamaru ② Amawari ③ *Uni*-Uhugusuku (Uhugusuku Kenyuu) ④ Oyake Akahachi
　⑤ Jana-*oyakata* Rizan

38. Prominent women of the Ryukyu Kingdom 83
　① Momoto-Humiagari ② Ogiyaka ③ Makan-*aji-ganashi*
　④ San'ai Isoba

Successive Dynasties of the Ryukyu Kingdom 86

Chapter2 From Ryukyu to Okinawa 87

1. Ryukyu and Okinawa 87

2. *Nintou-zei, Jintou-zei* (capitation tax) 88
　① Capitation tax ② The movement to abolish the capitation tax

3. Haihan-chiken(Abolition of the feudal domain) 90

4. *Ganko-tou* (Conservatives) and *Kaika-tou* (Reformists) 91

5. Ryukyu Disposition 91

6. *Banjo* (Local government offices in the Ryukyu Kingdom) 92

7. Basil Hall 93

8. Bettelheim 94

9. The arrival of Perry's fleet in Okinawa 95
　① Background　② Admiral Perry　③ William Board
　Incident, Tomari-*gaijin-bochi* (Cemetery for foreigners)
10. John Manjiro 98
11. *Murayaa* 99
12. Jahana Noboru 99
13. *Hougen-huda* (Dialect Disgrace Tag) 100
14. *Keibin* (*Keibin* railway) 101

Chapter3 Culture and Historic remains 102
1. *Niraikanai* 103
2. Amamikiyo/Shinerikiyo, Amamikiyo Tribe 104
　① Legend of Amamikiyo/Shinerikiyo　② The theory
　of maritime peoples who migrated north from the
　south　③ The theory of Amamikiyo tribe who landed in
　the northern part of Okinawa Island　④ The theory of
　migratory groups from the continent
3. *Gama* (natural cave made of Ryukyu limestone) ...106
4. *Utaki, Ibi (Ibe)* 107
5. *Kami-ashagi* 108
6. *Nii-yaa, Niin-chu* 108
7. *Nii-gan* 108
8. *Hinukan* (God of Fire) 109
9. *Onari-gami, Onari-gami* belief 110
10. Seifa-*utaki* 111
11. Kudaka Island...112
12. *Agari-umaai*...113
13. Nakijin-*nubui* (Nakijin-*umaai*) 114
14. *Kijimunaa* 115
15. Karate, *Kobujutsu* 115
16. *Kumi-odori* 116
17. *Ryuka* 117
18. *Ryubu* (Ryukyuan dance) 118
19. *Ryusou* (*uchina-sugai*) 118
20. *Bashou-fu* (*Bashou* cloth) 119
21. Ryukyu-*kasuri* 120
22. *Bingata*..121
23. *Shiisaa* 121
　① *Shiisaa* (stone lion) ② *Shishi-mai* (Lion dance)
24. *Uweeki* (*Uweekii*) 123
25. *Mou-ashibi* (night parties among young men and
　　women in the field) 124
26. *Hajichi* 125
27. *Ishigantou* 126
28. *Touteikun* 126
29. *Bijuru* worship.....................................127

30. Historic sites around Shuri Castle 128
　① Ryutan ② Enkan-*chi* ③ Bezaiten-*dou* ④ Enkakuji
　Temple Ruins ⑤ Sunuhyan-*utaki,* Sunuhyan-*utaki* Stone
　Gate ⑥ Benga-*dake* (Bin'nu-*utaki*) ⑦ Site of Uchaya-
　udun ⑧ *Bankoku-shinryo-no-kane* (Bell of the *Bankoku-
　shinryo*) ⑨ Site of Tenzan-*ryo* (royal tomb of the kings of
　the First Sho Dynasty) ⑩ Tama-*udun* (royal tomb of the
　Second Sho Dynasty successive kings and their families)
　⑪ Shurei-*mon* Gate
31. Shikina-*en* Garden....................................136
32. Sougenji Temple Ruins 137
33. Yarazamui-*gusuku* Ruins 138
34. Mii-*gusuku* Ruins 139
35. Omono-*gusuku* Ruins 139
36. Urasoe-*youdore* 140
37. Sashiki-*youdore* 141
38. *Nuchi-du-takara* (Above all else, human life is treasure)...147
39. *Shima-kutuba* (Ryukyu language) 142

Chapter4 Daily Life of Okinawans 143
1. The temperament of *Uchinanchu* 144
　① *Uchina*-time ② *Nankuru-naisa* ③ *Tee-gee* and *Tee-
　geeism* ④ *Ichariba-chodee*
2. *Champuruu* Culture 147
3. *Kyu-syougwachi* (Lunar New Year) 148
4. *Hachi-ukushi* 149
5. *Juuruku-nichii* (January 16th of lunar calendar) 149
6. *Hachika-shogwachi* (January 20th of the lunar
　calendar) 150
7. *Umachii* (fertility rites) 150
8. *Hamauri* 151
9. *Yuta*...152
10. *Munchu, Munchu-baka* (*Munchu* tombs) 153
　① *Munchu* ② *Munchu-baka*
11. *Yagou (Yaan'naa)* 155
12. *Shiimii-sai* (Seimei Festival) 156
13. *Tou-tou-mee* (memorial tablets) 157
14. *Haarii* (Okinawan dragon boat race) 158
　① Naha-*haarii* ② Itoman-*haaree*
15. *Tushibii* (Celebration of birth year) 160
16. *Kyu-bon* (*Obon* Festival) 161
17. *Eisaa*...162
18. *Tsuna-hiki* (tug of war) 163
19. *Yuimaaru, Moai* 164
20. *Awamori, Kuusu* and *Habu-shu* 165
21. Orion Beer 166

22. *Sanshin* 166

23. *Kacha-shii* 167

24. Ryukyuan (Okinawan)Cuisine 168

   ① Okinawa-*soba* ② *Champuruu* Cuisine ③ *Ina-muduchi* (*Ina-muruchi*) ④ *Juushii* (hard/soft) ⑤ *Nakami-jiru* ⑥ Yagi-*jiru* (*Hiijaa-jiru*) ⑦ *Toufu-yoh* ⑧ *Gouyaa* (Bitter melon) ⑨ *Shima-doufu* (Okinawan tofu) ⑩ *Kombu* (kelp),*Kuubu-irichii* ⑪ Taco-rice

25. Pork luncheon meat (canned pork).....................175

26. *Kamee! Kamee!* Attacks 175

27. Typical Okinawan sweets 175

   ① *Muuchii* ② Tan'nafa-*kuruu* ③ *Chinsukou* ④ *Saataa-andagii* ⑤ Okinawa's(Naha's) three major *manjuu* (buns) ⑥ *Kippan* ⑦ *Chimbin* ⑧ *Poh-poh*

28. Graves in Okinawa....................................182

   ① History and Characteristics ② *Horikomi-baka* (Dug-in grave /side-hole grave) ③ *Hahuu-baka* (Gable tomb) ④ *Kamekou-baka*/*Kikkou-baka* (Turtleback tomb)

Chapter5 Precious Species of Okinawa 185

1. Precious animals in Okinawa, the Galapagos of the Orient ...185

   ① *Habu* ② Mongoose ③ Iriomote *yamaneko* (wildcat) ④ Yambaru-*kuina*

2. Plants in Okinawa, prefectural flower, tree, bird, fish, and butterfly 189

   ① Ryukyu-matsu (Prefectural tree) ② *Deigo* (Indian coral tree) ③ Hibiscus ④ Noguchi-*gera* (Prefectural bird) ⑤ *Gurukun* (Double-lined fusilier)(Prefectural fish) ⑥ *Ohgomadara* (tree nymph butterfly),(Prefectural butterfly)

Chapter6 Battle of Okinawa 193

1. Features of the Battle of Okinawa.....................193

2. Tsushima Maru Distress Incident 194

3. *Juu-juu-kuushuu* (10. 10 Air Raids) 195

4. Ruins of the 32nd Army Headquarters bunker 196

5. Former naval command bunker 197

6. The ground battle....................................198

7. *Tetsu-no-bouhuu* (Iron Storm) 199

8. Mass suicide...200

9. *Himeyuri-no-tou* (*Himeyuri* Monument) 201

10. *Kenji-no-tou* (*Kenji* Monument) 202

11. *Kompaku-no-tou* (*Kompaku* Monument) 202

12. *Nanboku-no-tou* (*Nanboku* Monument) 203

13. *Kankara-sanshin*....................................204

14. *Kanpou-nu-kwee-nukusaa* 205

15. Memorial Day of the Victims of the Battle of Okinawa

(*Irei-no-hi*) 205

16. *Heiwa-no-ishiji* (the peace monument) 206

Chapter7 The Era of U. S. Military Rule 207

1. America-*yuu*(Governed by the U. S. military) 207

2. San Francisco Peace Treaty 209

3. High Commissioner 210

4. Major incidents and accidents related to the U. S. military 210

   ① Yumiko-*chan* incident ② Jet fighter crash at Miyamori Elementary School ③ A junior high school boy (Kokuba-*kun*) was run over and killed ④ B-52 crash ⑤ A housewife was run over and killed (in Itoman Town)

5. *Shimagurumi-tousou* (Island-wide Struggle) 215

6. *Sokoku-hukki-undou* (Return to the Motherland Movement) 216

7. Koza Anti-American Riot...............................217

8. Yara Chobyo 218

9. Senaga Kamejiro 219

10. Ahagon Syokou 220

11.Amerasian 222

Chapter8 Returning to Japan (reversion to our homeland) ...223

1. Incidents and accidents related to U. S. military bases after the reversion to Japan 224

   ① Assault of a young girl by an American soldier (September 4, 1995) ② The U. S. military helicopter crash at Okinawa International University

2. *Nana-san-maru* (Change in traffic rules with the return of Okinawa's sovereignty) 227

3. Okinawa International Ocean Exposition..............228

4.SACO agreement 229

5. Construction of a new base in Henoko 229

Chapter9 From Okinawa to the World 231

1. *Sotetsu-jigoku* (Hell of the Cycads) 231

2. Overseas immigration 232

   ① Japanese Overseas Immigration ② *Gan'nen-mono* (people who emigrated overseas in the first year of Meiji) ③ Overseas immigration from Okinawa

3. Okinawan immigration to Hawaii 235

4. Pigs came from the sea (*umi-kara-buta-ga-yattekita*) ...236

5. The Worldwide *Uchinanchu* Festival...................237

6. The World *Uchinanchu* Day (*Sekaino-Uchinanchu-no-hi*) 238

第１章　歴史

　奄美や沖縄では、本土のような縄文時代や弥生時代のような時代区分は行わず、先史時代は土器が出現する前の「旧石器時代」と、土器出現後の「貝塚時代」（紀元前 14,000 年〜 11 世紀）とに分けられる。旧石器時代から、続く貝塚時代までの約 12,000 年間の遺跡がほとんど発見されておらず、長らく空白期とされてきたが、近年ではサキタリ洞などでこの間の空白を埋める人骨や石器が発見された。

　沖縄の歴史について多くの歴史書は、先史時代は神話時代であり 1187 年に誕生した舜天王統から始まるというのが現在の歴史観である。しかし、有史時代以前の沖縄には山下洞人や港川人などもおり、その生活や歴史があったのは事実である。アマミキヨ族や日本武士団の流入など、彼らに続く古代人の歴史についても遺跡や伝承などが各地に残っている。その視点からの研究がまだ十分に行われておらず、解明されていないだけである。

　貝塚時代以降は「グスク時代」（12 世紀〜 16 世紀初め）、「三山時代」（1322 年〜 1429 年）、三山統一後の「琉球王国時代」（1429 年〜 1872 年）、「琉球藩」（1872 年〜 1879 年）、「沖縄県」（1879 年〜 1945 年）、「米国による沖縄統治時代」（1945 年〜 1972 年）、「日本復帰」（1972 年〜現在）と続く。

　沖縄の歴史について沖縄人（ウチナーンチュ）は「トウヌユーからヤマトゥヌユー、ヤマトゥヌユーからアメリカユー、アメリカユーからヤマトゥヌユー」（唐・中国の時代から大和・日本の時代、大和の時代からアメリカ時代、アメリカ時代から大和時代）と、各時代の盟主国名を冠して表現する。

Chapter 1 History

　In Amami and Okinawa, the prehistoric period is not divided into periods such as the *Jomon* and Yayoi periods as in the mainland Japan, but is divided into the "Paleolithic Period" before the appearance of pottery and the "Shell Mound Period" (14,000 B.C.-11th century) after the appearance of pottery. From the Paleolithic period to the subsequent shell mound period, almost no archaeological remains have been found for about 12,000 years, and the area has long been regarded as a blank period, but in recent years human remains and stone tools have been discovered in Sakitari Cave and other places that fill in the gaps.

　Many history books are telling that the Prehistoric era is a mythical era, and the history of Okinawa begins with the Shunten Dynasty, born in 1187, which is the current view of history. There are Yamashitadou-*jin* and Minatogawa-*jin* in prehistoric Okinawa, and it is true that they had their lives and history. The ruins and folklore of the ancients such as the influx of Amamikiyo and Japanese samurai corps following them remain in various places. Research from such a perspective has not yet been sufficiently conducted and has not been elucidated.

　Following the Shell Mound Period are the "*Gusuku* Period" (12th century-early 16th century), the "Sanzan (the Three Kingdoms) Period" (1322-1429), the "Ryukyu Kingdom Period" (1429-1872) after the unification of the Sanzan, the "Ryukyu Domain" (1872-1879), the "Okinawa Prefecture" (1879-1945), the "U.S. Rule of Okinawa Period" (1945-1972), and "Return to Japan" (1972-present).

　Okinawans (*uchinanchu*) describe the history of Okinawa by naming the allies of each era: "*Tounu-yuu kara Yamatunu-yuu, Yamatunu-yuu kara America-yuu, America-yuu kara Yamatunu-yuu*" (from the Tang/Chinese era to the Yamato/Japanese era, from the Yamato era to the American era, and from the American era to the Yamato era).

(1) 琉球・沖縄史の時代区分

　教科書による日本の歴史は、「原始」（旧石器・縄文・弥生）→「古代」（古墳・奈良・平安）「中世」（鎌倉・室町・戦国・安土桃山）→「近世」（江戸）→「近現代」（明治〜現在）の各時代に区分されている。しかし、これは本土を中心にした日本の歴史で、北海道ではアイヌ民族独自の時代区分があり、沖縄も独立国家・琉球王国独自の歴史を歩んだ。琉球・沖縄史の一般的な時代区分は、「先史時代」（旧石器時代・貝塚時代）→「古琉球」（グスク時代・第一尚氏時代・第二尚氏時代前期の薩摩侵攻まで）→「近世琉球」（薩摩侵攻から琉球処分まで）→「近代沖縄」（琉球処分から沖縄戦まで）→「現代沖縄」（沖縄戦後から現在まで）という区分である。沖縄の旧石器時代〜貝塚時代は、本土の旧石器時代〜平安時代に相当するが、沖縄ではまだ先史時代の文化である。この時代の先島諸島（宮古・八重山）は、沖縄諸島とは異なる南方系の先史文化であった。実在した王統とされる舜天王の即位は 1187 年、尚巴志による三山統一（琉球王国誕生）は 1429 年、薩摩侵攻は 1609 年、琉球処分は 1879 年、沖縄戦は 1945 年である。

琉球 ・ 沖縄の時代区分
Period Classification of Ryukyu/Okinawa

先史時代 *Prehistoric period*		古琉球 *Ko (Old)-Ryukyu*		近世 *Early Modern*	近代 *Modern*	戦後（現代） *Postwar (Present)*
7,000 *B.C.*　　1187		1429	1609	1879	1945	1972
旧石器時代 Paleolithic period	貝塚時代 Shell Mound period	グスク時代 *Gusuku* period	琉球王国 Ryukyu Kingdom	沖縄県 Okinawa Prefecture	アメリカ合衆国による沖縄統治 Period of United States Rule	
		三山時代 Sanzan period (1314 〜 1429) (1314、玉城王即位) (In 1314, King Tamagusuku ascended the throne)	第一尚氏王統 The 1st Sho Dynasty (1429 〜 1469)		沖縄県 Okinawa Prefecture 1972 〜	
			第二尚氏王統 The 2nd Sho Dynasty (1469 〜 1879)			
			薩摩藩による支配 Rule by the Satsuma Domain (1609 〜 1879)			
			琉球藩 Ryukyu Domain (1872 〜 1879)			

(1) Period Classification of Ryukyu/Okinawa History

　Japanese history according to textbooks is divided into the following periods: *Primitive* (Paleolithic, *Jomon*, *Yayoi*)→*Ancient* (Kohun, Nara, Heian)→*Medieval* (Kamakura, Muromachi, Sengoku, Azuchi-Momoyama)→*Early modern* (Edo)→*Modern* (Meiji to present). However, this is Japanese history centered on the mainland. In Hokkaido, the Ainu people had their own historical division of time, and Okinawa also had its own history as an independent nation, the Ryukyu Kingdom. The general period classification of Ryukyu/Okinawa history is : *Prehistory* (Paleolithic Period, Shell Mound Period) → *Ko*-Ryukyu (*Gusuku* Period, First Sho Dynasty Period, Up to the invasion of Satsuma in the early Second Sho Dynasty Period) → *Modern Ryukyu* (From the invasion of Satsuma to the disposition of the Ryukyu Islands) → *Modern Okinawa* (from the disposal of the Ryukyu Islands to the Battle of Okinawa) → *Contemporary Okinawa* (after the Battle of Okinawa to the present). The Paleolithic to Shell Mound Period in Okinawa corresponds to the Paleolithic to Heian period in mainland Japan, but the culture in Okinawa is still prehistoric. The Sakishima Islands (Miyako and Yaeyama) of this period were a southern prehistoric culture different from that of the Okinawa Island. The accession of King Shunten, who is believed to be the actual royal lineage, took place in 1187, and the unification of Sanzan (birth of the Ryukyu Kingdom) by Sho Hashi took place in 1429, the invitation of Satsuma was in 1609, the disposal of Ryukyu in 1879, and the Battle of Okinawa in 1945.

(2) 先史時代（せんしじだい）

　定義によると、先史時代とは文字を使用する以前、つまり文書記録が無い時代を指し、その後の時代は歴史時代（有史時代）と呼ばれる。以前は「文献によって知られる過去が歴史である」というのが伝統的な考え方であった。しかし、考古学的な調査の発達などによって、現代では「歴史は人間の誕生とともに始まる」と捉える。先史時代における歴史研究には、遺跡や遺物などの発掘を通じた考古学的分析の他、その地域に受け継がれる神話や伝承の社会的分析も必須となる。沖縄の島々に人間（沖縄人）が住み始めたのは今か

港川遺跡（港川フィッシャー）（八重瀬町港川）
Minatogawa Fissure Ruins(Minatogawa, Yaese Town)

ら約2万年から3万年前。その頃は海水面も今より低く、中国大陸と陸続きであった。人々も大陸から渡ってきたと考えられる。彼らはガマ（洞窟）を住み処にして森の動物や果物、海から魚を採集する漁労生活をした。港川人を代表とする旧石器時代に続く新石器時代は、沖縄では貝塚時代（紀元前7,000年～11世紀）と呼ばれ、これまでの時代を先史時代と称する。

(2) Senshi-*jidai* (The Prehistoric period)

　By definition, the prehistoric period refers to the period before the use of writing, i.e., the period without written records, and the period after that is called the historical period. In the past, the traditional view was that "the past known through literature is history". However, with the development of archaeological research and other factors, the modern view is that "history begins with the birth of man". In addition to archaeological analysis through the excavation of ruins and artifacts, social analysis of the myths and folklore passed down in the region is also essential for historical research in prehistoric times. It was about 20,000 to 30,000 years ago that humans (Okinawans) began to live on the islands of Okinawa. At that time, the sea level was lower than now, and the islands were connected to the Chinese continent. It is thought that the people came from the continent. They lived in caves, gathering animals and fruits from the forest and fish from the sea. The Neolithic Age, which followed the Paleolithic Age represented by the Minatogawa-*jin*, is called the Shell Mound Age (7,000 B.C. to 11th century A.D.) in Okinawa, and the period up to this point is called the Prehistoric Age in Okinawa.

(3) 山下洞人（やましたどうじん）

　日本最古の化石人骨は、那覇市山下町にある山下第一洞穴遺跡から 1968 年に発見され、山下洞人と命名された。8 歳程度の女児のものとみられる大腿骨、頸骨、腓骨の各 1 本が出土し、約 32,000 年前の旧石器時代の化石人骨と推定されている。人骨の分析結果によると、同年齢の現代人より筋肉の発達した体型はしているものの、現生人類（ホモ・サピエンス）と断定されている。人骨と同じ層からは鹿の骨や角の化石が多量に出土しており、その中には人為的に加工したと思われるものもみられる。山下洞人は、年代の確実な旧石器人であり、日本ばかりでなく東アジアにおいても重要な資料とされている。

山下第一洞穴遺跡 (那覇市山下町)
Yamashita Daiichi Cave Site （Yamashita-*cho*, Naha City)

(3) Yamashitadou-*jin*

　Japan's oldest fossil human bone was founded in 1968 at the Yamashita Daiichi Cave site in Yamashita-*cho*, Naha City, and named Yamashitadou-*jin*. One femur, one tibia, and one fibula, which are thought to belong to a girl about eight years old, were excavated. They are presumed to be a Paleolithic fossil human bone about 32,000 years ago. According to the results of the analysis of the human bones, it is determined to be a hominid (Homo sapiens), although it has a more muscular body shape than modern humans of the same age. A large amount of deer bones and antler fossils have been excavated from the same layer as human bones, and some of them appear to have been artificially processed. Yamashitadou-*jin* is a Paleolithic man of definite age, and is considered an important historical source not only in Japan but also in East Asia.

(4) 港川人 (みなとがわじん)

　港川人は 1968 年、八重瀬町港川の港川遺跡で大山盛保氏によって発見された化石人骨である。港川人は旧石器人を代表する 20,000 ～ 22,000 年前の人骨と言われ、7 体はほぼ完全な骨格が得られた。身長は男性で 153 ～ 155cm、女性は 144cm と小柄である。港川人は現在の人類ならば、オーストラリア先住民やニューギニアの集団に近いという分析結果が出ている。骨格の遺伝的特徴は現在の沖縄人に引き継がれているといわれる。しかし、DNA 分析の結果からは遺伝的に縄文人や現代日本人の直接の祖先ではないことが判明したが、日本人のルーツを巡る論争に一石を投じるものとなった。港川人のルーツについては、①中国江西省柳江県で発見された「柳江人」（りゅうこうじん）の頭蓋骨に似ていることから、港川人の祖先は中国南部から渡来したとする説②特徴がインドネシア・ジャワ島のワジャク人に似ていることからスンダランドからやって来た説③元々、日本列島やその周辺にいた人々が進化したとする説があり、港川人の故郷をめぐる問題は未解決である。

　石のように堅い人間の骨も 1 万年以上も経つと地中で酸

港川人（復元模型）
(提供：八重瀬町立具志頭歴史民俗資料館)
Minatogawa-*jin*(restoration model)

化して溶けてしまうが、琉球石灰岩で出来た洞窟（ガマ）では、時間が経つと炭酸石灰分が人骨に染みこみ、化石化してしまう。沖縄県には更新世の隆起サンゴ礁からなる石灰岩が広く分布しており、旧石器時代の人骨が多く発見される理由とされている。日本の化石人骨の 90％は沖縄で発見されていると言われる。

(4) Minatogawa-*jin*

Minatogawa-*jin* is fossil human bones, which was discovered by Oyama Seiho in 1968, at the Minatogawa Ruins in Minatogawa, Yaese Town. Minatogawa-*jin* is said to be a human skeleton representing the Paleolithic about 20,000 to 22,000 years ago, and seven bodies have almost complete skeleton. Height is 153 to 155cm for men and 144cm for women, and they are petite. Minatogawa-*jin* is analyzed as a human being close to the current natives of Australia and the people of New Guinea. It is said that the genetic characteristics of the bones of Minatogawa-*jin* are common to the current Okinawans. However, although the results of DNA analysis showed that they were not genetically the direct ancestors of the *Jomon* or modern Japanese, it has created a stir in the debate over the roots of the Japanese people. Regarding the roots of the Minatogawa-*jin*, (1) the theory that the ancestors of the Minatogawa-*jin* came from southern China because their skulls resemble those of the *Liujiang* people found in Liujiang County, Jiangxi Province, China, (2) the theory that they came from Sundaland because their characteristics resemble the *Wajak* people of Java, Indonesia, (3) the theory that people who originally lived in and around the Japanese archipelago evolved、and the question of the homeland of the Minatogawa-*jin* remains unresolved.

After more than 10,000 years, human bones, as hard as stone, oxidize and break down in the ground, but in caves (*gama*) made of Ryukyu limestone, carbonated lime soaks into human bones over time, turning them into fossils. Limestone rocks consisting of Pleistocene uplifted coral reefs are widely distributed in Okinawa Prefecture, which is considered to be the reason for the discovery of many human bones from the Paleolithic period. It is said that 90% of the fossil human remains in Japan have been found in Okinawa.

(5) サキタリ洞遺跡、世界最古の貝製釣り針（さきたりどういせき、せかいさいこのかいせいつりばり）

　沖縄県立博物館・美術館は 2016 年 9 月、南城市のサキタリ洞遺跡で、世界最古となる 23,000 年前（後期旧石器時代）の貝製の釣り針を発見したと発表した。それまで、東南アジアの島々では旧石器時代の人々が海の魚や貝を利用した証拠が見つかっていたが、それ以外の地域では殆ど発見されていなかった。本土や沖縄も例外ではなく、22,000 年前の港川人を始め、数々の旧石器人骨が見つかるものの、旧石器の発見は少なく、彼らの文化や暮らしぶりはよく分からなかった。

　サキタリ洞遺跡では、釣り針の他に小さな二枚貝に穴を開けたビーズや割れた海の貝殻も見つかった。石器制作に適した石が少ない沖縄島で、旧石器人が貝殻を割り、道具として使用していたことが明らかになった。

世界最古の釣り針が発掘されたサキタリ洞（南城市玉城前川）
Sakitari Cave where the world's oldest fishing hook was found
(Maekawa, Nanjyo City)

海にいるブダイやアイゴなど魚の骨も発見されたが、圧倒的に多いのが、モクズガニとカワニナの殻。それらはサキタリ洞の西側を流れる雄飛川で採れたものと考えられている。旧石器人というと、槍を片手に大型獣に挑む勇猛果敢な狩猟生活をイメージする。謎に包まれていた沖縄の旧石器人たちの生活が、サキタリ洞の発掘調査によって「季節に応じて川の幸を食べ、海に出かけて魚を捕らえ、豊富な貝殻を集めて釣り針や道具、ビーズを作る」という豊かで優雅な暮らしぶりが明らかになった。

(5) World's oldest shell fish hook at Sakitari Cave Site

The Okinawa Prefectural Museum & Art Museum announced in September 2016 the discovery of a 23,000-year-old (Late Paleolithic) shell fish hook, the oldest in the world, at the Sakitari Cave site in Nanjo City. Until then, evidence of the use of marine fish and shellfish by Paleolithic peoples had been found on the islands of Southeast Asia, but little had been found elsewhere. The mainland and Okinawa are no exception, and although numerous paleolithic human bones have been found, including those of the Minatogawa-*jin* 22,000 years ago, the discovery of paleolithic artifacts was scarce and their culture and lifestyle were not well understood.

At the Sakitari Cave site, in addition to fish hook, beads drilled into small bivalves and broken sea shells were also found. It is now clear that Paleolithic people on the island of Okinawa, where there are few stones suitable for stone tool production, broke shells and used them as tools. Bones of marine fish such as *budai* (parrotfish) and *aigo* (dusky rabbitfish) were also found, but the overwhelming majority were shells of *mokuzugani* (river crab) and *kawanina* (river mussel). They are believed to have been taken from the Yuuhi River, which flows west of Sakitari Cave. When we think of Paleolithic people, we imagine a life of valiant hunting, spear in hand, taking on large beasts. The lives of the Paleolithic people of Okinawa had been shrouded in mystery, but excavations at Sakitari Cave have revealed their rich and elegant lifestyle of "eating seasonal river food, going out to sea to catch fish, and collecting abundant shells to make fishing hooks, tools, and beads".

(6) 貝塚時代（かいづかじだい）

　沖縄でも以前は、石器時代の呼称が一般的だったが、この時代の遺跡が貝塚を形成していることが多いため、新石器時代を貝塚時代と呼んでいる。この時代は、旧石器時代の港川人から約 1 万年の時を経た次の文化段階である。この貝塚時代の人が現在のウチナーンチュの祖先とされているが、港川人との関係はよくわかっていない。貝塚時代は紀元前 7,000 年から 11 世紀頃で、早期・前期・中期・後期の 4 時期に区分される。早・前・中期は日本の縄文時代に、後期は弥生時代から平安時代にほぼ相当する。今のところ、沖縄最古の土器と考えられるのは「ヤブチ式土器」や「東原式土器」と呼ばれる「爪形文土器」で、今から約 6,600 年前（縄文時代）に作られたものである。本土の縄文時代の後に続くのは弥生時代だが、弥生文化の特徴は水稲農耕や金属器、弥生式土器などである。沖縄の貝塚時代後期の遺跡からも弥生式土器と鉄器が出土しており、沖縄での水稲農耕の始まりは 8 〜 10 世紀とされる。宮古・八重山諸島には縄文文化・弥生文化とも伝わってなく、先史時代の南西諸島には①南方文化の影響を強く受けて始まった宮古・八重山諸島②縄文文化・弥生文化の影響を

仲泊遺跡（恩納村仲泊）
Nakadomari Ruins (Nakadomari, On'na Village)

受けながらも独自の文化を築いていった沖縄諸島③日本文化の影響を強く受けた奄美諸島の 3 つの文化圏が存在した。それらは、12 世紀頃から始まったグスク時代に徐々に 1 つの文化圏形成に推移していく。

　貝塚時代には貝はとても重要で、特にタカラガイは古代中国では貨幣として使用され、主に南西諸島から運ばれた。ゴホウラガイは九州の重要な遺跡から装身具として発見されている。夜光貝は、貝類の中でも真珠層が厚く、色にも品格があり「琉球漆器」の螺鈿細工の材料として重用される。奄美諸島以南の熱帯海域に分布する。　　（例）仲泊遺跡（恩納村）、大山貝塚（宜野湾市）、荻堂貝塚（北中城村）

(6) *Kaizuka-jidai* (The Shell Mound Age)

　In Okinawa, the name "Stone Age" used to be more common, but the Neolithic Age is now called *Kaizuka-jidai* (the Shell Mound Age) because the remains from this period often form shell mounds. This period is the next cultural stage, about 10,000 years after the Minatogawa-*jin* (Paleolithic). It is believed that the people of this shell mound era are the ancestors of the current *uchinanchu*, but the relationship with the Minatogawa-*jin* is not well understood. The Shell Mound Period spans from 7,000 B.C. to the 11th century and is divided into four periods. The Founding, Early and Middle stage correspond to the *Jomon* period in Japan, and the Late period is roughly equivalent to the *Yayoi* to *Heian* periods in Japan. So far, the oldest earthenware in Okinawa is considered to be "*Tsumegatamon* pottery (nail-pattern pottery)," also known as Yabuchi-style pottery and Agaribaru-style pottery, which was made about 6,600 years ago (*Jomon* period). In the mainland, the *Yayoi* period followed the *Jomon* period, but the *Yayoi* culture was characterized by rice farming, metal tools, and *Yayoi*-style pottery. *Yayoi*-style pottery and ironware have also been excavated from the remains of the late shell mound period in Okinawa, and it is believed that rice farming in Okinawa began in the 8th to 10th centuries. The Miyako and Yaeyama Islands had neither *Jomon* nor *Yayoi* culture, and there were three cultural spheres in the prehistoric Southwestern Islands: 1. The Miyako and Yaeyama Islands, which were strongly influenced by southern culture; 2. The Okinawa Islands, which were influenced by *Jomon* and *Yayoi* culture but developed their own unique culture; and 3. The Amami Islands, which were strongly influenced by mainland Japanese culture. These three cultural groups gradually merged into one cultural zone during the *gusuku* period which began around the 12th century.

　Shells were very important during this period, in particular, *Takara-gai* (cowrie shells), was used as money in ancient China and was transported mainly from the Nansei Islands. *Gohuora-gai* have been found as accessories at important sites in Kyushu. *Yakou-gai* (Turban shells) have the thickest nacreous layer of all shells, and their dignified colors make them a valuable material for a *Raden* (mother-of-pearl inlays) used in Ryukyu lacquerware. It is distributed in tropical waters south of the Amami Islands.

　examples: Nakadomari-*iseki* (On'na Village), Oyama-*kaizuka* (Ginowan City), Ogidoh-*kaizuka* (Kitanakagusuku Village)

(7) マキヨ

　村落の古称で、御嶽を共有する氏子の村落は「マキヨ」と呼ばれ、個別の血縁集団で構成された。マキヨは守護神が祀られている御嶽によって護られ、元来は 1 集落（マキヨ）に 1 つの御嶽があった。マキヨはクダ、コダ、ムタとも呼ばれ、現在ではマキヨが音韻変化してマチュー、マキ、マクとして残っている。本土の日本海に面する山手方面にもマキ、マケという語が残っており、共通性がみられる。マキヨでは支配する者もなく、相互に助け合う平等的な横社会が形成されていたと考えられている。マキヨでは民主主義・祭祀一致が実践され、民衆を愛護する御嶽の神の意図に従い、首長の統制のもとに秩序ある社会であった。首長を「大グロー」（ウフグロー・ウフグル・ウフコロ）、成年男子は「若グロー」と呼ばれた。

(7) *Makiyo*

The ancient name of a village, the *ujiko* community that shared the *utaki* was called *makiyo* and consisted of individual blood-related groups. *makiyo* was protected by a *utaki* where the guardian deity is enshrined, and originally there was one *utaki* per village. *Makiyo* was also called *kuda, koda* or *muta,* and nowadays it remains as *machuu, maki,* and *maku* with phonetic changes. In the *Yamate* area of the mainland facing the Sea of Japan, the words *maki* and *maku* also remain, indicating a commonality. It is believed that in *makiyo*, there was no one to dominate, and

松尾御嶽（南城市南風原）
Matsuu-*utaki*(Haebaru, Nanjyo City)

an egalitarian horizontal society was formed where people helped each other. In *makiyo*, democracy and ritual unity were practiced, and the society was orderly under the control of the chief according to the intention of the god of the *utaki* who protected the people. The chief was called *uh-gurou, uhu-guru* or *uhu-koro*, and the adult male was called *waka-gurou.*

(8) 間切り (まぎり)

　間切りとは、古代から 1907 年までの長期にわたって存在した沖縄独自の行政区画単位。琉球王朝時代の土地分割で、現在の市町村に相当する。間切りが何時、どのような形で成立したのか詳しいことはわかっていない。按司は、間切りレベルの領域を有しており、間切りが元々は按司に主導される小政治圏を成していたとみられる。いくつかの村が集まって 1 つの間切りになった。間切りは琉球処分（1879 年）によって沖縄県が設置された以後も存続した。1899 年の官吏規定により「捌理」（さばくり・間切り番所の幹部役人）が廃止されて間切り長・書記・収入役が置かれ間切りの番所は「役場」と改称された。さらに 1908 年からは「沖縄県及び島嶼町村制」により、間切りは町村に、間切り長は町村長にそれぞれ改称された。この時から、間切りの呼称は沖縄の歴史から姿を消した。

　（例）高嶺間切、南風原間切、大里間切

(8) *Magiri*

Magiri is an administrative division unit unique to Okinawa that existed for a long period of time from ancient times until 1907. It was a division of land during the Ryukyu Dynasty, and it equivalent to cities, towns and villages currently. It is not known in detail when and how *magiri* was formed. It is believed that the *aji* had a territory of about *magiri*, and the *magiri* originally formed a small political zone led by *aji*. Several villages came together to form a single *magiri*. *Magiri* continued to exist even after the establishment of Okinawa Prefecture through the Ryukyu Disposition (1879). In 1899, according to the official regulations, *sabakuri* (senior officials of the *magiri-banjo*) was abolished, and the *magiri* chief, secretary, and revenue officer were appointed, and the *magiri-banjo* was renamed *yakuba*. Furthermore, from 1908, under the "Okinawa Prefecture and Islands Town and Village System," *magiri* were renamed as towns and villages, and *magiri* chief were renamed as mayors of towns and villages. From this time on, the name *magiri* disappeared from the history of Okinawa. examples: Takamine *magiri*, Haebaru *magiri*, Ozato *magiri*

(9) 按司 (あじ、あんじ)

　按司は琉球各地での支配者で、「主」（あるじ）が語源といわれ「アンジ」または「チャラ」とも称しほとんどの場合、城主を意味した。尚真王の中央集権化（1488 〜 1528）により按司たちは首里に居を移し、領地には按司掟（後の地頭代）を置いて支配した。近世には位階名となり、王、王子に次ぐ士族であった。12 世紀頃の沖縄島では、各地域の支配者は互いに競って自己の地位を保持し、勢力を拡大した。これらの支配者達が按司の始まりと考えられ、城塞としての「グスク」の発生も同時期とされている。　（例）佐敷按司、八重瀬按司、今帰仁按司、笠来若按司 (かさじわかちゃら)

(9) *Aji (Anji)*

　Aji were the rulers of the various regions of Ryukyu. The word *aji* is said to be derived from the word *aruji*, and was also called *anji* or *chara*, which in most cases meant the lord of a castle. With the centralization of power by King Sho Shin (1488-1528), the *aji* were moved to Shuri and ruled over their territories with *aji-ucchi* (later known as *jitu-dee*). In the early modern period, *aji* became the name of a rank, and was the second most important class of samurai after king and princes. On the island of Okinawa around the 12th century, the rulers of each region competed with each other to maintain their position and expand their power. These rulers are thought to be the beginning of the *aji*, and the *gusuku* as fortress is said to have arisen at the same time.
examples: Sashiki-*aji*, Eiji-*aji*, Nakijin-*aji*,Kasaji *waka-chara*

(10) グスク時代（ぐすくじだい）

　グスクが展開した時代はグスク時代と呼ばれ、考古学上の区分では 12 世紀ごろか 16 世紀の初めまでとされる。グスク時代になると、海岸砂丘地に居住していた人々が生活の場を琉球石灰岩の台地に形成するようになった。集落には「御嶽」と呼ばれる守護神を祀った聖域を構え、稲作と麦・粟を主とした畑作に牛の飼育を加えた複合農耕を営んだ。農耕社会は定住を前提としており、食料の備蓄を可能にしたため各地の人口は急速に増加していった。砦としての

具志川グスク跡（久米島町）
Gushikawa Castle Ruins (Kumejima Town)

グスクを有した按司たちは武力を背景に互いに抗争を繰り返し北山、中山、南山の三大勢力が形成された。この時代には本格的な農耕へと経済基盤が移行し、海外との交流が活発化した。1429 年、尚巴志による三山統一で琉球王国が誕生した。当初は各間切りに按司がおり、城を構えて領内を治めていたが、尚真王代（在位：1477 〜 1526）になって諸間切りの按司たちを首里城下に移し、代わりに按司家の家老格である「按司掟」（あじうっち）を派遣して間切り事務を監理させた。

(10) *Gusuku-jidai (Gusuku* period)

　The period in which the *gusuku* developed is called the *gusuku* period, which is archaeologically classified as from around the 12th century to the beginning of the 16th century. During the *gusuku* period, the people who had lived on the coastal dunes began to form their living space on the Ryukyu limestone plateau. A sanctuary called *utaki* was set up to enshrine the guardian deity in the village, and the people practiced multiple cropping systems, including rice cultivation, field cultivation of mainly wheat and millet, and cattle breeding. The agrarian society was based on the premise of settlement, and allowed for the stockpiling of food, which led to a rapid increase in the population of each region. The lords(*aji*) of the castles, whose *gusuku* served as fortresses, repeatedly fought against each other against the backdrop of their military power, and the three major powers of Hokuzan, Chuzan and Nanzan were formed. During this period, the economic base shifted to full-fledged agriculture, and exchanges with foreign countries became more active. In 1429, the Kingdom of Ryukyu was established with the unification of the Sanzan by Sho Hashi. In the beginning, there was *aji* at each *magiri*, who ruled the territory by setting up a castle, but in the reign of King Sho Shin (reigned 1477-1526), the *aji* of the various *magiri* were moved to Shuri Castle, and in their place, an *aji-ucchi*, a retainer of the *aji* family was dispatched to oversee the affairs of the *magiri*.

（11）グスク・石積み技法（いしづみぎほう）・城跡（じょうせき）

①グスク

　沖縄県や奄美諸島に約250〜300箇所あるといわれ、琉球王国時代の城または城塞のことをグスクという。一般に小高い丘の上に形成され、城壁などで囲われているが、それがないグスクも存在する。本土の城の石垣が直線的なのと対照的に、沖縄のグスクの石垣はうねるような曲線でつくられ、隅（コーナー）部分も直角に折れる本土の城とは異なり、ゆるやかな弧を描いて見事な造形美を醸し出している。石造りのアーチ門も見事で、中国の城門をイメージさせる。城壁に使用される琉球石灰岩は軽くて加工しやすいのが特徴で、琉球では本土に先駆けて石垣づくりの城が登場した。本土で石垣づくりの城が普及するのは織田信長や豊臣秀吉らが天下統一を目指した16世紀後半だが、琉球では100年以上も先駆けて総石垣のグスクが築かれていた。殆どのグスク内には御嶽と呼ばれる神聖な場所が存在する。このことから、グスクはもともと御嶽を中心とした集落であったものが発展し、城砦化したという説が有力である。グスクは琉球列島の村々や島々のほとんどに分布するが、特に沖縄本島南部に多い。琉球王国のグスク（首里城跡、勝連城跡、今帰仁城跡、中城城跡、座喜味城跡）と関連遺跡群は2000年、ユネスコの世界遺産に登録された。

（11）*Gusuku* and Stone masonry technique

① *Gusuku*

　A castle or fortress from the Ryukyu Kingdom era is called a *gusuku*, and there are said to be about 250-300 *gusuku* in Okinawa Prefecture and the Amami Islands. They are generally built on top of small hills and surrounded by walls, but there are also *gusuku* without walls. In contrast to the straight lines of castles on the mainland, the stone walls of Okinawan *gusuku* are made with undulating curves, and unlike castles on the mainland, which have right-angled corners, the stone walls of Okinawan *gusuku* have a gentle arc that creates a beautiful form. The stone arch gate is also magnificent, reminiscent of a Chinese city gate. Ryukyu limestone, which is used for castle walls, is light and easy to work with, and castles made of stonewalls appeared in Ryukyu ahead of those on the mainland. Stone-walled castles did not become popular on the mainland until the late 16th century, when Oda Nobunaga and Toyotomi Hideyoshi tried to unify the country, but in Ryukyu, *gusuku* with all-stone walls were built more than 100 years earlier. Most *gusuku* have a sacred place called a *utaki*. From this, it is widely believed that the *gusuku* was originally a village centered around a *utaki*, which developed into a fortress. *Gusuku* are distributed in most of the villages and islands in the Ryukyu Archipelago, but are especially common in the southern part of the main island of Okinawa. The Ryukyu Kingdom's *gusuku* (ruins of Shuri-*gusuku*, Katsuren-*gusuku*, Nakijin-*gusuku,* Nakagusuku-*gusuku*, and Zakimi-*gusuku*) and related sites were registered as a UNESCO World Heritage Site in 2000.

②石積み技法

　沖縄のグスクは、美しい曲線美を持つ城壁に石灰岩を使用しているが、その積み方には３つの技法がある。ほとんどのグスクが「琉球石灰岩」を用いているが、今帰仁城だけは「古生代石灰岩」を使用している。古生代石灰岩は硬くて加工しづらい石で、そのままの形を利用して積んでおり「野面積み」（のづらづみ）と呼ばれている一番古いタイプの石積み技法である。豆腐のように四角に加工した石を積み上げていく技法を「布積み」（ぬのづみ）という。五角形または六角形に加工した石を積み上げていく技法は「相方積み」（あいかたづみ）といい、一番強度が強く耐久性にも富み、最も新しい石積み技法である。中城城では、３種類の石積み技法が見られる。

野面積み（玉城グスク）*Nozura-zumi(*Tamagusuku*-gusuku)*

布積み（糸数グスク）*Nuno-zumi(*Itokazu*-gusuku)*

② Stone masonry technique

　The beautifully curved walls of Okinawan *gusuku* are made of limestone, and there are three different techniques for building them. Most of the *gusuku* are made of Ryukyu limestone, but only Nakijin Castle is made of Paleozoic limestone. Paleozoic limestone is a hard stone that is difficult to process, and it is piled using its original shape, which is the oldest type of masonry called *nozura-zumi*. Technique of stacking stones processed into squares like tofu is called *nuno-zumi*. The technique of piling up pentagonal or hexagonal stones is called *aikata-zumi*, and is the strongest, most durable, and newest type of masonry. At Nakagusuku Castle, three types of masonry techniques can be seen.

相方積み（中城グスク）*Aikata-zumi(*Nakagusuku*-gusuku)*

③今帰仁城跡（なきじんじょうあと）

　今帰仁村今泊の古生代石灰岩上、標高約 100m に位置する城址で、北山王統の居城である。北山城とも呼ばれ、連郭式のきわめて複雑な構造をもち、中城城跡より規模は広い。1962 年に修復された正門は「平郎門」と称し、南走平家との関連を指摘する歴史家もいる。築城年代は不明だが、発掘調査の結果からは 14 〜 16 世紀の遺跡であることが明らかになった。宅地造成が行われ屋敷内には掘立住宅の跡がある。武具や祭祀用具、遊具などが出土していることから、武士が家族単位で住んでいた屋敷跡と考えられている。1416 年（1422 年説もある）に尚巴志に滅ぼされた時の城主は攀安知王（はんあんちおう）で、その後、尚巴志は北部地域の管理のため「北山監守」を置き、強力な武将・護佐丸を初代監守に任じた。1422 年以降、グスクは歴代監守の居城として使用された。1609 年の薩摩軍による琉球侵攻で城は炎上した。1665 年、七代目監守のとき首里に引き揚げて廃城となった。

③ **Nakijin Castle Ruins**

The ruins of Nakijin Castle are located about 100 meters above sea level on Paleozoic limestone in Imadomari, Nakijin village, and was the residence of the Hokuzan royal family. Also known as Hokuzan Castle, it has an extremely complex structure with a series of walls and is larger than the Nakagusuku Castle ruins. The main gate, which was restored in 1962, is called Heirou-*mon* (Gate of Heirou), and some historians have pointed out its connection to the Nansou-Heike clan. The date of construction of the castle is unknown, but the results of excavation revealed that it was built

今帰仁城跡（今帰仁村今泊）
Nakijin Castle Ruins(Imadomari, Nakijin Village)

between the 14th and 16th centuries. The site was developed as a residential area and there are traces of dugout houses in the compound. It is thought to be the remains of a house where warriors lived as a family unit, as military equipment, ritual tools, and playground equipment have been excavated. When the castle was destroyed by Sho Hashi in 1416 (some say 1422), the lord of the castle was King Han Anchi, and later, Sho Hashi established the Hokuzan-*kanshu* to oversee the northern area, and appointed Gosamaru, a powerful warlord, as the first supervisor. After 1422, the *gusuku* was used as the residence of successive Hokuzan-*kanshu*. In 1609, the castle was burned down during the invasion of Ryukyu by the Satsuma army. In 1665, at the time of the seventh generation, the Hokuzan-*kanshu* withdrew to Shuri and the castle was abandoned.

④座喜味城跡（ざきみじょうあと）

築城の名手・護佐丸が、今帰仁城陥落後に北山監守として6年間、今帰仁城に配置されていた時に築いた城である。首里王府に対する勢力を監視する目的で造られ、1422年に完成した。規模はさほど大きくないが、難攻不落の今帰仁城を参考に築城したといわれる。城壁や城門（アーチ石門）の石積みの精巧さや美しさは沖縄の城の中でも随一といわれ、当時の石造建築技術の高さを示している。この城跡の最大の見どころは、沖縄戦の戦禍を逃れた、沖縄に現存する最古のアーチ門。門の強度を高めるために真ん中にクサビ石がある。座喜味城がある残波岬は崎枝（さきえだ）と呼ばれ、「崎の嶺」（さちんみ）に築城されたので「崎嶺グスク」（さちんみグスク）と称されたが、後に「座喜味グスク」と当て字されるようになった。築城工事では奄美諸島や慶良間列島からも人夫が集められ、山田城の石垣を取り壊して約5kmの距離を手渡しで運ばせたという。城を完成させた護佐丸は、城下の長浜港から大和や海外との交易を活発に行った。この時期に読谷発祥の織物「読谷山花織り」（ゆんたんざはなうい）のルーツとなる技法が東南アジアから伝わったと考えられている。1440年、護佐丸が中城城に移封された後は廃城になったといわれる。沖縄戦の際には日本軍の高射砲陣地になったため、アメリカ軍の集中攻撃を受けて破壊された。戦後も米軍のレーダー基地の建設のため、多くの城壁などが破壊された。

座喜味城跡（読谷村座喜味）
Zakimi Castle Ruins (Zakimi, Yomitan Village)

④ Zakimi Castle Ruins

This castle was built by Gosamaru, a master castle builder, while he was stationed at Nakijin Castle for six years as Hokuzan-*kanshu*, after the fall of Nakijin Castle. It was built for the purpose of monitoring the forces against the Shuri royal government, and was completed in 1422. Although not very large in scale, it is said to have been built based on the impregnable Nakijin Castle. The elaborate and beautiful masonry of the castle walls and gate (arch stone gate) is said to be the best among castles in Okinawa, showing the high level of masonry construction technology at that time. The main attraction of this castle ruin is the oldest surviving arch gate in Okinawa, which escaped the vortex of the Battle of Okinawa and has a wedge stone in the middle to strengthen the gate. Cape Zampa, where Zakimi Castle is located, is called Sakieda, and the castle was built on Sachinmi (Sakieda), so it was called Sachinmi-*gusuku*, but later it was called Zakimi-*gusuku*. It is said that during the construction of the castle, laborers were gathered from the Amami Islands and the Kerama Archipelago, and the stone walls of Yamada Castle were torn down and hand-carried over a distance of about 5 km. After completing the castle, Gosamaru actively traded with Yamato and overseas countries from Nagahama Port under the castle. It is thought that during this period, the technique that became the root of Yuntanza-*Hanaui*, a textile originating in Yomitan, was introduced from Southeast Asia. The castle is said to have been abandoned after Gosamaru was transferred to Nakagusuku Castle in 1440. During the Battle of Okinawa, it became an anti-aircraft gun position for the Japanese forces and was destroyed by concentrated attacks by the American forces. Even after the war, many of the castle walls were destroyed to make way for the construction of a U.S. military radar base.

⑤勝連城跡（かつれんじょうあと）

勝連城は、14 世紀初めに英祖王統二代
目・大成王の五男である勝連按司によっ
て築城され、最後の城主・阿麻和利に至
るまで 11 代の城主によって統治された。
5 つの郭からなり、オモロでは「きむたか」
（肝高）と謡われているように、日本本土
の京都や鎌倉にたとえられるほど繁栄し
ていたといわれる。城の南側に交易のた
めの港を備え、北側は田地として穀倉地
帯であった。城壁は、自然の地形を巧み
に利用しながら石灰岩の石垣をめぐらせ
ている。数回にわたる発掘調査の結果か

勝連城跡（うるま市勝連）
Katsuren Castle Ruins (Katsuren, Uruma City)

らは、岩盤を削って大がかりな土木工事が行われ、瓦葺き建物の存在が明らかになっている。当時は
板葺き屋根が主流であったが、瓦葺きの建物があったのは、現在のところ他には首里城と浦添城だけ
である。王権奪取の野望があった阿麻和利は 1458 年、国王（尚泰久王）の重臣・護佐丸（中城城主）
を滅ぼした後、首里城を攻めたが大敗して滅亡し、その後勝連城も廃城となった。

⑤ Katsuren Castle Ruins

Katsuren Castle was built in the early 14th century by Katsuren-*aji*, the fifth son of King Taisei, the second king of Eiso royal line, and ruled by eleven generations of lords until the last lord, Amawari. It consists of five castles, and is said to have been so prosperous that it is compared to Kyoto and Kamakura in mainland Japan, as it is chanted in the *Omoro-soushi* (collection of poems) as *kimutaka* (noble). The south side of the castle was equipped with a port for trade, while the north side was a rice field and a granary. The walls of the castle are made of limestone stone walls, making good use of the natural topography. The results of several excavations have revealed the existence of buildings with tiled roofs, which were constructed through extensive civil engineering work by cutting the bedrock. At that time, shingle roofs were the mainstream, but other than Katsuren Castle, Shuri Castle and Urasoe Castle are the only other castles with tile roofs at present. In 1458, Amawari, who had an ambition to take over the kingdom, attacked Shuri Castle after destroying Gosamaru (lord of Nakagusuku Castle), a chief vassal of the king (King Sho Taikyu), but was defeated and destroyed. Later, Katsuren Castle was also abandoned.

⑥中城城跡（なかぐすくじょうあと）

　中城湾に沿った標高 160m の琉球石灰岩上に、ほぼ南北に一直線の 6 連郭からなる山城である。眼下の屋宜湊で大和などとの交易で栄えていたことがオモロに謡われている。城壁は琉球石灰岩で積まれ、自然の岩石と地形的条件を巧みに生かしながら美しい曲線で構成されている。築城年代は不詳だが、14 世紀後半までに先中城按司が数世代にわたり城の主要部分である南の郭・西の郭・一の郭・二の郭を築き上げた。1440 年、座喜味城から移ってきた護佐丸によって三の郭と北の郭が最高の築城技術で増築され、現在の形が完成した。1458 年に阿麻和利の讒言によって首里王府軍に攻められ（護佐丸・阿麻和利の乱）、廃城となった。1609 年の薩摩藩の琉球侵攻後は「番所」として利用され、1879 年の廃藩置県後は中城村役場として戦前まで使用されて中城村の行政の中心となった。1853 年、ペリー提督一行がここを調査し、城壁やアーチ門の建築技術の高さに驚嘆。この城に関する詳細な絵図や測量図面などを残している。中城城は、琉球における築城技術を知る上で極めて高い価値があるとされている。戦後は、県下初の公園として動物園や遊園地が設置され、県民の憩いの場として利用された。

中城城跡（北中城村）
Nakagusuku Castle Ruins (Kitanakagusuku Village)

⑥ Nakagusuku Castle Ruins

　This is a mountain castle on Ryukyu limestone at an altitude of 160 meters along Nakagusuku Bay, consisting of a series of six castles that run in a straight line from north to south. In the *Omoro-sousi*, it is said that the Yagi Port below was prosperous in trade with Yamato and other countries. The castle walls are made of Ryukyu limestone and are composed of beautiful curves, skillfully taking advantage of the natural rock formations and topographical conditions. The date of construction is uncertain, but by the late 14th century, several generations of Sachinakagusuku-*aji* had built the main parts of the castle: the south wall, west wall, first wall, and second wall. In 1440, Gosamaru, who had moved from Zakimi Castle, added the third wall and the northern wall with the best construction techniques, completing the present shape of the castle. In 1458, the castle was attacked by the Shuri Royal Army due to Amawari's slander (the Gosamaru-Amawari Rebellion), and the castle was abandoned. After the invasion of Ryukyu by the Satsuma Domain in 1609, the castle was used as a *banjo*, and after the Haihan-chiken (the abolition of the domain) in 1879, it was used as the Nakagusuku Village Office until the war, and became the administrative center of Nakagusuku Village until before the war and became the center of Nakagusuku Village's administration. In 1853, Commodore Perry and his delegation surveyed the castle and were amazed at the high quality of the construction of the walls and arch gates, and left detailed drawings and survey plans of the castle. The Nakagusuku Castle is considered to be of extreme value in understanding the castle construction techniques in Ryukyu. After the war, it became the first park in the prefecture to have a zoo and an amusement park, and was used as a place for the people of the prefecture to relax.

⑦浦添城跡（うらそえじょうあと）

　浦添城は 13 世紀後半、当時の琉球国王「英祖王」（在位 1260 年〜 1299 年）が初めて築いた城である。浦添の語源である「うらおそい」は「津々浦々を襲う・支配する」という意味があり、当時は北西部にある牧港を利用した交易などで、大変勢力のある城として栄えていたといわれる。城内の建物は幾度も改築されているが、最後のものは 1609 年の薩摩軍の侵攻で焼失したと考えられている。英祖王在任中に、禅鑑（ぜんかん）という補蛇落僧（ふだらくそう）が流れ着いた。英祖王は彼の徳を重んじ、浦添城の西に極楽寺を建立したのが琉球における仏教の始まりとされている。城址の入り口から左側の道を下りていくと、英祖王と薩摩侵攻当時の国王・尚寧王が眠る「浦添ようどれ」に行き着く。中山王国は、後に首里の高台に首里城を築き王都としたが、当初の王城は浦添城であった。遷都の時期は英祖王統の次王統・察度王統の頃とも、尚巴志が中山・武寧王を滅ぼした（1406 年）後ともいわれている。貿易が国の柱だった琉球王国にとって港は重要で、大きな船が停泊できる那覇港に首里が近いことが遷都の主な理由であった。沖縄戦では 3 週間にも及ぶ日米両軍の激しい戦いが繰り広げられ、壊滅的なダメージを受けたが、戦後は幾度も修復されている。浦添城跡はハリウッド映画「ハクソー・リッジ」の舞台となった場所で、アメリカや韓国・中国などからも多くの観光客が訪れている。

浦添城跡のハクソー・リッジ（浦添市仲間）
Hacksaw Ridge in Urasoe Castle Ruins
(Nakama, Urasoe City)

⑦ Urasoe Castle Ruins

　Urasoe Castle was first built in the late 13th century by King Eiso (reigned 1260-1299), the king of Ryukyu at that time. The origin of the word *ura-osoi*, means "to attack or control all over the land," and it is said that the castle prospered as a very powerful castle at that time through trade using the Makiminato Port in the northwest. The houses inside the castle have been reconstructed many times, but the last one is thought to have been destroyed by fire during the invasion of Satsuma's army in 1609. During the reign of King Eiso, a monk named Zenkan, who was a complementary monk, washed ashore. King Eiso respected his virtue and built the Gokurakuji Temple on the west side of Urasoe Castle, which is said to be the beginning of Buddhism in Ryukyu. From the entrance of the castle ruins, go down the road on the left to reach the Urasoe-*youdore*, where King Eiso and King Sho Nei, who was the king at the time of the invasion of Satsuma Domain, are buried. The Chuzan Kingdom later built Shuri Castle on the hill of Shuri and made it the royal capital, but the original royal castle was Urasoe Castle. It is said that the relocation of the capital took place either during the Satto royal line, the next royal line after Eiso royal line, or after the destruction of King Bunei of Chuzan by Sho Hashi in 1406. The main reason for the relocation of the capital was the proximity of Shuri to Naha Port, where large ships could dock. A fierce three-week battle between the Japanese and U.S. forces during the Battle of Okinawa, the ruins of the castle were devastated, but have been repaired many times since the war. The ruins of Urasoe Castle were the setting for the Hollywood movie "Hacksaw Ridge," and many tourists from the U.S., South Korea, and China have visited the site.

⑧首里城（しゅりじょう）

　首里城は琉球王国の王都があった沖縄で最大規模の城で、かつて海外貿易の拠点であった那覇港を見下ろす琉球石灰岩上に築かれた山城である。首里城の創建年代は明らかではないが、発掘調査から最古の遺構は 14 世紀末のものと推定され、三山時代は中山の城として用いられていたことが確認されている。15 世紀初め、尚巴志が三山を統一し琉球王朝を確立すると、首里城を王家の居城として使用するようになった。以後、首里城は 450 年にわたる琉球王国の王城であったが、1879 年（明治 12）の「首里城明け渡し」で廃城となっ

1992 年に復元された首里城（那覇市首里）
Shuri Castle, restored in 1992 (Shuri, Naha City)

た。1929 年（昭和 4）には沖縄神社として歴代国王と源為朝が祀られ、旧国宝に指定された。沖縄戦と戦後の琉球大学建設により、ほぼ完全に破壊され僅かに城壁や建物の基礎など一部が残っている状態だった。1980 年代の琉球大学移転に伴い、1992 年に正殿などが復元された。2000 年 12 月、世界遺産に登録されたが、登録は「首里城跡」であり、復元された建物や城壁は世界遺産に含まれていない。史実に記録されている限りでも、首里城は数度にわたり焼失している。最初の焼失は、1453 年に第一尚氏王統の尚金福王の死後に発生した王位争い（志魯・布里の乱）であり、城は完全に破壊された。2019 年 10 月 31 日の火災では、正殿をはじめとする多くの復元建築や収蔵・展示されていた工芸品などが焼失または焼損した。建屋は国の所有で、2019 年 2 月以降、管理および運営が国から沖縄県に移管されたことになっているが、疑問も投げかけられている。

⑧ Shuri Castle

　Shuri Castle is the largest castle in Okinawa where the royal capital of the Ryukyu Kingdom was located. It is a mountain castle built on Ryukyu limestone overlooking Naha Port, which was once a base for overseas trade. The date of Shuri Castle's construction is not clear, but excavations suggest that the oldest remains date back to the end of the 14th century, confirming that it was used as a castle for Chuzan Kingdom during the Sanzan period. In the early 15th century, when Sho Hashi unified the Sanzan and established the Ryukyu Dynasty, Shuri Castle was used as the royal residence. From then on, Shuri Castle was the royal castle of the Ryukyu Kingdom for 450 years, but it was abandoned in 1879 when Shuri Castle was surrendered. In 1929, the castle was designated as Okinawa Shrine, enshrining successive kings and Minamoto-no Tametomo, and was designated as a former national treasure. Due to the Battle of Okinawa and the construction of the University of the Ryukyus after the war, the castle was almost completely destroyed and only a small portion of the castle walls and foundations of the buildings remained. With the relocation of the University of the Ryukyus in the 1980s, *seiden* (the main hall of Shuri Castle) was restored in 1992. It was registered as a World Heritage Site in December 2000, but the registration is for the "Shuri Castle Ruins" and the restored buildings and walls are not included in the World Heritage Site. As far as historical records go, Shuri Castle has been burned down several times. The first fire occurred in 1453 during a struggle for the throne (Shiro-Furi Rebellion) that followed the death of King Sho Kimpuku of the first Sho royal line, and the castle was completely destroyed. The fire on October 31, 2019 destroyed or burned down the *seiden* and many other restored buildings, as well as artifacts that were housed and displayed. The buildings are owned by the national government, but its management and operation are said to have been transferred from the national government to Okinawa Prefecture after February 2019, but questions have been raised.

⑨知念城跡（ちねんぐすくあと）

南城市知念の東方台地の中腹にある連郭式山城で、知念森城（ちねんむいぐすく）とも呼ばれる。『おもろさうし』に「ちねんもりぐすく　かみおれはじめのぐすく」（知念森城　神降り始めの城）と謡われており、グスク時代初期またはそれ以前の古いグスクである。グスクは「クーグスク」（古城）と「ミーグスク」（新城）と呼ばれる 2 つの郭からなり、その城壁の殆どが現存している。オモロに詠まれているのは東側にあるクーグスクで、石灰岩の「野面積み」による城壁である。ミーグスクは「あいかた積み」の城壁に石造りアーチ門でできた正門・裏門を配置している。築城年代については不明だが、

知念城跡（写真下方が「ミーグスク」で、上方が「クーグスク」）（南城市知念）
Chinen-*gusuku* Ruins.The lower part of the photo is Mii-*gusuku*,and upper part is *Kuu-gusuku* (Chinan, Nanjyo City)

12 世紀末から 13 世紀にかけて築城され、代々の知念按司の居城であったと考えられている。主な城主に内間大親がいるが、彼は金丸と内間ノロとの間にできた子といわれる。クーグスクはアマミキヨの時代に、ミーグスクは内間大親によって築かれたと伝わっている。城外には石畳をはさんで古屋敷跡やノロ屋敷跡が点在し、300m ほど離れた崖下には知念按司の墓がある。知念城城跡内には 1761 年〜 1903 年の間、知念間切の番所が置かれた。城跡は 1972 年 5 月 15 日に、国の史跡に指定されている。

⑨ Chinen-*gusuku* Ruins

It is also known as Chinen-*mui-gusuku*, a mountain castle with a series of walls located in the middle of the eastern plateau of Chinen, Nanjo City. In *Omoro-soushi*, it is said that *"Chinen-mori-gusuku, Kami-ore-hajime-no-gusuku"* (Chinen-*mui-gusuku* is the castle where the gods first descended), and is an old *gusuku*(castle) from the early *Gusuku* period or earlier. The *gusuku* is made up of two castles, called *Kuu-gusuku* (old castle) and Mii-*gusuku* (new castle), and most of its walls are still in existence. The one mentioned in the *Omoro-soushi* is *Kuu-gusuku*, which is located on the east side of the castle, and its walls are built of limestone using the *Nozura-zumi* technique. Mii-*gusuku* has the main and back gates made of stone arched gates using the *aikata-zumi* technique. The date of construction is unknown, but it is thought to have been built between the end of the 12th century and the 13th century, and is said to have been the residence of successive generations of Chinen-*aji*. The main lord of the castle was Uchima-*uhuya*, who is said to be the son of Kanamaru and Uchima-*noro*. It is said that *Kuu-gusuku* was created during the time of Amamikiyo and Mii-*gusuku* by Uchima-*uhuya*. Outside the castle, the ruins of old houses and *noro* residence are scattered across the stone pavement, and 300 meters away at the bottom of the cliff is the tomb of Chinen-*aji*. The *banjo* (village hall) of the Chinen *magiri* was located in the Castle ruins from 1761 to 1903. The ruins of the castle were designated as a national historic site on May 15, 1972.

⑩ミントン城跡（みんとんぐすくあと）

ミントングスクは琉球石灰岩からなる小高い丘（標高 110m）にあり、アマミキヨ族の住居跡と考えられている。一説によると、英祖王統四代目・玉城王の即位前の居城ともいわれている。このグスクは先史時代の遺跡で、石斧や貝塚時代中期の土器類などが採集されている。沖縄最古のグスクといわれるミントングスクは、県内各地に分布するグスクの発生や性格を知る上で貴重な遺跡である。ニライカナイからやって来た琉球開闢の祖・アマミキヨがヤハラヅカサから上陸して浜川御嶽に仮住ま

いした後、安住の地として居を構えた場所がこのグスクで、そこから子孫が繁栄して沖縄中に広がっていったという伝説がある。グスク内には「ニライカナイへの遥拝所」、「久高島への遥拝所」、「火の神」、「アマミキヨ・シネリキヨの墓」などの拝所や遥拝所があり、古くから由緒ある御嶽としても知られている。このグスクは沖縄県指定の史跡文化財だが個人の私有地内にあり、所有者である屋号「ミントン」（知念姓）はアマミキヨ直系といわれている。同家には戦前まで角が生えた鬼の面相をした木彫り

ミントン城跡（南城市仲村渠）
Minton-*gusuku* Ruins(Nakandakari,Nanjyo City)

面があったという。これは先祖の顔といわれるが、南方諸島には角や牙を出した仮面神が豊年を祝福する儀式があり、ミントン家の先祖も仮面を被って儀礼したものと考えられている。現在でも「東御回り」（アガリウマーイ）の巡拝地の一つで、久高島の人々との交流があり、参拝者が絶えない。

⑩ Minton-*gusuku* Ruins

Minton-*gusuku* is located on a small hill (110m above sea level) made of Ryukyu limestone and is thought to be the site of a residence of the Amamikiyo tribe. According to one theory, it is said to be the residence of King Tamagusuku, the fourth generation of the King Eiso royal line, before his accession to the throne. This *gusuku* is a prehistoric site, and stone axes and pottery from the middle of the shell mound period have been collected. The Minton-*gusuku* is said to be the oldest *gusuku* in Okinawa, and is a valuable site for understanding the origin and character of *gusuku* distributed throughout the prefecture. Legend has it that Amamikiyo, the founder of Ryukyu who came from *Niraikanai*, landed at Yaharazukasa and took up temporary residence at Hamagawa-*utaki*, and then settled down in this *gusuku* as a safe haven, and from there her descendants prospered and spread throughout Okinawa. Inside the *gusuku*, there are many *haisho* (a place of worship) and *youhaijo* (a place to bow in the direction of worship) such as *youhaijo* to *Niraikanai*, *youhaijo* to Kudaka island, *hinukan* (God of fire), and "tomb of Amamikiyo and Shinerikiyo," and it is also known as a historic *utaki* since ancient times. The *gusuku* is designated as a historical site and cultural asset by Okinawa Prefecture, but it is located on private property, and the owner, *yagou* Minton (family name Chinen), is said to be a direct descendant of Amamikiyo. The family is said to have had a wooden mask carved with the face of a horned demon until before the Battle of Okinawa, and the mask was said to be the face of the ancestor. In the Southern Islands, there is a ritual in which a masked god with horns and fangs is said to bless the harvest, and it is thought that the ancestors of *yagou* Minton also wore masks in the ritual. Even today, it is one of the pilgrimage sites called *Agari-umaai*, interaction with the people of Kudaka Island, and a constant stream of worshippers.

⑪玉城城跡（たまぐすくじょうあと）

築城年代は不明だが、『琉球国由来記』（1713年）によると、琉球の開闢神とされるアマミキヨが築きその子孫である天孫氏王統の城とされる。その後、英祖王統四代目の玉城王が王子時代に居城にしていたが、王位に就いた後は自分の弟を玉城按司として城を守らせ、この時代に城の修築・拡大を行ったと伝えられている。知念半島で最も高い断崖の上（標高179m）に築かれており、主郭・二の郭・三の郭からなる。二の郭跡・三の郭跡の石垣は、沖縄戦後の米軍統治下で隣接していた米軍基地の建築用石材に利用された。主郭の城壁はほぼ完全に近い形で残っており、自然の一枚岩をゴホウラ

ガイに模してくり抜かれた城門（太陽の門）がある。
夏至の日の出には、この門から差し込む朝日が城内
の「火の神」を一直線に照らす。東向きに開いたこ
の城門はそのまま「ニライカナイ」に通じる形になっ
ており、このグスクのシンボルとなっている。本丸
跡には「琉球開闢の七御嶽」の一つ「天つぎあまつ
ぎ御嶽」という拝所があり、この城は別名「アマツ
ヅ城」とも呼ばれる。この御嶽は琉球国王も参拝し
たといわれ、干魃の時、国王自ら雨乞いの儀式を行っ
たという記録も残っている。城跡の南側崖面には風
葬墓も多数確認され、崖下には「クラシミウジョウ」
という通路があり、聖域として重要な場所でもある。

玉城城跡の「太陽の門」（南城市玉城）
Tamagusuku Castle Ruins,the hole at the top of the
photo is the main gate "Gate of the Sun"

玉城城跡の北東（ゴルフ場内）には「タカラグスク」といわれる岩山があり、中腹には玉城王と西威
王（英祖王統五代目）の墓がある。玉城城は城としての規模はさほど大きくなく、軍事的な用途とい
うより祭祀的要素が大きかったのではないかと考えられている。このグスクは「東御廻り」（アガリ
ウマーイ）の聖地の一つであり、古代の祭祀を研究する上でも貴重とされている。

⑪ Tamagusuku Castle Ruins

　The date of construction of the castle is unknown, but according to the Ryukyu-koku-*yuraiki* (1713), it was built
by Amamikiyo, the goddess of the opening of the Ryukyu, and is believed to be the castle of her descendants,
the Tenson Dynasty. Later, it is said that King Tamagusuku, the fourth generation of the Eiso Dynasty, used the
castle as his residence when he was a prince, but after he ascended the throne, he had his younger brother guard
the castle as the anointed Tamagusuku-*aji*, and the castle was rebuilt and expanded during this period. It is built
on the highest cliff on the Chinen Peninsula (179 meters above sea level), and consists of the *shu-kaku*(main),
nino-kaku(second), and *sanno-kaku*(third) sections. The stone walls of the *nino-kaku* and *sanno-kaku* were used as
building stones for the adjacent U.S. military base after the Battle of Okinawa. The walls of the *shu-kaku* are almost
completely intact, and there is a gate (Gate of the Sun) made of a natural monolithic rock hollowed out to resemble
a *gohoura* mussel. At sunrise on the summer solstice, the morning sun shining through this gate illuminates the
hinukan (fire god) in the castle in a straight line. This gate, facing east, leads directly to *Niraikanai* and has become
the symbol of this *gusuku*. There is a place of worship called Tentsugi-amatsugi-*utaki*, one of the "Seven *utaki* of
the opening of the Ryukyu," at the site of the main castle, and the castle is also called Amatsuzu Castle. The king
of Ryukyu is said to have visited this *utaki*, and there is a record that the king himself performed a ceremony to
pray for rain during a drought. A number of wind burial tombs have also been identified on the southern cliff face
of the castle ruins, and there is a passage called *Kurasimi-ujoh* under the cliff, which is also an important place
for sanctuary. To the northeast of the Tamagusuku Castle ruins (now in the golf course) is a rocky hill known as
Takara-*gusuku*, and in the middle of the hill are the tombs of King Tamagusuku and King Irii (the fifth generation
of the Eiso Dynasty). Tamagusuku Castle was not very large, and is thought to have had more of a ritual element
than a military purpose. Tamagusuku Castle Ruins is one of the sacred sites of the *Agari-umaai*, and is considered
valuable for studying ancient rituals.

⑫島添大里城跡（しまそえおおざとじょうあと）

　南城市大里西原のほぼ東西に延びる琉球石灰岩丘陵の尾根部分（標高約 150m）を利用して構築さ
れている。基壇とその上に設けられた正殿建物を中心とする内郭と、それを取り巻いて巡らされた城

壁によって区画された外郭の二重構造となっている。島添大里城跡は大里城跡とも呼ばれ、2005 年の市町村合併以前の大里村の村名はこのグスク名に因んでいる。羽地朝秀が編纂した『中山世鑑』(1650 年)や蔡鐸が編纂した『中山世譜』(1701 年)などの歴史書では南山王の居城とされている。南山国王の居城は他にも南山城(島尻大里城)説があり、今でも見解が分かれている。「島添」とは「島々(村々)を支配する」という意味があり、城主・島添大里按司は大里・佐敷・知念・玉城地域を支配下に置き、眼下にある場天港を利用して明王朝とも貿易を行うほど大きな勢力を持っていた。外郭城壁の東側には突出部があり、そこには真手川原遺跡(マテガーバルいせき)を通り、場天港への通路が取り付けられていたとされる。最初の築城は 14 世紀頃と言われるが、1402 年、後に琉球王国の初代国王とな

る尚巴志によって攻め落とされた。尚巴志は大里城を拠点に、三山統一の足がかりとした。王都が首里に移った後は第一尚氏王統の離宮として 15 世紀後半まで使用され、首里城と並ぶほど壮麗な宮殿であったといわれる。沖縄戦では、島添大里城跡が立地する一帯の丘陵地には知念半島周辺の海岸から上陸する米軍に備えた大砲陣地や壕などが築かれ、日米間で激しい戦闘が繰り広げられた。城壁は戦後も復興資材に使われ、大半の遺跡が消失した。現在は廃墟となっているが、2012 年 1 月に国指定史跡となった。

島添大里城跡(南城市大里)
Shimasoe-Ozato Castle Ruins(Ozato, Nanjyo City)

⑫ Shimasoe-Ozato Castle Ruins

This *gusuku* was built on the ridge of a Ryukyu limestone hill (about 150m above sea level) extending almost east to west in Ozato Nishihara, Nanjo City. It has a double structure: an inner wall with the main hall built on top of the platform, and an outer wall that surrounds the inner wall. The ruins of Shimasoe-Ozato Castle are also called Ozato Castle Ruins, and the name of Ozato Village before the 2005 municipal merger is derived from the name of this castle. In history books such as Chuzan-seikan (1650) compiled by Haneji Choshu and Chuzan-seifu (1701) compiled by Sai Taku, it is said to be the residence of the king of the Nanzan Kingdom. There are other theories about the residence of the king of the Nanzan kingdom, such as Nanzan Castle (Simajiri-Ozato Castle), and opinions are still divided. shimasoe means "to rule islands (villages)," and the lord of the castle, Shimasoe-Ozato-*aji*, had the Ozato, Sashiki, Chinen, and Tamagusuku areas under his control, and was so powerful that he traded with the Ming Dynasty in China using the Baten Port located under the castle. There is a protrusion on the east side of the outer wall, where a passage was said to have been attached through the "ruins of Mategaa-*baru*" to the Baten Port. It is said that the first castle was built around the 14th century, but it was attacked in 1402 by Sho Hashi, who later became the first king of the Ryukyu Kingdom. Sho Hashi used the Ozato Castle as a foothold for the unification of the three kingdoms. After the royal capital was moved to Shuri, it was used as a detached palace of the First Sho Dynasty until the late 15th century, and is said to have been as magnificent as Shuri Castle. During the Battle of Okinawa, the hills around the site of Shimasoe-Ozato Castle were used to build artillery positions and dugouts to prepare for American troops landing from the coast around the Chinen Peninsula, and fierce battles were fought between the United States and Japan. The wall stones were used as reconstruction materials after the war, and most of the ruins were lost. It is now in ruins, but in January 2012 it was designated as a national historic site.

⑬豊見城城跡（とみぐすくじょうあと）

　豊見城市豊見城の標高 54m にあり、南山王（承察度王）の甥・汪応祖（ヤフス）が 14 世紀末～ 15 世紀初めに築城したといわれる。王府の正史『球陽』（1745 年）によると「汪応祖は中国の南京にある国子鑑に学び、帰国後、国場川を臨む丘に築城して城主となり、豊見城と名付けた」という。留学中に見た中国の竜舟競漕を伝え、1400 年頃、城下で爬竜船競漕（ハーリー）を行ったといわれる。城内に「豊見瀬之嶽」（ティミシヌタキ）と呼ばれる、豊見城ノロが雨乞いを祈願する御嶽がある。旧暦 5 月 4 日（現在は 5 月のゴールデンウィーク）に実施される那覇ハーリーでは、開始前にこの拝所を遥拝する儀式を行う。糸満ハーレーは、汪応祖が糸満市高嶺の南山城に移り、南山王に即位してから始まったといわれる。1429 年、尚巴志は南山城（他魯毎王）を攻撃する前に南山の前線基地である豊見城グスクを火攻めで落城させた。当時、他魯毎王の弟・豊見城按司が城主だったが、尚巴志側の「女性スパイ作戦」によって陥落した後は廃城となった。昭和 30 年代までは城壁やアーチ石門が残っていたが、1970 年頃に豊見城跡公園として整備する際に壊された。「空手発祥の地・沖縄」を国内外に発信し、空手の神髄を学ぶ拠点として、2017 年、沖縄空手会館が城跡内に開館した。

豊見城城跡内の豊見瀬御嶽（豊見城市豊見城）
Toyomise-*utaki* within the ruins of Tomigusuku Castle
(Tomigusuku, Tomigusuku City)

⑬ Tomigusuku Castle Ruins

　It is located at an altitude of 54 meters above sea level in Tomigusuku, City of Tomigusuku, and is said to have been built by Yahusu, a nephew of King Uhzatu (Nanzan kingdom), between the end of the 14th century and the beginning of the 15th century. According to Kyuyou (1745), the official history of the Shuri royal government, "Yahusu studied at *Kokushikan* in Nanjing, China, and after returning to Ryukyu, he built a castle on a hill overlooking the Kokuba River and named it Tomigusuku Castle. He is said to have introduced the Chinese dragon boat race that he saw while studying in China, and to have held a reptile boat race (*haarii*) under the castle around 1400. There is a *utaki* called Timishinu-*taki* in the castle, where Tomigusuku-*noro* prays for rain. The Naha-*haarii,* which is held on the fourth day of the fifth month of the lunar calendar (currently the Golden Week holiday in May), has a ceremony to worship the *utaki* before the start of the event. Itoman-*haaree* is said to have started after Yahusu moved to Nanzan Castle in Takamine, Itoman City, and ascended to the throne as King Nanzan. In 1429, before attacking Nanzan Castle (King Tarumii), Sho Hashi felled Nanzan's frontline base, Tomigusuku Castle, by fire attack. At that time, the lord of the castle was Tomigusuku-*aji*, the younger brother of King Tarumii, but the castle was abandoned after it fell due to the "female spy operation" by Sho Hashi. The castle walls and arched stone gates remained until the 1950s, but were torn down around 1970 when the area was developed as Tomigusuku Castle Ruins Park. In 2017, the Okinawa Karate-*Kaikan* was opened in the castle ruins as a base for promoting "Okinawa as the birthplace of karate" and learning the essence of karate.

⑭島尻大里城跡（しまじりおおざとじょうあと）

　島尻大里城は三山分立時代（14世紀頃）に栄えた南山王の居城とされ、南山城や高嶺城とも呼ばれる。糸満市教育委員会による発掘調査（1984年）によると、南山城は13世紀頃に築かれ、14～15世紀前半が特に栄えていたことが判っている。中国の史書『明実録』には、1380年に南山・承察度王が冊封を受け、1385年に明皇帝から南山王として銀印が下賜されことが記されている。糸満港を貿易港として冊封体制のもとで明国との交易や、朝鮮との交流もあったと思われる。1429年の中山・尚巴志王による南山王国滅亡後は伊覇按司二代目の弟・高嶺按司が南山監守として配置された。尚巴志の義弟に当たる高嶺按司は、700mほど北にあるタマターグスクの石垣を崩し、南山城の石垣を増築した。1915年（大正4）、城址内に散在していた御嶽や墓が東側に集められて納骨堂と鳥居が造られた。1927年（昭和2）に南山神社が創建されたが、現在の南山神社あたりが南山城正殿であったとみられている。沖縄戦後は、城址の大部分が高嶺小学校の敷地となり、按司墓や石積みの一部、古い香炉の他には往時の遺構はほとんど現存していない。

島尻大里城跡（糸満市大里）
Shimajiri-Ozato Castle Ruins(Ozato,Itoman City)

⑭ Shimajiri-Ozato Castle Ruins

　Shimajiri-Ozato Castle is said to be the residence of the King of Nanzan, which flourished during the period of the division of the three kingdoms (around the 14th century), and is also known as Nanzan Castle or Takamine Castle. According to an excavation conducted by the Itoman City Board of Education in 1984, Nanzan Castle was built around the 13th century and was particularly prosperous in the 14th to early 15th centuries. In the Ming-*jitsuroku*, a Chinese historical book, it is written that in 1380, King Sho Satto (Uhzatu) of Nanzan was granted a title of "King of Nanzan" and in 1385, the Ming Emperor bestowed a silver seal on him as King of Nanzan. With Itoman Port as a trading port, it is speculated that there was trade with the Ming Dynasty under the *sappuu-taisei* (Chinese Tributary System) and exchange with Korea. After the fall of the Nanzan kingdom by King Sho Hashi of Chuzan kingdom in 1429, Takamine-*aji*, the younger brother of Iha-*aji's* second generation, was assigned as the Nanzan-*kanshu* (governor). In 1915, *utaki* and tombs scattered in the castle ruins were gathered on the east side and an ossuary and a torii gate were built. The Nanzan Shrine was built in 1927, and the area where the current Nanzan Shrine is located is said to have been the *seiden* (main hall) of Nanzan Castle. After the Battle of Okinawa, most of the castle ruins became the site of Takamine Elementary School, and apart from the graves of *aji*, some masonry, and old incense burners, few other remains from the past have survived.

（12）英祖王統以前の王統　（えいそおうとういぜんのおうとう）

①天帝氏王統（てんていしおうとう）

　伝承によると、1世・明東天孫氏王の先祖は天帝氏で、高嶺間切（現・糸満市）の武順御嶽（ぶじゅんうたき）が居城であったといわれている。武順御嶽は糸満市の与座岳山頂にあり、麓には「武順ガー」が現存する。天帝氏の墓は浜比嘉島（うるま市）にあり、天帝氏時代は紀元前3世紀から西暦5世紀

まで続いたと考えられている。天帝氏王統の始祖は、秦の始皇帝の命を受けて不老長寿の薬草を求めて来琉した徐福であるという説もある。

(12) Dynasties before the Eiso Dynasty
① The Tentei Dynasty

According to tradition, the ancestors of King Minton-Tenson were the Tenteishi Clan, and their castle was located at Bujun-*utaki* in Takamine *magiri* (present Itoman City). Bujun-*utaki* is located at the top of Mount Yoza-*dake* in Itoman City, and Bujun-*gaa* still exists at the foot of the mountain. The tomb of the Tenson is located on Hamahiga Island (Uruma City), and the Tenteishi era is thought to have lasted from the 3rd century B.C. to the 5th century A.D. There is a theory that the founder of the Tenteishi Royal Descends was Xu Fu, who came to the Ryukyus in search of medicinal herbs for longevity under the order of Qin Shi Huang

武順御嶽（糸満市大里）
Bujun-*utaki*(Ozato, Itoman City)

②天孫氏王統（てんそんしおうとう）

　琉球王国として歴史書に登場する最初の王統は、1187 年に誕生した舜天王統である。1650 年に摂政・羽地朝秀によって編纂された正史『中山世鑑』によると、それ以前に天孫氏王統があり、25 世続いたと記されている。天孫氏王統の歴代王名は、第 1 世が明東天孫氏王で、最後の第 25 世は大里天孫氏王（大里思兼松金）となっている。第 25 世王の居城は大里間切（現・南城市）の義留森（ぎりむい）にあったが、家臣の利勇に滅ぼされ、10 男 2 女の子供たちは各地に亡命したという。初代・明東天孫氏王は、南城市仲村渠の屋号「明東」に祀られ、25 世・大里天孫氏王は南城市大里の屋号「大世」で祀られている。

義留森グスク（南城市大里）
Girimui-*gusuku*(Ozato, Nanjyo City)

② The Tenson Dynasty

The first royal lineage to appear in history books as the Kingdom of Ryukyu was the Shunten lineage born in 1187, and according to the Chuzan-seikan, the official history compiled by the regent Haneji Chosyu in 1650, there was an earlier lineage of the Shunten lineage that lasted for 25 generations. The first king of the lineage was King Minton Tenson , and the last king of the lineage was King Ozato Tenson (Ozato Umikani Machigani). The 25th king's castle was located at Girimui in Ozato *magiri* (present-day Nanjo City), but was destroyed by his vassal Riyuu, and his children, ten sons and two daughters, went into exile in various places. The first king, Minton Tenson, is enshrined at *yagou* Minton in Nakandakari, Nanjo City, and the 25th king, Ozato Tenson , is enshrined at *yagou* Uhuyuu in Ozato, Nanjo City.

③舜天王統（しゅんてんおうとう）

　逆臣・利勇を滅ぼした舜天を祖とする王統で、1187 年から 1259 年の間、3 代 73 年間にわたり「琉球国中山王」として王位に就いたとされる。舜天王統はそれ以前の伝説的王統とは異なり、実在した王統とされている。『中山世譜』（1701 年）に初代・舜天は源為朝の子と明記されているが、その実在を確証する史料はまったく残っていない。1185 年に「壇ノ浦の合戦」で水死したとされる安徳天皇が重臣とともに沖縄まで生き延び、舜天王として即位したという「南走平家伝説」も伝えられている。舜天王が統治していたとされる頃は、小規模のグスクが各地に点在し、沖縄本島全体を支配したとは考えられない。舜天王統は初代・舜天王、二代目・舜馬順熙王（しゅんばじゅんきおう）、三代目・義本王（ぎほんおう）と 3 代続いたが 1260 年、摂政の英祖に王位を奪われた。舜天王統三代の墓は北中城村仲順にある「ナス之御嶽」とされているが、他にも各地に存在する。

ナス之御嶽（北中城村仲順）
Nasu'no-*utaki*(Chunjun, Kitanakagusuku Village)

③ The Shunten Dynasty

　The royal line with Shunten as the ancestor who destroyed the adversary, Riyuu, is said to have reigned as the "King of Chuzan in Ryukyu Kingdom" for three generations for 3 years from 1187 to 1259. The Shunten lineage is considered to be a real lineage, unlike the legendary lineages before it. The "Chuzan-seihu" (1701) states that the first Shunten was the son of Minamoto-no Tametomo, but there are no historical documents to confirm the existence of the Shunten royal line, and the "legend of the Nansou-Heike" that Emperor Antoku, who was drowned in the "Battle of Dan'noura" in 1185, survived to Okinawa with his retainers and ascended to the throne as King Shunten is also a popular theory. There is also a popular theory that Emperor Antoku died at sea and survived to Okinawa with his chief retainer and ascended the throne as King Shunten. During the time when King Shunten was said to have ruled, there were many small *gusuku* scattered in various places, and it is not thought that he ruled the entire main island of Okinawa. The lineage of King Shunten lasted for three generations with the first King Shunten, the second King Shumba Junki, and the third King Gihon, but in 1260, the regent Eiso took the throne. The tombs of the three generations of King Shunten royal line are said to be Nasu'no-*utaki* in Chunjun, Kitanakagusuku Village, but they exist in various places.

(13) 南走平家（なんそうへいけ）

　平家は倶利伽羅峠の戦い（1183 年）、一の谷の戦い（1184 年）、屋島の戦い（1185 年 3 月）などの各戦いに敗れ、壇ノ浦での最終決戦（1185 年 4 月）でも源氏に敗れた。一連の源平合戦で敗北した平家は各地に敗走し隠れ住んだ。壇ノ浦の合戦で敗れ、京都から密かに移送された財宝や安徳天皇と共に奄美諸島、沖縄島、宮古・八重山諸島など南の島々に逃げ延びた平家は南走平家と呼ばれる。この説によると、壇ノ浦の戦いに赴いた平家は影武者で、安徳天皇を含む本隊は船団で南下して奄美諸島を経由して、沖縄で安徳天皇を初代の国王（舜天王）とする舜天王統を樹立。一部は宮古島や八重

山諸島にも逃れたという。首里王府の正史である『中山世鑑』には、舜天王統は 1187 年に設立され たと記されており、この年は壇ノ浦の戦いの 2 年後となる。『中山世鑑』を編纂した羽地朝秀は、源 為朝が琉球に渡ったという伝説を採用し、南走平家が琉球に来た痕跡を伏せた。しかし『中山世鑑』 は当然、薩摩藩の検閲を受けたものと考えられ、この記述は薩摩支配に対する羽地朝秀の政治的配慮 との見方がある。

(13) Nansou-Heike（Fallen Heike warriors fleeing to the south）

The Heike (the Taira clan) was defeated in various battles such as the Battle of Kurikara-*touge* (1183), the Battle of Ichinotani (1184), and the Battle of Yashima (March 1185), and were also defeated by the Genji (the Minamoto clan) in the final battle at Dan'noura (April 1185). The Heike, who was defeated in the series of battles between the Genji and Heike clans, fled to various places and lived in hiding. The Heike who was defeated in the Battle of Dan'noura and fled to Amami Islands, Okinawa Island, Miyako Islands, Yaeyama Islands, and other southern islands with treasures and Emperor Antoku that were secretly transported from Kyoto is called the Nansou-Heike. According to this theory, the Heike clan that went to the battle of Dan'noura were shadow warriors, and the main force, including Emperor Antoku, went south in a fleet of ships through the Amami Islands to establish the Shunten Dynasty with Emperor Antoku as the first king (Shunten King) in Okinawa, and some of them also escaped to Miyako Island and the Yaeyama Islands. In the Chuzan-seikan, the authentic history of the Shuri royal government, it is written that the Shunten Dynasty was established in 1187, which was two years after the Battle of Dan'noura. Haneji Chosyu, who compiled the Chuzan-seikan, adopted the legend that Minamoto-no Tametomo crossed over to the Ryukyu Islands and withheld the traces of the arrival of the Nansou-Heike to the Ryukyu Islands. However, the Chuzan-seikan is naturally considered to have been censored by the Satsuma Domain, and there is a view that this description was a political consideration by Haneji Chosyu for Satsuma's control.

(14) 久米（閩人）三十六姓 (くめ・びんじんさんじゅうろくせい)

久米三十六姓は、1392 年に明の光武帝より琉球王国に下賜されたとされる閩人（現・福建省の中 国人）の職能集団。琉球への渡来については『明実録』に、唐代に商売やその他の理由で移住した者 が自然発生的に唐人集落を形成したという記述がある。閩人三十六姓とも言われ、中国と琉球を往来 するための航海・造船等の技術を持ち、進 貢に不可欠な外交文書の作成や通訳、交易 を担い琉球王国を支えた。居住区域（現・ 那覇市久米町）を中国人自身は「唐栄・唐 営」（とうえい）と称したが、琉球側は久 米村（くにんだ）と呼びそこに暮らす人々 を久米村人（クニンダンチュ）または「ク ニンダー」と呼んだ。尚清王代後半から中 国の貿易政策で一旦は衰退したが、1609 年の薩摩の侵攻後、再び中国貿易が推進さ れて復興した。尚敬王代の三司官・蔡温や、 1609 年の薩摩藩による琉球侵攻後に薩摩 藩に従わず処刑された三司官・謝名親方利 山（鄭迵）も久米三十六姓の出身である。

久米村発祥の地（那覇市久米町）
Birthplace of *Kuninda* (Kume-*cho*, Naha City)

(14) Kume-*sanjuroku-sei* (Bin-*jin-sanjuroku-sei*)

The Kume-*sanjuroku-sei* was a professional group of Bin-*jin* (now Fujian Chinese) who are said to have been given to the Kingdom of Ryukyu by the Ming Emperor Guangwu in 1392. In the Min-*jitsuroku* (Records of the Ming Dynasty) there is a description of the arrival of the Ming people, who migrated for business or other reasons during the Tang Dynasty, and spontaneously formed a Tang settlement. The Kume-*sanjuroku-sei* also known as the Bin-*jin-sanjuroku-sei*, were skilled in navigation and shipbuilding to travel between China and the Ryukyu Islands, and supported the Ryukyu Kingdom by preparing diplomatic documents, interpreting, and trading, which were essential for paying tribute. The Chinese themselves called the area where they lived (now Kume-*cho*, Naha City) *Touei*, but the Ryukyuan side called it *Kuninda*, and the people living there *Kunindan-chu* or *Kunindaa*. From the latter half of the reign of King Sho Sei, the *Kuninda* declined due to China's trade policy, but after the invasion of Satsuma in 1609, China's trade was promoted again and the *Kuninda* was restored. Sai On, the *sanshikan* of the reign of King Sho Kei, and Jana-*oyakata* Rizan (Chinese name is Tei Dou), one of the *sanshikan* who was executed after the invasion of Ryukyu by the Satsuma Domain in 1609 for disobeying the Satsuma, were also from the Kume-*sanjuroku-sei*.

(15) 三山時代 （さんざんじだい）

沖縄本島では 1314 年、英祖王統第 4 代目・玉城王が即位すると、王統内で派閥争いが勃発した。1320 年頃から王統が乱れて分裂し、各地で城（グスク）を構えていた按司たちを束ねる強力な王が現われ 3 つの王国が誕生したといわれる。今帰仁グスクを中心とする北山王国、浦添・首里グスクを中心とする中山王国、島尻大里グスクを中心とする南山王国で、約 100 年間続いた。三山は互いに相争っていたので「三山鼎立時代」（さんざんていりつじだい）とも呼ばれる。三山はいずれも明皇帝から冊封を受け、それぞれ独立して朝貢〈進貢〉貿易を行った。15 世紀初頭に南山の佐敷按司（尚巴志）が台頭し、1405 年に中山を、1416 年に北山を、1429 年に南山を滅ぼして統一し、琉球王国が誕生した。中国の史書『明実録』や『明史』では三国名を「中山、山北、山南」と記しているが、首里王府の史書『中山世譜』などでは「中山、北山、南山」という表記となっている。そのため両方の名称が混在するようになったが、どちらの使用も正しい。

(15) Sanzan period

In 1314, when King Tamagusuku, the fourth in the line of King Eiso, ascended to the throne, factional conflicts broke out within the royal family. It is said that around 1320, when the royal family was in turmoil and divided, a powerful king emerged to unite the *aji* who had set up castles (*gusuku*) in various places, and three kingdoms were born. The period of three separate kingdoms lasted for about 100 years: the Hokuzan Kingdom centered on the Nakijin-*gusuku*, the Chuzan Kingdom centered on the Urasoe/Shuri-*gusuku*, and the Nanzan Kingdom centered on the Shimajiri-Ozato-*gusuku*. Since the three kingdoms were at odds with each other, this era is also known as the "Sanzan period". Three kingdoms received *sappuu* from the Ming emperor and conducted tribute trade independently of each other. In the early 15th century, Sashiki-*aji* (Sho Hashi) of Nanzan rose to prominence and unified the kingdom by destroying Chuzan in 1405, Hokuzan in 1416, and Nanzan in 1429, thus creating the Kingdom of Ryukyu. In the Chinese history books "Ming-*jitsuroku*" and "Ming-*shi*," the names of the three kingdoms are written as "Chuzan, San-hoku, San-nan," but in Chuzan Seihu, the history book of the Shuri royal government, the names are written as "Chuzan, Hokuzan, Nanzan". This led to a mixture of both names, but both uses are correct.

(16) 冊封体制（さっぷうたいせい）と進貢貿易（しんこうぼうえき）

①冊封体制

　中国皇帝との朝貢体制。この体制下では、琉球王国は中国の一員となったが、自治は保証された。1368 年に明朝を建国した光武帝は、アジア諸国に使者を送り朝貢を促した。中国皇帝に忠誠を誓う証として貢使を送り、貢物を捧げることを「朝貢」という。その見返りとして、「その国の王としての地位を認め、中国と交易ができる権利を与えること」を冊封という。国王が替わると皇帝の命を受けた冊封使が首里城に来て新国王を任命した。「御庭」（ウナー）と呼ばれる首里城正殿前の広場で行われたこの「冊封の儀式」は事

冊封の儀式（首里城御庭）
Sappuu Ceremony (*Unaa* in Shuri Castle)

実上の戴冠式であった。1372 年の中山・察度王以来、即位した王たちは競って冊封を受けた。1380 年には南山・承察度王が、1383 年には北山・怕尼芝王が朝貢した。冊封は 1875 年に明治政府によって禁止されたが、1372 年に察度王が最初に冊封を受けてから約 500 年間に 22 回行われた。

(16) *Sappuu-taisei* (The tribute system with the Chinese emperor) , Tribute trade

① *Sappuu-taisei*

　It is an Imperial Chinese Tributary System. Under this system, the Ryukyu Kingdom became a member of China, but its autonomy was guaranteed. Emperor Guangwu, who founded the Ming Dynasty in 1368, sent messengers to Asian countries to urge them to pay tribute. Sending a messenger and offering a tribute as proof of loyalty to the Chinese Emperor is called *chou-kou* in Japanese. In return for that, the emperor recognizes their status as the king of the country and grants them the right to trade with China. When the king of the Ryukyu kingdom took over, some messengers (*Sappuu-shi*) under the order of the Chinese Emperor came to Shuri Castle and appointed a new king. This *sappuu* Ceremony held in the plaza (*Unaa*) in front of the main hall of Shuri Castle was in effect a coronation ceremony. Since King Satto (Chuzan kingdom) received the *sappuu* in 1372, the kings who ascended to the throne competed and received the *sappuu*. In 1380, King Uhuzato (Nanzan kingdom) and King Haniji (Hokuzan kingdom) in 1383, were received the *sappuu*. Although *sappuu* was banned by the Meiji government in 1875, it was held 22 times in the 500 years since King Satto first received *sappuu* recognition from Ming China in 1372.

②進貢（朝貢）貿易

　王府時代の琉球と中国間の公的な貿易は進貢貿易（または朝貢貿易）と呼ばれ、中国皇帝への進貢（朝貢）の名目で行われた。進貢船には、皇帝への貢ぎ物（馬、刀、硫黄、貝、錫、南方産の蘇木など）の他に、一般貿易品が積まれた。琉球側からの進貢に対して皇帝からは、恩恵として絹織物などの返礼品が送られ、外交秩序を築いた。使節（朝貢使）による単なる儀礼的外交にとどまらず、随行する商人による一般貿易も多大な利益を上げて、俗に「唐一倍」などと言われた。当時は私的な貿易は許されず、公的な朝貢貿易のみが許された。

　ところで、琉球と中国の関係は儀礼的で、形式的なものであったといわれる。首里王府が、派遣した者たちに与えた文書の中には「進貢二番、買物一番」とか、「進貢は礼法の務めに過ぎないのであ

り、予定の品物を買い整えることが大事である」などと記されている。つまり、中国皇帝から冊封を受けたり、北京へ進貢使を派遣するのは、安定した貿易を維持するための儀式に過ぎなかったのである。進貢（朝貢）貿易は琉球王国の大きな財源となったが、薩摩の侵攻後は薩摩の管理下に置かれ、薩摩にその多くを吸い上げられた。

進貢船（模型）
Tribute ship (model)

② **Tribute trade**

The official trade between Ryukyu and China during the period of the royal government was called the tribute trade, and was conducted in the name of paying tribute to the Chinese emperor. The tribute ships were loaded with horses, swords, sulfur, shellfish, tin, and *soboku* (plants for dyes) as tribute to the Chinese emperor, as well as general trade goods. In response to the Ryukyu side's tribute, the emperor sent back silk fabrics and other gifts as a favor, establishing a diplomatic order. Not only was the diplomacy conducted by the tribute envoys a mere ritual, but the general trade conducted by the accompanying merchants was also very profitable, and was commonly referred to as *tou-ichibai* (great profit).

At that time, private trade was not allowed, only official tribute trade. By the way, it is said that the relationship between Ryukyu and China was ceremonial and formal. In a document given to those dispatched by the Shuri royal government, it is written, "The second duty is to pay tribute and the first duty is to buy," or "Tribute is nothing more than a ceremonial duty, and it is important to buy the planned goods well". In other words, receiving the *sappuu* from the Chinese emperor or sending the tribute envoys to Beijing was nothing more than a ceremony to maintain steady trade. The tribute trade was a major source of revenue for the Ryukyu Kingdom, but after the invasion by Satsuma, the Ryukyu Kingdom was placed under Satsuma's control, and Satsuma siphoned off much of the revenue.

③冊封使 (さっぷうし・さくほうし)

　冊封使とは、中国王朝の皇帝が附庸国の国王に爵号を授けるために派遣する使節をいう。琉球では国王の死後、中国皇帝にその訃を報じる使者が遣わされた。皇帝はこれを受けて冊封のための正・副使を任命した。冊封使一行は通常500人以上で、約 6 ヶ月間も琉球に滞在した。首里王府は、国賓としての接待のため那覇の浮島に天使館を造り、辻町に遊郭まで設定した。冊封使は儒学・詩文・書に長じており、琉球でも碑文・詩文・書を残した人が多い。名高い冊封使として、徐葆光（じょほこう）、李鼎元（りていげん）、周煌（しゅうこう）らがいる。

冊封使絵図
Sappuu-shi parade(pictured)

③ *Sappuu-shi*

The term *sappuu-shi* refers to an envoy sent by the emperor of Chinese Dynasty to confer a title on the king of a country. In Ryukyu, after the death of a king, an envoy was sent to inform the Chinese emperor of his death. In response to this, the emperor appointed regular and deputy envoys. The envoys usually numbered more than 500 and stayed in Ryukyu for about six months. The Shuri royal government built Tenshi-*kan* on Ukishima in Naha and even set up a red light district in Tsuji-*machi* to entertain them as state guests. They were skilled in Confucianism, poetry, and calligraphy, and many of them left inscriptions, poems and calligraphy in Ryukyu. The famous *sappuu-shi* include Xu Bohkou, Li Ding Yuan, and Zhou Huang.

(17) 天使館（てんしかん）

天使館絵図
Tenshi-*kan* (pictured)

　冊封使一行の宿泊所で、俗に「クヮンヤ」（館屋）と呼び、訛って「クヮーニャ」または「クヮーナ」と称した。現在の那覇市西消防署の近くにあり、建物はすべて中国風であった。大門は南面し、「天使館」と書かれた大額が掲げられていたという。天使館の創建は不明だが、王府の史書『球陽』には武寧王代（1396 ～ 1405）ではないかと記されている。天使館は王一代で一度だけ使用されたため、通常は砂糖座に流用され貢納のための砂糖樽の製造所にあてられていた。

(17) Tenshi-*kan*

This was the lodging place for the *sappuu-shi*, envoys of the Emperor of China, and was commonly called *kwanya*, which became *kwaa-nya* or *kwaa-na* in accent. It was located near the present-day Naha City Nishi Fire Station, and the buildings were all Chinese-style. The large south-facing gate is said to have had a large plaque with the words Tenshi-*kan* written in Chinese characters. The date of construction of the Tenshi-*kan* is unknown, but the royal history book Kyuyou says that it was probably built during the reign of King Bunei (1396 ～ 1405). Since the Tenshi-*kan* was used only once per king, it was usually diverted to the *satou-za* (department in charge of sugar) to be used as a place to manufacture sugar barrels for tribute payments.

(18) 天妃宮（てんぴぐう）

上の天妃宮跡（現・天妃小学校）
Ruins of Upper Tempiguu (now Tempi Elementary School)

　天妃廟とも呼ばれ久米村の一部・天妃町にあった。創建年は不明だが、永楽年間（1403 ～ 24）に建廟されたのは間違いないといわれている。航海安全の守護女神として信仰される媽祖（天妃）を祀り、上下 2 つの廟があった。「上の天妃宮」は現在の天妃小学校の地に、「下の天妃宮」は西消防署付近にあったという。1392 年に来琉した閩人三十六姓には航海業者も多く、彼らが神像を持ってきて建廟したと考えられている。天妃宮は沖縄戦で焼失したが 1975 年に復興。上下天妃宮の諸像は現在、那覇市久米町にある天尊廟内に合祀されている。

(18) Tempiguu temple (Tempi temple)

This temple, also called Tempi-*byo*, was located in Tempi-*cho*, a part of Kume Village. The year of its foundation is unknown, but it is said to have been built during the Yongle era (1403 ～ 24). The temple is dedicated to the goddess "Maso(Tempi)," who is believed to be the guardian of safe navigation, and had two temples, one above and one below. "The upper Tempiguu" is said to have been located at the site of the current Tempi Elementary School, while "the lower Tempiguu" was located near the Nishi Fire Station.

The Bin-*jin-sanjuroku-sei* (Fuzhou people) who came to Ryukyu in 1392 included many navigators, and it is thought that they brought this statue of the god with them when they built the temples. The Maso statues that were once in the upper and lower Tempiguu are now enshrined together in the Tenson Temple in Kume-*cho*, Naha City.

(19) 大交易時代 （だいこうえきじだい）

14 世紀末（1372 年）から 16 世紀半ばまでの約 150 年間のこの時代は「大交易時代」と呼ばれる。1368 年に誕生した明王朝は、中国を中心とした国際秩序の構築を目指した。近隣諸国に入貢を呼びかけるとともに、海禁政策によって自由貿易を禁止した。つまり中国を盟主とし、周辺諸国を臣下とする位置づけを明確にし、明の皇帝に忠誠を誓う国に対してのみ交易を許した。このように中国を中心とした東アジアの国際秩序は「冊封体制」と呼ばれ、琉球の他にも日本、シャム（現・タイ王国）、安南（現・ベトナム）、ルソン（現・フィリピン）なども明王朝から冊封を受けた。琉球は明王朝という強力な力を背景に、東アジアから東南アジアにまたがる地域を舞台に大交易を展開した。これらの地で買い入れた蘇木（そぼく）・香料・象牙などの南方産の品々や、琉球でとれる硫黄・馬・貝製品などを中国や韓国・日本で売りさばき、多大な利益をあげた。特に、当時の中国は火薬の原料である硫黄を大量に必要としており、琉球は農業生産力を高めるために鉄を必要としていた。明は自国の威厳を見せるために、朝貢してきた国に対し、その何倍もの高価な返礼品を贈った。琉球に大きな富をもたらした交易は 16 世紀初期（尚清王代）には徐々に衰えていった。理由は①明王朝の海禁策が緩み、中国商人が直接交易した②欧州勢のアジア進出で琉球の交易が阻害された③南米や日本から大量の銀が採掘され、通貨が銅銭から銀に代わった、などである。

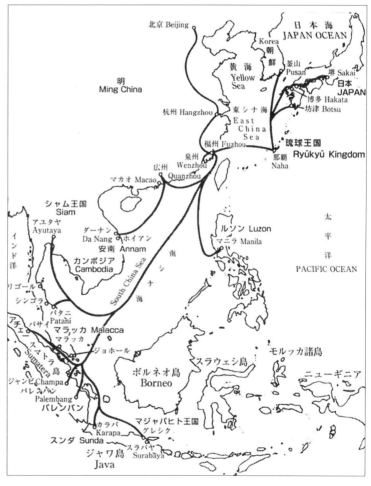

14 世紀末〜 16 世紀中期の琉球王国貿易ルート
（高良倉吉著『アジアのなかの琉球王国』）
Ryukyu Kingdom trade routes (late 14th century-mid 16th century)

(19) *Daikoueki-jidai* (The Great Trade Period)

This period of about 150 years, from the end of the 14th century (1372) to the mid-16th century, is called the *Daikoeki-jidai* (Great Trading Period). The Ming Dynasty, born in 1368, aimed to establish an international order centered on China, and called on neighboring countries to pay tribute to China, and prohibited free trade by adopting a sea ban policy. In other words, it clearly positioned China as the leader and neighboring countries as vassals, and allowed trade only with countries that pledged allegiance to the Ming emperor. This international order in East Asia centered on China was called the *sappuu-taisei* (tributary relationship), and in addition to Ryukyu, Japan, Siam (now the Kingdom of Thailand), Annam (now Vietnam), and Luzon (now the Philippines) also received *sappuu* recognition from the Ming Dynasty. Against the backdrop of the powerful Ming Dynasty, the Ryukyu Kingdom developed a large trade in the region spanning East and Southeast Asia. The Ryukyu Kingdom made huge profits by selling southern products such as *soboku* (plants that can get red dye), perfumes, and ivory purchased in those areas, as well as sulfur, horses, and shellfish from the Ryukyu Islands, to China, Korea, and Japan. In particular, China at the time needed large amounts of sulfur to make gunpowder, and the Ryukyu Kingdom needed iron to increase agricultural productivity. In order to show the dignity of their country, the Ming Dynasty gave many times more expensive returns to the countries that paid tribute to them. Trade, which had brought great wealth to Ryukyu, gradually declined in the early 16th century (the reign of King Sho Sei). The reasons for this were: (1) the Ming Dynasty's ban on sea trade was loosened, and Chinese merchants traded directly with them; (2) the expansion of European countries into Asia was hampering Ryukyu's trade; and (3) large amount of silver were being mined from South America and Japan, and silver was being used as currency instead of copper coins.

(20) 長虹堤 (ちょうこうてい)

　1451 年（尚金福王代）に造られた、安里橋（現在の崇元寺橋辺り）とイベガマ（松山交差点付近で現存していない）を結ぶ全長約 1km の海中道路で、浮道ともいう。現在の久米町や松山町などはかつて「浮島」と呼ばれる離島であり、那覇港に着いた冊封使一行は浅い海を渡って首里へと向かった。そのため王府は彼らを迎える際に国中の船を集めて舟橋とした。1452 年の冊封使来琉にむけて尚金福王は国相・懐機（かいき）に長虹堤の建造を命じた。工事は難航したため二夜三昼、神の加護を祈り、石橋 7 座を設けて完成した。懐機は神威に感謝して神社を建てて天照大神を奉じ、寺を建てて長寿寺と名付けた。長虹堤建設の際に亡くなった安波根ノロを堤防の畔に埋葬し、周囲に石垣を積んで祀った御嶽がイベガマといわれる。長虹堤の跡は現在、那覇市牧志の十貫瀬にわずかにみられる。

戦前の長虹堤（那覇市歴史博物館蔵）
Chokou-tei in prewar days

(20) *Chokou-tei*

A 1km-long underwater road built in 1451 (during the reign of King Sho Kimpuku) connecting Asato Bridge (around today's Sougenji Bridge) and Ibegama (said to be near Matsuyama intersection, but no longer exists), and it was also called *Ukimichi*. The present-day towns of Kume and Matsuyama were once remote islands called Ukishima, and when *sappuu-shi* (envoys from China) arrived at Naha Port, they crossed the shallow sea to get to Shuri. Therefore, when welcoming them, the royal government gathered all the boats in the country and lined them up to form a bridge. In preparation for the arrival of *sappuu-shi* in 1452, King Sho Kimpuku ordered his Minister of State, Kaiki, to build *Chokou-tei*. The construction work was difficult, but after two nights and three days of praying for divine blessings, it was completed with seven stone bridges.

In gratitude for the divine authority, Kaiki built a shrine dedicated to Amaterasu and a temple named Chojuji. There is a legend that Ibegama is a *utaki* where Ahagon-*noro*, who died during the construction of *Chokou-tei,* was buried by the bank of the embankment and enshrined with a stone wall around her. The remains of the *Chokou-tei* can now be seen only briefly around Jikkanji in Makishi, Naha City.

(21) 三司官（さんしかん）

首里王府の職名または位階名で、尚巴志王代に置かれたといわれるが不詳である。明らかなのは尚真王代に毛文英（沢岻盛里）が三司官に任ぜられた時からで、以後は常置の職となった。国政を司る３人の宰相で、重要な政務は協議のうえ国王の裁可を受け、軽易のものは３人で協議し決定した。その上に摂政（シッシー）（国相）がいるが、単なる形式的で、政治の実権は三司官が握っていた。古くは国王が任命したが、薩摩支配後は親方の中から親方衆はじめ要職にある者たちの投票で選任され、薩摩藩の承認を得て任命された。選挙権を持つ者は王族、上級士族ら200余名で、王族には選挙権はあるが被選挙権はなかった。ほとんどが向（しょう）・毛（もう）・馬（まー）・翁（おう）の各氏から選出され、士族の最高位である三司官は終身制であった。代表的な三司官には蔡温がいる。

切手に描かれた蔡温の肖像画
Portrait of Sai On on a postage stamp

(21) *Sanshikan* (Three prime ministers)

This is the name of a position or rank in the Shuri royal government, and is said to have been established during the reign of King Sho Hashi, but this is not known. However, it is clear that in the reign of King Sho Shin, Mou Bun'ei (Takushi Mouri) was appointed to the post of *sanshikan*, and from that time on it became a permanent position. The *sanshikan* was responsible for the administration of the state, and important matters were discussed and approved by the king, while minor matters were discussed and decided by the three ministers. There was *shisshii* (Regent, Minister of State) above them, but it was a mere formality, and the *sanshikan* held the real political power. In the old days, they were appointed by the king, but after the rule of Satsuma, they were voted in by the *oyakata* and other important officials, and appointed with the approval of the Satsuma Domain. More than 200 people, including royalty and senior samurai, were eligible to vote, but royalty had the right to vote but not to be elected. Most of them were elected from the clans of Sho, Mou, Maa, and Oh, and the *sanshikan*, the highest ranking of the samurai, were appointed for life. The representative *sanshikan* include Sai On.

(22) ノロ (ヌル、ヌール)

　沖縄で按司が出現した 8 ～ 9 世紀以後、按司のオナリ神はノロと呼ばれ、按司の支配地内での最高神女の地位を占めた。ノロは「ヌル又はヌール」とも呼ばれるが、「祈る」又は「祈る人」という解釈もある。第二尚氏王統の尚真王は、女神官組織を制定した。それによってノロは各村落の祭祀主として農耕儀礼を主導的に司祭して、宗教的に村落を管理支配した。国王から辞令書で任命され、「ノロクモイ地」や俸禄が支給されたノロは「公儀ノロ」と呼ばれた。ノロの継承は、集落の根屋の父系親族集団の世襲を原則とした。
（例）久高ノロ、南山ヌル、場天ノロ、安谷屋ノロ

ノロ　当初は死後、墓は別に造られた
Noro. Initially, after her death, the tomb was
made separately

(22) *Noro* (*Nuru, Nuuru*)

　After the 8th or 9th centuries, when *aji* appeared in Okinawa, the *onari-gami* of the *aji* was called *noro*, and she occupied the position of the highest deity within the *aji's* territory. *noro*, also known as *nuru* or *nuuru*, is also interpreted as "praying" or "one who prays". King Sho Shin of the Second Sho Dynasty established the organization of the Goddess Officers. As a result, *noro* took the lead in presiding over agricultural rituals as the ritual head of each village, and religiously controlled the village. *noro*, who were appointed by the king with a letter of appointment, were called *kuuji-noro* (official *noro*) and were given a *norokumoi-chi* (land for *noro*) and salary. The succession of *noro* was based on the principle of succession of patrilineal kinship groups of the *niiya* (the original family of the village).

　examples: Kudaka-*noro*, Nanzan-*nuru*, Baten-*noro*, Adan'na-*noro*

(23) 聞得大君 （きこえおおきみ）、三阿母志良礼 （さんあむしられ）

　1509 年、尚真王は女神官組織を編成した。沖縄各地に配置されたノロの頂点は聞得大君または「チフジン」と呼ばれ、国王の姉妹または后が就任した。古琉球（1609 年以前の琉球）では、王妃よりも格が上で、大きな影響力を持っていた。初代の聞得大君は尚円王と宇喜也嘉（おぎやか）の長女で、名を月清（げっせい）と称した。琉球王国にいる約 270 人のノロをまとめる女神官組織には、3 人の阿母志良礼が首里に配置された。中部地域を管轄する首里阿母志良礼が首里殿内に、北部地域を管轄する儀保（じーぶ）阿母志良礼は儀保殿内に、南部地域を管轄する真壁（まかん）阿母志良礼が真壁殿内に置かれた。3 人の阿母志良礼の下にそれぞれ 10 人の高級神女（ノロ）が置かれ「三十三君」（さんじゅうさんくん）と称された。「君南風」（ちんべー）、「アオリヤエ」、「踏揚」（ふみあがり）なども三十三君の一部である。最後の聞得大君は琉球王国最後の国王・尚泰王の長男・尚典の長女が第 18 代目として就任した。　【聞得大君の簪（口絵 1-23、P3 参照)】

(23) Kikoe Okimi (*Chifujin*) and *San-amushirare*

　King Sho Shin formed the Goddess Organization in 1509. The top of *noro*, placed in various parts of Okinawa, was called Kikoe Okimi or *Chifujin*, and the king's sister or queen was appointed. In *Ko*-Ryukyu (Ryukyu before 1609), they were of a higher rank than the queen and had a great deal of influence. The first Kikoe Okimi was the eldest daughter of King Sho En and Queen Ogiyaka, and her name was Gessei. In the organization of the goddess officers that united the approximately 270 *noro* in the Ryukyu Kingdom, *san-amushirare* (three *amushirare*) were assigned to Shuri under Kikoye Okimi. Shuri-*amushirare*, which had jurisdiction over the central region, was placed in Shuri-*dunchi*, Jiibu-*amushirare*, which had jurisdiction over the northern region, was placed in Jiibu-*dunchi* and Makan-*amushirare*, which had jurisdiction over the southern region, was placed in Makan-*dunchi*. Ten high-ranking goddesses (*noro*) were placed under each of the three *amushirare*, and they were called *sanju'san-kun*. *Chimbee*, *Aoriyae*, and *Humiagari* were also part of the *sanju'san-kun*. The last Kikoe Okimi was the eldest daughter of Sho Ten, the eldest son of King Sho Tai, the last king of the Ryukyu Kingdom, who became the 18th Kikoe Okimi. 【Kikoe Okimi's hairpin(Frontispiece, 1-23See page 3)】

(24) 聞得大君の「御新下り」儀式（きこえおおきみの「うあらうり」ぎしき）

　新しく就任した聞得大君は、南城市知念（久手堅）の斎場御嶽で「御新下り」の儀式を行う。斎場御嶽のある知念間切は代々、聞得大君の領地であり、「御新下り」とは「自分の領地へ新たに下る」という意味が語源とされている。御嶽内には久高島から運ばれた白砂が敷き詰められ、儀式は午前零時頃から始められた。久高ノロや知念ノロら70人のノロたちが「クェーナ」（人と神を結ぶ祈りの唄）

を謡うなか、大君は大庫理（ウフグーイ）の上座に着いた。午前4時頃、食事を済ませた後、大庫理の石畳の左部分にクバの葉で作られた「神家」で天から降りてくる神と一夜を共にした。新しい聞得大君と神のため、神家には2つの寝床が敷かれ黄金の枕が2個用意された。これは「神との結婚」を意味し、「セジ」（霊力）を授かる儀式である。朝8時頃、外間ノロら15人が新しい聞得大君に手を合わせて祈るとともに祝福し、儀式は終了した。儀式の中で久高島の外間ノロによって神名が与えられることによって、正式に聞得大君職に就任して国王を守護する神となったのである。

斎場御嶽の大庫理（南城市久手堅）
Uhuguui in Seifa-*utaki*, where the *kamiyaa* (God's house) made of palm leaves was prepared at the *Uara-uri* ceremony(Kudeken,Nanjyo City)

(24) *Uara-uri* of Kikoe Okimi (the inauguration ceremony of Kikoe Okimi)

　When Kikoe Okimi was newly appointed, a religious ceremony for inauguration was held at Seifa-*utaki*, in Kudeken, Nanjyo City. Chinen *magiri,* where Seifa-*utaki* is located, has been the domain of Kikoe Okimi for generations, and it is said that the word *uara-uri* was born from the meaning of "to land in her domain anew". The *utaki* was covered with white sand brought from Kudaka Island, and the ceremony started around midnight. While seventy *noro*, including Kudaka-*noro* and Chinen-*noro,* chanted *kweena* (a song of prayer that connects people to the gods), Okimi took her place at the upper seat of the *Uhuguui*. At around 4 a.m., after she had finished her meal, she spent the night with God descending from the heavens in *kamiyaa* (God's house) made of palm leaves prepared on the left part of the stone pavement in *Uhuguui*. Inside of bedroom in the *kamiyaa*, two tatami mattresses and two golden pillows were prepared for a new Kikoe Okimi and God. This ceremony meant "marriage with God" and was a ritual to receive *seji* (spiritual power) from God. At around 8:00 a.m., 15 *noro*, including Hokama-*noro*, prayed and blessed the new Kikoe Okimi with their hands, and the ceremony ended. In the ceremony, she was given a divine name by Hokama-*noro* of Kudaka Island, and thus was officially appointed to the position of Kikoe Okimi and became the guardian deity of the king.

(25) 位階制度（いかいせいど）

①位階（いかい）

　「位階」とは、基本的には地位、身分の序列、等級という意味で、位階制度は古代中国の政治行政における身分制度である。琉球王国における位階は身分序列で 1488 年、尚真王が中央集権を始めた頃に始まる。各間切の按司たちを首里に集め居住させて社会の「上層」とし、その従者たちを「中層」となし、一般の住民を「下層」として身分を区別した。1509 年には簪（ジーファー）によって貴賤の別が定められ、1524 年には 6 色の冠（ハチマチ）によって等級が制定された。近世の制度が確立したのは 1689 年（尚貞王代）に系図座を設け、家譜を編集するようになってからである。位階制度では、「王族」、「上級士族」、「一般士族」、「平民」に分れ、位階で身分が決まるのは上級・一般士族のみで、国王・王子・按司などの王族や平民は位階の上と下にそれぞれ位置した。呼称としては、国王の下に、王子（オウジ）、按司（アジ）、親方（ウェーカタ）、親雲上（ペーチン）、里之子（サトゥヌシ）、筑登之（チクドゥン）、子（シー）、仁屋（ニーヤー）の 8 つあり、細分化された 20 の位階に分かれていた。

琉球国王印 (1662 年、尚質王が清王朝から授かった国王印鑑。右側の文字は「琉球國王之印」と書かれており、左側の文字は満州文字。清朝は北方の満州系であったからといわれる)
Signature stamp of the King of Ryukyu (A king's seal given to King Sho Sitsu by the Qing Dynasty in 1662. The characters on the right side read "Ryukyu-Koku-Oh-No-In" (Seal of the King of Ryukyu),and the characters

(25) *Ikai* (rank) system

① *Ikai*

　The word *ikai* (rank) basically means position, order of status, or grade, and the rank system was the status system in political administration in ancient China. Rank in the Kingdom of Ryukyu is a hierarchy of status, which began in 1488 when King Sho Shin began the centralization of power. The *aji* of each *magiri* were gathered and made to live in Shuri to form the upper strata of society, their followers the middle strata, and the general population the lower strata. In 1509, the distinction between nobility and lowly was determined by the *jiifaa* (hairpin), and in 1524, the grades were determined by six-colored *hachimachi* (crowns). It was not until 1689 (during the reign of King Sho Tei) that the rank system of the early modern era was established, with the establishment of genealogical offices and the compilation of family records. The rank system was divided into "royalty," "upper class warriors," "general warriors," and "commoners". Only the upper class warriors and the general warriors were given status according to their rank, and the royal family, including kings, princes, and ajis, were placed above them, while the commoners were placed below them. Under the king, there were eight ranks: *ouji, aji, uweekata(oyakata), peechin, satunushi, chikudun, shii,* and *niiyaa*, which were divided into 20 subdivided ranks.

②王族（おうぞく）

　国王・王子・按司などは王族で、国王の親族である王子・按司は最高職である摂政（シッシー）を除けば、系図奉行や寺社奉行など政治には直接関わらない役職に就いた。王子・按司は 1 間切（今日の市町村）を領地として賜り、按司地頭と呼ばれた。王子・按司は領地名を家名にして、（例：北谷王子、本部按司）などと称した。邸宅は「御殿」（ウドゥン）と呼ばれ、これがそのまま家を指す尊称（例：北谷御殿、本部御殿）にも使われた。

② **Royalty**

The king, prince, and *aji* were royalty, while the prince and *aji*, who were relatives of the king, held positions that were not directly related to politics, such as genealogical magistrate and temple and shrine magistrate, except for the regent (*sisshii*), the highest position. Each of the princes and ajis were given 1 *magiri* (today's cities, towns, and villages) as their fiefdom, and were also called *aji-jitou*. Princes and *aji* were to use the name of their territory as their family name (e.g., Chatan-*ouji,* Mutubu-*aji*, etc.). The residence was called *udun*, which was also used as an honorific name of the family (e.g., Chatan-*udun*, Mutubu-*udun*).

琉球国王の王冠
Crown of the King of Ryukyu

③王子（おうじ）

　国王の子・王叔・王弟の称号および位階名は王子と呼ばれ、正室の子は直王子、側室の子を脇王子という。世子（世継ぎ）は中城間切を領地としたので、特に「中城王子」と呼ばれた。琉球で王子の称号が使われ出したのは、明の冊封を受けて王の称号が使用された以降であるが、実際に用いられたのは第二尚氏王統が始まってしばらく経ってからと考えられている。王子は一代限りで、王子の子は按司と称された。玉陵の碑文（1501年）には後の尚清王のことを「中くすくのあんし」と記されている。第一尚氏王統下でも、王の子たちは「あんし（按司）」と称していたが、後世の史書では国王の子はすべて王子と記されている。摂政や江戸登りの正使など、功績のあった按司なども王子の称号を賜った。羽地王子朝秀などがその例である。王子は赤地金入五色浮織冠を戴き、金簪を差した。

戦前の中城御殿（世子の住宅で、龍潭の向かいにあった）
Pre-war Nakagusuku-*udun* (residence of the next king, was across from the Ryutan Pond)

③ *Ouji* (Prince)

The title and rank of the king's son, uncle, or younger brother was called *ouji,* and the son of queen is called a "direct prince," and the son of a side wife is called a "side prince". The king's successor was especially known as Nakagusuku-*ouji* because he had Nakagusuku *magiri* as his domain. The title of *ouji* (prince) did not come into use in Ryukyu until after the acceptance of the Ming Dynasty's *sappuu* and the use of the title of king. But it is believed that the title as *ouji* was not actually used until some time after the beginning of the Second Sho Dynasty. The *ouji* was a title that lasts only one generation, and the son of prince had the title called *aji*. An inscription (1501) in Tama-*udun*, the mausoleum of the Second Sho Dynasty, refers to the future King Sho Sei as Nakagusuku-*anshi*. Even under the First Sho Dynasty, the king's sons were called *anshi (aji)*, but in later historical documents, all the king's sons were described as *ouji*. The title of *ouji* was also given to those who had distinguished themselves as *sisshii* (regents) or regular envoys to *Edo*. An example of such a person is Prince Haneji Chosyu. The *ouji* wore a floating crown of five colors, including gold on a red background, with a golden hairpin.

④按司（アジまたはアンジ）

　王族のうち王子に次ぐ称号および位階名で、王子や按司の嗣子（養子）が就いた。按司は王家の分家当主が賜るもので、日本の宮家当主に相当する。按司はアジまたはアンジと発音し主（あるじ）からの転訛ともいわれ、「按司」は単なる当て字である。元来、按司は地方の支配者やその家族など支配者階級の称号であったが、第二尚氏王統下になると、もっぱら王族の称号や位階名となった。玉陵の碑文に「きこえおおきみのあんし」と記されているように、王母や上級神女の敬称としても按司が使用されている。按司は大功があると王子位に昇ることができたが、歴代当主に功績がなければ、7代で士族に降格された。赤地金入五色浮織冠または黄地五色浮織冠を戴き、金簪を差した。

④ *Aji (Anji)*

　The second most important title and rank among royalty after prince, and the heir (adopted son) of prince and *aji*. The title was given to the head of a branch of the royal family, equivalent to the head of a court family in Japan. The word *aji* is pronounced *aji* or *anji* and is said to be a corruption of *aruji* (lord), and the Chinese character for *aji* is simply a guess. Originally, the title of *aji* was reserved for local rulers and their families, but under the Second Sho Dynasty, it became the title and rank of the royal family. As the inscription on the Tama-*udun* says, Kikoe Okimi-*no-anshi*, the name was also used as an honorific title for royal mothers and senior *noro*. *Aji* could ascend to the rank of *ouji* with great merit, but if successive heads of the family had no merit, they were demoted to warrior status after seven generations. *Aji* wore a floating crown of five-colored including gold on a red background, or a floating crown of five-colored on a yellow background, with a gold hairpin.

⑤上級士族（じょうきゅうしぞく）

　士族という用語は、1869年（明治2年）に明治政府が各藩の藩士を総称して用いたのが最初である。琉球では士族のことを「サムレー」といい、俗に「ユカッチュ」（良かる人）とも呼んだ。国政の要職を司ったエリート士族が上級士族である。親方となると1間切を領地として賜り、総地頭と呼ばれた。脇地頭とは、間切内の1村を領地として賜った地頭職であり、この場合は脇地頭親方と称した。脇地頭職の上級士族は特に「ペークミー」（親雲上）と称し、黄冠を戴いた。親方と親雲上（ペーチン）の邸宅、または親方家・親雲上家は殿内（トゥンチ）と呼ばれた。殿内は王族である御殿（ウドゥン）の下に位置し、高い格式を誇る家柄である。御殿と殿内は一括して「御殿殿内」（ウドゥントゥンチ）と呼ばれた。（例：伊江御殿、豊見城殿内、池城殿内）

伊江御殿跡（自然の岩山に大小の奇石を巧みにはめ込んでいるのは、中国庭園の影響と考えられている）
Ie-*udun* Ruins (the skillful incorporation of large and small stones into natural rock piles is thought to have been influenced by Chinese gardens)

⑤ *Joukyu-shizoku* (Senior samurai)

　The term *shizoku* (*samurai*, warriors) was first used by the Meiji government in 1869 as a generic term for the samurai of each domain. In Ryukyu, *shizoku* was called *samuree*, or also commonly called *yukacchu* (people of good character). The elite samurai who held important positions in the national government were the senior samurais. When a samurai became an *oyakata (uweekata)*, he received one *magiri* as his fief, and was called a *sou-jitou*. *Waki-jitou* was the position of a *jitou* who was given a village within a *magiri* as his territory, and in this case, he was called *waki-jitou-oyakata*. The *joukyu-shizoku* in the position of *waki-jitou* was specifically called *peekumii* and was crowned with a yellow crown. The residences of the *oyakata* and *peechin*, or the *oyakata* and *peechin* families, were called *tunchi*, and *tunchi* is a family of high prestige, under the royal family of *udun*. *Udun* and *tunchi* were collectively called *udun-tunchi*. (e.g., Ie-*udun*, Tomigusuku-*dunchi,* Ichigusuku-*dunchi)*

⑥親方（ウェーカタ）

　王族の下位、士族の最高位に位置する称号で、国政の要職に就いた。親方は世襲ではなく功績のある士族が昇ることになっていた。そのため、親方の子が必ずしも親方に昇進するとは限らなかったが、実際にはその大半が首里を中心とした門閥によって世襲されていた。親方は紫冠を戴き、花金茎銀簪を差した。さらに昇進すると金簪を差した。親方の称号は古くなく 17 世紀頃から使われ始め、それ以前は「かなぞめ親雲上」（紫の親雲上）と称され、紫冠に由来するといわれる。功績のある黄冠の士族に、特別に紫冠を賜ったのが親方の始まりといわれる。王族が儀典関係の職に就き、親方は政治の実務を担当し、投票で選ばれれば「三司官」に就任した。王子から親方までは 1 間切を領地としていたので「デーミョー」（大名）と呼ばれた。しかし、実際には脇地頭職に留まる脇地頭親方の方が多かった。琉球王朝末期（明治 6 年）の資料によると、総地頭職にある親方の数が 14 人に対して、脇地頭親方は 38 人で実に 2 倍以上であった。

⑥ *Oyakata (Uweekata)*

　Oyakata was a title that ranked lower than royalty, and the highest rank of *shizoku* (samurai)and was appointed to an important position in national politics. The position of *oyakata* was not hereditary, but was promoted by *shizoku* with meritorious achievements. As a result, the children of *oyakata* were not always promoted to the position of *oyakata*. However, in reality, most of them were handed down from generation to generation by prominent families centered in Shuri. The *oyakata* wore a purple crown and a hairpin with a design of gold flower and a silver stem, when he was promoted further, he wore a golden hairpin. The title *oyakata* is not old, but began to be used around the 17th century. Before that, it was called *kanazome-peechin* (purple *peechin*), which is said to be derived from the purple crown. It is said that the *oyakata* began when a special purple crown was given to a yellow-crowned *shizoku* with distinguished achievements. The royalty held ceremonial positions, while the *oyakata* was in charge of political affairs and, if elected by ballot, became the *sanshikan*. Those of the rank from prince to *oyakata* were called *deemyou* (feudal lords) because they had one *magiri* as their territory. However, in reality, there were more *waki-jitou-oyakata* who stayed in the *waki-jitou* position. According to data from the end of the Ryukyu Dynasty (1873), the number of *oyakata* in the position of *sou-jitou* was 14, while the number of *waki-jitou-oyakata* was 38, more than twice as many.

⑦親雲上（ペーチン・ペークミー）

　士族は一般に「ペーチン」（親雲上）と呼ばれ、主に中級士族に相当する者の称号だが、その中でも領地を賜った者、つまり地頭職にある者は「ペークミー」と称され区別された。親雲上に相当する階層を古琉球期では「大やくもい」（大屋子もい）と呼ばれた。「もい」は敬称接尾語で、「大やく」とは「大役」のことで、重要な役職に就いた者を意味するともいわれる。後世の親雲上（おやくもうえ・ペーチン）という称号は、この「大やくもい」の当て字である。それを何故ペーチンまたはペークミーと称するかについては諸説あって、定かでない。ペークミーも世襲ではなく、功績ある者が就いた。さらに功績を積めば親方の位にも昇格した。領地を持たず、領地名だけを賜った場合はペーチンと称した。親雲上は黄冠を戴き、銀簪を差した。

⑦ *Peechin (Peekumii)*

Shizoku (samurai) were generally referred to as *peechin*, which was mainly a title for those who were equivalent to mid class samurai. However, among them, those who had been given territories, in other words, those who held the position of *jito*, were called *peekumii* and were distinguished from others. The hierarchy corresponding to *peechin* was called *ouyaku-moi* in the Old Ryukyu period. The word *moii* is an honorific suffix, and *ouyaku* means "big role," which is said to mean a person who has held an important position. The title *peechin* in later times is an adaptation of the name *ouyaku-moi*. However, there are many theories as to why it is called *peechin* or *peekumii*, and it is not clear. The title of *peekumii* was also not hereditary, but was appointed to those who had distinguished themselves, and with further merit could be promoted to the rank of *oyakata*. If a person did not have a territory, but was given only the name of the territory, he was called a *peechin*. The *peechin* wore a yellow crown and a silver hairpin.

⑧ 一般士族（いっぱんしぞく）

　一般士族とは領地を持たない武士のことで、「ブンニン」と呼ばれ、上級士族に昇進するには大変な努力を要した。一般士族には、里之子家と筑登之家という2つの家格（家筋）があった。里之子家は中級士族、筑登之家は下級士族に相当する。里之子家では子（シー）→里之子（赤冠・銀簪）→里之子親雲上（黄冠・銀簪）→親雲上と出世していくのに対して、筑登之家は子→筑登之（赤冠・銀簪）→筑登之親雲上（黄冠・銀簪）→親雲上と出世。譜代武士の場合は、里之子家、筑登之家の両家筋とも最初は無位の子（シー）から始まったが、新参武士の場合は

守礼門を出発する、正装に身を包んだ士族たち（首里文化祭）
Warriors in formal attire departing from the Shurei-*mon* Gate
(at the Shuri Cultural Festival)

無位の「仁屋」（ニーヤー）が最初であった。「譜代」とは古くからの士族の家柄で、「新参」とは新たに士族になった家柄をいう。1689 年の家譜編纂の時に、尚寧王代以前から仕官していた家柄が譜代で、その後の仕官者は新参とされた。功績のあった平民や多額の献金を納めた者または私費で公共工事を行い、王府から認められた者たちは新参士族になった。

⑧ General-*shizoku* (General samurai)

General *shizoku* are unrelated warriors who do not have a territory and were called *bun-nin*, and it took a lot of effort to be promoted to a higher rank. There were two lines of families among the general samurai: the *satunushi* family and the *chikudun* family. The *satunushi* family was a middle class samurai family, while the *chikudun* family was a lower class samurai family. In the case of *satunushi* family, one rose through the ranks from *shii* to *satunushi* (red crown and silver hairpin) to *satunushi-peechin* (yellow crown and silver hairpin) to *peechin*, while the *chikudun* family rose through the ranks from *shii* to *chikudun* (red crown and silver hairpin) to *chikudun-peechin* (yellow crown and silver hairpin) to *peechin*. In the case of *hudai* samurai, both the *satunushi* and *chikudun* family lines started out as unranked *shii*, while in the *shinzan* samurai started out as unranked *niiyaa*. The term *hudai* refers to families that have been members of the samurai family for a long time, while *shinzan* refers to families that have newly joined the samurai family. At the time of the compilation of the family tree in 1689, the families that had served before the reign of King Sho Nei were considered to be *hudai*, while those that served afterwards were considered to be *shinzan*. Those commoners who had made meritorious contributions, those who had paid large sums of money, or those who had carried out public works at their own expense and had been recognized by the royal government became the *shinzan* samurai.

⑨里主（サトゥヌシ）

　里主は里之子と同じ発音だが、意味は異なる。里主とは総地頭家や脇地頭家の嗣子で、家督を継いだがいまだ黄冠以下の位階の低い者を指す。那覇の行政長官は那覇里主と称され、首里士族が任じられた。その役所は那覇里主所または那覇里主殿内と呼ばれた。那覇里主は薩摩の在藩奉行との交渉役でもあり、三司官候補の資格に必要な職であった。里主とは元来、領主を意味する。

⑨ *Satunushi*

　Satunushi (made up of two characters) is pronounced the same as *satunushi* (made up of three characters), but has a different meaning. The term *satunushi* (made up of two characters) here refers to heirs of the *sou-jitou* and *waki-jitou* families who have succeeded to the governorship but are still below the rank of yellow crown. The administrative head of Naha was called Naha-*satunushi*, and was appointed by the Shuri-*shizoku*. The office was called Naha-*satunushi-dokoro* or Naha-*satunushi-dunchi*. Naha-*satunushi* was also a negotiator with the Satsuma's Magistrate in Naha, a position necessary to qualify as a candidate for the *sanshikan*. The term *satunushi* originally meant a lord.

⑩筑登之（チクドゥン）

　王府の最下位の位階で、正式には下庫理筑登之と言う。筑登之家筋の士族は嫡子が 25 歳、次男以下は 28 歳になると筑登之に任じられた。本来は武官で、筑は一種の武器、登之は殿（とぅん）を意味する。子の最初の位は「里之子」または「筑登之」で、家柄の良い系統の里之子は最終的には親方や三司官の上級士族まで昇れた。一方、新参の系統である筑登之は王府内で顕著な勲功が無い限り、通常は中間管理職（親雲上）までしか昇進できなかった。

⑩ *Chikudun*

　It is the lowest rank in the Shuri royal government, and is officially called *shichaguui-chikudun*. The samurai of the *chikudun* family line, a legitimate son was appointed to the rank of *chikudun* at the age of 25, and the second son and younger at the age of 28. A samurai of the *chikudun* is essentially a military officer, where *chiku* means a kind of weapon and *dun* means *tun* (a structure). The first rank at which a *shii* was appointed was *satunushi* or *chikudun*, and a *satunushi* of good family lineage could rise to the *joukyu-shizoku* (Senior samurai), such as *oyakata* or *sanshikan*. On the other hand, the newcomer lineage, *chikudun*, was usually only promoted up to middle management positions (*peechin*) unless he had outstanding merits within the royal government.

⑪子（シー）、仁屋（ニーヤー）

　譜代士族の子弟で、無位の者を「子」と称し、カタカシラを結う（元服）と赤冠を戴き、銀簪を差した。新参士族の子弟で、無位の者は仁屋と呼ばれ、カタカシラを結うと緑冠を戴き、銅簪を差した。通常は士族の無位の者が子や仁屋と呼ばれたが、村役人などの上級平民の子弟で無位の者も仁屋と称した。

⑪ *Shii, Niiyaa*

　The children of *hudai*-samurai (hereditary samurai) who had no rank were called *shii*, and when reaching adulthood (age 13), they wore a hairstyle called *katakashira*, a red crown, and a silver hairpin on their head. The children of *shinzan*-samurai(newcomers), the unranked ones were called *niiyaa*, and after tying their hair into a *katakashira*, they were crowned with a green crown and a copper hairpin. Normally, unranked members of the samurai family were called *shii* or *niiiyaa*, but the children of high-ranking commoners such as village officials, who had no rank, were also called *niiyaa*.

(26) 平民（へいみん）

①百姓（ひゃくしょう）と地方役人（ちほうやくにん）

　琉球では、平民一般を百姓と呼んだ。首里・那覇・久米村・泊村に居住する者を「町百姓」、それ以外は「田舎百姓」と呼称された。田舎百姓のうち地方役人に取り立てられた者は「地方役人」（じかたやくにん）、「筆算人」（ひっさんにん）または「オエカ人」（オエカとは役職のこと）と呼ばれたが、系図を有しないので「無系」（むけい）ともいわれ、真鍮の箸を差した。地方役人の身分は百姓（平民）だが、上級役人になると「オエカ地」（役職に応じて与えられる土地）が与えられた。しかし身分の違いから、衣服や家、墓、その他あらゆる面で士族との落差は大きく、士族との婚姻や士族の家系への跡目入りなどは特に問題にされた。地方役人は「間切役人」と「村役人」の２つに分かれる。夫地頭になると村の百姓を年２回使役できるなど様々な特権があった。このため、中間搾取や地位を乱用する悪徳役人も多く、方言の「ウェーキ」（資産家）の語源はここから来ているといわれる。

系図座跡（1689 年に設置された系図座は系図・家譜を取り扱う役所であった）
Keizu-*za* Ruins(The genealogy office, established in 1689, was the office that handled genealogy and family records)

(26) *Heimin* (commoners)

① *Hyakusyo*(Peasants) and local officials

　In Ryukyu, commoners in general were called *hyakusyo*(peasants). Those who lived in Shuri, Naha, Kume, and Tomari were called *machi-hyakusyo*(town peasants), while the rest were called *inaka-hyakusyo*(country peasants). Of the country peasants, those who were appointed as local officials were called *jikata-yakunin*, *hissan-nin* or *oeka-nin* (*oeka* means position), but they were also called *mukei* because they did not have a genealogy, and they were plugging in a brass hairpin. The status of local officials was *hyakusyo*(commoner), but if they became senior officials, they were given *oeka-chi* (land given according to their position). However, due to the difference in status, there was a large gap between the samurai and the local official in terms of clothing, houses, tombs, and all other aspects, and marrying into the samurai family or becoming an heir to the samurai family was a particular problem. Local officials were divided into two categories: *Magiri* officials and Village officials. Those who became *bu-jitou* had various privileges, such as being able to use the peasants of the village twice a year. As a result, there were many corrupt officials who exploited middlemen and abused their positions, and this is said to be the origin of the word *uweeki* (wealthy) in the dialect.

②地頭代 （ジトゥデー）

　薩摩侵攻（1609 年）以後の 1629 年から 1879 年にかけて、各間切（現在の市町村に相当）の地頭（領主）の代官として地方行政を担当した役職名で、現代の村長に相当する。役奉（役料）としては「オエカ地」と呼ばれる耕作権をもつ役地と、夫（ぶー：使役）を遣う権利があった。選任方法は、総耕作当（そ

うこうさくあたい：間切における耕作責任者）や総山当（そうやまあたい：間切における山林事業の責任者）の中から、総地頭の内申、三司官の上奏をへて国王が任命した。任期は、建前上は 5 年で、内規で 3 年とされた。身分は百姓だが、在任中は親雲上（ペーチン）の称号を許され、黄冠を戴いた。間切の長は、1879 年の沖縄県誕生後に地頭代から間切長（まぎりちょう）、さらに市町村長に改称され現在に至っている。

② *Jitudee*

After the invasion of Satsuma (1609), from 1629 to 1879, it was the name of the position that was in charge of local administration as the deputy of the head of the land (*jitou*, lord) of each *magiri* (equivalent to today's municipalities), and it is equivalent to the current head of a municipality. The role fees of *jitudee* included the right to cultivate the land, called *oeka-chi*, and the right to use the labor of the farmers(*buu*). *Jitudee* were appointed by the king from among *sou-kousaku-atai* (cultivation manager in *magiri*) and *sou-yama-atai* (head of forest operations in *magiri*), after an informal request from *sou-jitou* and a report from *sanshikan*. The term of office was five years in principle, but according to the bylaws, it was to be three years. *Jitudee's* status was that of *hyakusyo*, but during their tenure they were allowed the title of *peechin* and were crowned with the Yellow Crown. The name of the chief of *magiri* was changed from *jitudee* to *magiri'cho* after the birth of Okinawa Prefecture in 1879, and then to the mayor of the municipality, where it remains today.

③夫地頭（ぶじとう・ブージトー）

夫地頭（ぶじとう、方言でブージトゥー）は、「捌理」の上、「地頭代」の下に位置した。一定の職務はなく非常勤で、地頭代の補佐役であった。または「掟」（うっち）を兼ねて「村屋」（むらやー）に務める者もいた。夫地頭には「首里大屋子」（しゅりおおやこ）から地頭代になる者と、掟から捌理を経ずに夫地頭になる者の 2 種類があり、後者はこれ以上の昇進はなく地頭代にはなれなかった。夫地頭の任期は基本的に 3 年で、定員は間切の規模によって異なり、2 ～ 8 人だった。

③ *Bu-jitou (Buu-jitou)*

Bu-jitou (buu-jitou in dialect) was located above *sabakuri* and below *jitudee*. It was part-time, with no fixed duties, and was an assistant to *jitudee*. Or there were those who worked for the *murayaa* (village office) and also served as *ucchi* position. There were two types of *bu-jitou*: those who were promoted to *jitudee* from Shuri-*uhuyaku* and those who became *bu-jitou* without going through *sabakuri*, the latter of which did not get any further promotion and could not become *jitudee*. The term of office was basically three years, and the number of employees ranged from two to eight, depending on the size of the *magiri*.

④捌理（さばくり・さばくい）

間切番所の幹部役人である首里大屋子（シュイウフヤク）、大掟（ウフウッチ）、南風掟（フェーウッチ）、西掟（ニシウッチ）の 4 者は捌理（さばくり、方言でサバクイ）と呼ばれた。捌（さばく）とは裁く、処理する意味の方言で、事務を処理するという意味と推察される。捌理は地頭代の指揮を受けて番所の庶務に従事した。捌理の初級である西掟から南風掟、大掟、首里大屋子を経て地頭代に昇進する。定員は各掟とも 1 人で、任期はなく、国王が任命する。捌理のトップである首里大屋子は元来、首里王府と交渉する役からきた名称だが、地頭代が現在の村長に該当すれば助役にあたる。

④ *Sabakuri(Sabakui)*

The four senior officials of the *magiri* office, *Shui-uhuyaku, Uhu-ucchi, Fee-ucchi,* and *Nishi-ucchi,* were called *sabakuri* (*sabakui* in dialect). The word *sabaku* is a dialect word meaning "to judge" or "to process," and it is presumed to mean "to handle affairs". Under the direction of the *jitudee, sabakui* was engaged in the general affairs of the *magiri* office. They were promoted to the rank of *jitudee* from *Nishi-ucchi*, which was the beginner level of *sabakui* position, through *Fee-ucchi, Uhu-ucchi,* and *Shui-uhuyaku*. There was no fixed term of office, and the king appointed one person to each *sabakui* position. The head of *sabakui, Shui-uhuyaku*, was originally named after his role in negotiating with the Shuri royal government, but if a *jitudee* was the current village mayor, he would be an assistant mayor.

⑤文子（ティクグ）

　文子は、最下位の地方役人で現在の書記にあたり、間切役人の振り出しはまず文子である。文子になるには筆算稽古人からなる者と、御殿・殿内での奉公人を経てなる者がいた。初級の文子は給仕業務で、番所内の掃除は文子、外は馬番がするという内規もあった。任期はなく、賦税は免除されたが無給もいた。階級や職種によって大文子、島文子、相附（あいつけ）文子、脇文子、若文子、見習文子などの呼称があり、人数は比較的多かった。西原間切の 66 人、宜野湾間切の 63 人という記録がある。

⑤ *Tikugu*

　The *tikugu* was the lowest-ranking local civil servant, corresponding to today's scribe, and the first position to be appointed as an official was the *tikugu*. There were two types of people who became *tikugu*: those who practiced writing and calculating, and those who became *tikugu* after working as an apprentice in the *uduntunchi*. There was an internal rule in the office that the novice *tikugu* was in charge of serving, and the *tikugu* was responsible for cleaning inside the office, while the horse staff(*uma-ban*) was in charge of the outside. There was no term of office, and some were exempt from taxation but without pay. Depending on their rank or job title, they were called *Uhu-tikugu, Shima-tikugu, Aitsuke-tikugu, Waki-tikugu, Waka-tikugu, Minarai-tikugu*, and their numbers were relatively large. There are records of 66 people at Nishihara *magiri* and 63 people at Ginowan *magiri*.

(27) 帕（冠）（はちまち）

　王府時代の冠服制度の一つで、尚真王時代に士族が位階に応じて帕（冠）の色（浮織、紫、黄、赤、青色など）が規定された。浮織は、国王に次ぐ位を示し王子・王弟・按司が使用。紫は、高級官僚の位で親方の肩書きを持つ者。黄は、中・高級官僚の位で親雲上（ペーチン）の肩書きを持つ者。赤は、下級官僚の位で、里之子（サトゥヌシ）や筑登之（チクドゥン）の肩書きを持つ者。青色は、最下級の者で位階に上る前の位。国王の冠は「皮弁冠」または「タマンチャーブイ」と呼ばれ、琉球国王が中国皇帝に冊封され正式の国王となった後に着用した。「皮弁冠」は本来、明王朝までの中国皇帝が儀式等で着用した冠で、明王朝では皇帝や王子、郡王などに限られ、冊封関係にあった外国君主にも下賜された。国王の服は「皮弁服」と呼ばれ、琉球国王は郡王とほぼ同列に扱われた。ハチマキは当初、頭を布で巻くターバン式であったが、尚寧王（1589 〜 1620）の時代から帽子のように被る冠になった。ハチマキは主に儀式の時に用いられ、通常はハチマキバクと呼ばれる丸櫃型の箱に収納され、持ち運びされた。　【冠（口絵 1-27、P3 参照）】

(27) *Hachimachi* (Crown)

　One of the crown clothing systems of the kingdom period, the color of the crown (*ukiori*, purple, yellow, red, blue, etc.) was prescribed for the warriors according to their rank during the reign of King Sho Shin. *Ukiori*

indicated the rank next to the king and was used by princes, royal brothers, and *aji*; purple was used by high-ranking officials with the title of *oyakata*; yellow was used by middle-and high-ranking officials with the title of *peechin*; red was used by lower-ranking officials with the title of *satunushi* or *chikudun*; and blue was used by those who were at the lowest level and had not yet ascended the ranks. The king's crown was called *hibenkan* or *taman-chaabui* and was the official crown worn by the King of Ryukyu after he was appointed by the Chinese Emperor and became the official king. *Hibenkan* was originally a crown worn by Chinese emperors up to the *Ming* Dynasty for ceremonial purposes, and in the Ming Dynasty it was limited to the emperor, princes, and county kings, and was also given to foreign monarchs with whom the emperor had a *sappuu* relationship. The king's clothes were called *hibenfuku*, and the Ryukyu kings were treated almost on a par with the county kings. Initially, the *hachimachi* was worn as a turban type with a cloth wrapped around the head, but it became a crown worn like a hat during the reign of King Sho Nei (1589-1620). *Hachimachi* was mainly used during ceremonies, and was usually stored and carried in a round chest-shaped box called a *hachimachi-baku*.
【Crowns(Frontispiece 1-27, See page 3)】

(28) ジーファー (簪)

　琉球王朝時代、髪にさした簪（かんざし）で、様々な素材が使用された。長さは各階級でもだいたい 10cm だが、1509 年（尚真王代）には位階の違いで素材が決められた。王族は金、士族は銀、百姓は真鍮（しんちゅう）、木、べっ甲などと定められた。男女によって形状が異なり、女性用はスプーン状に窪ませた頭部と六角形の胴体でできており、その形は女性の姿を表しているといわれる。男性用は龍、水仙、牡丹など位階によって違う形をした。ジーファーは女性の分身とも言われ、肌身離さず身につけた。国王の黄金簪は、花（頭）の部分が向竜頭で中央を

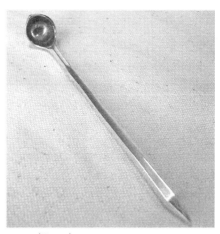

銀のジーファー　Silver *Jiifaa*

丸く膨らませた円盤状のものと、竜頭を立体的に彫ったものの 2 種類。王妃や聞得大君は、普段は半月形の黄金簪を差したが、大礼時には王妃は「鳳凰型黄金簪」、聞得大君は「竜文黄金簪」を使用した。ほとんどの百姓は木簪（キージーファー）で、貴族に仕える者や富者は、礼装時にはべっ甲簪（カーミヌクージーファー）を差した。漁民は魚(海の哺乳類)の骨で作られた「イユヌジーファー」を使った。

(28) *Jiifaa* (hairpin)

　Jiifaa were hairpins used in the Ryukyu Dynasty, and a variety of materials were used. The length was about 10 cm for each rank, but in 1509 (the reign of King Sho Shin), the material was decided according to rank: gold for the royal family, silver for the warrior class, and brass, wood, or tortoiseshell for the *hyakusyo*(peasants). The shape differs depending on the gender, with the female version made up of a spoon shaped depressed head and a hexagonal body, which is said to represent the female form. The male version had different shapes depending on the rank, such as dragon, narcissus, and peony. The *jiifaa* was said to be the alter ego of the woman, and was always worn. The king's golden hairpin came in two types: one with a disc-shaped head with opposing dragon heads and a round bulge in the middle, and another with a three-dimensional carved dragon head. The queen and Kikoe Okimi usually wore a half-moon shaped golden hairpin, but during the Grand Salute, the queen used a phoenix-shaped golden hairpin and the Kikoe Okimi used a golden hairpin with a dragon design. Most peasants wore wooden hairpins*(kii-jiifaa)*, while those who served the nobility and the wealthy wore tortoiseshell hairpins(*kaami'nu-kuu-jiifaa*) for ceremonial occasions. Fishermen used *iyu'nu-jiifaa* made from the bones of fish (sea mammals).

(29) カタカシラ

　王府時代の成人男子の髪型で、士族も百姓も同じ髪型をした。丸結という幼少期の髪型からカタカシラに変わる儀式（15歳）は上流社会では「元服」、一般では「カタカシラユーイ」と呼ばれ成人式に相当した。頭頂部を中剃りし、周囲の髪をかき上げて結い簪で止めた。簪の種類で身分が区別された。『李朝実録』（16世紀）や冊封使の使録に「琉球の人は左耳上に結髪する」と記されている（『球陽』には「右側」と記載）。片頭に結っていたものが、後に中央部に移された。女性一般にみられる髪型は「ウチナーカラジ」（沖縄髪）である。首里結い・那覇結い・辻結い・田舎アン小結いに大別され、身分の違いで形が変化した。

　沖縄における断髪は、本土の断髪令（1871年）にならってすすめられたが、1888年頃から官吏や教師・学生を中心に行われた。しかしこれに対する批判は強く、特に首里・那覇の旧士族層を中心に反対する者が多く、頑なにカタカシラを切ることを拒否した。しかし、日清戦争での日本の勝利を境に断髪するようになり、20世紀に入る頃までにはカタカシラ姿はほとんど姿を消した。

カタカシラ（琉球の成人男性の髪型。士族も百姓も同じ髪型をした）
Kata-Kashira (Ryukyuan adult male hairstyle.Both samurai and peasants wore the same hairstyle)

(29) *Katakashira*

　This was the hairstyle for adult men during the Ryukyu Kingdom, and both samurai and peasants wore the same hairstyle. The ceremony of changing from the childhood hairstyle called *maruyui* to *katakashira* was called *gempuku* in the upper class society and *katakashira-yuui* in the general public, and was equivalent to the coming-of-age ceremony. The top of the head was shaved, and the surrounding hair was brushed up and tied with a hairpin. The type of hairpin was used to distinguish the status of the person. In the *"Lee Chou Jitsuroku"* (official record of Korea in16th century) and in the records of the *sappuu-shi* (Chinese envoys), it is written that "people in Ryukyu tie their hair above the left ear" (the Kyuyou says "on the right side"). It used to be tied on one side of the head, but was later moved to the center. The general hairstyle of women was *Uchina-karaji* (Okinawan hairstyle). It was roughly classified into Shuri-*yui*, Naha-*yui*, Tsuji-*yui*, and *Inaka-angwaa-yui*, and its shape changed depending on the status.

　Haircutting in Okinawa was promoted in accordance with the mainland's haircutting order (1871), but from around 1888, it was mainly practiced by government officials, teachers and students. However, there was strong criticism of this, especially from the old samurai families of Shuri and Naha, who stubbornly refused to cut the *katakashira*. But, after Japan's victory in the *Sino-Japanese War* (1894-1895), they began to cut their hair, and by the beginning of the 20th century, the *katakashira* hairstyle had almost disappeared.

(30) 日琉同祖論（にちりゅうどうそろん）

　日琉同祖論とは、日本人と琉球（沖縄）人は、その起源において民族的には同一であるとする説である。日本人と沖縄人の人種的・文化的同一性を学術的に立証することによって民族的一体性を強調する理論である。日琉同祖論は、16世紀に京都の僧侶等によって唱えられた源為朝の琉球渡来説に

端を発し、それが琉球へ伝わり 1650 年に摂政・羽地朝秀が編纂した首里王府の正史『中山世鑑』に影響を与えた。羽地はこの中で、王家だけでなく琉球の人々の祖先が日本から来た渡来人であると記している。さらに明治時代以降は、沖縄学の大家・伊波普猷によって詳細に展開されたが、源為朝の琉球渡来説が史実的根拠を欠いた伝説の域を出ないのは確かである。日琉同祖論は、源氏の流れを汲む薩摩藩による琉球支配を正当化する理論だが、現在では、羽地朝秀が当時の因習を打破するために用いたレトリック（巧みな言い回し）であるとする説が定説となっている。

伊波普猷
Iha Huyuu

(30) *Nichiryu-douso-ron*

Nichiryu-douso-ron is the theory that the Japanese and Ryukyus (Okinawans) are ethnically identical in their origins, and it is a theory that emphasizes ethnic unity by academically proving the racial and cultural identity of the Japanese and Okinawans. The theory originated in the 16th century, when monks in Kyoto advocated the theory that Minamoto-no Tametomo had come to Ryukyu, which was transmitted to Ryukyu and influenced the Chuzan-seikan, the official history of the Shuri royal government compiled by Haneji Chosyu (regent) in 1650. In it, Haji writes that the ancestors of the people of Ryukyu, as well as the royal family, were immigrants from Japan. In addition, after the Meiji era, the theory was developed in detail by a great scholar of Okinawan studies, Iha Huyuu, but it is certain that the "Theory of Minamoto-no Tametomo's arrival in Ryukyu" does not go beyond the realm of legend lacking a historical basis. The *Nichiryu-douso-ron* is a theory that justifies the rule of the Ryukyu Islands by the Satsuma Domain, which is descended from the Minamoto clan (the Genji), but the current theory is that it was a rhetorical device used by Haneji Chosyu to break down the conventions of the time.

(31) 薩摩藩島津氏による琉球侵攻（さつまはんしまづしによるりゅうきゅうしんこう）

　琉球侵攻は、薩摩藩が 1609 年に行った琉球王国に対する軍事行動のことである。島津氏は、関ヶ原の戦い（1600 年）で敗れていたこともあり、江戸幕府の信任を得る機会を伺っていた。その他にも、相次ぐ戦乱で破綻した財政の再建と、分散していた内部権力を藩主・島津家久のもとに再編しなければならなかった。こうした問題を解決するために企てられたのが琉球の領土である奄美群島を奪い取ることであった。1609 年 3 月下旬、薩摩藩島津氏は約 3,000 の兵と 100 隻余の軍船を琉球に差し向けた。鉄砲隊を主軸に戦いに長けた薩摩軍は奄美大島・徳之島・沖永良部島を次々と攻略し、3 月末には沖縄島北部の運天港に上陸して今帰仁城を陥落させた。勢いづいた薩摩軍は、さらに中部の読谷を攻略し、陸路と海路から那覇・首里に攻め入り、4 月 1 日、首里城に達した。対する首里王府は，一部で抵抗し戦闘が行われたものの一貫して和睦を求める方針をとり、全面的な抵抗を試みることはなかった。4 月中旬に薩摩に連行された尚寧王と三司官は、1611 年、「琉球は古来、島津氏の付属国である」と記された起請文に署名させられた。その後は、琉球王国の中国との貿易を薩摩藩が管轄・監督することとなった。薩摩藩は、第二尚氏王朝を存続させながら、那覇に在藩奉行所を置いて琉球王国を間接支配するようになった。

(31) Invasion of the Ryukyu Islands by Shimazu clan, the Satsuma Domain

The invasion of Ryukyu was a military action by the Satsuma Domain against the Ryukyu Kingdom in 1609. The Shimazu clan had been defeated in the Battle of Sekigahara (1600) and was looking for an opportunity to gain the confidence of the Edo Shogunate. In addition, they had to rebuild their finances, which had been ruined by a series of wars, and reorganize their dispersed internal power under the leadership of Shimazu Iehisa, the feudal lord. The solution to these problems was to seize the Amami Islands, a Ryukyu territory. In early March 1609, the Shimazu clan of the Satsuma Domain sent about 3,000 soldiers and more than 100 warships to the Ryukyu Kingdom. The Satsuma army, skilled in battle and led by its artillery, captured Amami Oshima, Tokunoshima, and Okinoerabu Island one after another, and at the end of March, they landed at Unten Port in the northern part of Okinawa Island and felled Nakijin Castle. The Satsuma army, now in full force, attacked Yomitan in the central part of the country and then invaded Naha and Shuri by land and sea, reaching Shuri Castle on April 1. In response, the Shuri royal government resisted and fought in some areas, but consistently adopted a policy of seeking peace and did not attempt to put up a full-scale resistance. Taken to Satsuma in mid-April, King Sho Nei and *sanshikan* were forced to sign a pledge in 1611 stating that Ryukyu had always been an appendage of the Shimazu clan. Thereafter, the Satsuma Domain assumed jurisdiction and supervision of the Ryukyu Kingdom's trade with China. The Satsuma Domain came to indirectly control the Ryukyu Kingdom with the establishment of the *Zaihan-bugyosyo* (Satsuma clan magistrate's office) in Naha, while keeping the Second Sho Dynasty alive.

(32) 喜安日記 (きあんにっき)

　喜安（1566 ～ 1653）は、17 世紀に琉球で活躍した日本（堺出身）の茶人で和歌や漢詩にも通じており、尚寧王の侍従となった。1609 年の薩摩の琉球侵攻では捕虜となった国王に付き添い、薩摩側との折衝役を務めた。帰国後の 1611 年には御茶道職に任じられ、日本式の茶道が琉球に広まった。その後も薩摩には度々交渉で渡り、晩年には親方の位を授けられた。病没するまで御茶道職にあり、彼の死後も同職は琉球王府の官職として続いた。次の尚豊王の時代に、薩摩との開戦前から王の帰国までの 2 年半を回想した『喜安日記』を著した。日記は全体として、日次ぎの記録というよりも事件の全貌を把握した後の回想となっている。原本は現存しないが、原本に近い「尚家本」が那覇市歴史博物館にある。『喜安日記』は薩摩の琉球侵攻に関する重要な資料で、同事件を琉球側の視点で記した唯一の史料である。

(32) Kian-*nikki* (Kian diary)

Kian (1566 ～ 1653) was a Japanese (from Sakai) tea master who was active in Ryukyu in the 17th century. He was also well versed in Japanese poetry and Chinese poetry, and became the chief attendant of King Sho Nei. During the Satsuma invasion of Ryukyu in 1609, he accompanied the captive king and acted as a negotiator with the Satsuma side. After returning to Ryukyu, in 1611, he was appointed to the position of tea ceremony official, and the Japanese style tea ceremony spread to Ryukyu. He continued to travel to Satsuma frequently for negotiations, and in his later years he was given the rank of *oyakata*. He held the position of tea ceremony official until his death due to illness, and this position continued as an official position in the Ryukyu royal government after his death. In the reign of the next king, Sho Hou, he wrote the Kian-*nikki*, which recalled the two and a half years from before the outbreak of war with Satsuma until the king's return. The diary as a whole is not so much a daily record as it is a recollection of the incident after it has been fully understood. The original does not exist, but the Sho-ke-bon(a manuscript preserved by the Sho family), which is close to the original, is in the Naha City Museum of History. The Kian-*nikki* is an important document on the Satsuma invasion of Ryukyu, and is the only historical document that describes the incident from the Ryukyu side.

(33) 首里王府の編纂書 (しゅりおうふのへんさんしょ)

①おもろさうし（おもろそうし）

　首里王府が奄美、沖縄に伝わる歌を意味する「オモロ」を少なくとも 3 回にわたって採録した沖縄最古の歌謡集で、全 22 巻(1554 首)からなる。第 1 巻は 1531 年（尚清王代）、第 2 巻は 1613 年、第 3 巻〜 22 巻は 1623 年（尚豊王代）に編纂された。オモロの語源は「ウムイ」といわれている。ウムイは「思い」の転訛であり、「言う」や口に出して「唱える」という意味の古語「思ふ」を原義として、神の言葉という意味を包含するものといわれている。「さうし」を漢字表記すれば「草紙」となり、大和の「草紙」に倣って命名された

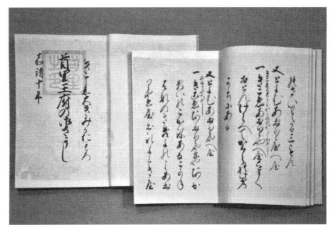

おもろさうし
Omoro-saushi

ものと考えられている。初期のオモロの主題は神や太陽であり、祭祀儀礼が中心。按司時代には、築城、造船、貿易、按司の讃美などが多い。王府時代になると、国王の礼讃、建寺、貢祖、航海、属島成敗などの非農村的な主題が多くなった。主題は奄美・沖縄諸島、宮古・八重山、本土の鎌倉・京都、さらに唐、ベトナム、タイまで空間的な広がりを持ち、恋を詠んだオモロは極めて少ない。本格的なオモロ研究は、180 余年眠っていた『おもろさうし』を田島利三郎が 1894 年に発見してからである。古文献の少ない沖縄で『おもろさうし』は、沖縄の古代を研究する有力な資料として注目されているが、解読作業はまだ進行途上である。

(33) Compiled books by the Shuri Royal Government

① *Omoro-saushi* (*Omoro-soushi*)

　This is the oldest collection of Okinawan poems, consisting of 22 volumes (1554 poems), in which the Shuri royal government collected *omoro*, meaning songs from Amami and Okinawa, at least three times. The first volume was compiled in 1531(during the reign of King Sho Sei), the second in 1613, and the third through 22nd volumes in 1623 (during the reign of King Sho Hou). The origin of the word *omoro* is said to be *umui*. The word *umui* is a corruption of *omoi*, and the ancient word *omou* has the original meaning of "to say" or "to recite aloud," and is said to include the meaning of the word of God. The word *saushi* is written in Chinese characters as *soushi*, which is thought to have been named after the Yamato word (Japanese)*soushi*. The subject matter of the early *omoro* was the gods and the sun, and rituals were central. During the *aji* period, there was much about building castles, shipbuilding, trade, and praise of the *aji*. During the kingdom era, there were more non-rural themes such as praise of the king, construction of temples, paying taxes, voyages, and the defeat of the gentry islands. The subjects of *omoro* poems spread spatially from Amami and Okinawa islands, Miyako and Yaeyama, Kamakura and Kyoto on the mainland, to the Tang Dynasty (China), Vietnam, and Thailand, and there are very few *omoro* poems about love. Full-scale research on *omoro* began in 1894, when Tajima Risaburo discovered *Omoro-soushi*, which had been lying dormant for more than 180 years. In Okinawa, where there are few ancient documents, the *Omoro-soushi* is attracting attention as a powerful source for studying the ancient history of Okinawa, but the work of deciphering it is still in progress.

②歴代宝案（れきだいほうあん）

　1424 年（尚巴志王代）から 1867 年（尚泰王代）までの 440 余年にわたる、中国を中心として朝鮮やシャム、ベトナム、スマトラなど東南アジア諸国との外交文書を漢文で記録した琉球王国の外交文書を集成したものである。明・清国の対中国関係文書が大半を占める『歴代宝案』は、中近世外交史の史料的価値がある。『歴代宝案』は 2 部作成され、1 部は首里王府に、もう 1 部は久米村の天妃宮で保管されていた。王城で保管されていた原本は明治政府による琉球処分により東京の内務省へ移管されたが、関東大震災（1923 年）で焼失した。久米村で保管されていた原本は、1933 年に沖縄県立図書館に保管されたときに副本が制作された。その原本は沖縄戦で焼失したが、副本が那覇市歴史博物館などに残っており、2022 年に訳注本（全 15 冊）の刊行作業が完了した。

② Rekidai-houan

　This is a collection of diplomatic documents of the Kingdom of Ryukyu, written in Chinese, covering more than 440 years from 1424 (the reign of King Sho Hashi) to 1867 (the reign of King Sho Tai), mainly with China, but also with Korea, Siam, Vietnam, Sumatra and other Southeast Asian countries. The majority of the documents are from the Ming and Qing dynasties' relations with China, making the Rekidai-houan a great valuable historical document in the history of diplomacy in the middle and early modern ages. Two copies of the Rekidai-houan were made, one kept at the Shuri Royal Office and the other at the Tempiguu Temple in Kume Village. The original kept at the Shuri Royal Office was transferred to the Ministry of Interior in Tokyo when the Meiji government disposed of the Ryukyu Islands, but it was destroyed by fire in the Great Kanto Earthquake (1923). The other original kept in Kume Village was transferred to the Okinawa Prefectural Library in 1933, and a duplicate copy was produced then. The original copy was destroyed by fire during the Battle of Okinawa, but the duplicate copy remains in the Naha City Museum of History and other places, and in 2022, work was completed on the publication of the translated book (15 volumes in total).

③中山世鑑（ちゅうざんせいかん）

　羽地朝秀が、王府の命により薩摩支配下の 1650 年に編纂した琉球王国最初の正史である。琉球開闢から尚清王代まで記した全 5 巻からなるが、その前代の尚真王代の記載が全く除かれている理由は不明とされている。中国年号や和暦が使用され、和文体で書かれている。後の史書の開闢神話に関する記述は、すべて『中山世鑑』に基づいている。源為朝が琉球に逃れその子が琉球王家の始祖「舜天」になったと記されており、この話が後の歴代の史書に踏襲されている。『中山世鑑』は史実としては不備があるとされ後に蔡鐸によって漢文体に訂正され、さらにその子・蔡温は、中国の史書などの史料を使って漢文体で改訂した。蔡鐸と蔡温親子によって記された漢文体の両正史が『中山世譜』である。

中山世鑑
Chuzan-seikan

③ Chuzan-seikan

　This is the first official history of the Kingdom of Ryukyu, compiled by Haneji Chosyu in 1650 under the rule of Satsuma at the order of the royal government. It consists of five volumes covering the period from the founding of Ryukyu to the reign of King Sho Sei, but the reason for the complete omission of his predecessor, King Sho Shin, is unknown. Chinese years and Japanese calendars are used, and the text is written in a Japanese style. The descriptions of the creation myth in later historical books are all based on the Chuzan-seiken. It is written that Minamoto-no Tametomo fled to Ryukyu and his son became Shun Ten, the founder of the Ryukyu royal family, and this story was followed in later historical books. After that, Sai Taku revised Chuzan-seikan in Chinese because it was inadequate as a historical fact, and his son, Sai On, further revised it in Chinese using Chinese historical materials. The two authentic histories in Chinese style written by father and son, Sai Taku and Sai On, are Chuzan-seihu.

④中山世譜（ちゅうざんせいふ）

羽地朝秀によって編纂された『中山世鑑』を、蔡鐸（さいたく）が 1701 年に漢文体に改訂したもので、俗に蔡鐸本ともいわれる。この書の特徴は①『中山世鑑』の誤りを『歴代宝案』の記述を元にして訂正していること②新しく伝承を取り入れていること③疑わしいことはとらないこと、などである。蔡鐸本は幻の本と考えられていたが、1972 年 11 月、蔡温本とともに県立図書館の蔵書から発見された。

蔡鐸によって編纂された『中山世譜』を息子の蔡温（さいおん）がさらに改訂して 1725 年、蔡温本と呼ばれる『中山世譜』を編纂した。蔡温は『隋書』や『宗史』、『元史』や冊封使録などの中国側の史料を参照して蔡鐸本の誤りを訂正した。記述にあたり、彼はできるだけ伝承の類いを避けた。琉球と薩摩との関係は、中国に知られないようにとの気遣いから別冊にまとめられている。蔡温本は信憑性の高い史料を駆使して編集してあるので、最も信頼のおける史書といわれている。

④ Chuzan-seihu

Sai Taku revised the Chuzan-sheikan compiled by Haneji Choshu into Chinese style in 1701, and it is also commonly known as "Sai Taku-*bon*". This book is characterized by the following: (1) errors in the Chuzan-seikan are corrected based on the descriptions in the Rekidai-houan, (2) some new lore is incorporated, and (3) no questionable information is taken. The Sai Taku-*bon* book was thought to be a phantom book, but in November 1972, it was discovered in the collection of the prefectural library along with the Sai On-*bon*.

The Chuzan-seihu written by Sai Taku was further revised by his son, Sai On, and in 1725, a new edition of the Chuzan-seihu called "Sai On-*bon*" was published. Sai On corrected the errors in the Sai Taku-*bon* by referring to historical documents from the Chinese side, such as the "History of the Sui Dynasty," the "History of the Zong Dynasty," the "History of the Yuan Dynasty," and the "Records of *sappuu-shi*". In describing, he has avoided as much as possible any kind of folklore. The relationship between Ryukyu and Satsuma was compiled in a separate volume out of concern for not letting China know about it. The "Sai On-*bon*" is said to be the most reliable history book because it is compiled using highly credible historical materials.

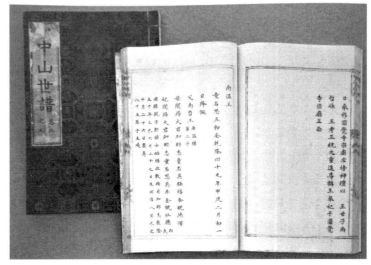

中山世譜
Chuzan-seihu

⑤琉球国由来記（りゅうきゅうこくゆらいき）

首里王府が編集した琉球最古の体系的な地誌で、全21巻からなる。当時（尚貞王代）は、諸行事や儀式に関する文献が王府内になく、毎年毎月に行う儀式・行事についての由来が不明確であった。そこで1703年、それを正すために王命によって琉球各地の旧記や由来記が収集され、『琉球国由来記』が1713年（尚敬王代）に完成した。王府から各間切りの番所に命じて、管内の旧事や由来を調査・報告させ、その中から取捨選択して編纂した。第11巻の数カ所には『琉球神道記』（1605年）を参照した記述もある。琉球国由来記には王城の公式行事や官職制度のほか、各地の旧記・由来、御嶽などが記されており、伝統的な琉球社会を知る上で欠くことのできない資料といわれる。

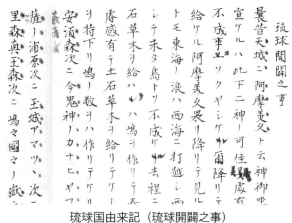

琉球国由来記（琉球開闢之事）
Ryukyu-koku-*yuraiki*
(Description of the creation of Ryukyu)

⑤ **Ryukyu-koku-*yuraiki*(Ryukyu Kingdom Origin Story)**

The oldest systematic geography of the Ryukyu, edited by the Shuri royal government, consisting of 21 volumes. At that time (the reign of King Sho Tei), there were no documents on various events and ceremonies in the royal government, and the origin of the ceremonies and events held every month or year was unclear. Therefore, in 1703, in order to correct this situation, the old records and origin stories from various parts of Ryukyu were collected by order of the King, and the Ryukyu-koku-*yuraiki* (Ryukyu Kingdom Origin Story) was completed in 1713 (during the reign of King Sho Kei). The Shuri royal office ordered the *magiri-banjo* (village offices) to investigate and report on the old events and origins of the area, and then selected and compiled the information from among them. In many places in Volume 11, there are some descriptions that is based on the Ryukyu *Shintou-ki* (1605). The Ryukyu-koku-*yuraiki* contains information on the official events of the royal castle and the governmental office system, as well as old records, origins, and *utaki* in various regions, and is said to be an indispensable source for understanding traditional Ryukyu society.

⑥球陽 (きゅうよう)

尚敬王代の1743年から45年にかけて、王府の命を受けた鄭秉哲（ていへいてつ）が編纂した琉球王国の正史である。本巻（22巻）と外巻（3巻）から成り、それぞれに付巻（4巻と1巻）がついており全文が漢文で書かれている。『球陽』という書名は琉球処分以降に広まったもので、それ以前は『球陽記事』または単に『記事』と呼ばれていた。「球陽」とは琉球の美称であり、長崎を「崎陽」（きよう）、岐阜を「岐陽」（きよう）と呼称したのと同類と考えられている。外巻は特に『遺老説伝』（いろうせつでん）とも呼称され、別の文献として扱われることもある。本巻には歴代琉球国王の治世と政治経済、天変地異、社会風俗、外交関係などが詳細に記される一方で、日本、特に薩摩藩との関係については清国に配慮して付巻に記している。一方、琉球王国成立以前の歴史については簡略した記述となっている。1745年には一旦完成したが、その後も1876年まで追記が及んでいる。『球陽』は旧琉球王家に秘蔵された正本の他にも写本が流布していたが、沖縄戦の戦火で大部分が消失した。その後、球陽研究会によって研究が続けられ、1974年に角川書店より刊行された。この歴史書は、琉球歴史研究のほか民族、民話など多方面の研究資料となっている。

⑥ **Kyuyou**

This is the official history of the Kingdom of Ryukyu, compiled by Tei Heitetsu under the order of the royal government between 1743 and 1745 during the reign of King Sho Kei. It consists of the main volume(22volumes) and the outer volume (3 volumes), each of them has an appendix (four volumes and one volume), and the entire text is written in Chinese. The title Kyuyou became popular after the disposal of Ryukyu, and before that it was called Kyuyou-*kiji* (Kyuyou articles) or simply *Kiji* (articles). The word kyuyou is a beautiful name for Ryukyu, and is considered to be the same as the name Kiyou for Nagasaki and Kiyou for Gifu. The outer volume is also called Irou-Setsuden and is sometimes treated as a separate document. The main volume contains detailed information on the reigns of successive Ryukyu kings, political economy, natural disasters, social customs, and diplomatic relations, but relations with Japan, especially with the Satsuma Domain, are described in a supplementary volume in consideration of the Qing government. On the other hand, the history before the establishment of the Ryukyu Kingdom is briefly described. It was once completed in 1745, but additions were made until 1876. In addition to the original manuscript kept by the former Ryukyu royal family, there were other copies of Kyuyou in circulation, but most of them were lost in the fires of the Battle of Okinawa. Later, research was continued by the Kyuyou Study Group, and the book was published by Kadokawa Shoten in 1974. This history book has become a research resource for many fields, including ethnic groups and folktales, as well as Ryukyu history research.

(34) 琉球王国の英傑たち （りゅうきゅうおうごくのえいけつたち）

①舜天王（しゅんてんおう）(1166 ～ 1237)

　幼少期に尊敦（そんとん）と呼ばれた舜天（1166 ～ 1237）は、琉球の正史では初代琉球国王と位置づけられている。伝承によると、舜天は源為朝と大里按司の妹との間に生まれ、1180 年に衆望を得て浦添按司になったといわれる。1187 年、天孫氏王統を滅ぼした逆臣・利勇（りゆう）を討ち、推されて 22 歳で琉球国中山王に即位したとされるが、実在を証明する史料は全く残っていない。『おもろさうし』にも彼を讃えるオモロは見当たらない。王といっても、当時の琉球全体を統治する存在ではなく、浦添を中心とする地域の覇者にすぎなかったともいわれる。舜天

食栄森御嶽 （南城市南風原）
Iimui-*utaki*(Haebaru, Nanjo City)

は右耳上頭部に瘤（こぶ）があり、これを隠すために髪を結んだことから民衆もこれにならい「カタカシラ」の髪型がおこったという由来譚がある。舜天王の墓は北中城村の「ナスの御嶽」や南城市大里にある「食栄森（いいむい）御嶽」に存在する。舜天王統は 3 代・73 年間続いた。

(34) Heroes of the Ryukyu Kingdom

① **King Syunten(1166 ～ 1237)**

Syunten, who was called Sonton in his childhood, is positioned as the first King of Ryukyu in the authentic history of Ryukyu. According to the legend, Syunten was born to Minamoto-no Tametomo and the sister of Ozato-*aji*, and became Urasoe-*aji* in 1180 with the support of the people. In 1187, he is said to have defeated

Riyuu, a vassal who had destroyed the Tenson Dynasty, and was recommended and enthroned as the king of Chuzan in Ryukyu at the age of 22, but there are no historical documents to prove his existence, and there is no *omoro* (description)in *Omoro-soushi* to praise him either. Even though he was a king, it is said that he was not the ruler of the entire Ryukyu Kingdom at that time, but only a champion of the region centered on Urasoe. Sunten had a bump on the upper head of his right ear and tied his hair up to hide it, and the people followed suit and the *katakashira* hairstyle was said to be born. What is said to be the tomb of King Shunten can be found at the Nasu'no-*utaki* in Kitanakagusuku Village and the Iimui-*utaki* in Ozato, Nanjo City. The Sunten Dynasty lasted for three generations and 73 years.

②英祖王（えいそおう）(1229 ？〜 1299)

　英祖王の誕生について琉球王国の最初の正史『中山世鑑』（1650 年）に以下のように記されている。「舜天王統三代目の義本王代の沖縄は、大飢饉や疫病が蔓延し死者が多数出た。義本王はそれを自らの徳のなさが原因だと思い、王政を任せる摂政を探した。家臣達は伊祖城の英祖を推した。英祖が摂政になって数年のうちに災危がなくなり、民心も彼を慕うようになると義本王は王位を禅譲した」。しかし「天孫氏王統の末裔」である英祖が、「大和系」の義本王を追放したのが史実とされている。正史によると、母親

伊祖グスク跡（浦添市伊祖）
Ruins of Iso-*gusuku*（Iso,Urasoe City)

が太陽を宿す夢をみて懐妊し、産まれた男子（英祖）は「ティダコ」（太陽の子）と呼ばれたという。英祖は『おもろさうし』で「いくさもい」と詠われているように、武勇に優れ数年で沖縄全島を統治した。租税の公平化をはかり農業に力を入れたので、国力も徐々に充実した。大和から来琉した僧・禅監（ぜんかん）の教えに帰依した英祖王は、浦添城の北側に「極楽寺」を建て、自らの墓である「浦添ようどれ」を建造した。英祖王統は 5 代・90 年間続いた。

② King Eiso(1229 ？〜 1299)

　The birth of King Eiso is described in the first official history of the Kingdom of Ryukyu, Chuzan-seikan (1650), as follows. "During the reign of King Gihon, the third generation of the Syunten Dynasty, Okinawa experienced a great famine and plague that caused many deaths. King Gihon thought it was due to his lack of virtue and looked for a regent to take charge of the monarchy. His retainers recommended Eiso of Iso Castle. Within a few years of Eiso becoming regent, the disasters ceased and the people's hearts began to adore him, so King Gihon relinquished the throne to him". However, it is said that the historical fact is that King Eiso, a descendant of the Tenson Dynasty, banished King Gihon, a Japanese bloodline. According to the authentic history, his mother had a dream that she was pregnant with the sun, and the baby boy (King Eiso) was called *Tidako* (son of the sun). As described as *Ikusamoi* in *Omoro-soushi*, a collection of poems by the Shuri royal court, King Eiso was a man of great military prowess and ruled the entire island of Okinawa in a few years. He made taxation fair and focused on agriculture, so the country's strength gradually increased. King Eiso, who took refuge in the teachings of Zenkan, a monk from Yamato (Japan), built Gokurakuji Temple on the north side of Urasoe Castle and constructed his own tomb, Urasoe-*youdore*. The Eiso Dynasty lasted for five generations and 90 years.

③察度王（さっとおう）（1321〜1396）

　1321年生まれで、父は浦添間切謝名村の奥間大親（おくまうふや）、母は天女と伝えられるが、天女の正体は英祖王統三代目・恵慈王の次女・真銭金（まじにがに）といわれる。察度は牧港に来港する日本商船から鉄を買い入れ、耕者には鉄を与えて農機具を作らせた。これによって人心を得て浦添按司に推挙され、1350年、英祖王統最後の西威王を廃して中山王に推された。1372年、察度は明の洪武帝の招愉に応じ、弟の泰期（たいき）を遣わして初めて進貢した。1387年頃からは南蛮貿易を開拓し、胡椒や蘇木（そぼく＝染料の一種）など南方産の物質が重要な貢物になった。さらに朝鮮とも意欲的に交易

黄金宮・察度王の屋敷跡（宜野湾市大謝名）
Kugani-naa(ruins of the residence of King Satto)
(Ohjana, Ginowan City)

を行うなど諸国との貿易が活発になると、琉球船の北上や堺・博多・対馬などから来琉する船も多く、中継貿易地として栄えるようになった。宮古・八重山が服属したのもこの頃といわれる。1392年には３人を初めて中国の「国子監」（近代以前の中国の最高学府）に留学させるなど、経済面ばかりでなく文化面の功績も大きい。晩年は首里城に移ったという説もある。察度王統は２代・56年間続いた。

③ King Satto（1321〜1396）

　King Satto was born in 1321, and his father is said to be Okuma-*uhuya* of Urasoe *magiri* Jana village, and his mother is said to be a celestial maiden, but the true identity of the celestial maiden is said to be Majinigani, the second daughter of King Eiji, the third generation of the Eiso Dynasty. He bought iron from the Japanese merchant ships that came to Makiminato Port, and gave the iron to the cultivators so that they could make agricultural implements. By doing so, he won the hearts of the people and was promoted to the position of Urasoe-*aji*, and in 1350, he was nominated as King of Chuzan, dethroning King Irii, the last king of the Eiso Dynasty. In 1372, at the invitation of the Hongwu Emperor of the Ming Dynasty, Satto sent his younger brother Taiki to pay tribute for the first time. From around 1387, he began to develop trade with the south, and materials from the south such as pepper and *soboku* (a type of dye) became important tributes. As trade with other countries became more active, such as with Korea, Ryukyu ships came north and many ships from Sakai, Hakata, Tsushima, etc. came to Ryukyu, and the area flourished as a transit trade area. It is said that it was around this time that Miyako and Yaeyama were subjugated to Chuzan. In 1392, he was the first to send three students to study at China's *Guozijian* (the highest school in China before the modern era), making him a great contributor not only to the economy but also to culture. Some say that he moved to Shuri Castle in his later years. The Satto Dynasty lasted for two generations and 56 years.

④尚巴志王（しょうはしおう）（1372〜1439）

　尚巴志は1372年、第一尚氏王統初代・尚思紹王の長男として佐敷上グスクで生まれた。伝承によると、幼年のとき名剣を造らせ、その剣と異国船が満載してきた鉄とを交換し、その鉄を庶民に与えて人望を得たという。1402年に島添大里按司を滅ぼして東四間切（佐敷・大里・知念・玉城）を支配下におさめて勢力を拡大した。その後、三山と呼ばれる３つの勢力（中山・北山・南山）を次々に攻略し、琉球で最初の統一王国を成立させたカリスマ的な天下人である。1406年に中山・武寧王を倒して父・尚思紹を中山王に即位させて拠点を浦添から首里に移し、1416年には北山・攀安知王を攻略した。1421年の父の薨去にともない翌1422年に中山王として即位した。1427年には安国山に樹華木を

植え、龍潭池を掘り、中山門を創建して外苑を整備するとともに、首里城を拡張整備して王城にふさわしい城とした。1429 年には南山・他魯毎王を滅ぼして第一尚氏王統による琉球王国最初の統一王朝を樹立した。この頃、福建省から甘蔗（サトウキビ）を、南蛮から薯萸（サトイモの類）を輸入して盛んに栽培した。那覇港を整備し、中国（明）をはじめ日本、朝鮮、南アジア諸国との交易を盛んに行い、琉球の繁栄の基礎をもたらした。間切制度（現在の市町村に相当する）を確立し、首里王府と地方を結ぶ国道「宿道」を整備した。墓は当初、首里の天山陵にあったが、金丸（後の尚円王）のクーデター（1469 年）の際に天山陵の破壊を恐れた親族によって遺骨が持ち出され、現在の場所（読谷村伊良皆）に移された。尚、「佐敷ようどれ」と呼ばれる父・尚思紹王や母の墓は航空自衛隊知念分屯基地内にある。第一尚氏王統は 7 代・64 年間続いた。

尚巴志王の墓（読谷村伊良皆）
Tomb of King Sho Hashi(Iramina, Yomitan Village)

④ King Sho Hashi（1372 ～ 1439）

Sho Hashi was born in 1372 at Sashiki-*Uwii-gusuku* as the eldest son of King Sho Shisho, the first king of the First Sho Dynasty. According to tradition, he had a famous sword made when he was a child, and traded the sword for iron that was loaded on foreign ships and gave it to the common people, gaining popularity. In 1402, he destroyed the Shimasoe-Ozato-*aji* and expanded his power by taking control of *Agari-yumajiri* (the four eastern districts：Sashiki, Ozato, Chinen, and Tamagusuku). After that, he was a charismatic natural ruler who established the first unified kingdom in Ryukyu by conquering the three forces known as Sanzan (Chuzan, Hokuzan, and Nanzan) one after another. In 1406, he defeated King Bunei of Chuzan, enthroned his father Sho Shisho as King of Chuzan, and moved his base from Urasoe to Shuri, and in 1416, he conquered King Han Anchi of Hokuzan. After the death of his father in 1421, he ascended to the throne as King Chuzan in 1422. In 1427, he planted trees and flowers on Ankoku-*zan*, dug the Ryutan Pond, built the Chuzan Gate and developed the outer garden, and also expanded and developed Shuri Castle to make it suitable for a royal castle. In 1429, he destroyed King Tarumii of Nanzan and established the first unified Dynasty of the Ryukyu Kingdom under the First Sho Dynasty. Around this time, sugar cane was imported from Fujian Province in China, and *taro* from Southeast Asian countries, and began to be actively cultivated. He developed Naha Port and actively traded with China (Ming Dynasty), Japan, Korea and other South Asian countries, laying the foundation for Ryukyu's prosperity. He established the *magiiri* system (equivalent to today's municipalities) and developed the *shukumichi*, a national road connecting the Shuri royal government and the provinces. His tomb was originally located at the Tenzan Mausoleum in Shuri, but during the *coup d'etat* by Kanamaru (later King Sho En) in 1469, his relatives, fearing the destruction of the Tenzan Mausoleum, took his remains and moved them to the present location (Iramina, Yomitan Village). The tomb of his father, King Sho Shisho, and his mother is called Sashiki-*youdore* and is located in the Air Self-Defense Force Chinen Air Base. The First Sho Dynasty lasted for 7 generations and 64 years.

⑤尚円王（しょうえんおう）(1415 〜 1476)

　尚円王は即位前の名を「金丸」（かなまる）といい、以下のような伝承が残っている。「父・尚櫻（しょうしょく）、母・瑞雲（ずいうん）の長男として伊是名村諸見で生まれた。20 歳の時に両親を亡くした彼はしばらく農業を励んでいたが、村人たちとのトラブルが絶えなかった。耐えかねて 24 歳の時、15 歳年下の弟と妻とともに沖縄本島の国頭村へ逃亡した」。しかし、第一尚氏の尚巴志の祖父・鮫皮大主の伝説と類似しているこの伝承は後世の作り話といわれる。一説によると、金丸は南山・他魯毎王の子で尚巴志による南山攻略時に伊是名島へ亡命。国頭間切や久志間切を経て南下し、頃合いを見て首里に乗り込んだという。首里では越来王子（後の尚泰久王）に見出

尚円王の御後絵
Portrait of King Sho En

され、家臣となった。10 年後には高官に抜擢され西原間切内間村の領主に任命された。尚泰久王の絶大な信頼を得て順調に出世し、1459 年には御物城御鎖側（貿易長官）に就任した。尚泰久王が薨去し尚徳王が即位（1461 年）すると、金丸は政策面などで幾度も衝突し領地の内間御殿に隠避した。1469 年、クーデターで尚徳王一族を追放。世子として冊封を受け尚円王を名乗り、1879 年の廃藩置県までの 410 年にわたる第二尚氏王統の初代国王となった。彼は歴代の琉球国王の霊を祀るための国廟・崇元寺を建てたが、第一尚王統の祟りを恐れたのがその理由といわれる。1476 年に薨去した尚円王は第二尚氏王統の王墓・玉陵に眠っている。第二尚氏王統は 19 代・410 年続いた。

⑤ King Sho En（1415 〜 1476 ）

　King Sho En's name before his accession to the throne was Kanamaru, and the following legend remains. He was born in Shomi, Izena Village, the eldest son of Sho Shoku, his father, and Zuiun, his mother. His parents died when he was 20 years old, and he worked hard at farming for a while, but had a lot of trouble with the villagers. At the age of 24, he fled to Kunigami village on the main island of Okinawa with his younger brother, 15 years younger, and his wife. However, this legend, which is similar to the legend of Samekawa-*uhunushi*, the grandfather of Sho Hashi of the First Sho Dynasty, is said to be a later fabrication. According to one theory, Kanamaru was the son of King Tarumii of Nanzan and fled to Izena Island when Sho Hashi invaded Nanzan. He is said to have moved south via Kunigami and Kushi *magiri*, and arrived in Shuri when the time was right. In Shuri, he was promoted to Prince Goeku (later King Sho Taikyu) and became his vassal. Ten years later, he was selected as a high official and appointed as the lord of Uchima village, Nishihara *magiri*. He gained the great trust of King Sho Taikyu and rose steadily, and in 1459, he was appointed as the *Umunu-gusuku-usashinusuba* (Minister of Trade). After the death of King Sho Taikyu and the accession of King Sho Toku in 1461, Kanamaru had numerous conflicts over policy and other issues and went into hiding at Uchima-*udun* in his domain. In 1469, he ousted King Sho Toku and his family in a *coup d'etat*. He was approved by the Ming emperor as his successor and took the name of King Sho En, becoming the first king of the Second Sho Dynasty, which lasted 410 years until the abolition of the domain in 1879. He built a national temple, Sougenji Temple, to enshrine the spirits of successive Ryukyu kings, said to be because he feared that the First Sho Dynasty would be haunted. King Sho En, who passed away in 1476, rests in the royal tomb of the Second Sho Dynasty successive kings and their families, Tama-*udun*. The Second Sho Dynasty lasted for 19 generations and 410 years.

(35) 沖縄の五偉人（おきなわのごいじん）

　伊波普猷（いはふゆう）が発表した論文「沖縄の代表的政治家」をベースに、真境名安興（まじきなあんこう）が加筆して 1916 年に発刊した単冊本に収録されている琉球史上の 5 名の人物である。

(35) Five Great People of Okinawa (Five politicians representing Okinawa)

　These are five people in Ryukyu history who are included in a single volume book published in 1916 based on the article "Representative Politicians of Okinawa" published by Iha Huyuu with additions by Majikina Ankou.

①儀間親方真常（ぎまうぇーかたしんじょう）（中国名：麻平衡）

　1557 年に垣花で生まれ、1593 年に真和志間切儀間村の地頭に任じられた。1605 年に野国総管が中国から持ち帰ったサツマイモの普及に尽力し、黒砂糖の製造法の習得と普及に努めた。1609 年に捕虜となった尚寧王の日本行きにも随行。薩摩に赴いた際に木綿の種子を持ち帰り、木綿栽培と木綿織の技法を広め、琉球絣の基礎を築いた。中でも砂糖は、その後の琉球の経済を支える重要産物となり、甘藷は後に薩摩藩を経て日本全国へと広がり、「サツマイモ」の名前で知られるようになった。これらの功績から「沖縄産業の恩人」と称され、奥武山公園内にある世持神社に祀られている。1644 年（88 歳）に亡くなり墓は那覇市大道にある。

儀間真常の墓（那覇市大道）
Tomb of Gima Shinjo(Daidou,Naha City)

① Gima-*oyakata* Shinjo (Chinese name: Ma Heikou)

　He was born in Kakinohana in 1557, and was appointed as *jitou* (landowner) of Gima village in Mawashi *magiri* in 1593. He was instrumental in popularizing the sweet potatoes brought back from China by Noguni-Soukan in 1605, and worked to learn and popularize the brown sugar production method. In 1609, he accompanied the captive King Sho Nei to Japan. When he went to Satsuma, he brought back cotton seeds, spread cotton cultivation and cotton weaving techniques, and laid the foundation for Ryukyu-*kasuri*. In particular, sugar became an important product that supported the Ryukyu economy, and later, sweet potatoes spread throughout Japan via the Satsuma Domain and became known as "Satsuma-*Imo*". Because of these achievements, he is called the "Benefactor of Okinawan industry" and is enshrined at the Yomochi Shrine in Ohnoyama Park. He died in 1644 (at the age of 88) and his grave is in Daidou, Naha City.

②羽地朝秀（はねじちょうしゅう）（中国名：尚象賢）

　尚真王の長男・尚維衡の血筋を引く名家で、1617 年に生まれた沖縄の歴史を代表する政治家の一人である。1640 年に家督を継いで羽地間切の総地頭となり、国王の命を受けて 1651 年に『中山世鑑』を編纂した。薩摩へは幾度となく出張したが、中国へ使節として赴いたことは一度もない。1666 年には摂政に就任し、退職するまでの 7 年間、国政に敏腕をふるい王子の位階を与えられた。羽地朝秀の時代は、薩摩や明清交代期の中国との対外問題や、経済的・政治的に弱体化した琉球の再建という内政問題に直面していた。彼の政策は「羽地仕置」という布達によって実行された。その政策は薩摩側の強い支持を得ていたが、琉球の伝統を大きく改革する面で、琉球内の守旧派の強い反発にさらされた。激しい気性や周到な戦術家の羽地は、一定の妥協を含みながらも反対派を押さえて強引に施策

を展開した。彼の思想として「日琉同祖論」が指摘されるが、それは国王の久高島参詣を廃止するための理論補強であり、周到な戦術家としての羽地朝秀の側面と捉える説もある。那覇市末吉町にある墓は国王から拝領されたもので、葬儀には国王（尚貞王）も臨席した。

羽地朝秀の墓（那覇市末吉町）
Tomb of Haneji Choshu (Sueyoshi-*cho*, Naha City)

② Haneji Choshu (Chinese name: Sho Shoken)

He was born in 1617 in a prominent family descended from King Sho Shin's eldest son, Shou Ikou, and is one of the most representative politicians in the history of Okinawa. In 1640, he succeeded to the governorship of his family and became *sou-jitou* (general landowner) of Haneji *magiri*, and compiled the Chuzan-seikan (the first official history book of the Shuri royal government), in 1651 at the order of the king. He made numerous business trips to Satsuma, but never once went to China as an envoy. In 1666, he was appointed *shisshii* (regent), and for seven years until his retirement, he administered the affairs of state with great skill and was given the rank of prince. During the reign of Haneji Chosyu , the Ryukyu Kingdom faced both external problems with Satsuma, and China during the changeover between the Ming and Qing dynasties, and internal problems of rebuilding the economically and politically weakened Ryukyu Kingdom. His policy was carried out by means of a notification called Haneji-*shioki*, which was strongly supported by the Satsuma side, but was strongly opposed by the Ryukyu's old guard because it was a major change in Ryukyu tradition. A man of fierce temperament and careful tactician, Haneji forcefully implemented measures that included a certain amount of compromise but also suppressed opposition. His ideology of *Nichiryu-douso-ron* has been pointed out, but some consider it to be a reinforcement of the theory to abolish the King's visit to Kudaka Island, and another aspect of Haneji Chosyu as a careful tactician. His tomb, located in Sueyoshi-*cho*, Naha City, was given to him by the king, and the king (King Sho Tei) was present at the funeral.

③名護親方寵文（なごうぇーかたちょうぶん）（中国名：程順則）

　1663年に久米村で生まれた詩人・儒学者で、沖縄名を寵文という。父は進貢使として清国に赴いたが、内乱で福建省へ戻れず、1676年に蘇州で客死したので、母の教育のもとで育った。21歳で通事として謝恩使とともに渡清し、一度は琉球に戻るが、再度渡清して程朱学（朱子学の一種）と漢詩を数年間学んだ。帰国後は中城御殿に宿泊しながら王子の教育係となった。その後、進貢使として数回、清国へ赴くが、1706年の渡清時にかつて留学中に感銘を受けた『六諭衍義』（りくゆえんぎ）に序と後書を添えて私費で刊行した。1714年、謝恩使の一員として江戸に赴く際に薩摩藩藩主に献上した。66歳で名護間切の総地頭となり、名護親方を名乗った。琉球で最初の公的教育機関となる「明倫堂」（めいりんどう）の創設を建議し、琉球の教育に大きく貢献した。彼が福州で刊行した六諭衍義は、後に日本各地の寺子屋の教科書として広く普及し、教育勅語にも影響を与えた。墓は那覇市識名にある。

名護親方の銅像（名護市東江）
Bronze statue of Nago *oyakata*
(Agarie, Nago City)

③ Nago-*oyakata* Chobun (Chinese name: Tei Junsoku)

A poet and Confucian scholar born in Kume Village in 1663, whose Okinawan name is Chobun. His father went to the Qing Dynasty as a tribute envoy, but could not return to Fujian due to the civil war, and died as a guest in Suzhou in 1676, so he grew up with his mother's education. At the age of 21, he traveled to the Qing Dynasty as an interpreter, with a gratitude envoy, once returned to Ryukyu, but then went back to China to study neo-Confucianism (a type of Cheng-Zhu) and Chinese poetry for several years. After returning to Ryukyu, he stayed at the Nakagusuku-*udun* (the residence of the prince) and became the prince's educator. Later, he went to the Qing Dynasty several times as a tribute envoy, and when he went to the Qing Dynasty in 1706, he added a preface and afterword to the moral book Rikuyu-Engi, which had impressed him during his studies in China, and published it at his own expense. In 1714, when he went to Edo (present-day Tokyo) as a member of a gratitude envoy, he presented the Rikuyu-Engi to the lord of the Satsuma Domain. At the age of 66, he became the *sou-jitou* (general landowner) of Nago *magiri* and called himself Nago-*oyakata*. He contributed greatly to the education of Ryukyu by advocating the establishment of Meirindo, the first public educational institution in Ryukyu. The moral book he published in Fuzhou, Rikuyu-Engi, was later widely used as a textbook in *terakoya* (a private elementary school in the Edo period) throughout Japan, and later influenced the Imperial Rescript on Education. His tomb is located in Shikina, Naha City.

④具志頭親方文若（ぐしちゃんうぇーかたぶんじゃく）（中国名：蔡温）

　1682 年に蔡氏十世・蔡鐸（さいたく）の次男（正室の子）として生まれたが、彼には 2 歳年上の兄（側室の子）がいた。後継ぎをめぐり、そのことが蔡温少年に影響を与えたといわれ、自伝によると少年期は反抗的で怠け者であったという。しかし 17 歳になると学問に目覚め、20 歳頃までには論語など多くの書物を読破した。27 歳で現地での通事として福州に赴任した時、「書物を読み知識だけを習得しただけでは何の役にも立たない」と指摘され、実学の思想に目覚めた。尚敬王が即位し「国師」に任命された彼は実学を重んじ、物事を現実的にとらえ自ら行動した。特に中・北部の山林保全や、羽地大川などの河川改修では現地に赴き自ら指揮を執ることが多かった。当時の琉球は薩摩藩の支配下にあり社会全体が停滞していたが、蔡温は薩摩藩に従う利点を説き、現実的な対応を指導。内政では羽地朝秀の改革を継承し、近世的な民衆支配の制度を確立した。その一方で、対立していた平敷屋朝敏とその配下 15 人が処刑されるという事件も起きている（平敷屋・友寄事件）。1762 年、80 歳で死去した蔡温の墓は首里大名町にある。

蔡温の墓（那覇市首里大名町）
Tomb of Sai On(Shuri Ohna-*cho*,Naha City)

④ Gushichan-*oyakata* Bunjaku
　　(Chinese name: Sai On)

He was born in 1682 as the second son (son of the main family) of Sai Taku, the tenth generation of the Sai family, but he had an older brother (a concubine boy) who was two years older than him. The issue of succession is said to have influenced the boy Sai On, and according to his autobiography, he was rebellious and lazy as a boy. However, at the age of 17, he became interested in learning, and by the time he was 20, he had read many books, including the Analects of Confucius. At the age of 27, when he was transferred to Fuzhou as an interpreter, he was awakened to the idea of practical learning when it was pointed out to him that merely reading books and gaining knowledge would not help him. When King Sho Kei ascended to the throne and appointed him as the "National

Teacher," he emphasized practical learning, took a realistic view of things, and acted on his own. In particular, he often went to the field and personally led the conservation of forests in the central and northern parts of Ryukyu and the renovation of rivers such as the Haneji River. At the time, Ryukyu was under the control of the Satsuma Domain and society as a whole was stagnant, but Sai On explained the advantages of obeying the Satsuma Domain and guided Ryukyu to take practical measures. In domestic affairs, he succeeded the reforms of Haneji Choshu and established a modern system of people's rule. On the other hand, there was an incident in which Heshikiya Choubin and 15 of his men were executed for opposing Sai On (Heshikiya-Tomoyose Incident). The tomb of Sai On, who died in 1762 at the age of 80, is located in Ohna-*cho*, Shuri.

⑤宜湾親方朝保（ぎわんうぇーかたちょうほ）（中国名：向有恆）

　1823 年生まれで、琉球処分直前の三司官として琉球の近代化への扉を開いた。私人としては和歌に親しみ、当代きっての歌人であった。生家の宜湾家は向氏小禄御殿の分家で、宜野湾間切の総地頭家であった。1868 年に明治政府が成立すると、1871 年に慶賀使の副使として上京した。明治政府から琉球国王・尚泰を琉球藩王にするとの命を受け、喜んで帰国した。しかし、明治政府は約束を反故にし、琉球併合を断行した。1875 年に琉球処分が具体化し始めると、維新慶賀使の責任として世の非難を浴び三司官を辞職した。翌年、失意のうちに 54 歳の生涯を閉じた。墓は首里大名町にある。

⑤ Giwan-*oyakata* Choho (Chinese name: Sho Yuukou)

　Born in 1823, he opened the door to the modernization of Ryukyu as one of *sanshikan* just before the disposal of Ryukyu. He was a private citizen. As a private citizen, he loved *waka* poetry and was one of the most popular poets of his time. His birthplace, the Giwan family, was a branch of Oroku-*udun* (Sho family), and was *Soujitou* (the general landowner) of Ginowan *magiri*. When the Meiji government was established in 1868, he went to Edo (now Tokyo) in 1871 as a deputy of the *keigashi* envoy, and when he received an order from the Meiji government to recognize Sho Tai, the King of Ryukyu, as the King of the Ryukyu Domain, he gladly returned to Ryukyu. However, the Meiji government reneged on its promise and annexed Ryukyu. In 1875, when the disposal of Ryukyu began to take shape, he resigned from *sanshikan*, facing public condemnation for his responsibility as a *keigashi* envoy. The following year, he died of a broken heart at the age of 54. His grave is in Ohna-*cho*, Shuri.

宜湾朝保の墓（那覇市首里大名町）
Tomb of Giwan Choho(Shuri Ohna-*cho*,Naha City)

(36) 野国総管（のぐにそうかん）

　進貢船の総管となって福建省に渡り 1605 年、蕃薯（ばんしょ、現在のサツマイモ）の苗を鉢植えにして持ち帰った北谷間切野国村の人。氏名や生没年は未詳とされているが、彼の位牌から名前は与那覇松・中国名「總世健」（そうせいけん）で、1557 年生まれの儀間真常より 10 歳ほど若かったとされる。総管とは、進貢船で水夫を管理する職名である。当職は普通、久米村人が担当したが、何故、彼が総管職となったかは不明とされている。帰国後は野国村で試作したが、苗は悪天候に左右されず土地によく根付いた。村の農民に広められ、これによって餓死など凶作による村人の災難は防がれた。この情報を得た王府役人・儀間真常は野国に会い、苗を譲ってもらい栽培法を教わった。その後、彼は五穀に代わる重要作物として琉球各地に

広めた。尚豊王代（1621 〜 40）に甘藷は薩摩に伝わり、やがて青木昆陽らによって関東はじめ日本中に広まった。野国総管の墓は米軍嘉手納マリーナ内にあり、那覇市奥武山町にある世持神社に蔡温、儀間真常とともに「沖縄産業の恩人」として祀られている。

野国総管の墓（嘉手納町・嘉手納マリーナ）
Tomb of Noguni-*soukan*(Kadena marina, Kadena Town)

(36) Noguni-*soukan*
(General Officer of Noguni Village)

A man from the village of Noguni, Chatan *magiri*, who went to Fujian Province (China) in 1605 as the *soukan* of a tribute ship and brought back potted sweet potato seedlings. His name and the year of his birth and death are unknown, but his tablets indicate that his name was Yonaha Matsu and his Chinese name was Sou Seiken, and that he was about 10 years younger than Gima Shinjo, who was born in 1557. *Soukan* is the name of the position that manages the sailors on the tribute ships. This position is usually held by a *Kunindaa* (Kume villager), but it is unclear why he was appointed to the position. After returning to Ryukyu, he made a trial crop in Noguni village, and the seedlings took root well in the land regardless of bad weather. The seedlings were spread among the farmers in the village, and this prevented the villagers from starving to death and other disasters caused by bad harvests. Upon receiving this information, Gima Shinjo, an official of the royal government, met Noguni, who gave him the seedlings and taught him how to grow them. Later, he spread it throughout Ryukyu as an important alternative crop to the five grains. During the reign of King Sho Hou (1621 〜 40), sweet potatoes were introduced to Satsuma, and eventually spread throughout Japan, including the Kanto region by Aoki Konyo and others. Noguni-*soukan's* grave is located in Kadena Marina on the U.S. military base, and he is enshrined at Yomochi Shrine in Ohnoyama-*cho*, Naha City, along with Sai On and Gima Shinjo as "benefactors of Okinawan industry".

(37) 琉球王国の有名な武将（りゅうきゅうおうごくのゆうめいなぶしょう）

①護佐丸（ごさまる）

中国名は毛国鼎（もうこくてい）、正式名称は中城按司護佐丸盛春で生年不詳だが、山田グスクで生まれた。娘は尚泰久王の妃である。1416 年、中山（尚巴志）軍の武将として北山（今帰仁城）討伐に従軍し、今帰仁城の攻略後は初代の北山監守として同地に駐屯した。その間に座喜味城を築き、山田グスクから居城を移した（1422 年）。築城の際、山田グスクの石材を手渡しで運ばせたという逸話は有名である。その後、1440 年には王府の命で中城グスクに移転したが、1458 年、阿麻和利の計略による王府軍の攻撃で自刃したといわれる（護佐丸・阿麻和利の乱）。この乱やその後に創作された「組踊り」などで「忠臣・

護佐丸の墓（中城城址東方の山中）
Tomb of Gosamaru(In the forest of eastern part of the Nakagusuku Castle site)

護佐丸」の人物像が作られたが、『おもろさうし』に護佐丸を称えるオモロが一首もないのは不思議である。護佐丸は尚泰久王の岳父、阿麻和利の妻は尚泰久王の娘で、両者は王家を挟んで姻戚関係にあった。「護佐丸・阿麻和利の乱」は首里王府に匹敵する勢力を誇る護佐丸と阿麻和利を排除するための王府サイドの陰謀という見方もある。護佐丸の墓は中城グスク東方の山中にある。

(37) Famous Warlords of the Ryukyu Kingdom
① Gosamaru

His Chinese name is Mou Kokutei, and his official name is Nakagusuku-*aji*, Gosamaru Seisyun, although his date of birth is unknown. He was born in Yamada-*gusuku*, and his daughter was the consort of King Sho Taikyu. In 1416, as a general in the Chuzan (Sho Hashi) army, he participated in the defeat of Hokuzan (Nakijin Castle), and after the capture of Nakijin Castle, he was stationed there as the first generation of Hokuzan-*kansyu* (supervisor). In the meantime, he built Zakimi Castle and moved his residence from Yamada-*gusuku* (1422). There is a famous anecdote that when the castle was built, stones from Yamada-*gusuku* were hand-carried. Later, in 1440, he was relocated to Nakagusuku Castle by the order of the royal government, but in 1458, he is said to have committed suicide in an attack by the royal army under the scheming of Amawari (the Gosamaru-Amawari Rebellion). This rebellion and the *kumi-odori* created afterwards established the image of the "Loyal retainer Gosamaru," but it is curious that *Omoro-saushi* does not contain a single poem in praise of Gosamaru. Gosamaru was the father of King Sho Taikyu, and Amawari's wife was the daughter of King Sho Taikyu, and they were related across the royal family. Some believe that the "Gosamaru-Amawari Rebellion" was a conspiracy on the part of the royal government to get rid of Gosamaru and Amawari, who were as powerful as the Shuri royal government. The tomb of Gosamaru is located in the mountains east of Nakagusuku Castle.

②阿麻和利（あまわり）

出自については諸説あるが、1429年の南山滅亡の際、中山軍の武将として参戦した屋良大川按司が、捕虜として屋良大川グスクに連れてきた兼城若按司（南山の武将）の娘との間に生まれた男子という説が有力である。阿麻和利は、悪政を強いる茂知附按司（勝連グスク城主）を攻め滅ぼして第11代目勝連城主となった。日本や東アジアとの貿易を促進して急速に頭角を現した阿麻和利の力を恐れた尚泰久王は、娘の百度踏揚を娶らせ懐柔策とした。国王の娘婿となった阿麻和利は1458年、中城グスク城主の護佐丸を王の命令で討った（護佐丸・阿麻和利の乱）。

阿麻和利の墓（読谷村古堅）
Tomb of Amawari(Hurugen, Yomitan Village)

さらに、首里城攻略の野望を抱いていたが、夫人・百度踏揚と鬼大城に事前に知られ、鬼大城を総大将とする王府軍に攻め滅ぼされた。この乱やその後の創作劇（組踊り）などにより「逆臣」という強いイメージが作られた。その後、近代の『おもろさうし』研究などにより、海外貿易により繁栄する勝連グスクや阿麻和利を讃美するオモロの存在が明らかになり「農民の信望を集めた英雄」などと再評価された。

② **Amawari**

There are various theories about his origins, but the prevailing one is that he was a boy born between Yara Ohkawa-*aji*, who participated in the battle as a warlord of the Chuzan army when Nanzan was destroyed in 1429, and the daughter of Kanegusuku *waka-aji* (a warlord of Nanzan) who was brought to Yara-*gusuku* as a prisoner of war. Amawari became the 11th Lord of Katsuren Castle after attacking and destroying the evil government of Mochizuki-*aji* (Lord of Katsuren Castle). Fearing the power of Amawari, who was rapidly gaining prominence by promoting trade with Japan and other East Asian countries, King Sho Taikyu had Amawari marry his daughter, Momoto-Humiagari, in order to win Amawari over to his side. Amawari, who became the king's son-in-law, defeated the lord of Nakagusuku Castle, Gosamaru, on the king's orders in 1458 (Gosamaru-Amawari Rebellion). In addition, he had ambitions to capture Shuri Castle, but his wife, Momoto-Humiagari, and *Uni*-Uhugusuku knew about it in advance, and he was attacked and destroyed by the Royal Army with *Uni*-Uhugusuku as its commander-in-chief. This rebellion and the subsequent creative drama (*kumi-odori*) created a strong image as "Treacherous retainer". Later, modern research on *Omoro-saushi* and other sources revealed the existence of Katsuren-*gusuku*, which prospered due to overseas trade, and *omoro*, which praised Amawari, and he was reevaluated as a "hero who gained the trust of the farmers".

③鬼大城（うにうふぐすく）

　尚泰久王（在位 1454 ～ 60）に仕えた武将で、英祖王の後裔・喜屋武按司（二代目）の長男。本名は大城賢勇（中国名は夏居数）という。史書『球陽』に「忠義剛直にして武勇無比、骨格は人と異なり勢狼虎の如し」と人物像が記されており、人々に「鬼大城」と呼ばれた。勝連城主・阿麻和利討伐（1458年）では首里王府軍の総大将を任され、大功をたてた。第一尚氏王統による三山（琉球）の実質的な統一は、この時点で達成された。この功績によって越来グスク城主となり、王女・百度踏揚を妻に娶った。1469 年に成立した第二尚氏王統の転覆を謀ったが、最後は知花グスクの中腹にある洞窟に追い込まれ、火攻めの末に殺されたという。その洞窟が彼の墓とされる。鬼大城が阿麻和利を斬ったとされる刀が昭和初期まで伝来していたが、沖縄戦以降は不明である。

鬼大城の墓（沖縄市知花、知花グスク中腹）
Tomb of *Uni*-Uhugusuku
(Halfway up Chibana-*gusuku*) (Chibana, Okinawa City)

③ *Uni*-Uhugusuku (Uhugusuku Kenyuu)

He was a military commander in the service of King Sho Taikyu (reigned 1454-60), the eldest son of Kyan-*aji* (the second generation), a descendant of King Eiso, and his real name was Uhugushuku Kenyuu (his Chinese name was Ka Kyosuu). His character is described in the historical book Kyuyou as "loyal and upright, with unparalleled bravery and courage, and a frame that differs from that of a man and is like a wolf and a tiger". When he defeated Amawari, the lord of Katsuren Castle (1458), he was entrusted as the commander-in-chief of the Shuri Royal Army and did a great job. The substantial unification of Sanzan (Ryukyu) by the First Sho Dynasty was achieved at this point. For this achievement, he became the lord of Goeku-*gusuku* and took the princess Momoto-Humiagari as his wife. He plotted to overthrow the Second Sho Dynasty, which was established in 1469, but in the end, he was driven into a cave in the middle of Chibana-*gusuku* and killed after a fire attack. The cave is said to be his tomb. The sword with which *Uni*-Uhugusuku is said to have killed Amawari was handed down until the early Showa period, but it has not been found since the Battle of Okinawa.

④オヤケアカハチ

　15 世紀末、八重山大浜村で豪勇として知られ、近隣を制圧し宮古勢とも対立した。年貢を拒否し首里王府に反旗を翻したが、逆徒として王府征討軍により誅殺された。伝承によると、波照間島で生まれ、幼少の頃より風貌が怪異で、長じては筋骨逞しく威名隆々たるものがあった。野望を抱いて石垣島の大浜村に居を構え、全島制圧の勢いを見せた。石垣島の酋長・長田大主の妹を娶り、大主と盟約して王府への反抗を企てた。しかし、大主はじめ他の有力酋長もアカハチに従わなかったため、殺されたり追われたりした。1500 年、アカハチは奮戦したが尚真王の軍勢（3000 人）に誅伐された。乱の原因を、王府側の記録ではアカハチ個人的粗暴な性格、王府への年貢拒否という逆徒とみている。他方、地元では正義感が強く、島民解放のため先頭に立って権力に立ち向かい、大浜村の人々から太陽と崇められ信望を集めていた「英雄」と語り継がれている。史籍に「オヤケアカハチホンガワラ」や、「オヤケアカハチ」と「ホンガワラ」として別人の人物名が出てくる。このことから首謀者を 2 人とみて「アカハチ・ホンガワラの乱」とする説が近年、有力になりつつある。石垣市大浜の崎原公園に「オヤケ赤蜂之碑」が建立されている。

オヤケアカハチの銅像（石垣市大浜、崎原公園）
Bronze statue of Oyake Akahachi
(Sakihara Park in Ohama,Ishigaki City)

④ Oyake Akahachi

　At the end of the 15th century, he was known for his bravery in the village of Ohama in Yaeyama, where he conquered the neighborhood and confronted the Miyako forces. He refused to pay tribute and rebelled against the Shuri royal government, but was killed by the royal conquering forces as a rebel. According to legend, he was born on Hateruma Island and had a strange appearance from an early age, becoming more muscular and dignified as he grew older. With ambition, he settled in Ohama village on Ishigaki Island and showed great vigor to conquer the entire island. He married the sister of the chieftain of Ishigaki Island, Nagata-*uhushu*, and made a pact with *uhushu* to rebel against the royal government. However, *uhushu* and other influential chiefs did not follow Akahachi, so they were killed or chased away. In 1500, Akahachi fought hard but was defeated by the army of King Sho Shin (3,000 men). According to the records of the royal government, the cause of the rebellion was Akahachi's own violent personality and his refusal to pay tribute to the royal government. On the other hand, the locals say that he was a "hero" with a strong sense of justice, who stood up against the authorities to liberate the islanders and was worshipped as the sun by the people of Ohama Village. In the historical records, the names of different people appear as Oyake Akahachi Hongawara, Oyakeakahachi and Hongawara. From these facts, the theory that there were two ringleaders and that it was the "Akahachi-Hongawara Rebellion" has been gaining popularity in recent years. The "Oyake Akahachi Monument has been erected at Sakihara Park in Ohama, Ishigaki City.

⑤謝名親方利山（じゃなうぇーかたりざん）

　琉球王国の政治家で、三司官の一人として対日本外交で強便姿勢をとり、1609 年の薩摩藩による琉球侵攻後、薩摩で処刑された。謝名親方の名で知られており、中国名は鄭迥（ていどう）。久米村出身で 1566 年、南京の国子監へ入学した後は進貢使者として数度渡唐した。1609 年の薩摩侵攻の際、三司官の一人として尚寧王、具志頭王子とともに薩摩に連行された。1611 年、薩摩藩は尚寧王および三司官に島津氏に忠誠を誓う起請文と、琉球が今後守るべき法度「掟十五条」（おきてじゅうごじょう）への署名を強要したが、謝名は琉球国の誇りと威厳をもって断固抵抗。独りだけ署名しなかったので斬首された。手（空手）の達人で、処刑の際に薩摩の番兵を何人か道連れにしたという言い伝えもある。

謝名は、長崎に来航した中国船に密かに明国の救援を願ったが、失敗に終わった。中国側は、謝名を「国難に殉じた忠臣」として評価している。謝名親方利山の墓はないが、鄭氏の一族によって建てられた顕彰碑が那覇市若狭町の旭が丘公園にある。

謝名親方利山の顕彰碑（那覇市旭が丘公園）
Monument in hornor of Jana *oyakata* Rizan
(Asahigaoka Park,Naha City)

⑤ Jana-*oyakata* Rizan

A politician of the Kingdom of Ryukyu, he took a strong stance in diplomacy against Japan as one of the *sanshikan* (three governors), and was executed in Satsuma after the invasion of Ryukyu by the Satsuma Domain in 1609. He was known by the name of Jana-*oyakata*, and his Chinese name was Tei Dou (Zheng Deng). He was born in Kume Village, and after entering the Kokushikan (Guozi Academy) in Nanjing in 1566, he traveled to China several times as a tribute messenger. During the invasion of Satsuma in 1609, he was taken to Satsuma with King Sho Nei and Prince Gushichan as one of the *sanshikan*. In 1611, the Satsuma Domain forced King Sho Nei and the *sanshikan* to sign a document pledging allegiance to the Shimazu family, and the *Okite-juugo-jou*,a law that Ryukyu would have to abide by in the future. Jana resisted resolutely with the pride and dignity of the Ryukyu nation, and was beheaded because he was the only one who did not sign the document. He was an expert in karate, and legend has it that he killed several Satsuma guards at the time of his execution. Jana secretly sought relief from the Ming Dynasty through a Chinese ship that came to Nagasaki, but was unsuccessful. The Chinese side evaluates Jana as a "loyal retainer who martyred himself for the national cause". There is no grave for Jana-*oyakata* Rizan, but there is a monument built by the Tei clan in Asahigaoka Park in Wakasa-*cho*, Naha City.

(38) 琉球王国の著名な女性たち（りゅうきゅうおうごくのちょめいなじょせいたち）

①百度踏揚（ももとふみあがり、むむとぅふみあがり）

　絶世の美女に纏わる悲劇の伝説は何処の世界にもあるが、琉球王国にも悲劇の運命をたどった美女がいた。その一人が「百度踏揚」である。第一尚氏王統の第 6 代目国王・尚泰久の長女である彼女は歴史の荒波に翻弄され、琉球歴史上、最も悲哀な生涯を送った女性といわれる。1429 年に尚巴志によって統一されて誕生した琉球王国だが、まだ地方には強力な按司がおり国の体制は盤石ではなかった。とりわけ中城城主・護佐丸や勝連城主・阿麻和利の存在は首里王府にとっては脅威であった。そこで尚泰久王（尚巴志王の七男）は護佐丸の娘を妃にする。つまり政略結婚だが、こうして生まれた王女が百度踏揚である。一方、勝連城では若き阿麻和利が台頭し王府の脅威となっていた。これを封じるための政略結婚で彼女は阿麻和利に嫁ぐのだが、1458 年、「護佐丸・阿麻和利の乱」が勃発する。百度踏揚にとって護佐丸は祖父であり、阿麻和利は夫であったのだが、結果的には両者とも王府軍によって滅ぼされた。乱の後、彼女は付き人の剣豪・鬼大城（うにうふぐすく）と再婚する。しかし、今度はかつての家臣・金丸がクーデターによって新王統（第二尚氏王統）を樹立した

百度踏揚の簪と鏡（南城市冨里）
Hairpin and Mirror of Momoto-Humiagari
(Husato, Nanjo City)

ため、旧体制の遺臣・鬼大城も新王府軍に滅ぼされた。第一尚氏王統末期の混迷期に生きた百度踏揚は2度夫を失い、その後は兄たちが落ち延びていた玉城の地に身を寄せ、ひっそりと余生を過ごしたという。

(38) Prominent women of the Ryukyu Kingdom
① Momoto-Humiagari

Everywhere in the world there are tragic legends about beautiful women, but in the Ryukyu Kingdom there were also beautiful women who suffered from tragic fate, and one of them was Momoto-Humiagari. The eldest daughter of Sho Taikyu, the sixth king of the First Sho Dynasty, she was tossed about by the ravages of history and is said to have lived the most sorrowful life in Ryukyu history. The Kingdom of Ryukyu was united by the Sho Hashi in 1429, but there were still powerful governors(*aji*) in the provinces and the system was not yet solid. In particular, Gosamaru, the lord of Nakagusuku Castle, and Amawari, the lord of Katsuren Castle, were threats to the Shuri royal government. Therefore, King Sho Taikyu (the seventh son of King Sho Hashi) took the daughter of Gosamaru as his wife. In other words, it was a political marriage, and the princess born in this way was Momoto-Humiagari. Meanwhile, at Katsuren Castle, the young Amawari was rising to prominence and becoming a threat to the royal government. To contain this threat, she was forced into a political marriage with Amawari, but in 1458, the "Gosamaru-Amawari Rebellion" broke out. For Momoto-Humiagari, Gosamaru was her grandfather and Amawari was her husband, but both were ultimately destroyed by the royal army. After the rebellion, she remarried her valet, a swordsman named *Uni*-Uhugusuku. However, his former vassal Kanamaru established a new royal Dynasty (the Second Sho Dynasty) through a *coup d'état*, and the vassal of the old regime, *Uni*-Uhugusuku, was also destroyed by the new royal army. Momoto-Humiagari, who lived during the chaotic period at the end of the First Sho Dynasty, lost her husband twice, and after that, it is said that she hid herself in Tamagusuku, where her brothers had escaped before her, and lived the rest of her life in seclusion.

② 宇喜也嘉（オギヤカ）

美貌のオギヤカ（1445～1505）は20歳の時に金丸（当時50歳、後の尚円王）へ嫁いだ。1476年に尚円王が薨去すると王弟の尚宣威が即位し、半年後に首里城正殿前の広場「御庭」（うなー）で即位式が行われた。ところが、大神（キミテズリ）によって新王を讃えるはずの「キミテズリの儀式」では、神意を伝えるノロたちが尚宣威ではなく、オギヤカの子・尚真を讃えるオモロを唱えたのである。王府の女官を掌握していたオギヤカの陰謀であったとされている。尚真王は即位時にはまだ13歳の幼少であり、母后・オギヤカが実権を握った。1509年、尚真王は女神官組織を編成し、全琉球のノロを統轄する聞得大君という役職を設け、妹または姉（オギヤカの長女）を任じた。これもオギヤカの意向とされており、「王（息子）による政治支配」と聞得大君（娘）による「神の神託」という形態で民衆を統治した。

第二尚氏王統の墓所「玉陵」にある埋葬資格者を記した「玉陵の碑文」では、尚円王とオギヤカの子孫だけに限定し、その血筋以外の者の埋葬を厳しく禁じている。碑文は権力を握っていたオギヤカの意向で書かれたとされるが、第二尚氏王統の初代王の妃にもかかわらず彼女自身は王墓に祀られていない。王府の正史にも存在が認知されていないオギヤカは、琉球王国最強の女帝といわれる。

玉陵の碑文
Inscription on the Tama-*udun*

② Ogiyaka

The beautiful Ogiyaka (1445-1505) married Kanamaru (then 50 years old, later King Sho En) at the age of 20. When King Sho En passed away in 1476, his younger brother Sho Sen'i ascended the throne, and six months later the coronation ceremony was held at *Unaa*, the square in front of the main hall of Shuri Castle. However, at the "*Kimitezuri* Ceremony," that the new king was supposed to be praised by the Great God (*Kimitezuri*), the *noro* who conveyed the divine will chanted *omoro* in praise of Sho Shin, the son of Ogiyaka, instead of Sho Sen'i. But, it is said to have been a conspiracy by Ogiyaka, who had taken control of the ladies of the royal court. King Sho Shin was only 13 years old when he ascended the throne, and his mother, Ogiyaka, took control of the kingdom. In 1509, King Sho Shin organized the Goddess Organization and created the position of Kikoye Okimi, who was in charge of all Ryukyu *noro*, and appointed his sister (the eldest daughter of Ogiyaka). This is also believed to have been her intention, and the Ogiyaka ruled the people in the form of "political rule by the king (son)" and "divine oracle" by Kikoe Okimi (daughter).

The inscription on Tama-*udun*, which describes who is eligible for burial at Tama-*udun,* the cemetery of the Second Sho Dynasty, limits burial to the descendants of King Sho En and Ogiyaka, and strictly forbids the burial of anyone outside of that lineage. The inscription is said to have been written at the behest of Ogiyaka, who held power, but she herself is not enshrined in the tomb, despite being the first queen of the Second Sho Dynasty. Ogiyaka, whose existence is not even recognized in the official history of the royal government, is said to be the strongest empress of the Ryukyu Kingdom.

③真壁按司加那志（まかんあじがなし）

　世界には中国の「西太后」（清王朝・咸豊帝の妃）や「楊貴妃」（唐王朝・玄宗皇帝の妃）、「アグリッピナ」（ローマ帝国・皇帝ネロの母親）など悪女と呼ばれる女性たちがいるが、琉球王国時代にもそのような女性がいた。最も有名なのは前出の「オギヤカ」だが、他にも存在していた。それが尚貞王の継妃であった「真壁按司加志」である。彼女は勝ち気さと美貌で国王（第2尚氏王統11代目・尚貞王、在位1669～1709）の側室となり、王を虜にした。そのことに正妃が嫉妬して感情的に彼女と対立。正妃は離婚された上に王に遠ざけられ、失意のうちに死亡すると、尚貞王は真壁按司加志を継妃とした。王妃は死後、玉陵に葬られるが、前妃（正妃）もそこに葬られることになる。そこで彼女は「正妃と同じ墓に葬られるのは嫌だ。あの女を玉陵に入れないで欲しい」と王にせがんだ。彼女にメロメロな王は彼女の言い分を聞き入れ、離婚した正妃を玉陵に葬らないことにした。それに対して長男の尚純（王妃の子）は泣きながら「そんな非情なことはしないで下さい」と父親（尚貞王）に懇願した。さすがに王は真壁按司加志のワガママを聞き入れることが出来ず、前言を取り消した。正妃の葬儀を王とともに見物した時、正妃との思い出が蘇り涙した王をみて、嫉妬心から激怒した。「この白髪頭、恥を知りなさい」と言って、持っていた煙管で国王の頭を叩いたといわれる。国王を虜にした彼女だが、王位を継いだのは尚純の子・尚益であった。

③ Makan-*aji-ganashi*

In the world, there were women called "bad women" such as "Empress Dowager Xi" (Queen of the Xianfeng Emperor, Qing Dynasty), "Yang Guifei" (consort of Emperor Xuanzong of the Tang Dynasty), and "Agrippina" (mother of Emperor Nero of the Roman Empire), but there were also such women in the Ryukyu Kingdom. The most famous of these was the Ogiyaka mentioned above, but there were others, including "Makan-*aji-ganashi* " who was the step-queen of King Sho Tei. With her winning spirit and good looks, she became the side wife of King Sho Tei, (the 11th in the Second Sho Dynasty, reigned 1669-1709) and captivated him. The queen was jealous of this and confronted her emotionally. When the queen died of a broken heart after being divorced and kept away from the king, King Sho Tei took Makan-*aji-ganashi* as her successor. The queen had been supposed to be buried in Tama-*udun* after her death, and the former queen was also supposed to be buried there. So she begged the king not to bury her in Tama-*udun* because she did not want to be buried in the same tomb as the queen. The king, who was very fond of her, listened to her arguments and decided not to bury the divorced queen in Tama-*udun*. In response, the eldest son, Sho Jun (the queen's son), cried and pleaded with his father (King Sho Tei), "Please don't do such a terrible thing". As expected, the king could not accept the selfishness of Makan-*aji-ganashi* and retracted his previous statement. When she and the king watched the funeral of the former queen, she saw the king in tears, recalling his memories of the former queen, and became furious out of jealousy. She is said to have said, "You gray-headed!!, you should be ashamed of yourself!!," and struck the king on the head with a smoking pipe she was carrying. She captivated the king, but it was Sho Jun's son Sho Eki who succeeded to the throne.

④サンアイイソバ

　生没年は不詳だが、15 世紀末に与那国島のサンアイ村で生まれ、女酋長として君臨した実在の人物といわれる。「サンアイ」とは与那国島の言葉で「ガジュマル」を意味し、ガジュマルが生い茂る森を切り開いて村を建設したのでそれが村名となった。人々からは親しみと敬意を込めて「サンアイイソバ」と呼ばれて与那国島を侵略から救った英雄として今も語り継がれている。伝承によると、イソバ女傑は身長が 2m に達するほど巨体で怪力の持ち主。4 人の兄弟をそれぞれ村々に配置し統治させた。自らは島の中央台地にある「ティンダバナ」に住居を構え、新村建設や開拓など内治につくす一方、宮古島と貿易を行っていた。当時、琉球王国（尚真王代）は宮古島や石垣島を既に支配しており、残るは与那国島だけになっていた。1501 年、首里王府の命を受けた宮古軍が侵略した際には 4 人の兄弟が殺害され集落が焼き払われた。それを知ったイソバは阿修羅のごとく凶変。恐るべき腕力を発揮して宮古軍を撃退したが、彼女の権力は失墜し、勢力を増していた「鬼虎」（ウニトゥラ）が新しい酋長となった。多少、脚色された伝承だが、彼女は一種の司祭的存在で、政教両面を主宰した人物であったといわれる。

サンアイイソバ碑（与那国町）
Monument of San'ai Isoba (Yonaguni Town)

④ San'ai Isoba

　Her birth and death dates are unknown, but she is said to be a real person who was born at the end of the 15th century in the village of San'ai on Yonaguni Island and reigned as a female chieftain. San'ai means "banyan tree" in the language of Yonaguni Island, and the name of the village was derived from the fact that it was built by cutting through a thick forest of banyan trees. She was called San'ai Isoba by the people with affection and respect, and is still spoken of as the heroine who saved Yonaguni Island from invasion. According to the legend, Isoba was a huge and powerful woman, standing up to two meters tall, and had her four younger brothers to rule over the villages. She lived in Tindabana on the central plateau of the island, where she devoted herself to internal affairs such as building new villages and cultivating the land, while at the same time trading with Miyako Island. At that time, the Ryukyu Kingdom (during the reign of King Sho Shin) had already taken control of Miyako and Ishigaki Islands, leaving only Yonaguni Island. In 1501, four brothers were killed and the villages were burned to the ground when the Miyako army invaded on the orders of the Shuri royal government. When Isoba knew this fact, she was furious and defeated the Miyako army with her fearsome prowess, but her power was lost, and Unitura who had been gaining strength became the new chieftain. This tradition has been somewhat adapted, but she is said to have been a kind of priestess, who had control over both politics and religion.

琉球王国の歴代王統（円内数字は王位継承の歴代数）
Successive Dynasties of the Ryukyu Kingdom
(Numbers in circles are the successive generations in the succession to the throne)

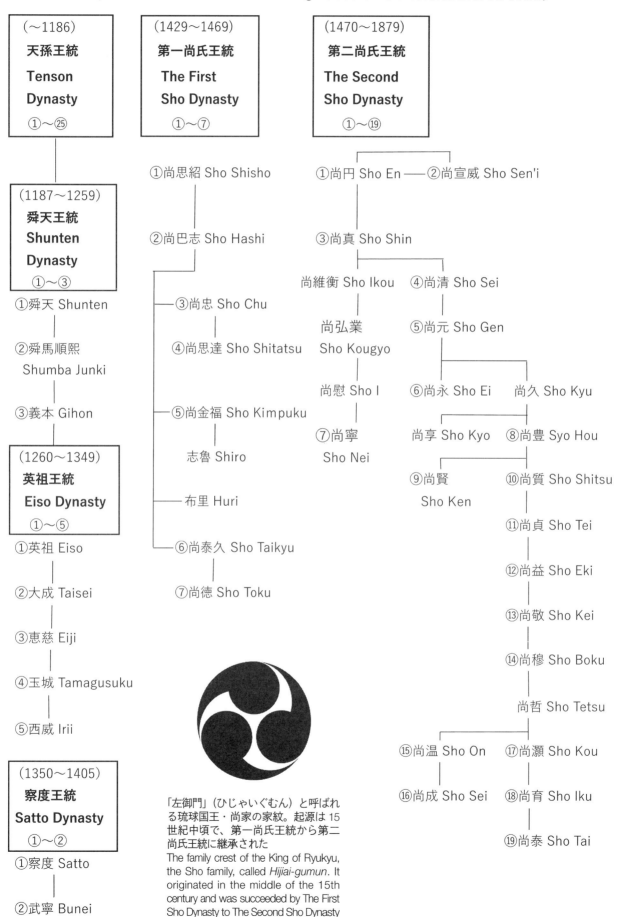

（～1186）
天孫王統
Tenson
Dynasty
①～㉕

（1429～1469）
第一尚氏王統
The First
Sho Dynasty
①～⑦

（1470～1879）
第二尚氏王統
The Second
Sho Dynasty
①～⑲

（1187～1259）
舜天王統
Shunten
Dynasty
①～③

①舜天 Shunten

②舜馬順熙
Shumba Junki

③義本 Gihon

（1260～1349）
英祖王統
Eiso Dynasty
①～⑤

①英祖 Eiso

②大成 Taisei

③恵慈 Eiji

④玉城 Tamagusuku

⑤西威 Irii

（1350～1405）
察度王統
Satto Dynasty
①～②

①察度 Satto

②武寧 Bunei

①尚思紹 Sho Shisho

②尚巴志 Sho Hashi

③尚忠 Sho Chu

④尚思達 Sho Shitatsu

⑤尚金福 Sho Kimpuku

志魯 Shiro

布里 Huri

⑥尚泰久 Sho Taikyu

⑦尚徳 Sho Toku

①尚円 Sho En ── ②尚宣威 Sho Sen'i

③尚真 Sho Shin

尚維衡 Sho Ikou　④尚清 Sho Sei

尚弘業
Sho Kougyo　⑤尚元 Sho Gen

尚慰 Sho I　⑥尚永 Sho Ei　尚久 Sho Kyu

⑦尚寧
Sho Nei　尚享 Sho Kyo　⑧尚豊 Syo Hou

⑨尚賢
Sho Ken　⑩尚質 Sho Shitsu

⑪尚貞 Sho Tei

⑫尚益 Sho Eki

⑬尚敬 Sho Kei

⑭尚穆 Sho Boku

尚哲 Sho Tetsu

⑮尚温 Sho On　⑰尚灝 Sho Kou

⑯尚成 Sho Sei　⑱尚育 Sho Iku

⑲尚泰 Sho Tai

「左御門」（ひじゃいぐむん）と呼ばれる琉球国王・尚家の家紋。起源は15世紀中頃で、第一尚氏王統から第二尚氏王統に継承された
The family crest of the King of Ryukyu, the Sho family, called *Hijiai-gumun*. It originated in the middle of the 15th century and was succeeded by The First Sho Dynasty to The Second Sho Dynasty

第２章　琉球から沖縄へ

（１）琉球と沖縄（りゅうきゅうとおきなわ）

琉球と沖縄の名称はどちらも古くからあり、歴史的にみると琉球は中国から、沖縄は日本からの呼称として使われてきた。琉球は７世紀に編纂された中国の正史『随書倭国伝』の中に「流求」という表記で初めて登場する。しかし、それが現在の沖縄を指した地名かどうかは不明で、台湾などを含め東シナ海の島々全体を「流求」と呼んでいたのではないかといわれる。明の時代には沖縄を「大琉球」、台湾のことを「小琉球」と区別した記録も残っている。1429 年に尚巴志による統一された王国が出現するが、この王朝が「琉球」と称したのは、当時は日本より中国との結びつきが強かったからといわれる。廃藩置県の時、「琉球県」の名称も検討されたが、中国（清）の宗主権を完全に排除し日本帰属の意思を明確にするため、古くからの日本の呼び名「沖縄」に決まったといわれる。沖縄の地名は、廃藩置県以前までは沖縄本島のみを指していたが、沖縄県設置により宮古・八重山を含む琉球諸島が沖縄と呼ばれるようになった。戦後、沖縄を占領したアメリカ軍は、琉球ナショナリズムを煽り立てるために公立の施設名を「沖縄」ではなく「琉球」と付けた。琉球政府や琉球大学などである。今日ではどちらも併用して一般に用いられている。

琉球王国最後の国王「尚泰王」
Last King of the Ryukyu Kingdom, King Sho Tai

Chapter 2 From Ryukyu to Okinawa

（1）Ryukyu and Okinawa

Both the names Ryukyu and Okinawa have been around for a long time. Historically, Ryukyu has been used as a name from China and Okinawa as a name from Japan. Ryukyu first appeared as Ryukyu in the Chinese history Zuisho-Wakoku-Den compiled in the 7th century. However, it is unclear whether it was a place name referring to the present-day Okinawa or not, and it is said that the islands in the East China Sea as a whole, including Taiwan, were called Ryukyu. In the Ming Dynasty, there are records that distinguish Okinawa as "Greater Ryukyu" and Taiwan as "Lesser Ryukyu". In 1429, the unified kingdom by Sho Hashi emerged, and this dynasty was called "Ryukyu" because it had stronger ties with China than Japan at that time. When the feudal system was abolished, the name "Ryukyu Prefecture" was considered, but in order to completely eliminate the suzerainty of China (Qing Dynasty) and to clarify the intention of belonging to Japan, it is said that the old Japanese name Okinawa was chosen. The place name Okinawa used to refer only to the main island of Okinawa before the abolition of the domain, but with the establishment of Okinawa Prefecture, the Ryukyu Islands including Miyako and Yaeyama came to be called Okinawa. After the war, the U.S. forces that occupied Okinawa named public facilities Ryukyu instead of Okinawa in order to incite Ryukyu nationalism. This included the Ryukyu government and the University of the Ryukyus. Today, both are commonly used in combination.

（２）人頭税（にんとうぜい・じんとうぜい）

①人頭税

　人頭税とは、ヨーロッパやインドなど多くの国で古くから採用されていた税制で、納税能力に関係なく、すべての住民に一定額を課すものである。薩摩藩の琉球侵攻（1609 年）により、琉球王国は薩摩藩に支配され重税を課されることになった。1637年、財政的に困窮した首里王府は宮古・八重山地方へ厳しい人頭税を課した。両地方は 1390 年に中山・察度王に入貢して以来、尚真王の中央集権化に伴って支配力が強化された。さらに薩摩藩の琉球侵攻を

久部良バリ（与那国町与那国）
Kubura-*bari* (Yonaguni,Yonaguni Town)

契機に統治機構はいっそう整備された。1636 年には人口調査が行われ、翌年から 15 歳から 50 歳までの人頭に対して課税されるようになった。首里王府は両地方を補地とみなし、沖縄本島とは異なる扱いをし、明らかに差別していた。男は穀物、女は織物が税金として課された。年齢によって納める税に違いはあるものの、個人の能力や体力は考慮されなかった。身体の不自由な人、病人、怪我人なども納税の対象となった。人頭税の負担軽減のために赤子の圧殺や堕胎などによる間引き、逃亡して盗賊になる者、あるいは役人の下男下女となって人頭税を逃れた話なども伝わっている。

　凄惨を極める人減らしの悲劇として与那国島の「久部良バリ」（クブラバリ）がある。そこは幅３㍍、深さ７〜８㍍の岩の裂け目で、妊婦はそこを飛び越えることを余儀なくされた。大半の妊婦が岩の底に落ちて死に、たとえ飛び越えたとしても腹を打ったりして流産するのがほとんどだったといわれる。それでも人口が減らないので、男に対しても凄惨な人減らしがあった。突然、村中に銅鑼が鳴り響くと男たちは直ぐに「人桝田」（トゥングダ）と呼ばれる田んぼに駆け込んだ。制限時間内にたどり着けないような者や溢れた男は、住民の合意のもとに惨殺された。沖縄の人頭税は廃藩置県後も続き、1903 年（明治 36 年）に廃止された。

　宮古・八重山には「上布（じょうふ）」と呼ばれる苧麻（ちょま）を原料にした織物がある。これは女性に課された貢納布で、徹底した役人の管理下で織られたため、必然的に高級な織物として重宝されるようになった。特に宮古上布は、「東の越後、西の宮古」と呼ばれ、1978 年には国の重要無形文化財に指定されている。

(2) *Nintou-zei, Jintou-zei* (capitation tax)

① Capitation tax

　Capitation tax is a tax system that had long been used in many countries, including Europe and India, that imposes a fixed amount on all residents, regardless of their ability to pay taxes. After the invasion of Ryukyu by the Satsuma Domain in 1609, the Kingdom of Ryukyu was controlled by the Satsuma Domain and heavily taxed. In 1637, the financially troubled Shuri royal government imposed a severe capitation tax on the Miyako and Yaeyama regions. Both regions paid tribute to King Satto of Chuzan in 1390, and their control was later strengthened by the centralization of power by King Sho Shin. In addition, the Satsuma domain's invasion of Ryukyu led to the further development of the governance structure. In 1636, a population census was conducted, and from the following year, taxes were levied on the head of the population between the ages of 15 and 50. The Shuri royal government considered these two areas as lands of supplementary lands and treated them differently from the main island of Okinawa, clearly discriminating against them. As taxes, men were assigned grain and women were assigned textiles. Although there were differences in the taxes paid according to age, individual ability and fitness were not taken into account. The disabled, the sick, and the injured also became taxable counterparts. There are stories of babies being crushed to death or aborted to reduce the burden of the per capitation tax, deserting to become bandits, or having become servants of officials to evade the per capitation tax.

One of the tragedies of the terrible people reduction measures is the Kubura-*bari* on Yonaguni Island. It is a rocky crevice, 3 meters wide and 7 to 8 meters deep, through which pregnant women were forced to be jumped it over. It is said that most pregnant women fell to their deaths at the bottom of the rocks, and even if they jumped over, they were almost always hit in the stomach or suffered miscarriages. Still, the population did not decrease, so, there was a horrendous man reduction policy for men as well. When the gongs suddenly sounded throughout the village, the men immediately rushed into the rice field known as Tunguda. Those who could not reach that rice field within the time limit or overflowed were killed with the consent of the inhabitants. The *nintou-zei* in Okinawa continued after the Haihan-chiken (abolition of the domain) and was abolished in 1903.

In Miyako and Yaeyama, there is a fabric made from Ramie called *joufu*. This was a tribute cloth imposed on women, and since it was woven under the strict control of officials, it inevitably came to be valued as a high-class fabric. Miyako-*joufu*, in particular, is called "Echigo in the East, Miyako in the West," and was designated as an important intangible cultural property of Japan in 1978.

②人頭税廃止運動

　苛酷な人頭税からの解放を求める運動が宮古島から起きた。沖縄県当局への不信などから、城間正安（製糖指導員・那覇出身）、中村十作（真珠養殖業者・新潟県人）および農民代表の西里蒲、平良真牛の両名が上京し直接、帝国議会に請願書を提出した。1894 年 12 月に開会した貴衆両院議会で請願が可決され、沖縄県政改革の建議がなされた。1903 年（明治 36）1 月、「地租条例」の公布によって、宮古・八重山の島民は 260 年余にわたる苛酷な「人頭税」から解放された。請願団 4 名の顕彰碑が宮古島市城辺に建てられている。

人頭税撤廃運動顕彰碑（宮古島市城辺）
Monument in honor of the movement to abolish the capitation tax(Gusukube,Miyakojima City)

② The movement to abolish the capitation tax

A movement to free the people from the harsh capitation tax arose from Miyako Island. Because of their distrust of the authorities in Okinawa Prefecture, Shiroma Seian (a sugar refinery instructor from Naha City), Nakamura Jussaku (a pearl farmer from Niigata Prefecture), and two representatives of the farmers, Nishizato Kama and Taira Moushi, went to Tokyo and directly submitted a petition to the Imperial Diet. In December 1894, both the House of Peers and the House of Representatives of the Imperial Diet passed the petition and made a request to Okinawa Prefecture for policy reform. In January 1903, with the promulgation of the "Land Tax Ordinance," the people of Miyako and Yaeyama Islands were freed from the harsh "capitation tax" that had been imposed for more than 260 years. A monument honoring the four petitioners was erected in Gusukube, Miyakojima City.

（3）廃藩置県（はいはんちけん）

　1429 年に尚巴志が三山（南山王国・中山王国・北山王国）を統一して、琉球王国が対外的に誕生した。1609 年に日本の薩摩藩の侵攻を受けた後も、独立国家としての体裁を保ち続け、日本の明治

新政府の廃藩置県によって沖縄県となるまでの 450 年間、諸国に翻弄されながら王国は続いた。日本では 1871 年、藩が廃止されて道府県制度が導入された。この制度改革は廃藩置県と呼ばれる。独立国であった沖縄では 1872 年、琉球王国が廃止され琉球藩を設置、琉球国王は「琉球藩王」と称された。さらに 1879 年、琉球藩が廃止され沖縄県が誕生した。明治新政府による一連の政治過程は「琉球処分」と呼ばれる。琉球王国は沖縄県として日本に強制的に組み込まれたことで、これまで実質的に許されなかった住民の移動が自由になり、ウチナーンチュは小さな沖縄から海外に移住するようになった。

(3) Haihan-chiken（Abolition of the feudal domain）

In 1429, the Kingdom of Ryukyu was born externally when Sho Hashi unified the Sanzan (Nanzan Kingdom, Chuzan Kingdom, and Hokuzan Kingdom). Even after being invaded by the Satsuma Domain of Japan in 1609, the kingdom continued to maintain the appearance of an independent state, and was at the mercy of other countries for 450 years until it became Okinawa Prefecture with the abolition of the domain by the new Meiji government. In 1871, Japan abolished the domain system and introduced the prefecture system. This reform is known as the Haihan-chiken. In 1872, the Kingdom of Ryukyu was abolished and the Ryukyu Domain was established, and the King of Ryukyu was named "King of the Ryukyu Domain". In 1879, the Ryukyu domain was abolished and Okinawa Prefecture was born. The series of political processes by the new Meiji government is known as the Ryukyu-*shobun*(disposition). The Ryukyu Kingdom was forcibly incorporated into Japan as Okinawa Prefecture. As a result, *uchinanchu* began to migrate from tiny Okinawa to foreign countries, as the movement of residents, which had been practically unacceptable in the past, became freer.

(4) 頑固党と開化党（がんことうとかいかとう）

明治新政府による琉球処分によって琉球王国の消滅に不満を抱いた一部の旧支配者層（上級士族が主体）は、非合法のうちに清国に亡命した。彼らは「脱清人」と呼ばれ、清政府に「琉球王国の再興」を働きかけた。沖縄では琉球王国の再興を求める「頑固党」とそれに反対する「開化党」が対立した。開化党は親日派で下級士族が多かった。沖縄の同化政策や「皇民化教育」を支持し、明治政府による琉球処分に積極的に協力した。当然、頑固党は彼らを裏切り者として嫌った。1894 年に始まった日清戦争では、頑固党は清国戦勝祈願祭を行い、開化党は日本の戦勝祈願祭を催したが、結果は清の敗北。これによって琉球王国再興の道が絶たれ、同時に頑固党も力を失っていった。その後、「日本の主権を認める代わりに、尚家による沖縄統治を求める」という「公同会運動」が起こる。この運動では開化党と頑固党が協力したが、明治政府に却下され、当運動は終息した。頑固党の中心的指導者は亀川盛武親方（三司官）で、幸地朝常（向徳宏）、国頭盛乗（毛精長）、名城春傍（林世功）らがいる。開化党の代表的な人物としては、大湾朝功、仲吉良春、太田朝敷（琉球新報元社長、首里元市長）らがいる。

1896 年（明治 29）に中国（清）に渡った頑固党の人々
（那覇市歴史博物館）
Stubborn Party people who went to China (Qing) in 1896 (Meiji 29)

(4) *Ganko-tou* (Conservatives) and *Kaika-tou* (Reformists)

Some of the former ruling class (mainly senior samurai), who were dissatisfied with the disappearance of the Ryukyu Kingdom due to the disposal of Ryukyu by the new Meiji government, defected to the Qing Empire illegally. They were known as the *Dassin-nin* (Defectors to the Qing) and lobbied the Qing government to "revive the Ryukyu Kingdom". In Okinawa, there was a confrontation between the *Ganko-tou*, which called for the revival of the Ryukyu Kingdom, and the *Kaika-tou*, which opposed it. The *Kaika-tou* was pro-Japanese, and many of its members were lower class samurai. They supported the assimilation policies and "imperialist education" in Okinawa, and actively cooperated with the Meiji government in the disposal of Ryukyu. Naturally, the *Ganko-tou* hated them as traitors. In the Sino-Japanese War that began in 1894, *Ganko-tou* and *Kaika-tou* held victory rituals to pray for victory for the Qing Empire and for Japan, respectively, but the result was the defeat of the Qing Empire. This cut off the path to the revival of the Ryukyu Kingdom, and at the same time the *Ganko-tou* lost its power. Later, the *Koudoukai*-movement started, which demanded that the Sho family rule Okinawa in exchange for recognition of Japanese sovereignty. In this movement, the *Kaika-tou* and the *Ganko-tou* cooperated, but were rejected by the Meiji government, and this movement came to an end. The main leaders of the *Ganko-tou* were Kamegawa Seibu-*oyakata (sanshikan)*, with Kouchi Chojou (Sho Tokukou), Kunigami Seijou (Mou Seicho), and Nashiro Shumbou (Lin Seikou). Representative figures of the *Kaika-tou* included Ohwan Chokou, Nakayoshi Ryoshun, and Ohta Chohu (former president of Ryukyu Shimpo and former mayor of Shuri).

（5）琉球処分（りゅうきゅうしょぶん）

松田道之・琉球処分官（前列中央）
Matsuda Michiyuki, the officer in charge of disposing of the Ryukyu Kingdom(front row, center)

　明治政府によって、琉球王国が日本の近代国家の中に強制的に組み込まれていく一連の政治過程を琉球処分という。1872 年（明治 5）の琉球藩設置から始まり、1879 年の廃藩置県を経て、分島問題が起こる 1880 年までの 9 年間にまたがる。明治政府の方針が強権をもって一方的に押しつけられる形で行われたので「処分」といわれる。琉球藩の設置では、当時の尚泰王を「琉球藩主」として華族に列し、琉球藩を設置した。これにより、これまで鹿児島県（薩摩藩）の管轄下にあった琉球は明治政府の直轄に移った。首里王府内では王国の再興を主張する勢力（頑固党）と、それに反対する勢力（開化党）に分かれた。琉球王国の消滅に不満を抱いた頑固党の一部（脱清人）は清国に亡命して事態を挽回しようと画策した。清朝は日本の一方的な対琉施策に抗議し、旧態に戻すように日本政府に申し入れたが、日本側はそれを無視した。両国間の外交交渉の中で日本が提案したのが、宮古・八重山諸島を中国領とし、沖縄本島以北を日本の領土とする分島案。結局その案は流れて、琉球諸島すべてが日本の領土となった。これによって琉球王国という独立国は滅び、沖縄県となった。

(5) Ryukyu Disposition

The Ryukyu Disposition is a series of political processes in which the Kingdom of Ryukyu was forcibly incorporated into the modern state of Japan by the Meiji government for a period of nine years, starting with the establishment of the Ryukyu Domain in 1872, followed by the abolition of the domain in 1879, and ending with the issue of the division of the Ryukyu Islands in 1880. It is called a "disposition" because the policy of the Meiji government was unilaterally imposed by force. In the establishment of the Ryukyu Domain, the then King Sho Tai was listed among the nobility as the "Lord of the Ryukyu Domain" and the Ryukyu Domain was established. As a result, the Kingdom of the Ryukyu, which had previously been under the jurisdiction of Kagoshima Prefecture (Satsuma Domain), was transferred to the direct control of the Meiji government. Within the Shuri royal government, the forces were divided between those who advocated the revival of the kingdom *(Ganko-tou)* and those who opposed it *(Kaika-tou)*. Dissatisfied with the disappearance of the Ryukyu Kingdom, some of the *Ganko-tou* defected to the Qing Empire in an attempt to redress the situation. The Qing Dynasty protested against Japan's unilateral policy toward the Ryukyu and asked the Japanese government to restore the islands to their original state, but the Japanese side ignored the request. During the diplomatic negotiations between the two countries, Japan proposed a bifurcated island plan in which Miyako and Yaeyama Islands would be Chinese territory and Okinawa Island and northward would be Japanese territory. In the end, the proposal was rejected and the entire Ryukyu Islands became Japanese territory. As a result, the Ryukyu Kingdom, an independent country, died and became Okinawa Prefecture.

（6）番所（ばんじょ）

　琉球王朝時代、市町村にあたる行政区域は間切（まぎり・まきり）と呼ばれていた。番所は、間切の行政の拠点となった役所で現在の市町村役場にあたる。番所には地頭代（現在の市町村長）以下の間切役人が交代で詰めて、王府への納税など地方行政全般にわたって執り行い、首里との交通・通信網の拠点としても用いられた。王府の命を各地に伝達することを宿次（しゅくつぎ）と称し、当初は間切内の行政機関というより、宿次制を整備するためのものであった。従って番所は、宿道（国道）沿いに位置した。

喜名番所跡（読谷村喜名）
Ruins of Kina *Banjo* (Kina, Yomitan Village)

番所の始まりは尚巴志時代（15 世紀）といわれるが、1897 年（明治 30）、「間切島吏規程」の発布で廃止され、名称が役場に変わった。敷地の遺構がうかがえるものとして読谷村の喜名番所跡があり、往時の建物が復元されている。

(6) *Banjo* (Local government offices in the Ryukyu Kingdom)

　During the Ryukyu Dynasty, the administrative areas of cities, towns and villages were called *magiri* or *makiri*. The *banjo* was the administrative center of the *magiri*, equivalent to today's municipal offices. *jitudee* (the current mayor of the municipality) and other *magiri* officials were stationed in *banjo* in shifts, and it was also the base of the transportation and communication network with Shuri. Conveying the orders of the royal government to the various provinces was called *shukutsugi*, and in the beginning it was more for the development of the *shukutsugi* system than as an administrative body within *magiri*. Therefore, *banjo* was located along the *shukumichi* (national highway). The *banjo* system is said to have originated in the 15th century during the reign of Sho Hashi, however, it was abolished in 1897 with the promulgation of the "Regulations for Officials of the *magiri*" and its name was changed to the town office. The remains of the site can be seen at the site of the Kina-*banjo* in Yomitan Village, where a *banjo* from the past has been restored.

（7）バジル・ホール

　1788 年生まれのバジル・ホールはイギリスの海軍将校で、作家でもあった。1816 年、清国に通商を迫るために英国全権大使ら外交団を北京に送りとどけた。その時、東シナ海海域の調査のために朝鮮の西海岸と琉球王国に寄港し、那覇に 40 余日間滞在した。徹底した海禁政策のため拒絶対応を受けた朝鮮と違い、琉球では中国語が話せる通事の協力を得て、非常に好印象を抱いた。一行は調査や観測を徹底して行い、1 週間余りで全島地図を完成させた。帰国後の 1818 年にその記録を『朝鮮・琉球航海記』に記した。琉球の人々との交流を好意的な視点から描いた本書は当時、ヨーロッパ諸国で大きな反響を呼び、数カ国語に翻訳された。1826 年の第 3 版ではナポレオン皇帝との会見録が追加された。この中でホールは、武器を見かけなかったことを理由に、琉球が非武装であることを欧米諸国に印象づけた。2016 年、バジル・ホール来琉 200 年を記念して泊港広場に記念碑が建立された。

バジル・ホール来琉 200 年記念碑
（那覇市泊港）
Basil Hall Stone monument memorating
the 200th anniversary of the arrival of the
Ryukyus (Tomari Port, Naha City)

（7）Basil Hall

　Born in 1788, Basil Hall was a British naval officer and author who sent a diplomatic delegation, including the British plenipotentiary, to Beijing in 1816 to press the Qing government for trade. At that time, he stopped at the west coast of Korea and the Kingdom of Ryukyu to survey the waters of the East China Sea, and stayed in Naha for more than 40 days. Unlike Korea *(Chosen)*, which had a strict sea ban policy that caused rejection, the Kingdom of Ryukyu, with the help of a Chinese-speaking interpreter, made a very favorable impression on the group. The group conducted thorough surveys and observations and completed a map of the entire island in a little over a week. After returning to England in 1818, they recorded their findings in the "Voyage to Korea and the Ryukyu Islands". This book, which describes the interaction with the people of Ryukyu from a favorable perspective, had a great response in European countries at the time and was translated into several languages. In the third edition published in 1826, a transcript of the meeting with Emperor Napoleon was added. In this transcript, Hall impressed upon the Western countries that Ryukyu was unarmed because he did not see any weapons. In 2016, a monument was erected at Tomari Port Plaza to commemorate the 200th anniversary of Basil Hall's arrival in Ryukyu.

（8）ベッテルハイム

　1846 年から 54 年にかけて那覇で布教活動した、日本最初のプロテスタント宣教師で医師。1845 年に英海軍の琉球伝道会の宣教師となり、妻と娘を伴い 46 年 4 月に那覇に到着した。外国人の琉球滞在を拒否する王府に抗して上陸を強行して以後、8 年余、波の上の護国寺に逗留した。厳重な監視の下での伝道と医療活動は困難を極めたが、数人の受礼者を得て、種痘法の導入などの医療行為を行った。特に貧民のあいだではその医療事業は人気があり、「波の上の眼鏡」（ナンミンヌガンチョウ）という綽名で親しまれた（彼の顕彰碑が当寺の境内に建立されている）。1847 年の尚育王の葬儀のとき暴徒に殴打された後は、彼の活動は極度に困難になった。ペリーの日本遠征中に琉米双方の仲介となり、彼の行動も比較的自由になった。1854 年にペリー艦隊で沖縄を離れ、南北戦争では軍医として従軍した。

(8) Bettelheim

First Protestant missionary to japan and physician who proselytized in Naha from 1846 to 1854. In 1845, he became a missionary for the Royal Navy's Ryukyu Mission, and arrived in Naha in April 1846 with his wife and daughter. In defiance of the royal government's refusal to allow foreigners to stay in Ryukyu, he forced his way ashore and stayed at the Gokokuji Temple in Naminoue for more than eight years. His evangelistic and medical work under close surveillance was extremely difficult, but he gained a few recipients, and introduced the vaccination method and other medical practices. His medical services were especially popular among the poor, and he was nicknamed *"Nanmin-nu-gancho"* (the man with the glasses at Naminoue). A monument in his honor has been erected in the precincts of the Gokokuji Temple. After he was beaten by a mob at the funeral of King Sho Iku in 1847, his activities became extremely difficult. He left Okinawa with Perry's fleet in 1854 and served as a military doctor in the Civil War.

ベッテルハイム居住地跡で説明を受けるベッテルハイムの曾孫（左）
Bettelheim's great-granddaughter receiving an explanation at the ruins of Bettelheim's residence(left)

（9）ペリー艦隊の来琉（ぺりーかんたいのらいりゅう）

①背景

　産業革命によって大量生産された工業品の輸出拡大の必要性から、西ヨーロッパ諸国は、インドを中心に東南アジアと中国大陸（清）への市場拡大を競っていた。しかし、それは後に熾烈な植民地獲得競争となった。イギリス、フランス、スペイン、オランダなどが南アジアや東南アジアに進出し、戦争などを伴って各種条約を結び、アジア各地を獲得していった。幕末当時、インドや東南アジアに拠点を持たないアメリカ合衆国は西ヨーロッパ諸国に出遅れていた。アメリカは1835年、東インド艦隊を設立し日本や清との条約締結のために特使を派遣することとした。1833年当時、アメリカの人口は約1,416万人、日本が2,760万人、清は約4億人で巨大市場であった。

　産業革命によって欧米の工場は夜間でも稼働するようになり、機械の潤滑油や照明用として主にマッコウクジラの油が使用されていた。その重要性から欧米各国は日本沿岸を含む世界中の海で捕鯨を盛んに行った。長期の捕鯨活動には大量の薪・水・食料が必要で、太平洋におけるそれらの補給拠点が求められた。その点からも太平洋に面する日本との条約締結は有利であった。18世紀末から19世紀中頃にかけ、ペリー艦隊の来航（1853年）以前にもすでに欧米諸国の軍艦や捕鯨船が数多く来日していた。中国に対したのと同様にペリーは、日本への来航に際して「恐怖に訴える方が、友好に訴えるよりより多くの利点があるだろう」という方針で任務を遂行した。そのため4隻の軍艦のうち3隻は大型の蒸気軍艦が使用された。

ペリー提督上陸地（那覇市泊）
Admiral Perry's Landing Site (Tomari, Naha City)

(9) The arrival of Perry's fleet in Ryukyu

① Background

Due to the need to expand exports of industrial goods mass-produced by the Industrial Revolution, Western European countries competed to expand their markets to Southeast Asia and mainland China (Qing), with India at the center. However, it later became a fierce competition for colonies. Britain, France, Spain, the Netherlands, and other countries expanded into South and Southeast Asia, and through war and other means, concluded various treaties and acquired various parts of Asia. At the end of the Edo period, the United States, without a base in India or Southeast Asia, lagged behind Western European countries. In 1835, the U.S. established the East India Squadron and decided to send envoys to sign treaties with Japan and China (Qing). In 1833, the population of the United States was about 14.16 million, Japan 27.6 million, and Qing was a huge market with about 400 million people.

With the Industrial Revolution, factories in Europe and the United States began to operate at night, and sperm whale oil was mainly used to lubricate machinery and for lighting. Because of its importance, Western countries actively engaged in whaling in the world's oceans, including the coast of Japan. Long-term whaling activities require large amounts of firewood, water, and food, and a supply base in the Pacific Ocean was required. From this point of view, it was advantageous to conclude a treaty with Japan, which faced the Pacific Ocean. From the end of the 18th century to the middle of the 19th century, even before the arrival of Perry's fleet (1853), many warships and whaling ships from Western countries had already visited Japan. Just as he had done with China, Perry carried out his mission to Japan with the policy that "an appeal to fear would be more advantageous than an appeal to friendship". For this reason, three of the four warships used were large steam warships.

②ペリー提督

米国海軍大佐で、1852 年に日本開国交渉のための特命全権大使に任命された。日本遠征の目的は、米難破船員の保護のための協定を結び、石炭および必需品の補給地を確保し、可能ならば交易のため開国させることであった。その他、日本沿岸および隣接国や諸島を探検し、その地の社会・政治・商業状況などできる限りの情報収集が求められた。1853 年 5 月 26 日に那覇に初来港した。以後、遠征中にペリーは 5 度も那覇に寄港・滞在し、条約交渉のための基地として利用した。もし日本開国に失敗すれば琉球、小笠原または台湾北部の占領も意図していた。滞琉中は首里城を強行訪問し、海陸を調査した後もペリーの日本への中継地として活用した。1853 年 7 月の江戸幕府との交渉後には那覇市泊に貯炭所を確保した。1854 年 1 月に那覇経由で江戸に向かい、同年 3 月に日米和親条約を結び、7 月には那覇で琉米修好条約を締結した。

マシュー・カルブレイス・ペリー
Matthew Calbraith Perry

② Admiral Perry

He was a colonel in the U.S. Navy and was appointed ambassador extraordinary and plenipotentiary to negotiate the opening of Japan in 1852. The purpose of the expedition was to conclude an agreement for the protection of American shipwrecked sailors, to secure a supply of coal and other necessities, and to open Japan to trade if possible. In addition, he was required to explore the coast of Japan and neighboring countries and islands to gather as much information as possible about the social, political, and commercial conditions there. The ships first arrived in Naha on May 26, 1853. Thereafter, during his expedition, Perry stopped and stayed in Naha five times, using it as a base for treaty negotiations. If he failed to open Japan to the outside world, he intended to occupy Ryukyu, the Ogasawara Islands, or northern Taiwan. During his stay in the Ryukyu Islands, he made a forced visit to Shuri Castle, and after surveying the land and sea, he continued to use Ryukyu as a staging post for Perry's visit to Japan. After negotiations with the Edo Shogunate in July 1853, he secured a coal storage facility in Tomari, Naha City. In January 1854, he went to Edo via Naha, and in March of the same year, he signed the Treaty of Amity between Japan and the United States, and in July, he concluded the Ryukyu-U.S. Treaty of Amity at Naha.

③ウィリアム・ボード事件、泊外人墓地

　1854 年、泊港沖に停泊していたペリー艦隊の残留水兵「ウィリアム・ボード」が酔っ払ったあげく、那覇の民家に押し入り婦人（54 歳）に暴行し、その息子らに撲殺された事件。事件については「大声で助けを求める女性の声で駆けつけた数人の地元青年が石を投げて追いかけ、ボードが崖から墜落死した」という説もある。日本から帰ったペリーはボードの非を認めながらも、犯人の引き渡しを要求した。王府は家族の生活の面倒をみるなどの条件を付けて希望者を募った。希望者は直ぐに現われ王府は犯人を引き渡そうとしたが、ペリーは琉球国法で裁くようにと伝えてきた。王府は犯人を流刑にする

ウィリアム・ボードの墓 (右側の小さい方)（那覇市泊・外人墓地内）
William Board's tomb(smaller one on the right)（In Foreigner Cemetery, Tomari, Naha City）

とした判決文をデッチあげてペリーに提出し、了解を得て一件落着とした。事件は、外国人による日本人婦女暴行事件の第 1 号である。ボードの墓は泊外人墓地内にあるが、埋葬を手伝ったのがベッテルハイム（宣教師）であった。ボードの墓の左隣は病死した水兵の墓で、両者の墓標の大きさは明らかに異なり、ボードが不名誉な死に方をしたのがその理由といわれる。

　泊外人墓地は久米村に近く、元来は中国人移住者たちの墓地であったが、後には米兵を中心として埋葬されるようになった。この墓地で最も古いのは 1718 年に埋葬された中国人である。当墓地内には他にもペリー提督の部下たちの墓があるが、この中に 1 つだけ墓標のないものがある。この墓に眠っているのは黒人水兵といわれる。この外国人墓地は、18 世紀以降の琉球と諸外国との交流を知る史跡として重要で、1987 年（昭和 62 年）に那覇市の文化財（史跡）に指定された。

③ William Board Incident, Tomari-*gaijin-bochi* (Cemetery for foreigners)

In 1854, William Board, who had remained off Tomari Harbor as a sailor in Perry's fleet, got drunk and broke into a house in Naha, assaulted a 54-year-old woman, and was beaten to death by his sons and the others. Another theory is that "Board crashed off the cliff and died as several local youths, who had rushed to his aid at the woman's loud shout, chased him, throwing stones at him. When Perry returned from Japan, he admitted that Board was at fault but demanded that the perpetrators be extradited. The royal government invited applicants with conditions such as taking care of their family's living needs. The applicants showed up immediately and the royal government tried to hand over the culprits, but Perry told them to be tried under Ryukyuan law. The royal government faked a sentence that the culprits were to be exiled and submitted it to Perry, who agreed and settled the matter. This incident is the first case of assault on a Japanese woman by a foreigner. Board's grave is in the Tomari-*gaijin-bochi* (Cemetery for foreigners), and it was Bettelheim (a missionary) who helped with the burial.

To the left of Board's grave is the grave of a sailor who died of illness, and the size of the two grave markers are clearly different, which is said to be the reason why Board died in disgrace.

Tomari-*gaijin-bochi* is located near Kume Village and was originally a cemetery for Chinese immigrants, but later became a burial ground for mainly American soldiers. The oldest burial in this cemetery is that of a Chinese in 1718. There are other graves of Commodore Perry's men in this cemetery, but only one of them has no grave marker. This grave is said to be that of a black sailor. This foreigner's cemetery is important as a historical site that provides information on the exchange between Ryukyu and other countries since the 18th century, and was designated as a cultural asset (historical site) of Naha City in 1987.

(10) ジョン万次郎

　ジョン万次郎こと中浜万次郎は、1827 年に現在の高知県土佐清水市中浜で貧しい漁師の次男として生まれた。9 歳の時に父を亡くし、母と兄が病弱であったため幼い頃から働いて家族を養った。1841 年 1 月、14 歳の万次郎は 4 人の仲間と共に漁に出たが突然の強風で遭難し、数日間の漂流後、無人島に漂着した。漂着から 143 日後の同年 6 月、アメリカの捕鯨船ジョン・ハウランド号に仲間と共に救助された。当時の日本は鎖国政策で帰国するすべがなく、彼らは捕鯨船に同乗してアメリカへ向かわざるをえなかった。船長のウィリアム・

ジョン万次郎上陸の地（糸満市大度海岸）
John Manjiro Landing Site (Ohdo Beach, Itoman City)

ホイットフィールドは、宣教師の計らいによって 4 人をハワイで降ろし、気に入った一番若い万次郎だけを本人同意でアメリカへ連れて行った。この時、船名に因んで「ジョン・マン」という愛称をつけた。

　万次郎は船長の養子となり、船長の故郷・フェアヘーブン（マサチューセッツ州）の学校で英語・数学・測量・航海術・造船技術などを学んだ。優秀な成績で卒業した後は捕鯨船に乗り、数年の航海を経た後、日本への帰国を決意。ゴールドラッシュに沸くカリフォルニアの金鉱で働いて得た帰国資金を持ってハワイに寄り、2 人の漂流仲間とともに上海行きの商船に乗り込んで日本に向かった。万次郎はアメリカで、民主主義や男女平等など日本人にとって新鮮な概念に触れる一方で、人種差別も経験した。

　1851 年、実質的に薩摩藩領であった琉球の大渡浜海岸（現・糸満市大渡）に上陸した。万次郎らは、豊見城間切翁長村の高安家に留め置かれた時、牧志朝忠から英語で取り調べを受けている。その後、薩摩藩経由で鎖国中の日本へ帰国した万次郎らは、西洋文物に興味のあった藩主・島津斉彬の厚遇を受けた。さらに長崎奉行所での尋問を受けた後、1852 年、土佐藩に引き取られた。1853 年のペリー提督による黒船来航への対応として江戸幕府は、万次郎を招聘し旗本の身分を与えた。万次郎は勝海舟や福沢諭吉らとともに日米修好条約の締結のため再度渡米するなど、幕府の開国決定に寄与したほか、通訳・英語教師などで活躍し日本の英語教育の創始者となった。1898 年、71 歳で波瀾万丈の生涯を閉じた万次郎の墓は東京都豊島区の「雑司ヶ谷霊園」（ぞうしがやれいえん）にある。

　首里王府の命によって万次郎が半年間滞在した豊見城市翁長には 2010 年 9 月、記念碑が建立された。さらに 2018 年 2 月には、カウボーイハットを被り、ベストやジーンズを着用し、右手で故郷の土佐清水市を指さしているアメリカ帰りの万次郎（24 歳）の銅像が上陸地・大渡浜海岸に設置されている。

(10) John Manjiro

Nakahama Manjiro, a.k.a. John Manjiro, was born in 1827 in Nakahama, Tosashimizu City, present-day Kochi Prefecture, as the second son of a poor fisherman. His father died when he was nine years old, and his mother and brother were sickly, so he worked from an early age to support his family. In January 1841, fourteen-year-old Manjiro and his four companions went fishing, but a sudden strong wind caused them to be lost, and after drifting for several days, they drifted to an uninhabited island. In June of the same year, 143 days after drifting ashore, he and four others were rescued by an American whaling ship, the John Howland. At the time, Japan's isolationist policy meant that there was no way for them to return home, so they were forced to board a whaling ship and head for the United States. The captain of the ship, William Whitfield, dropped off the four men in Hawaii by arrangement with the missionaries, and took only the youngest Manjiro, whom he liked, to America with his permission. At this time, the captain gave him the nickname "John Mung" after the ship's name.

Manjiro was adopted by the captain and studied English, mathematics, surveying, navigation, and shipbuilding skills at a school in the captain's hometown of Fairhaven, Massachusetts. After graduating with honors, he joined a whaling ship, and after a few years of sailing, he decided to return to Japan. With the money to return home after working in the gold mines of California during the gold rush, he stopped in Hawaii and boarded a merchant ship bound for Shanghai with two other castaway fellows, heading for Japan. In the U.S., Manjiro was exposed to concepts that were new to Japanese people, such as democracy and gender equality, but he also experienced racism.

In 1851, they landed on the coast of Odohama (now Odo, Itoman City) in the Ryukyu, which was practically the territory of the Satsuma clan. He was interrogated in English by Makishi Chochu when he was detained at the Takayasu family in Onaga village Tomigusuku *magiri*. Later, Manjiro and others returned to Japan which was still closed to the outside world, via the Satsuma Domain, and were treated well by Shimazu Nariakira, the feudal lord who was interested in Western culture. After further interrogation at the Nagasaki Magistrate's Office, he was taken in by the Tosa Domain in 1852. In 1853, in order to respond to Commodore Perry's arrival of black ships, the Edo Shogunate invited Manjiro and gave him a position as *Hatamoto* (one of the statuses of samurai directly under the Shogun). Manjiro, together with Katsu Kaishu and Fukuzawa Yukichi, went to the U.S. again to conclude the Treaty of Amity between Japan and the U.S. and contributed to the Shogunate's decision to open the country to the outside world, and was also active as an interpreter and English teacher, and became the founder of English education in Japan. The grave of Manjiro, whose checkered life ended in 1898 at the age of 71, is located at Zoushigaya Cemetery in Toshima ward, Tokyo.

In September 2010, a monument was erected in Onaga, Tomigusuku City, where Manjiro stayed for six months by order of the Shuri royal government. In addition, in February 2018, a bronze statue of Manjiro (age 24), who returned from the United States wearing a cowboy hat, vest and jeans, and pointing with his right hand to his hometown of Tosashimizu City, was set up on the coast of Odohama at the landing site.

(11) 村屋（むらやー）

　間切内の各村を管理するための機構または建物を指し、近くに広場と拝所があるのが一般的で、ムラの中心であった。沖縄島や周辺離島では「ムラヤー」と呼ばれたが、宮古・八重山諸島では「村番所」といわれた。村屋は独立した行政機能を持たず、常に番所（現在の市町村役場）の指導を受け、掟（現在の区長）も番所から派遣された。かつては「ムラヤー」の前を通るときは村役人への敬いとして馬を下り、かぶり物をとるべきとされていた。1908 年（明治 41）、間切が村へ、村が字に改称されると村屋事務所となり、戦後は社会教育で公民館活動が盛んになると「公民館」と呼ばれるようになった。

(11) *Murayaa*

This refers to the mechanism or building for managing each village within a *magiri*, and was the center of the village, usually with a plaza and a place of worship nearby. In Okinawa Island and the surrounding islands, it was called *murayaa*, but in Miyako and Yaeyama Islands, it was called *mura-banjo*. *Murayaa* did not have independent administrative functions, but were always under the guidance of the *banjo* (present-day municipal offices), and the *ucchi* (present-day ward chiefs) were dispatched from the *banjo*. In the old days, people had to get off their horses and take off their hats when passing by a

むらやー（那覇市識名公民館）
Murayaa (Shikina Community Center, Naha City)

murayaa to show respect to the village officials. In 1908, when *magiri* was renamed as a village and the village was renamed as an aza, it became the *murayaa* office, and after the war, when community center activities became popular for social education, it became known as the *kouminkan*.

(12) 謝花昇（じゃはなのぼる）

　行政官、社会運動家で 1865 年に東風平間切東風平村の農家で生まれた。1882 年（明治 15）、太田朝敷、岸本賀昌らとともに第 1 回県費留学生として上京したが、士族出身でないのは謝花のみであった。学習院中等科に入学した彼は中江兆民の教えも受けた。沖縄県令（現・知事）からの要請で東京山林学校に特別入学し、東京農林学校を経て、帝国農科大学（現・東京大学農学部）で学び科学的農業を修めた。1891 年の大学卒業後は、鹿児島県等の県外出身者が多数を占めていた沖縄県庁に技師として入り、沖縄の農政改革に努めた。1892 年、「琉球王」と綽名された薩摩藩出身の専制的な「奈良原繁」が第四代沖縄県知事に赴任した。1893 年に土地調査委員に任命された謝花は、旧特権階級や支配者層を優遇する「杣山問題」で奈良原知事と対立し、その翌年、開墾主任を解任された。1898 年に県庁を退職した謝花は上京し、自由民権運動の主導者で当時内務大臣であった板垣退助に面会して奈良原知事の更迭を求め、内諾を得た。しかし、第 1 次大隈重信内閣が倒れたため、約束が果たされることはなかった。

謝花昇
Jahana Noboru

　翌 1899 年に当山久三らと「沖縄倶楽部」を結成し、県政批判・土地整理問題・参政権獲得の 3 点を中心に農民層の立場に立った活動を展開したが数々の妨害にあって、挫折した。1901 年、新しい職を得て赴任地（山口県の農業試験場）へ向かう途中、神戸駅で精神に異常を来した。東風平に帰郷したが、以来回復することなく 1908 年、44 歳の若さで亡くなった。「階級打破の象徴」や「沖縄の自由民権運動の父」として民衆の尊敬を集めた謝花昇の銅像は 1964 年に建立され、現在は八重瀬町の東風平運動公園内に設置されている。

(12) Jahana Noboru

A government official and social activist, he was born in 1865 in a farmhouse in Kochinda village, Kochinda *magiri*. In 1882, he went to Tokyo as the first prefectural scholarship student, along with Ohta Chohu, Kishimoto Kasho, and others, and Jahana was the only one not from a samurai family. He entered *Gakushuin* Secondary School, where he was taught by Nakae Chomin. At the request of the governor of Okinawa

Prefecture, he specially enrolled in the Tokyo *Sanrin Gakkou*, and after attending the Tokyo Agricultural and Forestry School, he studied at the Imperial University of Agriculture (now the University of Tokyo's Faculty of Agriculture), where he mastered scientific agriculture. After graduating from university in 1891, he joined the Okinawa Prefectural Government as an engineer, where most of the employees were from Kagoshima and other prefectures, and worked to reform Okinawa's agricultural policy. Appointed as a member of the Land. In 1892, the tyrannical Narahara Shigeru from the Satsuma domain, who was nicknamed the "King of Ryukyu," was appointed as the fourth governor of Okinawa. Survey Committee in 1893, Jahana came into conflict with Governor Narahara over the "*somayama* issue," which favored the former privileged class and the ruling class, and was dismissed as chief cultivator the following year. After resigning from the prefectural government in 1898, Jahana went to Tokyo and met with Itagaki Taisuke, then Minister of Home Affairs and a leader of the Civil Liberties Movement, and asked for and received his informal consent to remove Governor Narahara. However, the first Okuma Shigenobu cabinet collapsed, and the promise was never fulfilled.

The following year, in 1899, he formed the "Okinawa Club" with Toyama Kyuzo and others, and developed activities from the standpoint of the peasant class, focusing on three points: criticism of the prefectural government, land consolidation issues, and the acquisition of suffrage, but was frustrated by numerous obstacles. In 1901, on his way to his new position at the Agricultural Experiment Station in Yamaguchi Prefecture, he suffered a psychotic episode at Kobe Station. He returned to his hometown of Kochinda, but never recovered and died in 1908 at the young age of 44. The bronze statue of Jahana Noboru, who was respected by people as a "symbol of breaking the class" and the "father of the freedom and civil rights movement in Okinawa," was erected in 1964 and is currently located in Kochinda Sports Park in Yaese Town.

(13) 方言札（ほうげんふだ）

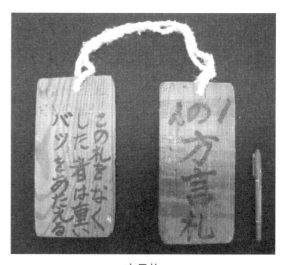

方言札
Hougen-huda(dialectal tag)

　沖縄における標準語（日本語）普及の問題は、廃藩置県に伴う新しい学校制度の発足（1880 年）とともに、性急かつ強硬策によって進められた。当時の沖縄では、標準語は外国語同様の言語でしかなく、特に昭和 10 年代になると、国家主義の高揚に伴ってこの傾向は強くなった。1940 年（昭和 15）に県当局が推進した「標準語励行運動」は、強制、禁止、懲罰などの過激な方法が貫かれたので、一般に「方言撲滅運動」と受けとられた。当運動は、方言の侮蔑、抑圧につながり、県民に屈辱感を与える恐れがあるなど、方言論争が展開された。方言札は、標準語励行の強硬手段として沖縄各地の学校で用いられた罰札である。方言を使った生徒は罰則として「方言札」と書かれた木札を首に掛けさせられ、これを持った者は方言を話している他の生徒を見つけて手渡していくという方法であった。この指導法はもともと標準語普及のための方便であったが、方言軽視による沖縄文化の否定につながり、逆に子どもたちに劣等意識を植え付けることになった。「方言札」は戦後もしばらく用いられ、1960 年代半ばまで使用した地域もあった。

(13) *Hougen-huda* (Dialect Disgrace Tag)

The issue of the spread of the standard Japanese language in Okinawa was pursued with hasty and heavy-handed manner, along with the inauguration of a new school system (1880) following the abolition of the domain. In Okinawa at that time, standard Japanese was only a language similar to a foreign language, and this tendency became especially strong from the mid-1930s with the rise of nationalism. In the 1940s, the prefectural authorities promoted a campaign to encourage the use of standard Japanese, which was generally regarded as a "dialect eradication campaign" because of its radical methods of coercion, prohibition, and punishment. The movement was met with controversy over the dialect, including the fear that it would lead to contempt and suppression of the dialect and humiliate the Okinawans. *Hougen-huda* (dialectal tags) were used as punishment tags in schools throughout Okinawa as a heavy-handed way to enforce the standard language. As a penalty, students who spoked in their dialects (*hougen*) were made to hang a wooden tag around their necks with a *hougen-huda* written on it, and those who held the tag would find other students who were speaking dialects and hand it to them. This was originally a way to promote the use of the standard Japanese, but it led to the denigration of Okinawan culture through the neglect of dialects, and in turn, instilled a sense of inferiority in the children. The *hougen-huda* continued to be used for a while after the war, with some areas using it until the mid-1960s.

(14) 軽便鉄道（けいびんてつどう）

　一般車両より軌間が短い軽便鉄道だったので、県民からは「ケイビン」または「ケービン」の名で親しまれていた。まず与那原線が 1914 年 12 月に開業。次の嘉手納線が 1922 年、最後の糸満線は 1923 年 7 月にスタートした。1920 年頃から戦時中にかけて、嘉手納—名護間の建設計画が持ち上がったが、実現しなかった。 3 線が開業したが、経営状況は芳しくなく一時は国有化の話もあった。太平洋戦争末期になると軍事輸送が本格化して、1940 年 7 月には通常ダイヤによる営業を終了し、実質的な軍用鉄道と

軽便鉄道与那原駅跡（与那原町与那原）
Ruins of Yonabaru Station on the Keibin Railway

なった。1944 年 10 月 10 日の空襲によって那覇駅が焼失し、12 月には糸満線の稲嶺駅付近で列車爆発事故が発生した。戦争の激化で 1945 年 3 月には運行を停止し、その後は米軍によって破壊された。

(14) *Keibin* (*Keibin* railway)

Since it was a light railroad with a shorter gauge than a regular railroad car, it was called Keibin or Keebin by the people of the prefecture and was well known. First, the Yonabaru Line opened in December 1914. The next line, the Kadena line, opened in 1922, and the last line, the Itoman line, opened in July 1923. From around 1920 to the end of the war, a plan to build a line between Kadena and Nago was proposed, but it never came to fruition. Three lines were opened, but the business situation was not good and at one point there was talk of nationalization. Toward the end of the Pacific War, military transport became a full-scale business, and in July 1940, the line ceased operating on a regular schedule, becoming essentially a military railroad. Naha station was burned down in an air raid on October 10, 1944, and in December there was a train explosion near Inamine station on the Itoman line. With the escalation of the war, it ceased operation in March 1945, and was subsequently destroyed by the U.S. military.

第３章　文化・史跡

　1879 年に消滅し、日本の一部としての沖縄県が誕生するまでこの地は琉球王国という独立国であった。琉球王国時代には中国、日本、東南アジア諸国との貿易が活発に行われ、この時期に三線、泡盛、紅型などの琉球文化の基礎が流入したと考えられている。さらに、沖縄戦後の 27 年間に及ぶアメリカ軍の占領によって新たな沖縄文化も誕生した。そのため、沖縄県は日本の他の地域と異なる独自の文化を持っており、しばしば「チャンプルー文化」とも呼ばれる。

Chapter 3 Culture and Historic remains

　Okinawa was an independent country called the Ryukyu Kingdom until 1879, when it ceased to exist and Okinawa Prefecture was created as part of Japan. During the period of the Ryukyu Kingdom, trade with China, Japan, and Southeast Asian countries was active, and it is believed that the foundation of Ryukyu culture, such as *sanshin*, *awamori*, and *bingata*, was introduced during this period. In addition, the 27-year occupation by the U.S. military after the Battle of Okinawa gave birth to a new Okinawan culture. As a result, Okinawa Prefecture has a unique culture that is different from the rest of Japan, often referred to as the "*champuruu* culture".

（1）ニライカナイ

　海の彼方または地の底にあり、人間が住む世界とは異なる神々が住む異次元世界をニライカナイと呼ぶ。ニライは「根の方」という意味に捉える説が有力で、「カナイ」には「ニライ」に対する韻をとるための無意味な言葉という説や「彼方」を意味するなど諸説ある。仏教でいう浄土は西にあるとされているが、ニライカナイは東方の海上または海底にあると考えられている。生命だけでなくあらゆる豊穣やエネルギーが東方からもたらされるという沖縄の東方信仰をニライカナイ思想という。琉球王府にとっては、ニライカナイは首里の東方にある久高島の彼方にあり、そこには太陽が生まれ出る「てぃだが穴」（太陽の穴）があると信じられた。久高島のほぼ中央にある

クボウ御嶽（琉球王国時代の７御嶽の１つで、イザイホーなどの神事が行われる久高島最高の聖地。男子禁制）（南城市久高島）
Kubou-*utaki* (One of the seven *utaki* from the Ryukyu Kingdom era, this is the most sacred place on Kudaka Island where *Izaihou* and other rituals are held. Men are forbidden to enter) (Kudaka Island, Nanjo City)

「クボウ御嶽」が「てぃだが穴」とみなされ、亡き王が太陽神として生まれ出て復活する場所とされていた。琉球神道には太陽神（てぃだ）を最高神とする信仰「太陽子思想」が根底にあり、太陽の子である国王の権力は神聖で不可侵であるとされた。

　沖縄の祭祀にはニライカナイの神を迎えたり、祀ったりする行事が多くあり、奄美諸島から八重山の島々まで広く分布している。沖縄本島北部で旧暦７月に行われる「ウンジャミ」（ウンガミ・海神祭）はニライカナイからの来方神にまつわる祭祀。八重山地方の「アカマタ・クロマタ」や宮古島の「パーントゥ」は仮装して現世に表れた来方神である。沖縄の祭りには「ミロク」（ミルク）がよく登場する。ミロクは来世に衆生を救済するために出現する仏教の弥勒菩薩のことだが、沖縄では在来のニライカナイ信仰と融合しながら、海の彼方の楽土からユー（豊穣・幸福・富）を運んでくる五穀の神と考えるようになった。豊年のことを「ミルクユー」（弥勒世）や「ミルクユガフ」（弥勒世果報）と称するのはこのためである。

(1) *Niraikanai*

Niraikanai is an interdimensional world beyond the sea or at the bottom of the earth, where gods live that is different from the world inhabited by humans. The most popular theory is that *nirai* means "direction of the roots," but there are many theories about *kanai*, such as that it is just a meaningless word that rhymes with *nirai* or that it means "beyond". The Pure Land in Buddhism is considered to be in the west, while *Niraikanai* is considered to be on the sea or at the bottom of the ocean in the east. The Okinawan "belief in the east" that not only life, but also all kinds of fertility and energy are brought from the east, is called the *Niraikanai* philosophy. For the royal government of the Ryukyu Kingdom, *Niraikanai* existed beyond Kudaka Island, east of Shuri, where it was believed that there was a *Tidaga-ana* (hole for the sun) where the sun was born and came out. *Kubou-utaki*, located almost in the center of Kudaka Island, was considered to be *tidaga-ana*, the place where deceased kings were born and resurrected as sun gods. The Ryukyu Shinto religion was based on the "Sun Child Concept," a belief that the sun god (*Tida*) was the supreme deity, and the power of the king, the son of the sun, was considered sacred and inviolable.

In Okinawa, there are many events to welcome and worship the gods of *Niraikanai*, and they are widely distributed from Amami Oshima to Yaeyama Islands. *Unjami* (Sea God Festival), held in the northern part of Okinawa Island in July of the lunar calendar, is a ritual related to the gods that come from *Niraikanai*. *Akamata-kuromata* in the Yaeyama region and *Paantuu* in Miyako Island are said to be the figures of gods who appeared in this world from another world. *Miroku (Miruku)* often appears in Okinawan festivals. *Miroku* refers to the Maitreya Bodhisattva, a saint believed in Buddhism who appears on earth at the end of a degenerate age to save the common people. In Okinawa, the myth of *Miroku* was blended with the native *Niraikanai* faith is some unknown time with the result that *Miroku* is believed to be the god of the five grains who brings "*yuu*" (fertility, happiness, and wealth) from the paradise beyond the sea. That is why the year of a rich harvest is called *Miruku-yuu* or *Miruku-yugahu*.

(2) アマミキヨ・シネリキヨ、アマミキヨ族

①伝説

ヤハラヅカサ（南城市百名海岸）
Yaharazukasa
(Hyakuna Beach, Nanjo City)

　アマミキヨは琉球神話における開闢神（女神）で、男神・シネリキヨとともに「アマミキヨ・シネリキヨ」と対語で呼ばれる。アマミキヨはニライカナイ（東方の彼方にある神々の住む理想郷・神の国）から「ヤハラヅカサ」に上陸してミントングスクを築いたという伝説がある。1605年に編纂された琉球王国最古の歴史書『中山世鑑』によると、アマミキヨはそこでシネリキヨとの間に3男2女をもうけ、長男は国王の始めの「天孫氏」となり、次男は按司の始め、三男は百姓の始め、長女は聞得大君となり、次女はノロの始めになったと伝えられている。琉球神話では、天孫氏はアマミキヨが築いたとされる玉城城を居城にして25代続いたとされる。アマミキヨやシネリキヨの墓といわれるものがミントングスクなど、各地に存在する。方言で「チュ」とも発音される「キョ」とは「人」の意で、アマンチュ、アマミチュ、すなわち「奄美人」の意ととられ、北方（奄美方面）から農耕文化を始めとする異文化を持ち込んだ渡来人の総称というのが現在の定説になっている。

(2) Amamikiyo/Shinerikiyo, Amamikiyo Tribe
① Legend of Amamikiyo/Shinerikiyo

Amamikiyo is the creator god (goddess) in Ryukyu mythology, and together with the male deity Shinerikiyo, they are referred to as Amamikiyo-Shinerikiyo. Legend has it that Amamikiyo landed at Yaharazukasa from *Niraikanai* (the ideal land of the gods in the far east) and built Minton-*gusuku*. According to the oldest history book of the Ryukyu Kingdom, Chuzan-seikan, compiled in 1605, Amamikiyo is said to have had three sons and two daughters with Shinerikiyo there, and the eldest son was the first of the kings to establish the Tenson Dynasty, the second son became the first of *aji*, the third son became the first of the peasants, the eldest daughter became the first of Kikoe Okimi, and the second daughter became the first of *noro*. According to Ryukyu mythology, the Tenson Dynasty lasted for 25 generations, settling in Tamagusuku Castle, which is said to have been built by Amamikiyo. The tombs of Amamikiyo or Sinelikiyo are said to be located in various places, including Minton-*gusuku*. The word *kiyo* is also pronounced as *chu* in the dialect and means people, which can be taken to mean "*Aman-chu*" or "*Amami-chu*," in other words, "Amami people". The current prevailing theory is that Amamikiyo is a generic name for people who came from the north (Amami area) and brought with them different cultures, including agricultural culture.

②南方から北上した海洋民族説

アマミキヨ族の渡来については学問的にまだ解明されていない。沖縄各地や奄美諸島にアマミキヨ族に関する幾多の伝説があるが、いずれも、太古の昔にニライカナイから船に乗ってきたという共通点をもつ。多くの歴史書によると、1187 年に舜天が琉球王として即位した舜天王統が沖縄の有史時代の始まりで、それ以前は神話時代とされる。約 10,000 年前～ 6 世紀頃までは、南海から北上してきた「海洋民族（アマミキヨ族時代）」、7 世紀～ 1186 年までが天孫氏王統、1187 年～ 1259 年が舜天王統で、次の英祖王統（1260 年～ 1349 年）へ続くとされる。

② The theory of maritime peoples who migrated north from the south

The academic details of the Amamikiyo tribe arrival in Okinawa have not yet been elucidated. There are many legends about the Amamikiyo tribe in various parts of Okinawa and the Amami Islands, all of which have in common that they came from *Niraikanai* on a ship in prehistoric times. According to many history books, the Shunten Dynasty, in which Shunten ascended to the throne as King of Ryukyu in 1187, was the beginning of the prehistoric period in Okinawa, and before that, it was the mythical period. From about 10,000 years ago to the 6th century, it was the "Amamikiyo period," a maritime people who migrated northward from the South Sea; from the 7th century to 1186, it was the Tenson Dynasty; and from 1187 to 1259, the Shunten Dynasty, which continued into the next Eiso Dynasty (1260 to 1349).

③本島北部上陸説

1972 年 4 月 7 日発行の琉球新報に、沖縄文化財保護委員会や辺土名高校の郷土研究クラブらによる沖縄古代人の住居跡（国頭村辺土の宇佐浜貝塚）の発掘調査に関する記事が紹介されている。それによると、貝塚からは住居跡や石器、石皿、土器片などが見つかり、次のことが推測されている。「年代はほぼ 2,300 年前の中期貝塚時代にあたる」「奄美大島の宇宿貝塚の上層文化と同一系統」で、「従って沖縄に農耕文化をもたらしたアマミキヨ族の最初の上陸点と思われる」と結論づけている。

③ The theory of Amamikiyo tribe who landed in the northern part of Okinawa island

The April 7, 1972 issue of the Ryukyu Shimpo introduced an article on the excavation of an ancient Okinawan dwelling site (Usahama shell mound in Hedo, Kunigami Village) by the Okinawa Cultural Properties Protection Committee and the Hentona High School Local Studies Club. According to the article, the shell mound revealed the remains of a dwelling, stone tools, stone plates, and pottery fragments, and the following is inferred. It is dated to the middle shell mound period of Okinawa, about 2,300 years ago, and is of the same lineage as the upper culture of the Ushuku shell mound on Amami-Oshima Island. And the study concluded, "Thus, it appears to be the first landing site of the Amamikiyo tribe, who brought their agricultural culture to Okinawa".

④大陸からの渡来集団説

　アマミキヨ族は、大陸からの渡来集団という説がある。宋の時代の中国には遠洋航海の出来る木造船の造船技術や航海術が既に発達していた。宋に代わったモンゴル帝国（元朝）の日本侵攻（元寇）では、当時世界最大規模の艦隊による大軍が、2度にわたって九州北部を襲っている。1274年（兵数約4万）と1281年（兵数14万～15万）のモンゴル（元）軍の日本襲来はそれぞれ「文永の役」、「弘安の役」とも呼ばれる。元寇の襲来では2度とも神風が吹いたためモンゴル軍は遭難・漂流し、日本軍が勝利したとされるが、この時、大軍の一部が沖縄に漂着したと考えられている。10世紀以前の沖縄人の骨と10～13世紀以降の沖縄人の骨が大分、異なるといわれる。沖縄本島南部の墳墓からは、身長が1.7m近い人骨が発掘されている。アマミキヨ族は、中国大陸でのモンゴルなどの騎馬遊牧民族の侵入に伴う動乱による民族移動や、その後の元寇、モンゴル帝国滅亡時の王族などが集団的に沖縄に渡来した人々とする説である。この説によると、アマミキヨ族の渡来時期は前述の他説と時代的に大きな差異がある。

④ The theory of migratory groups from the continent

　There is a theory that the Amamikiyo tribe is a migratory group from the continent. In China during the Rong Dynasty, shipbuilding technology and navigation techniques for wooden vessels capable of long-distance voyages were already well developed. During the Mongol invasion of Japan (*Genkou*) by the Mongol Empire (Yuan Dynasty), which replaced the Rong Dynasty, a huge army with the largest fleet in the world at the time attacked northern Kyushu on two occasions. The Mongol (Yuan) invasions of Japan in 1274 (with about 40,000 troops) and 1281 (with 140,000-150,000 troops) are also called "*Bun'ei-no-eki*" and "*Kouan-no-eki*," respectively. It is said that the Mongolian army was lost and adrift because of *kamikaze* winds (divine winds) on both occasions during the *Genkou* attacks, and that the Japanese army was victorious, however, it is thought that a part of the large Mongolian army drifted to Okinawa at that time. It is said that the bones of Okinawans before the 10th century differ greatly from those of Okinawans from the 10th to 13th centuries onward. Human bones nearly 1.7 meters tall have been excavated from tombs in the southern part of the main island of Okinawa. This is the theory that the Amamikiyo tribe is a people who came to Okinawa in groups during the upheavals in mainland China, including ethnic migrations due to the invasion of Mongolian and other nomadic horsemen to China, the subsequent *Genkou* invasion, and royalty at the time of the collapse of the Mongol Empire. According to this theory, the timing of the arrival of the Amamikiyo tribe differs significantly in time from the other theories mentioned above.

（3）ガマ（洞窟）

　沖縄県に多く見られる自然洞窟のこと。沖縄本島には石灰岩でできた約2,000の鍾乳洞があり、沖縄方言で「ガマ」と呼ばれている。ガマは数十万年もの年月が創り出した自然の芸術で、ダイナミックで幻想的であるが古代から風葬や洞窟葬、生活の場所として使われてきた。死者は現在では火葬され墓

地に埋葬されるが、明治時代に行政から禁止され
るまで沖縄では風葬が行われていた。風葬では遺
体はまず崖や洞窟（ガマ）に置かれて自然の腐敗
を待ち、適当な時期に洗骨して納骨する。沖縄で
は崖やガマは古来、現世と後生の境界の世界とさ
れ「聖域」であると同時に「忌むもの」とされてきた。
祖霊を崇める一方で、死はあくまで「穢れ」と捉
えられているのである。鍾乳洞の美しい景観が残っ
ているガマは人気観光地としても有名だが、沖縄
戦においては住民や日本兵の避難場所として、ま
た野戦病院として利用された。そこでは、しば
しば集団自決などの悲劇が起きた。シムクガマ

チビチリガマ（読谷村波平）
Chibichiri-*gama* (Namihira, Yomitan Village)

（読谷村）、チビチリガマ（読谷村）、アブチラガマ（南城市）、轟ガマ（糸満市）などが有名で、今日
では平和学習にも利用されている。

(3) *Gama* (natural cave made of Ryukyu limestone)

A natural cave often found in Okinawa Prefecture. There are about 2,000 limestone caves on the main island
of Okinawa, and they are called *gama* in Okinawan dialect. Limestone caves(*gama*) are the natural artifacts of
hundreds of thousands of years, dynamic and fantastic, but they have been used since ancient times for wind
burials, cave burials, and as places for people to live. Today, the dead are cremated and buried in cemeteries, but
in Okinawa, wind burial was used until the government banned it in the Meiji era. In wind burial, the body is
first placed on a cliff or in a cave (*gama*) to wait for natural decomposition, and then washed at an appropriate
time and delivered. In Okinawa, cliffs and caves have long been considered the boundary between this world
and the next, and have been regarded as both "sanctuaries" and "abominations". While ancestral spirits are
revered, death is regarded as a "defilement". *Gama*, with its beautiful limestone caves, is famous as a popular
tourist destination, but during the Battle of Okinawa, it was used as a refuge for residents and Japanese soldiers
and as a field hospital, where tragedies such as mass suicides often occurred. Shimuku-*gama* (Yomitan Village),
Chibichiri-*gama* (Yomitan Village), Abuchira-*gama* (Nanjo City), Todoroki-*gama* (Itoman City), etc. are famous
and are also used for peace education today.

(4) 御嶽 (うたき)、イビ（イベ）

琉球における祖先崇拝信仰で、祖先に対す
る多大な崇敬の念を抱くための儀式を行う聖
地または場所。奄美諸島では「オガミヤマ、
オボツヤマ」、宮古諸島では「グスク、ムトゥ」、
八重山諸島では「オン、ワー」などと呼ばれ
るが、そのような聖地を総称して沖縄では「ウ
タキ」と称する。御嶽はもともと古代社会に
おいて集落があった場所と考える説が有力で
ある。御嶽の近くから遺骨が見つかる例が多
く、祖先崇拝と強く関係していると考えられ
ている。沖縄の御嶽には一般的に建造物はな

安居御嶽（石垣市真栄里）
Angun-*on* (Maesato, Ishigaki City)

いが、地域によっては神女が神に近づくために夜籠もりをする建物がみられる。八重山の御嶽では石組みにより聖域を取り囲む構造となっている。御嶽の内奥にある最も神聖な場所は「イビ」または「イベ」と呼ばれる。本来はそこに祀られている神名で、イビには香炉が置かれている。その背後には巨岩・クロツグやクバ（ビロウ）などの神木、墓などがあるが、これらは本来、神が降臨する標識であり御神体とは異なる。本土の神社などと違って、御嶽には御神体や偶像は無く、実体を持たない「神聖な空間」が御嶽の中核である。つまり空間そのものが霊的な場である。

（例）斎場（せーふぁ）御嶽、武順（ぶじゅん）御嶽、カニマン御嶽、アングンオン（安居御嶽）

(4) *Utaki, Ibi* (*Ibe*)

A sacred site or place where rituals are held to inspire great reverence for ancestors in the Ryukyu Islands. In the Amami Islands, it is called *ogamiyama* or *obotsuyama*; in the Miyako Islands, *gusuku* or *mutu*; in the Yaeyama Islands, *on* or *waa*; etc. Such sacred places are collectively called *utaki* in Okinawa. There is a popular theory that *utaki* was originally the location of a village in ancient society. There are many cases where remains are found near *utaki,* and it is believed that they are strongly related to ancestor worship. *Utaki* in Okinawa generally does not have any structures, but in some areas, there are structures where goddesses stay at night in order to get closer to the gods. The *utaki* in Yaeyama is a structure that surrounds the sanctuary with masonry. The most sacred place in the inner part of the *utaki* is called *ibi* or *ibe*. It is originally the name of the deity enshrined there, and an incense burner is placed in the *ibi*. Behind it, there are huge rocks, sacred trees such as *kurotsugu* and *kuba* (*birou*), and tombs, but these are essentially signs to which the deity descends, and are different from the *goshintai* (an object of worship believed to contain the spirit of a deity). Unlike shrines in the mainland, there is no deity or idol in *utaki*, and the core of *utaki* is a "sacred space" without substance. In other words, the space itself is a spiritual place.

examples: Seifa-*utaki*, Bujun-*utaki*, Kaniman-*utaki*, Angun-*on*.

(5) 神アシャギ（かみあしゃぎ）

　村々において神を招いて祭祀を行う場所をいう。本来、建物の有無とは関係ないが、そこに建てられた祭祀用建物も「神アシャギ」と呼ばれるようになった。建物は壁がない4本または6本柱造りの竹茅葺き屋根（今ではコンクリート作りや赤瓦屋根もある）で、沖縄本島北部では軒が低く、奄美諸島では軒が高い。神アシャギの呼称は沖縄本島北部や奄美諸島のノロ分布圏内に限られており、沖縄本島中南部では「殿」（とぅん）と呼ばれる。母屋に向かって右手前にある客を歓待する建物はアシャギと呼ばれる。神アシャギの語源は、神へ「アシー」（飲食物）を差し上げて歓待する場所の意味から付いたともいわれるが、来訪した神が「足を上げて」くつろぎながら村人たちと歓談する場所という説もある。

神アシャギ（国頭村比地）
Kami-ashagi（Hiji,Kunigami Village）

(5) *Kami-ashagi*

A place in villages where gods are invited to perform rituals. Originally, it had nothing to do with the presence or absence of structures, but the ritual structures built there also came to be called *kami-ashagi*. The structures are made of four or six pillars without walls, and roofs are made of bamboo and thatch (nowadays concrete and red tile roofs are also available), with low eaves in the northern part of Okinawa Island and high eaves in the Amami Islands. The name *kami-ashagi* is limited to the *noro* distribution area in the northern part of Okinawa Island and the Amami Islands, and is called *tun* in central and southern Okinawa Island. The house in the right foreground facing the main house is called *ashagi*, where guests are entertained. The word *kami-ashagi* is said to have originated from the meaning of a place where people entertain the gods by giving them *ashii* (food and drink), but there is also a theory that it is a place where the visiting gods relax and chat with the villagers while "putting their feet up".

(6) 根屋（にーやー）、根人（にーんちゅ）

　根屋は、沖縄本島とその周辺離島で村落の創始者の家筋とされ、村落の祭祀の中心となる家で、根処（ニードゥクル）とも呼ばれる。根屋の当主は代々、「根人」（ニーンチュ）と称される。根屋は、村落創設や村落祭祀の役割から、他の家々より上位にあるのが普通で、村落の祭祀場である「神アシャギ」や「殿」（トゥン）などとも近接する位置にある。沖縄本島の根屋に相当するものとして、奄美地域の「イネヤ」があり、宮古・八重山地域では「ムトゥ」と称する草分け筋の家がある。

(6) *Nii-yaa, Niin-chu*

Nii-yaa, also known as a *nii-dukuru*, is the family lineage of the founder of a village and the center of village rituals on the main island of Okinawa and the surrounding outlying islands. The head of the *nii-yaa* is called *niin-chu* for generations. Because of its role in the founding of the village and village rituals, the *nii-yaa* usually ranks higher than the other families, and is in close proximity to the village ritual site, such as the *kami-ashagi* or *tun*. The *ineya* in the Amami region corresponds to the *nii-yaa* in the main island of Okinawa, and there is a pioneering house called *mutu* in the Miyako and Yaeyama regions.

(7) 根神（にーがん）

　沖縄本島地域の村落では、根屋の長男は「根人」（ニーンチュ）、その姉妹（ほとんどの場合は長女）は「根神」（ニーガン）と呼ばれる。ニーガンは村落の血縁集団から選ばれた神女・神役たちから成る祭祀組織の頂点に立つ。ニーンチュとニーガンはエケリ（兄弟）とオナリ（姉妹）の関係にあり、姉妹が兄弟を霊的に保護し優越した位置に立つという「オナリ神」信仰が根底にある。ニーガンは、門中などの血族レベルにおいては血縁集団の構成員と祖先神の中間に立つ司祭者・媒体者である。同時に、村落の根屋のオナリ神として、村落の農耕儀礼など祭祀行事のリーダーでもある。尚真王代（1477～1527）に確立した聞得大君を頂点とするノロ制度では、各地のノロが国王から任命された。各地にノロが配置されると、村落のニーガンは他の神女たちとともにノロの統轄下におかれた。

(7) *Nii-gan*

In the villages of the main island of Okinawa, the eldest son of the *nii-yaa* is called *niin-chu*, and his sisters (mostly the eldest daughters) are called *nii-gan*. *Nii-gan* stands at the top of the ritual organization consisting of female deities selected from blood-related groups in the village and those in charge of the ritual. *Niin-chu* and *nii-gan* have a relationship of *ekeri* (brothers) and *onari* (sisters), which is based on the *onari-gami* belief that sisters protect and have spiritual superiority over their brothers. At the level of the blood group, such as the *munchu*, *nii-gan* is the priest or medium who stands between the members of the blood group and the ancestral deity. At the same time, At the same time, *nii-gan* is also the leader of the village's agricultural rituals and other ritual events as the *onari-gami* of the village's *nii-yaa*. In the *noro* system, which was established during the reign of King Sho Shin (1477-1527) and headed by Kikoe Okimi, *noro* of each region was appointed by the king. When *noro* was assigned in each area, the *nii-gan* of the village, along with other goddesses, were placed under *noro's* control.

（8）火の神（ひぬかん）

台所にある火の神（八重瀬町世名城）
Hinukan in the kichen
(Yonashiro, Yaese-*cho*)

　本土では、「火の神」とは火を統制し管理する神のことで火そのものを信仰することはない。火の神を「荒神」（こうじん）や「三宝」（さんぽう）荒神と呼ぶ地域は広く、竈（かまど）や囲炉裏（いろり）を対象にした「火の神信仰」は全国的にみられる。仏教が浸透している本土では、今では火の神を知らない人が多くなったが、沖縄では今日でも火の神（ヒヌカン）はどこの台所にもいる身近な神様である。

　沖縄の信仰は「琉球神道」とも言われ、独自の世界観を持っており、超自然の神々の国の存在を前提とする「ニライカナイ思想」に基づく。人間の魂は、神々のいるニライカナイから来て死後またそこへ帰り、守護神となって子孫の元へ還ってくるというのが沖縄の生死観である。沖縄の「火の神」は、台所を司る「竈の神」であるが、ニライカナイの大王・君真物（キンマムン）の分身であり、人間が交信するためのお通し役とも考えられている。御香炉（ウコール）の灰に宿っているとされる火の神は、台所や火を司る神様だけに主に女性が拝む。「ウミチムン」とも呼ばれる火の神は家の守り神でもあり、ニライカナイの神々に対する感謝・祈願とともに家族の報告を旧暦の１日・15日（ティータチ・ジュウグニチ）などに定期的に行う。

(8) *Hinukan* (God of Fire)

　In the mainland, the "god of fire" refers to the god who controls and manages fire, and fire itself is not worshipped. There are many areas where the god of fire is called *koujin* or *sanpou-koujin*, and the "belief in the god of fire," which is the god of the cooking stove and hearth, is found all over Japan. On the mainland, where Buddhism is more widespread, many people are now unaware of the god of fire, but in Okinawa, the god of fire *(hinukan)* is still a familiar deity in every kitchen.

　Okinawan beliefs, also known as "Ryukyu Shinto," have a unique worldview and are based on the "*Niraikanai* philosophy," which is based on the existence of a supernatural land of gods. The Okinawan view of life and death is that the human soul comes from *Niraikanai*, where the gods reside, and returns there after death to become a guardian deity and return to its descendants. The Okinawan *hinukan* is thought to be the "god of the hearth" who controls the kitchen, as well as an alter ego of *Kinmamun*, the great king of *Niraikanai*, and a mediator of communication between humans and *Kinmamun*. *Hinukan*, that is said to reside in the ashes of the incense burner *(ukouru)*, is worshipped mainly by women as the god of the kitchen and fire. *Hinukan*, also known as *umichimun*, is also the guardian deity of the house, and prayers and thanks to the gods of *Niraikanai* are made regularly on the 1st and 15th days of the lunar calendar *(chii-tachi juugu-nichi)* to report the status of the family.

（9）オナリ神、オナリ神信仰

　兄弟を守護するといわれる姉妹の霊を「オナリ神」という。「オナリ」は、兄弟から姉妹を指す言葉で、姉妹から兄弟を指す「エケリ」に対応する。オナリ神の主な機能は兄弟の守護や祝福をすることで、兄弟が危機に陥ったときに顕在する。戦争や旅に出るときはお守りとして姉妹の髪や手巾（ティーサージ）を持って行った。姉妹が存在しない場合、その機能は通常、父系親族内の女性が代行した。その場合は「ウバ神」（叔母神）と呼ばれた。他方で、兄弟は姉妹に対して俗的保護の役割を果たすことが期待される。「根神と根人」、「ノロと按司」、「聞得大君と王」の関係もそれである。

オナリ神
Onari-gami

　「オナリ」が「エケリ」を霊的に守護すると考え、オナリの霊力を信仰する沖縄地方の信仰を「オナリ神信仰」という。かつて琉球王国の版図であった奄美群島から先島まで広く見られるが、唯一、宮古島では「オナリ神信仰」は希薄である。現代では、琉球の信仰（琉球神道）の一要因として捉えられているが、オナリ神信仰を基盤とした祭政一致社会は、日本本土の邪馬台国や古奄美など広範に見られる。

(9) *Onari-gami, Onari-gami* belief

　The spirit of the sisters who is said to protect the brothers is called *onari-gami*. The word *onari* refers to the sisters from the brothers, and corresponds to the word *ekeri* which refers to the brothers from the sisters. The main function of the *onari-gami* is to protect and bless the siblings, and they become manifest when the siblings are in danger. When they went to war or on a journey, they took their sisters' hair or handkerchiefs *(tii-saaji)* with them as a talisman. If there were no sisters, the function was usually performed by a woman in the patrilineal family. In this case, she was called *uba-gami*. Brothers, on the other hand, were expected to play a secular protective role over their sisters. This was also the case with the relationship between the *nii-gan* and the *niin-chu,* between the *noro* and the *aji*, and between the Kikoe Okimi and the King.

　The Okinawan belief in the spiritual power of *onari* is called the *"onari-gami* belief" because *onari* is believed to spiritually protect *ekeri*. The belief in the *onari-gami* is widespread from the Amami Islands to the Sakishima Islands, which were once part of the Ryukyu Kingdom, only in Miyako Island is less common. In modern times, it is seen as a factor in the beliefs of the Ryukyu Islands (Ryukyu Shinto), but ritualistic and political societies based on the belief in the *onari-gami* can be found in a wide range of places in mainland Japan, such as the Yamataikoku and ko(old)-Amami.

(10) 斎場御嶽（せーふぁうたき）

　琉球開闢の神・アマミキヨが造った国始めの7御嶽の一つと伝えられ、琉球王国最高の聖域。男子禁制で国王さえ中に立ち入ることができなかった。首里城の東方に位置し、ニライカナイに真向かう久高島へのお通し御嶽である。また、聞得大君の就任式「お新下り」（ウアラウリ）や、国の豊穣祈願、雨乞い祈願、国の吉凶を占う儀式などが行われ、王府が直接管理した。御嶽内にある6箇所の霊域のうち、「大庫理」（ウフグーイ）、「寄満」（ユインチ）、「三庫理」（サングーイ）はいずれも首里城内に同名の建物や部屋があり、往時の首里城と斎場御嶽との深い関わりを示している。

「大庫理」とは大広間や一番座という意味を持ち、「お新下り」儀式の際には聞得大君が、琉球の創造神「キミテズリ」との聖婚によって霊力（セジ）を身体に宿す場所であった。「寄満」とは首里城の「台所」を意味するが、ここでの意味は「寄せて満ちる」の文字どおり、貿易で栄えた琉球王国に寄せられ、満ちた交易品の数々が集まった場所とされている。「お新下り」儀式の際にはここで料理が作られた。「三庫理」は、2つの巨岩が絶妙なバランスで支え合う空間である。岩の隙間を抜けた広間からは東方に久高島が望める。近年この広場で黄金の勾玉が見つかっており、重要な場所であったことを示している。

斎場御嶽の三庫理（南城市久手堅）
Sanguui in Seifa-*utaki* (Kudeken, Nanjyo City)

　巨石奇岩が多い霊威（セジ）高いこの御嶽は元来、地元の漁労祭祀の重要な斎場で、南方にあった集落の腰当森（クサティムイ＝集落を保護する森）であった。御嶽背後にある巨岩「アンドゥン」にはウフジチュウ（網を作る神）の墓がある。近隣の安座真・久手堅集落では、「ウフジチュウのお祝い」という漁労祭祀が行われる。アンドゥンの隣には幻のグスク「ナーワンダー」がある。ナーワンダーは、支配する曲輪（くるわ）の意の「ナデルワ」の転訛といわれ、古代集落の祭祀遺跡である。斎場御嶽は 2000 年 12 月、世界遺産リストに登録された。

(10) Seifa-*utaki*

　It is said to be one of the first seven *utaki* built by Amamikiyo, the creator god of the Ryukyu Islands, and is the highest sanctuary of the Ryukyu Kingdom. It was forbidden to men and even the king was not allowed to enter. It is located to the east of Shuri Castle and is the *utaki* for worshipping Kudaka Island, located directly in front of *Niraikanai,* from a distance. The *utaki* was also used for the inauguration ceremony of Kikoe Okimi called *Uarauri*, prayers for fertility of the country, prayers for rain, and rituals to predict the fortune of the country, which were directly managed by the royal government. Of the six sacred areas in the *utaki*, *Uhuguui*, *Yuinchi*, and *Sanguui* all have structures and rooms with the same name in Shuri Castle, indicating the deep relationship between Shuri Castle and Seifa-*utaki* in the past. The word *uhuguui* means "great hall" or "first room," and it was the place where the new Kikoe Okimi was married to Kimitezuri, the creator god of the Ryukyu Islands and received the spiritual power*(seji)*, during the *uarauri* ceremony. The word *yuinchi* means "kitchen" in Shuri Castle, but in this case it means "to gather and fill with goods," and it is said to be a place where many trade goods were gathered and filled in the Ryukyu Kingdom, which flourished through trade. This is where the food was prepared during the *uarauri* ceremony. The *Sanguui* is a space where two huge rocks support each other in a perfect balance. Passing through the gap between the two huge rocks, from the square you can see Kudaka Island to the east. Recently, a golden jade was found in this square, indicating that it was an important place.

　This *utaki*, which has many huge and strange rocks, was originally an important place for local fishermen's rituals and was the *kusatii-mui* (a forest that protects the village) of the village located in the south. There is a tomb of Uhujichu (the god who makes nets) on the giant rock Andun behind the *utaki*. In the neighboring villages of Azama and Kudeken, a fishing ritual called "Uhujichu's Celebration" is held. Next to Andun, there is a fantastic *gusuku* called *Naawandaa*. *Naawandaa* is said to be a corruption of the word *naderuwa*, which means a ruling citadel, and is a ritual site of an ancient village. Seifa-*utaki* was registered on the World Heritage List in December 2000.

（11）久高島（くだかじま）

久高島は沖縄本島の南東端に位置する知念岬の東海上 5.3km にある周囲 8 km の細長い島で、2020 年 4 月現在、人口 238 人、世帯数 153 世帯である。公有地などを除き、土地は集落名義で登記され全体の所有となっており、琉球王朝時代の地割制度が唯一、今でも残っている。家を建てるときは、集落総会の許可を得なければならない。通常、土地は自宅や畑として使用できるが、島を出る際には集落へ返す。琉球開闢の聖地といわれるこの島では 12 年に一度、午年（うまどし）の旧

イザイホー（南城市久高島）
Izaihou(kudaka Island, Nanjyo City)

暦 11 月に行われる「イザイホー」と呼ばれる祭事が有名である。この島で生まれた 30 歳から 41 歳の女性たちは、ノロが主宰する 3 晩、4 日間にわたるこの祭りを通じて村の祭祀集団の一員となる。祭りに参加し、神女として認証された女性たちは「家族の守り神」としての霊力が更に高まるのである。

琉球開闢の祖・アマミキヨが天から舞い降りてきて、ここから国造りを始めたといわれる琉球神話の聖地で、「神が宿る島」としても知られる神秘に満ちた離島である。特に島中央にある「クボー御嶽」は久高島第一の聖地であり、男子禁制である。久高島には現在でも「久高ノロ」と「外間ノロ」という 2 人のノロがいて、琉球王朝時代に作られた「ノロ制度」を継承。民俗学的にも重要な島である。ノロは祭祀を司る報酬としてこの島の特産物「エラブウミヘビ」（イラブー）を捕る権利や私有地が与えられている。この島には五穀豊穣が異界「ニライカナイ」からもたらされたという伝説があり、琉球王国時代には、国王が聞得大君を伴って参拝したが、後には斎場御嶽から遥拝する形式に変わった。

（11）Kudaka Island

Kudaka Island is a long, narrow island with a circumference of 8 km, located 5.3 km east of Cape Chinen on the southeastern tip of the main island of Okinawa, and as of April 2020, the city has a population of 238 and 153 households. Except for public land, the land is registered in the name of the village and is owned by the whole village. It is the only place where the land division system of the Ryukyu Dynasty era still remains. When building a house, permission must be obtained from the village assembly. Normally, the land can be used as a home or farm, but when leaving the island, it is returned to the village. The island, which is said to be the sacred place of the founding of Ryukyu, is famous for a secret festival called *Izaihou*, which is held once every 12 years in November of the lunar year of the horse. Women between the ages of 30 and 41 born on the island become part of the village ritual group through this three-night, four-day festival presided over by *noro*. Women who participate in the festival and are certified as divine maidens will have their spiritual power further enhanced as "guardians of the family".

This island is a holy place where Amamikiyo, the founder of Ryukyu, is said to have descended from the heavens and started the creation of the country from here, and is also known as "the island where the gods dwell" and is full of mysteries. In particular, Kubou-*utaki*, located in the center of the island, is the most sacred place on Kudaka Island and is forbidden to men. Kudaka Island still has two *noro*, Kudaka-*noro* and Hokama-*noro*, who inherit the *Noro* System created during the Ryukyu Dynasty, making it an important island in terms of folklore. As a reward for presiding over the rituals, *noro* are given the right to catch the island's special product, the "Erabu sea snake" *(irabuu)*, as well as private property. There is a legend that the five grains were brought to this island from the other world *Niraikanai*, and during the time of the Ryukyu Kingdom, the king accompanied Kikoe Okimi to Kudaka Island to worship. Later, the style was changed to worshipping from Seifa-*utaki*.

(12) 東御廻り（あがりうまーい）

　琉球の創世神「アマミキヨ」がニライカナイから渡来して住みついたと伝えられる聖地を巡拝する行事のこと。聖地は、「東四間切」（あがりゆまじり）といわれた知念・玉城・佐敷・大里（以前、与那原は大里の一部であった）の4間切に点在する。尚巴志王（1372～1439）の聖地巡礼が起源とされ、琉球王国の繁栄と五穀豊穣を祈願する行事として始められた。この行事は王族から士族、民間へと広がっていった。聞得大君を伴って国王が自ら参加する本来の東御廻りは、200年以上も続いたが、羽地朝秀の改革によって廃止されて以降は、聞得大君による行事となった。沖縄には祖先を敬い、自然

御殿山（聞得大君の「御新下り」の儀式の際、首里を出発して最初の休憩地として仮御殿が建てられた場所）（与那原町与原）
Udunyama(The place where a temporary palace was built as the first resting place after leaving Shuri during the "Uarauri ceremony" of Kikoe Okimi)(Yobaru,Yonabaru Town)

の恵みに感謝して祀ってきた長い歴史と文化がある。東御廻りは、そんな琉球の精神文化にふれる旅といわれる。現在伝えられているコースは、首里の園比屋御嶽（スヌヒャンウタキ）を出発して与那原、佐敷、知念、玉城にある拝所を経て、玉城グスクをゴールとする計14ヶ所の聖地を巡る。これは首里王府が国家的祭祀ルートとして指定したものである。

(12) *Agari-umaai*

　This is a pilgrimage to sacred places where Amamikiyo, the founding god of Ryukyu, is said to have come from *Niraikanai* and settled. The sacred sites are scattered in the four *magiri* of Chinen, Tamagusuku, Sashiki, and Ozato (Yonabaru used to be a part of Ozato), which are known as the *Agari-yumajiri* (four *magiri* of the east). It is said to have originated from the pilgrimage of King Sho Hashi (1372~1439) to the holy ground, and was started as an event to pray for the prosperity of the Ryukyu Kingdom and a good harvest. This event spread from the royal family to the warrior class and then to the general public. The original *agari-umaai*, in which the king personally participated accompanied with Kikoe Okimi, lasted for over 200 years, but was abolished during the reforms of Haneji Chosyu, and has since been conducted by Kikoe Okimi. Okinawa has a long history and culture of honoring ancestors and worshipping them with gratitude for the blessings of nature. *Agari-umaai* is said to be a journey to experience such spiritual culture of Ryukyu. The current course of the pilgrimage starts from Sunuhyan-*utaki* in Shuri, passes through worship sites in Yonabaru, Sashiki, Chinen, and Tamagusuku, and finishes at Tamagusuku-*gusuku*, visiting a total of 14 sacred sites. This was designated by the Shuri royal government as a national ritual route.

(13) 今帰仁上り（今帰仁御廻り）（なきじんぬぶい・なきじんうまーい）

　「東御廻り」に対して「今帰仁上り」は、今帰仁城内外の聖地・旧跡を巡礼する行事で「今帰仁御廻り」（なきじんうまーい）ともいう。東御廻りが国家行事を起源とするのに対し、今帰仁上りは民間起源といわれ、門中が必ず行うべき行事とされていた。アマミキヨ族が北山を開いたとされ、今帰仁城も信仰の対象となったのである。当行事の起源は定かではないが、第一・第二尚氏王統の発祥地で

ある伊平屋・伊是名両島を擁する旧北山国領と、その首府があった今帰仁には王族のルーツも多くあることが理由と考えられている。琉球開闢の伝説に関わる御嶽、三山時代の旧跡、村落のノロ殿内、北山監守時代の墓などが主な巡拝地である。「東御廻り」と同様に、巡礼することで祖先の霊に感謝し祖霊との結びつきをより緊密なものにしようとする精神世界の習わしである。神拝みの時期は、旧暦の8月から10月頃までの農閑期で、祖神たちもこのころ天下りして回遊すると信じられている。

百按司墓（第一尚氏系北山監守などが埋葬されていると推定されている）（今帰仁村運天）
Mumujana-*baka* (It is estimated that Hokuzan-*kanshu* a member of the First Sho clan, and others are buried there),(Unten, Nakijin Village)

(13) Nakijin-*nubui* (Nakijin-*umaai*)

In contrast to *Agari-umaai*, Nakijin-*nubui* is a pilgrimage to sacred and historic sites inside and outside of Nakijin Castle, also known as Nakijin-*umaai*. While the *Agari-umaai* originated as a national event, Nakijin-*umaai* is said to have originated in the private sector, and was considered a must-perform event for all *munchu*. It is said that the Amamikiyo tribe carved out Hokuzan, and Nakijin Castle became an object of worship. The origin of this event is not known, but it is thought to be due to the fact that many of the royal families have their roots in the former Hokuzan Kingdom, which includes the islands of Iheya and Izena, the birthplace of the First and Second Sho Dynasties, and Nakijin, where its capital was located. The main sites of pilgrimage are *utaki*, which is related to the legend of the founding of Ryukyu, old sites from the Sanzan period, ruins of *noro* houses in the villages, and old tombs in the period when the Hokuzan supervisor was established. Like *agari-umaai*, it is a spiritual practice to thank the ancestral spirits and make a closer connection with them through pilgrimage. The god worshipping period is from August to October of the lunar calendar, which is the "off-season for farming," and it is believed that the ancestral gods descend from heaven and migrate around this time.

(14) キジムナー

　沖縄本島と周辺で伝承されている伝説上の妖怪で、古木に住みついているといわれる樹木の精霊である。地域によって「ブナガヤ」「アカガンター」などとも呼ばれる。人から恐れられることはあまりなく「体中が真っ赤な子ども」、「赤髪の子ども」、「赤い顔の子ども」、「長髪で全身毛だらけ」などの姿で現われるといわれる。男女の区別があり、大人になって結婚し子どもを産んで家族連れで出現することもあるとされる。魚の目が好物で、仲良くなれば漁師の舟に同乗して漁を手伝うが、捕れた魚は必ず片目がないという。夕食時には竈（かまど）の火を借りに来たり、年の瀬には一緒に過ごすなど、人間とは「ご近所」的な存在であるという伝承が多い。人間と敵対することは殆どないが、住み処の老木を切ったりしてひとたび恨みを買えば、家畜を全滅させたり海で船を沈めて溺死させるなど、徹底的に祟られるといわれる。キジムナーに気に入られた家は繁栄し、嫌われた家は滅びると伝えられている。

キジムナーが住んでいそうな古くて大きなガジュマル（南風原町神里）
An old, large banyan tree that looks like a *kijimunaa* might live there (Kamisato, Haebaru Town)

(14) *Kijimunaa*

Kijimunaa is a legendary specter handed down in and around the main island of Okinawa, and is said to be a tree spirit that lives in old trees. Depending on the region, they are also called *Bunagaya* or *Aka-gantaa*. They are not often feared by people, and are said to appear as "children with bright red bodies," "children with red hair," "children with red faces," or "children with long hair and hair growing all over their bodies". It is said that there is a distinction between male and female, and that when they grow up, they get married, have children, and sometimes the whole family appears together. They like the eyes of fish, and if they get along well with the fishermen, they will ride with them on their boats to help them fish, but it is said that the fish they catch are always missing one eye. Many legends say that they are "neighbors" with humans, coming to borrow the fire of the cooking stove at dinner time and spending time together at the end of the year. It is said that *kijimunaa* are rarely hostile to humans, but if you cut down old trees where *kijimunaa* live, they are said to thoroughly haunt you by wiping out your livestock or sinking your boat at sea and drowning you. It is said that a house that is favored by *kijimunaa* will prosper, while one that is disliked will perish.

(15) 空手 (からて)、古武術（こぶじゅつ）

沖縄県無形文化財「沖縄の空手・古武術」保持者の故・仲里周五郎の直弟子、伊福文徳師範（沖縄少林琉）。（八重瀬町具志頭出身）
Master Ifuku Buntoku (Okinawa Shorin Ryu) is a direct disciple of the late Shugoro Nakazato, holder of the Okinawa Prefecture Intangible Cultural Property "Karate and *Kobujutu* of Okinawa" (From Gushichan, Yaese Town)

　空手は武器を一切使わず、素手のみで護身をはかる武道である。琉球古来の武術「手」と中国伝来の「拳法」が融合し、発展したものといわれる。王国時代、空手は門外不出として秘密裏に行われ、決しておおっぴらに教えることはなく、夜陰に乗じて密かに行うことが常であった。「空手に先手なし」と言われるように、形の動作はすべて「受け」から始まり、技にしてもむき出しの闘争心は極力避ける工夫がみられるといわれる。尚真王（1477～1526)による中央集権化政策と1609年の薩摩藩による琉球侵攻。空手が沖縄で顕著に発達したのはこの2度にわたる禁武政策が時代的背景にあったというのが定説だが、確証はない。第二次世界大戦後は、米国軍人によって国際的に普及発展し、諸流派の海外進出も盛んになっている。2021年夏に行われた東京オリンピックで空手競技が初めて採用され、「空手発祥の地・沖縄」出身の喜友名諒選手が金メダルを獲得した。彼の快挙は、いろんな不条理の中にある沖縄県民に勇気と希望を与えた。現在、世界に1億3000万人の空手愛好家がおり、スポーツとしての空手の注目度は高まりつつある一方、沖縄では後継者不足も深刻となっている。沖縄県は、2022年の日本復帰50年に合わせ、沖縄空手のユネスコ無形文化遺産登録を目指している。

　古武術は手に何らかの武器や武具を持って行う沖縄伝統の武術。鎌や杖、船の櫂（かい）など日常の民具を使用し、空手とともに護身術として普及した。棒、サイ、ヌンチャク、トゥンファー、カイ（櫂）、鎌などの武術がある。1997年に、「沖縄の空手・古武術」が県の無形文化財に指定された。

(15) Karate, *Kobujutsu*

Karate is a martial art that uses only bare hands for self-defense without using any weapons. It is said to have developed from the fusion of the ancient martial arts of Ryukyu (*tii*) and China (*kempou*). In the days of the kingdoms, karate was practiced in secret and was not allowed to be seen outside the gates, and it was never openly taught, but was usually done secretly in the shadows of the night. As the saying goes, "there is no first move in karate," all *kata* movements begin with *uke*, and it is said that even in the art of fighting, the artist avoids the bare fighting spirit as much as possible. The centralization of power by King Sho Shin (1477-1526) and the invasion of Ryukyu Kingdom by the Satsuma Domain in 1609 led to the development of karate in Okinawa. It is theorized that the development of karate in Okinawa was due to these two policies, but there is no proof of this. After World War II, karate was popularized and developed internationally by U.S. military personnel, and various schools began to expand overseas. In the summer of 2021, the Tokyo Olympics adopted karate for the first time, and Kiyuna Ryo, from "Okinawa, the birthplace of karate," won the gold medal. His accomplishment gave courage and hope to the Okinawans who are in the midst of various absurdities. Today, there are 130 million karate enthusiasts in the world, and karate as a sport is gaining more and more attention, but in Okinawa, there is a serious shortage of successors. Okinawa Prefecture is aiming to register Okinawan karate as a UNESCO Intangible Cultural Heritage in time for the 50th anniversary of Okinawa's return to Japan in 2022.

Kobujutsu is a traditional Okinawan martial art that is performed with some kind of weapon or armor(weapon-like) in hand. Using daily folk tools such as sickles, canes, and boat paddles, it became popular as a self-defense technique along with karate. There are martial arts using sticks, *sai* (a weapon with two or three prongs), *nunchaku*, *tunfaa* (40-50cm-long, rectangular stick with a grip), paddles and sickles, etc. In 1997, Okinawan karate and *kobujutsu* were designated as "intangible cultural assets" of the prefecture.

(16) 組踊り（くみおどり）

組踊りは玉城朝薫によって創作された沖縄の伝統的な歌劇で、琉球王国の国劇と呼ばれている。1719 年に尚敬王の冊封のために首里城を訪れた冊封使を歓待する目的で上演されたのが最初である。組踊りには、朝薫が江戸上りの時に見聞した日本の能楽や歌舞伎などの様式が取り入れられている。琉球の歴史や説話などを題材とした物語に、三線や琉球舞踊を融合した。台詞には琉球古語が使用され、独自の琉球芸能が生まれた。組踊りは現在でも浦添市の「国立劇場おきなわ」などで上演される。
【組踊り（口絵 3-16、P3 参照】

(16) *Kumi-odori*

Kumi-odori is a traditional Okinawan opera created by Tamagusuku Choukun (1684～1734), and is called the national drama of the Ryukyu Kingdom. It was first performed in 1719 to welcome the *sappuu-shi* who came to Shuri Castle for the appointment of King Sho Kei. The *kumi-odori* incorporates the styles of Japanese *Noh* and *Kabuki*, which Choukun saw and heard when he was in Edo. The stories were based on Ryukyu history and tales, and were combined with *sanshin* and Ryukyu dance. Old Ryukyuan languages were used for the dialogues, and a unique Ryukyuan performing art was born. The *kumi-odori* is still performed at the National Theater Okinawa in Urasoe City and other places.
【*Kumi-odori*(Frontispiece 3-16, See page 3)】

(17) 琉歌（りゅうか）

琉歌は主に沖縄諸島および奄美群島で歌われ、宮古諸島や八重山諸島では不定型の短詩型歌謡が歌われたが、何れも叙情短詩型の歌謡である。日本本土の和歌と同様に「ウタ」ともいわれるが、奄美群島では主に「島唄」と称される。琉歌は古くからあり、沖縄語（ウチナーグチ）で三線（サンシン）

に乗せて歌うのが特徴。内容としては、その土地の自然や植物、風俗、恋愛、社会的事象などである。和歌（31音）や俳句（17音）と違い、基本的には「八・八・八・六」の30音から成り、「サンパチロク」ともいわれる。民間歌謡や琉球古典音楽の多くがこの形式で歌われる。

　北谷モウシ、吉屋チルー、恩納ナビィは琉球の三大女流歌人と称される。北谷モウシは「絶世の美声の持ち主」の唄者で、「空を飛んでいる鳥もその美声に聴き惚れて、しばらく羽を休めて歌を聴いた」という伝説がある。読谷山間切久良波（現・恩納村山田）出身の吉屋チルーは8歳の時、貧しさゆえに那覇の遊郭「吉屋」に遊女として売られたが、一人の恋人を想い続けて絶食し18歳で果てた薄幸の歌人。恩納ナビィは、ダイナミックで自由奔放な表現で恋を歌った女流歌人として有名である。

恩納ナビィの歌碑（写真中央の右奥に恩納岳が見える）（恩納村恩納）
Un'na Nabii's Song Monument (On'na-*dake* can be seen in the back right of the center of the photo) (On'na, On'na Village)

(17) *Ryuka*

Ryuka were mainly sung on the Islands of Okinawa and Amami, while indefinite short poem-type songs were sung in the Miyako and the Yaeyama Islands, all of which are lyrical short poem-type songs. Like *waka* in mainland Japan, it is also called "*uta*," but in the Amami Islands it is mainly called *shima-uta*. *Ryuka* have been around for a long time, and are characterized by Okinawan (*uchina-guchi*) lyrics sung on the *sanshin*, and are about local nature, plants, customs, love, and social events. Unlike *waka* (31 syllables) and *haiku* (17 syllables), it basically consists of 30 syllables (8, 8, 8, 6) and is also called *san-pachi-roku*. Many folk songs and Ryukyu classical music are sung in this form.

Chatan Moushi, Yoshiya Chiruu, and Un'na Nabii are considered the three greatest female poets of the Ryukyu Islands. Legend has it that Chatan Moushi was a singer with "an immensely beautiful voice" and that even the birds flying in the sky were so fascinated by her beautiful voice that they rested their wings for a while to listen to her singing. Yoshiya Chiruu, a native of Kuraha, Yomitan *magiri* (now Yamada, On'na Village), was sold as a prostitute to a brothel in Naha called "Yoshiya" at the age of eight due to poverty. However, despite being a prostitute, she was a thin-skinned poetess who fasted for the sake of one lover and died at the age of 18. Un'na Nabii is famous as a female poet who sang about love with dynamic and free-spirited expression.

(18) 琉舞（りゅうぶ）

　琉球舞踊は、琉球、沖縄県内で継承されている舞踊の総称で、俗に琉舞とも称される。歌舞伎舞踊や上方舞、京舞と並び、琉球舞踊は2009年に重要無形文化財に指定されている。古来、琉球舞踊は神女らが神事・祭事の中でオモロ（古謡）を歌いながら舞った祭祀舞踊であったとみられている。この祭祀舞踊が長い歴史の中で時代に応じ、日本芸能や東南アジアなど周辺地域の舞踊の影響を受けつつ発展し、首里城や識名園・御茶屋御殿などの離宮で披露される宮廷芸能となったと考えられている。近世に入ると、首里王府は踊奉行（おどりぶぎょう）という奉行を設け、首里士族の子弟による踊り手・演奏者が任命された。冊封使をもてなすための「御冠船踊り」（おかんせんおどり）と呼ばれる

芸能が今日で言う「古典舞踊」である。沖縄県誕生（1879 年）によって庶民の民謡や生活などを題材にした踊りが作られるようになった。これが「雑踊り」（ぞうおどり）であり、アップテンポな琉球民謡が取り入れられた。さらに明治・大正期に入ると、芝居小屋の中で男性の役者らによって、大衆的な「雑踊り」が発達して「創作舞踊」が生まれた。舞台で演じられるこれらの舞踊の他に、「獅子舞」や「エイサー」、「祭祀舞踊」など、各地で伝承されている「民俗舞踊」がある。
【琉舞（口絵 3-18、P3 参照）】

(18) *Ryubu* (Ryukyuan dance)

Ryukyuan dance is a general term for dances inherited in Ryukyu and Okinawa Prefecture, and is also commonly called *ryubu*. Along with *Kabuki* dance, *Kamigata* dance, and Kyoto dance, Ryukyu dance was designated as an important intangible cultural property in 2009. In ancient times, Ryukyuan dance is thought to have been a ritual dance performed by divine maidens while singing *omoro* (ancient songs) during rituals and ceremonies. It is thought that this ritual dance developed over a long period of time, influenced by Japanese arts and dances from Southeast Asia and other regions, and became a courtly art form performed at Shuri Castle, Shikina-*en* Garden, Uchaya-*udun* Palace, and other remote palaces. In the early modern period, the Shuri royal government appointed a magistrate called *odori-bugyo* and promoted children of Shuri warriors as dancers and performers. The entertainment called *okansen-odori* to entertain the *sappuu-shi* (envoys from China) is what we call "Ryukyuan classical dance" today. With the birth of Okinawa Prefecture (1879), dances based on the folk songs and daily lives of the common people began to be created. This was called *zou-odori*, and it incorporated up-tempo Ryukyu folk songs. Furthermore, in the Meiji and Taisho periods, *sousaku-buyou* (creative dance) was born in theaters developed by male actors who developed the popular *zou-odori*. In addition to these dances performed on the stage, there are also "folk dances" that have been handed down in various regions, such as the *shishi-mai* (Lion dance), *eisaa*, and "Ritual dance". 【*Ryubu*(Frontispiece 3-18, See page 4)】

(19) 琉装（りゅうそう）

琉球王国時代における成人男女の民族衣装で、方言で「ウチナースガイ」といい、着物は「チン」と呼ばれる。琉球王国は、薩摩藩の侵攻後は江戸幕府の支配下になった。この時は同時に、中国の明・清国の冊封国でもあった。その時期に日中間の文化をとり続けて、日本の和服と中国の漢服の特徴や着方、織り方を融合し、独自の服装文化が生まれた。琉装は亜熱帯の気候風土に合わせてゆったりした縫い方となっており、いろいろな形状がある。和服と違い太帯で固定せずに着られ、下着の中に押し込んで着る女性の着付け方は「ウシンチー」と呼ばれる。肌と着衣との間にたっぷりと隙間ができて風通しが良く、暑い沖縄の風土に適した着付けだが、労働する女性たちには不向きで細い帯を用いる。薩摩藩の侵攻（1609 年）以降、本土の和服が流入して琉球王国内は服装乱立となったが、1800 年代から琉球国王による「服装規定」が幾度も発出された。それによって地域や身分によって服装が強制的に規定され、それぞれ独特な着用方法が決められた。基本的に身分の高い者だけが絹製の衣装が許された。【琉装（口絵 3-19、P4 参照）】

(19) *Ryusou* (*uchina-sugai*)

This was the national costume of adult men and women during the Ryukyu Kingdom era, and is called *uchina-sugai* in dialect, and also the Okinawan kimono is called *chin*. The Ryukyu Kingdom came under the control of the Edo Shogunate after the invasion by the Satsuma Domain in 1609. At the same time, it was also under the control of the Ming and Qing Dynasties in China. During this period, it continued to take culture from Japan and China, and fused the characteristics, wearing styles and weaving methods of Japanese kimono and Chinese traditional clothing to create a unique clothing culture. Ryukyuan costumes (*ryusou*) are sewn loosely to suit the subtropical climate, and come in a variety of shapes. Unlike in mainland kimono, it can be worn without being secured with a thick *obi* (belt), and the women's way of dressing by pushing it into their underwear is called *ushinchii*. This style of dressing is suitable for the hot climate of Okinawa, as it leaves plenty of space between the skin and the garment, allowing for good air circulation. However, it is not suitable for working women, so a thin *obi* is used. After the invasion by the Satsuma clan in 1609, Japanese kimono entered the Ryukyu Kingdom, and clothing became disorderly. So, from the 1800s, the King of Ryukyu issued "dress regulations" over and over again. As a result of this, clothing was forcibly regulated according to region and status, and each had its own unique way of wearing it. Basically, only those of high status were allowed to wear silk costumes. 【*Ryusou* (Frontispiece 3-19, See page 4)】

(20) 芭蕉布（ばしょうふ）

　イトバショウの繊維で織った布を芭蕉布といい、一反の着物を織るのに 200 本の糸芭蕉が必要とされる。1546 年という古い明確な記録があることから、芭蕉園は王府の管理下にあり、約 500 年前から良質の芭蕉布が織られていたことを示している。15 〜 16 世紀の交易が盛んな時代、芭蕉布は中国への貢ぎ物にも登場した。17 世紀以降の江戸上りの際には献上品として贈答され、当時の絵図を見ると、ほとんどの随行員が芭蕉布を身につけている。原料の栽培から糸績みまでの製糸工程と、布にでき上がるまでの全行程を含め、地元ですべて手作業によって行われる沖縄特有の織物である。空気のように軽やかで「幻の布」と呼ばれる芭蕉布は、トンボの羽のように透けるほど軽いと評される。さらりとした肌触りが特徴で、風を通す心地よい生地は、高温多湿の沖縄で暮らす人々にとってはなくてはならないものであった。沖縄戦が激しくなるまでは沖縄各地で織られ、夏衣としてあらゆる階層の人々に愛用された。かつて木綿や絹が贅沢品とされていた頃は、冬でも芭蕉衣を重ね着したという。戦争末期以降、沖縄を占領した米軍によって「蚊の繁殖を防止するため」として多くのイトバショウが切り倒され、絶滅の危機に瀕した。現在では「芭蕉布の里」として知られている大宜味村喜如嘉を中心に生産され、「喜如嘉の芭蕉布」として国の重要無形文化財（工芸技術）に指定されている。【喜如嘉の芭蕉布（口絵 3-20、P4 参照）】

(20) *Bashou-fu* (*Bashou* cloth)

　Bashou-fu is a cloth woven from the fiber of the *ito-bashou* plants, and it is said to take 200 *ito-bashou* plants to make one *tan* of kimono (one *tan* is one length of kimono cloth). The fact that there is a clear record as old as 1546 indicates that the *Ito-bashou* garden was under the control of the royal government and that good quality *bashou-fu* was woven there for about 500 years. Between the 15th and 16th, during which Okinawa was actively engaged in trading, *bashou-fu* was taken to China as tribute. From the 17th century onward, it was presented as a gift when Okinawan magistrates went up to Edo (now Tokyo), and illustrations from that time show that most of the attendants were dressed in *bashou-fu*. *Bashou-fu* is a unique Okinawan textile that is made entirely by hand in the local area, including the entire process from the cultivation of raw materials to the spinning of yarn, and all the way to the finished cloth. Light as air, *bashou-fu* is called "fantastic cloth," and is described as being so light that it is transparent like the wings of a dragonfly. The fabric, which is characterized by its light and smooth texture and allows the breeze to flow through it, was indispensable to the people living in Okinawa, a hot and humid place. Until the Battle of Okinawa intensified, it was woven in many parts of Okinawa and was used as summer clothing by people of all classes. In the past, when cotton and silk were considered luxury items, people wore *bashou-fu* garments in layers even in winter. After the end of the war, many *ito-bashou* were cut down by the U.S. troops who occupied Okinawa "to prevent mosquitoes from breeding" and were in danger of extinction. Today, it is produced mainly in Kijoka, Ogimi Village, which is known as the "home of *bashou-fu*," and is designated as an important intangible cultural property (craft technique) by the government as "Kijoka'*no-bashou-fu*".

【*Bashou-fu* in Kijoka(Frontispiece 3-20, See page 4)】

(21) 琉球絣（りゅうきゅうかすり）

　近世の琉球では、王府の政策により日本から綿花栽培や養蚕技術が導入され、絣などの織物技術が確立した。17 世紀前半に租税として貢納する制度が導入されると、米の代わりに宮古・八重山では上布が、久米島では紬が貢納布として納付させられた。王府は市場での評価を得るため、図案帳を手本にしてより精緻な布を織らせ、王府や薩摩への貢納品とした。この方策は染織技術を発展させたが、同時に島々の女性たちは苛酷なまでの労働を強いられることになった。

　絣の起源は 7 ～ 8 世紀にインドで発生し、シャムやジャワに伝播し、沖縄に入ったのはこれらの国々と交易していた 14 ～ 15 世紀頃である。沖縄に入った絣はまったく独自の発展をみせ、単純ですっきりした美しさが特徴といわれる。繊維には木綿・麻・絹が使われ、図柄は日常生活から取り入れられている。約 600 種という多彩でさわやかな清涼感を誘う図柄は、琉球王朝時代から伝わる「御絵図帳」（みえずちょう）を元にしている。それに加え今日では、職人達が現代の感覚を取り入れて作り上げている。琉球絣は、薩摩絣、久留米絣など日本の絣のルーツとなった。琉球王朝時代から絣の生産地と知られた南風原町は、たゆまぬ技術導入・改良や職人達の努力を積み重ねた。現在、「琉球絣」の殆どが南風原町で作られている。【南風原町の琉球絣（口絵 3-21、P4 参照)】

(21) Ryukyu-*kasuri*

In the Ryukyu Islands during the early modern period, cotton cultivation and sericulture techniques were introduced from Japan through the policies of the royal government, and textile techniques including *kasuri* were established. When the system of paying tribute as taxes was introduced in the first half of the 17th century, instead of rice, *joufu* was used in Miyako and Yaeyama, and *tsumugi* was used in Kumejima as tribute cloth. In order to gain a good reputation in the market, the royal government had more elaborate cloths woven based on the design books, which were then delivered as tribute to the royal government and the Satsuma domain. This strategy developed the art of weaving and dyeing, but it also forced the women of the islands to work harder and harder.

Kasuri originated in India in the 7th and 8th centuries and spread to Siam and Java, and entered Okinawa around the 14th and 15th centuries when Okinawa was trading with these countries. The *kasuri* that came to Okinawa developed in a completely unique way and is said to be characterized by its simplicity and clean beauty. Cotton, linen, and silk were used as fibers, and the patterns were taken from everyday life. The diverse and refreshingly cool designs, which number about 600, are based on the *Miezu-chou* (design books), which has been handed down since the Ryukyu Kingdom. In addition to this, today's artisans have incorporated modern sensibilities into their creations. Ryukyu-*kasuri* has become the root of Japanese-*kasuri* such as Satsuma-*kasuri* and Kurume-*kasuri*. Since the days of the Ryukyu Kingdom, the town of Haebaru has been known for its production of *kasuri*, and in this town, artisans have been working tirelessly to introduce and improve new technologies. Today, most of the Ryukyu-*kasur*i is made in Haebaru Town.

【Ryukyu-*kasuri* in Haebaru Town (Frontispiece 3-21, See page 4)】

(22) 紅型（びんがた）

　沖縄の代表的な染め物である紅型は、王族や士族の礼服として着用された。身分や年齢によって模様の種類や、大小、地色の違いがあった。模様の大きなものや、着物に一つの連続模様がつけられたものは、王族や上級士族の女性に限って着用された。中位の士族は中柄の模様、その下位は藍型などと決まっていた。色に関しては、王族の衣装は黄色地、貴族は水色が用いられた。一般庶民は縞か絣で、しかも縦縞・経絣に限られていたが、「組踊り」で使われる衣装は例外で、大柄の鎖模様が用いられている。

　「紅」（びん）は色全体を意味し、「型」（かた）は様々な模様を指しており、その起源は 13 世紀頃と推定されている。紅型の特徴的な魅力は、鮮明な色彩、大胆な配色、図形の素朴さが挙げられ、中国的な豪華さと日本的な優雅さを持ち合わせている。着用が王族・士族に限られていたので、1879 年の廃藩置県以後、紅型は急速に衰退していった。【紅型（口絵 3-22、P4 参照）】

(22) *Bingata*

　Bingata, the most representative of Okinawa's traditional dyed textiles, was worn as formal wear by royalty and samurai. Depending on the status and age of the person, there were different types of patterns, large and small, and different ground colors. A textile with large designs or a single continuous pattern was exclusively for the royal family and women of the upper samurai class. Mid-sized patterns were meant for the middle samurai class, indigo color for the classes lower than that, and so forth. As for colors, yellow background was used for royal costumes and light blue for nobles. The ordinary people of Okinawa were allowed to wear kimono with simple cross stripes or stripes, for which only the warp was dyed, but the costumes used in the *kumi-odori* (Okinawa Opera) were an exception, with large chain patterns.

　The word *bin* refers to the entire color, and *kata(gata)* refers to the various patterns, which are estimated to have originated around the 13th century. The characteristic appeal of *bingata* is the vivid colors, bold color schemes, and simplicity of the patterns, combining Chinese luxury with Japanese elegance. Since the wearing of *bingata* was limited to royalty and samurai, it rapidly declined after the Haihan-chiken in 1879.
【*Bingata*(Frontispiece 3-22, See page 4)】

(23) シーサー

　石や瓦、漆喰などで作られた石獅子や、正月や盆などで演舞される獅子舞の獅子。同じルーツを持つ両者だが、沖縄ではどちらも「シーサー」と呼ばれ、それぞれ役割は異なる。シーサーは紀元前のスフィンクスにルーツを持つといわれる。中国と琉球の交流が盛んになった 13 ～ 15 世紀頃に、シルクロード経由で中国から伝わったものといわれ、沖縄の地はそのルートの中で重要な役割を果たしていた。その姿は変遷しながら沖縄のシーサー、神社のこま犬へと伝播された。

(23) *Shiisaa*

　Stone lions made of stone, tiles, plaster, etc., and lions of the lion dance performed at New Year and *bon* festivals. Although they are thought to have the same roots, both are called *shiisaa* in Okinawa, but they play different roles. *Shiisaa* is said to have its roots in the Egyptian Sphinx, which was created in B.C. *Shiisaa* is said to have been introduced from China via the Silk Road around the 13th to 15th century, when exchanges between China and Ryukyu became active, and the land of Okinawa played an important role in this route. The figure was transformed and propagated to *shiisaa* in Okinawa and *koma-inu* in shrines.

①石獅子（いしじし）

　沖縄では門扉に 2 つ並んだ陶器製や、民家の屋根に座している瓦や漆喰でできた石獅子をよく見かける。漆喰で作られたシーサーが普及したのは、家を作る際に余った瓦や漆喰で職人が作ったのが始まりと言われている。屋根に獅子を据えて魔除けとする習俗には「ヒーゲーシ」（火返し）と「ヤナカジゲーシ」（悪霊返し）の目的がある。それ以前のシーサーは石（琉球石灰岩）でできており、集落の守り神や魔除けとして集落入り口に置かれた。魔除け獅子で建造物とかかわりのあるものでは、1477 年に首里城の正門・歓会門が築造された時、正門の両脇に添えたのが始まりとされている。玉陵の屋根や墓室内部

御茶屋御殿のシーサー（那覇市首里崎山町）
Shiisaa at Uchaya-*udun*
(Shuri Sakiyama-*cho*, Naha City)

にも見られる。建造物と無関係なものでは、1677 年（尚貞王代）の建造と思われる御茶屋御殿の石獅子や 1689 年の建造といわれる八重瀬町富盛の石彫大獅子が古い。石獅子は沖縄本島や周辺離島では確認できるが、宮古・八重山の地域では見られない。

① *Shiisaa* (stone lion)

  In Okinawa, it is common to see two ceramic *shiisaa* lined up on a gate, or sitting on the roof of a private house, made of tiles or plaster. It is said that plastered *shiisaa* first became popular when craftsmen made *shiisaa* out of leftover tiles and plaster when building houses. The custom of placing a *shiisaa* on the roof has two purposes: *hii-geeshi* (to protect the house from fire) and *yanakaji-geeshi* (to keep evil spirits away).Before that, *shiisaa* were made of stone (Ryukyu limestone) and were placed at the entrance of the village as a guardian deity or to ward off evil. As for the *shiisaa* to ward off evil spirits that are related to constructions, it is said that they were first placed on both sides of the main gate (Kankai-*mon*) of Shuri Castle when it was built in 1477. *Shiisaa* can also be found on the roofs of royal tombs (Tama-*udun*) and inside tomb chambers. The older one that are not related to constructions are the *shiisaa* in Uchaya-*udun,* which is thought to have been built in 1677 (during the reign of King Sho Tei), and the large *shiisaa* made of Ryukyu limestone in Tomori, Yaese Town, which is said to have been built in 1689. *Shiisaa* can be found on the main island of Okinawa and the surrounding islands, but not in the regions of Miyako and Yaeyama.

②獅子舞（ししまい）

　獅子舞はお正月や晴れの日に、獅子頭を頭にかぶって舞う民俗芸能の一つで日本各地にある。いつ頃から演じられたかは不明だが、中国から伝わってきたといわれ、沖縄では主に旧暦 6 月から 8 月にかけての豊年祭や旧盆に行われる。百獣の王である獅子はその威力が信じられ、獅子を舞わすことによって悪霊を祓い幸福の世を招来し、五穀豊穣と地域の繁栄がもたらされると考えられている。獅子舞が最も盛んに行われるのは稲の収穫を終えた村遊び（豊年祭）の時で、それは日頃、村を守ってくれた獅子に対する村人の感謝の気持ちといわれている。通常、獅子は沖縄本島や周辺離島では 1 頭獅子だが、宮古・八重山諸島では雌雄の 2 頭獅子である。沖縄各地の獅子は、王朝時代には首里王府から授けられたと言われ、演舞にはそれぞれ特徴がある。

獅子舞
Shishi-mai(Lion dance)

② *Shishi-mai* (Lion dance)

Lion dance *(shishi-mai)* is a folkloric art in which a lion's head is placed on a person's head and danced on New Year's Day or other happy occasions, and is found in many parts of Japan. It is not known when it was first performed, but it is said to have been introduced from China. In Okinawa, it is mainly performed from June to August of the lunar calendar during harvest festivals and lunar *obon* festivals. The lion, the king of a hundred beasts, is believed to be powerful, and it is believed that the lion dance will exorcise evil spirits and bring about a world of happiness, a bountiful harvest, and prosperity for the community. The lion dance is most popular during the village festival after the rice harvest, and it is said that this is the villagers' way of expressing their gratitude to the lions that protect their village on a daily basis. Usually, the lion dance is performed with a single lion on the main island of Okinawa and the surrounding islands, but in Miyako and Yaeyama Islands, it is performed with two lions, one male and one female. The lions of the lion dance in various parts of Okinawa are said to have been given by the Shuri royal government during the dynastic period, and each performance has its own characteristics.

(24) ウェーキ（ウェーキー）

船越上門（南城市船越）
Hunakoshi Uwiijo(Hunakoshi, Nanjo City)

ウェーキとは富豪のことで、土地をはじめとする財産を多く所有している。ウェーキは自ら農業経営者であり、土地の一部を小作に出したり、金銭や家畜を貸し付けたりした。ウェーキ経営で借金などの代償に提供される労働のうち、住み込みで衣食住の一切を依存して労働するのは「イリチリ」と呼ばれ、決められた特定の日時にのみ労働するのは「シカマ」と称される。従属度が強い「イリチリ」は、身売り同然の形態であり、漁業における糸満売り（身売り百姓）や遊郭におけるジュリ（遊女）と類似している。「グスクマ・ナーカ」（浦添間切城間村）、「イズルン・アサト」（中城間切伊舎堂村）、「ゲンガ・ウェーキ」（名護間切源河村）、「フナコシ・ウィージョウ」（玉城間切船越村）は、琉球の「四大ウェーキ」と称された。

(24) *Uweeki* (*Uweekii*)

Uweeki is a wealthy person who owns a lot of land and other property. *Uweekii* was a farmer himself, giving out part of their land to small farmers and lending money and livestock to them. Among the labor offered in exchange for debt or other compensation, work that is live-in and dependent on the *uweekii* for all food, clothing, and shelter was called *irichiri,* while work that is done only on specific, set dates and times was called *shikama. Irichiri,* with its strong subordination, was a form of human trafficking, similar to the Ichiman-*ui* (peddling peasant) in the fishing industry and the *juri* (prostitute) in the brothel. Gusukuma Naaka (Gusukuma village, Urasoe *magiri*), Izurun Asato (Ishadou village, Nakagusuku *magiri*), Genga *Uweeki* (Genga village, Nago *magiri*), and Hunakoshi Uwiijyo (Hunakoshi village, Tamagusuku *magiri*) were known as the "Four Great *Uweeki*" of Ryukyu.

(25) 毛遊び（もーあしび）

　かつて沖縄で広く行われていた男女交際の一方法である。主として村外れの原野（モー）がその場所だったので「モーアシビ」と呼ばれ、ほぼ毎晩おこなわれた。参加資格は男女とも一人前とされる 14,15 歳から結婚するまでで、結婚すると参加しなくなる。村内の男女のみで構成するのが本来の形だが、幾つかの村の連合で行うこともあった。三線を弾きながら、男女の掛け合いをしたり踊ったりして楽しい夜を過ごした。毛遊びでの選択で結婚に至る例が多いが、毛遊びへの参加は認めるが結婚相手は親が決めるケースもあった。特に士族系は結婚を親が決めたので、娘の毛遊びへの参加は認めなかった。明治後半から昭和 10 年（1935 年）にかけて、風紀上問題があるという理由で警察や教育界からの圧力が強化され、次第に消滅していった。

毛遊びの名所「アカバンター」（南城市手登根）
Akabantaa, a famous place for *mou-ashibi*
(Tedokon, Nanjo City)

(25) *Mou-ashibi* (night parties among young men and women in the field)

　This is one of the group dating methods that used to be widely practiced in Okinawa. It was mainly held in the wilderness (*mou*) on the outskirts of the village, so it was called *mou-ashibi* and was held almost every night. Both men and women participated from the age of 14 or 15, when they were considered to be on their own, until they got married, after which they stopped participating. The original form of the parties was for men and women from within the village, but it was also sometimes held by a coalition of several villages. Men and women danced and enjoyed conversation the night away while playing the *sanshin* (a three-stringed Okinawan folk instrument). In many cases, the choices made at the *mou-ashibi* led to marriage, but in other cases, parents decided who to marry, although they allowed their children to participate in the *mou-ashibi*. Especially in samurai families, parents decided who to marry and did not allow their daughters to participate in the *mou-ashibi*. From the latter half of the Meiji era to the 10th year of the Showa era, pressure from the police and educational circles intensified on the grounds that it was a problem for public morals, and it gradually disappeared.

(26) 針突き (はじち)

　ハジチとは、琉球王国時代から明治末期まで沖縄で広く行われていた成人女性限定の刺青であり、沖縄固有の風習である。成人女性の儀礼として指から手の甲、肘にかけて施された。7 ～ 10 歳の間で始め、15 歳から結婚直前までに完成した。紋様は地方によって微妙な違いがあり、それぞれの紋様には太陽や矢など様々な意味が込められていた。ハジチは既婚者の証であり、「ハジチのない女性はあの世で成仏できない」や「ハジチはニライカナイへの通行手形」などの意味合いが込められていたという。記録が残るのは 1534 年に冊封正使として琉球王国を訪れた

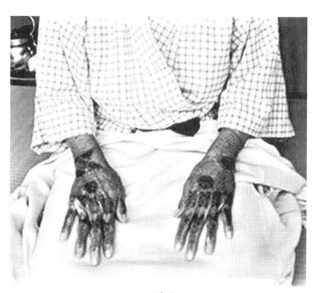

ハジチ
Hajichi

陳侃（ちんかん）が後に記した『使琉球録』にさかのぼる。1899 年、日本政府によって入れ墨禁止令が出たが、その後も隠れてハジチを入れた多くの女性たちが逮捕された。沖縄ではハジチを施す者が昭和の初期までみられ、1980 年代まで生存者がいた。台湾原住民族の複数の民族にもタトゥーの風習があった。沖縄と同様に施術が規制され一時は途切れたが、原住民族の権利運動の高まりなどにより再び「民族の印」として復活しつつあるといわれる。沖縄では戦後、禁止令が解除されたが、「野蛮な風俗」との烙印は消えず、新たにハジチを入れる人は殆どいなくなった。

(26) *Hajichi*

Hajichi is a tattoo that was widely practiced in Okinawa from the time of the Kingdom of Ryukyu until the end of the Meiji era (1868-1912) for adult women only, and is a custom unique to Okinawa. It was applied from the fingers to the back of the hands and elbows as a ritual for adult women, and was started between the ages of 7 and 10 and completed between the ages of 15 and just before marriage. The patterns differed slightly from region to region, and each pattern had various meanings, such as the sun and arrows. It is said that the *hajichi* was a sign of marriage, and that it also meant that "women who did not have *hajichi* would not be able to attain Buddhahood in the afterlife" or "*hajichi* was passport to *Niraikanai*. Records date back to 1534, when Chen Kan visited the Kingdom of Ryukyu as a main envoy to the Ryukyu Kingdom, and later wrote the *Shi-Ryukyu-Roku* (Records of Envoys). In 1899, a ban on tattoos was imposed by the Japanese government, but even after that, many women were arrested for secretly getting *hajichi*. In Okinawa, the practice of *hajichi* continued until the early Showa period, and there were women with their *hajichi* until the 1980s. Several ethnic groups of Taiwanese aborigines also had tattooing customs. As in Okinawa, tattooing was regulated and temporarily discontinued, but it is said to be making a comeback as a "mark of the people" due to the growing rights movement of the natives. In Okinawa, the prohibition was lifted after the war, but the branding of *hajichi* as a "barbaric custom" remained, and few new people are getting *hajichi* anymore.

(27) 石敢當（いしがんとう）

中国起源の除災招福の石柱で、後には駆邪が目的となった。日本と同じく、石に対する信仰に基づき、災危を除く意味を明示するために「石敢當」と刻んだものといわれ、中国古代の武人名とするのは俗説である。西暦770 年に中国福建省甫田県の県知事が県内の除災や無事繁栄を祈って造立したのが最古とされる。雲南省では、石獅子の胸部に石敢當と刻んで屋根上に置いた。沖縄では、T 字路の突き当たりや道の曲がった場所に立てる。マジムン（魔物）は直進する性質があるため、T 字路や三叉路などの突き当たりに石敢當を設け、魔物の進入を防ぐ。魔物は石敢當に当たると砕け散ってしまうといわれる。沖縄には石敢當以外にも様々な魔除けがあり、よく知られた「シーサー」やススキの葉を結んで作る「サン」などがあり、何れも玄関の両脇に置くことによって魔物の侵入を防御する。石敢當は北海道から日本全国にあるが、沖縄県がダントツに多い。1575 年に建立されたとされる日本最古の石敢當が大分県臼杵市にあるが、何度か立て

泰山石敢當（那覇市首里）
Taizan-*Ishigantou*（Shuri,Naha City）

替えられており、現存のものは 1877 年に立て替えられたものと考えられている。1733 年に作られた久米島にある「泰山石敢當」は県内で最古のものとされている。

(27) *Ishigantou*

This is a stone pillar of Chinese origin used to ward off evil and bring good fortune, but later it was used to ward off evil. As in Japan, it is said that the name *ishigantou* was carved on the stone in order to express the meaning of getting rid of disasters, based on the belief in stones, and it is just a popular belief that *ishigantou* is the name of an ancient Chinese warrior. The oldest *ishigantou* is said to have been in 770 A.D. by the governor of Futian County, Fujian Province, to pray for disaster prevention and prosperity of the county. In Yun'nan Province, China, *ishigantou* was carved into the chest of a stone lion and placed on the roof. In Okinawa, an *ishigantou* is placed at the end of a T-junction or at a bend in the road. Since demons have a tendency to move in a straight line, *ishigantou* is placed at the end of T-junctions and three-way junctions to prevent them from entering. It is said that if a demon hits the stone, it will be shattered. In Okinawa, there are many other types of amulets, including the well-known *shiisaa*, and *san* made by tying silver grass leaves together, which are placed on either side of the entrance to protect against evil. *Ishigantou* can be found all over Japan from Hokkaido, but Okinawa Prefecture has the largest number of them. The oldest *ishigantou* in Japan, said to have been erected in 1575, is located in Usuki City, Oita Prefecture, but it has been rebuilt several times, and the existing one is thought to have been rebuilt in 1877. The Taizan-*ishigantou* in Kume Island, made in 1733, is considered the oldest in the Okinawa prefecture.

(28) 土帝君（トーテークン）

　古代中国の土地関係の神の一種で、3 世紀から村落の守り神とされ、一般に土地神と呼ばれる。台湾では土地公（トティコン）や伯公（パックン）と呼ばれ、他の東南アジア諸国にも現存する。11 世紀から広く信仰されたが、今では農民は農業神、漁民は大漁の神、商人は商売繁盛の神など、それぞれの職業に結びつけられている。各地で功労があった高徳の人が死後に土地神になるとされ、他の一般の神々と性格を異にする。御利益は豊作、健康、村の繁栄が中心である。現在、土帝君の神像はほとんど盗難にあっているが、古像は中国の土地公に酷似しているといわれる。土帝君は現在、南城市佐敷地域に多く見られるが沖縄各地で祀られている。その中でも瀬底島の「瀬底土帝君」は最大規模を保つ礼拝施設で、土帝君信仰をよく保つ代表的な遺構として高く評価されている。中国の土地神の誕生日といわれる旧暦 2 月 2 日を祭日とするところが多く、中国伝来を思わせる証拠の一つである。奄美諸島には土帝君信仰はない。

(28) *Touteikun*

A type of land-related deity in ancient China, it has been regarded as a guardian deity of villages since the 3rd century and is generally referred to as a land deity. In Taiwan, it is called *totikong* or *pakkun*, and it also exists in other Southeast Asian countries. It has been widely worshipped since the 11th century, but nowadays it is associated

土帝君（南城市手登根）
Touteikun（Tedokon, Nanjo City）

with different occupations: farmers with the god of agriculture, fishermen with the god of great catches, and merchants with the god of prosperity. It is said that a person of great virtue who has made meritorious deeds in each area becomes the god of the land after death, which is different in character from other common gods. The main benefits are good harvest, health, and prosperity of the village. Today, most of the statues of the *touteikun* gods have been stolen, but the ancient statues are said to closely resemble the Chinese Land Deity. *Touteikun* is now mostly found in the Sashiki area of Nanjo City, but is also worshipped throughout Okinawa. Among them, Sesoko-*touteikun* on Sesoko Island is the largest worship facility, and is highly regarded as a representative relic that preserves the belief in *touteikun*. In many places, the festival is held on the second day of the second month of the lunar calendar, which is said to be the birthday of the Chinese god of the land. In the Amami Islands, there is no worship of *touteikun*.

(29) ビジュル信仰（びじゅるしんこう）

泡瀬ビジュル（沖縄市泡瀬）
Awase *Bijuru*(Awase,Okinawa City)

　ビジュル信仰とは、「ビジュル」と呼ばれる霊石を祀る習俗。ビジュルは「ビンズル」や「ビンジリ」とも称され、高さ 15cm ～ 1 m くらいの自然石で、人型（ダルマ型）のものが多い。ビジュルを安置した洞穴・石祠・神殿は「ティラ（又はテラ）」とも呼ばれる。一般には旧暦 9 月 9 日を例祭とする。お釈迦様の特に優れた 16 人の弟子は「十六羅漢」と呼ばれるが、賓頭盧（ビンズル）はその中の筆頭である。羅漢とは、「煩悩をすべて断ち切り、最高の境地に達した人（悟りを開いた人）」を指す言葉。本土におけるビンズルは撫で仏で、撫でることで御利益があるとされる。沖縄のビジュルはビンズルの訛りで、仏像ではなく霊石が信仰の対象である。豊作、豊漁、雨乞い、航海安全、健康など、ビジュルに対する祈願の内容は多様である。

(29) *Bijuru* worship

Bijuru worship is the practice of worshipping a sacred stone called a *bijuru*. *Bijuru*, also known as *binjuru* or *binjiri*, is a natural stone about 15cm to 1m high, and is often human-shaped (dharma-shaped). The cave, stone shrine, or temple where the *bijuru* is enshrined is also called a *tira* (or *tera*). The festival is generally held on the 9th day of the 9th lunar month. The sixteen outstanding disciples of Buddha are called the Sixteen *Arhats*, of which *binjuru* is the first. The term *Arhat* refers to "a person who has attained the highest state of enlightenment, having cut off all worldly desires. In the mainland, *binjuru* is a caressing Buddha, and it is believed that stroking it will bring benefits. In Okinawa, *bijuru* is an accent of *binjuru*, and the object of worship is not a Buddha statue but a sacred stone. Various prayers are offered to the *bijuru*, such as for a good harvest, good fishing, rain, safe voyages, and good health.

(30) 首里城周辺の史跡（しゅりじょうしゅうへんのしせき）

①龍潭（りゅうたん）

　1427 年（尚巴志王代）に国相・懐機（かいき）が造った池。1425 年に来琉した冊封使が尚巴志に城北に池を作るように勧めたのが契機となり、懐機を明国に派遣し造園技術を学んで造ったとされている。明国の首都・北京をはじめ中国各地には龍潭池があるという。面積 7,575 ㎡の龍潭は、かつては

魚が多くいたので「魚小堀」（いゆぐむい）とも呼ばれた。ここでは中国皇帝の使者・冊封使を歓待する船遊びの宴も行われた。この人工池・龍潭は幾度も浚渫され、1942年（昭和17年）の工事では市民、学生ら約２万人が勤労奉仕に参加した。当時は沖縄も太平洋戦争勃発以来の非常体制下であったため、この池を養魚池として活用することが目的であった。付近に建てられていた沖縄最古の碑文「安国山樹華木記」（あんこくざんじゅかぼくき）には、「安国山に龍潭を堀り、香りのする木や花を植え、万人が利用できるようにして太平の世のシンボルとして永遠の記念とした」などと記されている。

龍潭の上でカラフルな鯉のぼりが泳ぐ
（2022年５月、那覇市首里）
Colorful carp streamers are swimming over Ryutan, May 2022
(Shuri, Naha City)

(30) Historic sites around Shuri Castle

① Ryutan

This pond was built in 1427 (during the reign of King Sho Hashi) by Kai Ki, the Minister of State. The *sappuushi* (envoys of the Chinese emperor) came to the Ryukyu Kingdom in1425, recommended that Sho Hashi build a pond in the north of the castle, which led to the dispatch of Kai Ki to Ming Dynasty to learn landscaping techniques and build the pond. It is said that there are Ryutan Ponds in Beijing, the capital of the Ming Dynasty, and other places in China. Ryutan, with an area of 7,575 square meters, was once called *Iyugumui* (fish small moat) because of its abundance of fish. The pond was also the site of a boating party to welcome the *sappuushi*. The artificial pond, Ryutan, has been dredged many times before, and about 20,000 citizens and students participated in the service work during the construction in 1942. At the time, Okinawa was also under a state of emergency since the outbreak of the Pacific War, so the purpose was to use this pond as a fishpond. The oldest inscription in Okinawa, Ankokuzan-*jukabokuki*, which was erected in the vicinity of the pond, says, "We dug Ryutan in Ankokuzan, planted fragrant trees and flowers, and made it available for all to use as an eternal memorial as a symbol of the peaceful era".

②円鑑池（えんかんち）

円鑑池は1502年に造られた人工池で、首里城や円覚寺からの湧水・雨水が集まる仕組みになっている。ここから溢れた水が隣の池「龍潭」へ流れている。池の中央にある赤瓦の堂は「弁財天堂」で、池の水深は３ｍ程である。円鑑池と龍潭の間の水路に掛けられたアーチ状の橋は「龍淵橋」（りゅうしんきょう）と呼ばれ、天女橋と同年代の建造と推定されている。この池は薩摩の侵攻（1609年）や沖縄戦（1945年）で幾度も破壊されたが、1968年に現在の姿に修復された。

円鑑池と弁財天堂（那覇市首里）
Enkan-*chi* and Bezaiten-*dou*(Shuri,Naha City)

② Enkan-*chi*

Enkan-*chi* is a man-made pond built in 1502, and the system is designed to collect spring water and rainwater from Shuri Castle and Enkakuji Temple. The water overflowing from this pond flows into the neighboring pond, Ryutan. The red-tiled structure in the center of the pond is called Bezaiten-*dou* and the depth of the pond is about 3 meters. The arched bridge that spans the waterway between Enkan-*chi* and Ryutan is called Ryushinkyo, and is estimated to have been built in the same year as *Ten'nyo-bashi*. This pond was destroyed many times during the invasion of Satsuma (1609) and the Battle of Okinawa (1945), but was restored to its present state in 1968.

③弁財天堂（べざいてんどう）

弁財天堂は航海安全を司る水の女神「弁財天」を祀っていた。弁財天は「べんざいてん」または「べざいてん」と発音され、もともとインド神話の「サラスバティ」が漢字訳され女神の姿に造形化したもので、仏教に取り入れられた。日本では「七福神」の1つに数えられ、貧困を救い財物を与える天女や女神として信仰されている。弁財天堂は、朝鮮王から贈られた方冊蔵経（ほうさつぞうきょう・仏教の経典）を納めるために尚真王が 1502 年に建立したが、1609 年の薩摩侵攻で破壊された。1629 年に修復された時に、円覚寺にあった弁財天像を安置した。その後、荒廃したため 1685 年に薩摩から新像を移した。しかし沖縄戦で破壊され 1968 年に復元された。堂に渡る小橋は「天女橋」（てんにょばし）と呼ばれ、中国南部の駝背橋（だはいきょう＝中国の技術を巧みに組み合わせた駱駝の背中に似たアーチ橋）の形式を取っている。「ニービヌフニ」と呼ばれる細粒砂岩が用いられている欄干は、日本の木造の組み合わせ技術が取り入れられており、蓮の彫刻などが施されている。

③ Bezaiten-*dou*

Bezaiten-*dou* enshrines the goddess of water, Benzaiten, who is responsible for safe navigation. Bezaiten, pronounced "Benzaiten" or "Bezaiten," was originally Goddess translated into Chinese character of the Indian mythology Sarasvati, which was sculpted into the form of a goddess and introduced into Buddhism. In Japan, she is one of the *Shichi-hukujin* (Seven Gods of Good Fortune) and is worshipped as a heavenly maiden or goddess who saves people from poverty and gives them wealth. Bezaiten-*dou* was built in 1502 by King Sho Shin to house the *Housatsu-zoukyo* (Buddhist scriptures) presented by the King of Korea, but was destroyed during the invasion of Satsuma in 1609. When it was restored in 1629, a statue of Bezaiten from Enkakuji Temple was enshrined here. Later, it fell into disrepair, so a new statue was moved from Satsuma in 1685. However, it was destroyed during the Battle of Okinawa and was restored in 1968. The small bridge that crosses the Bezaiten-*dou* is called *Ten'nyo-bashi* and has the characteristics of a *Dahaikyou* (the bridge, the form of a camel-back arch bridge which is a skillful combination of Chinese techniques) in southern China. The stone balustrade, made of fine sandstone called *niibinu-huni*, is a combination of Japanese wooden techniques, with lotus carvings on it.

④円覚寺跡（えんかくじあと）

かつて首里城周辺には仏教寺院や御殿（うどぅん）と称される王族や家臣の屋敷などが多くあり、王都の雰囲気を醸し出していた。その中でも代表的なものが「円覚寺」である。この寺は 1494 年に創建された沖縄における臨済宗の総本山で、第二尚氏王統歴代国王の菩提寺であった。寺は、禅宗の「七堂伽藍」（しちどうがらん）の形式で建造され、境内には多くの建物が配置されていた。中でも仏殿は琉球建築の粋を集めた建築物で、中央の須弥壇（しゅみだん）には仏像が安置され、装飾が施されていた。1933 年に山門や仏殿など計 9 件が国宝に指定されていたが、すべて沖縄戦で破壊された。1968

年より復元整備が行われ現在、総門や放生池（ほうじょうち）などが復元された。なお、池に架かる放生橋は往時のもので、国指定重要文化財である。

円覚寺跡（那覇市首里）
Enkakuji Temple Ruins (Shuri, Naha City)

④ Enkakuji Temple Ruins

In the past, the area around Shuri Castle had many Buddhist temples and the residences of the royal family and their vassals, known as *udun*, which created the atmosphere of a royal capital. The most representative of these was Enkakuji Temple. Founded in 1494, this temple was the head temple of the Rinzai sect of Buddhism in Okinawa, and was the family temple of the successive kings of the Second Sho Dynasty. The temple was built in the style of Zen Buddhism's *Shichido-garan* (seven halls), and many buildings were arranged in the temple grounds. Among them, the Buddha Hall was a masterpiece of Ryukyu architecture, with an ornately decorated altar in the center where a Buddha statue was enshrined. A total of nine items were designated as national treasures in 1933, including the temple gate and Buddh Hall, but all were destroyed during the Battle of Okinawa. The main gate and the Houjou-*chi* (pond) have been restored since 1968. The Houjou-*bashi* (bridge) over the pond was built in the old days and is designated as a national important cultural property.

⑤園比屋武御嶽、園比屋武御嶽石門（すぬひゃんうたき・いしもん）

　石門の背後にあるのが園比屋武御嶽である。国王が外出する時には必ずこの御嶽で安全祈願し、聞得大君の就任に際して最初に礼拝した国家の聖地でもあった。尚氏王統ゆかりの島・伊平屋島の神「ソノヒヤブ」を勧請し、祀られている。首里城正門・歓会門と守礼門の間にある園比屋武御嶽石門がこの御嶽の礼拝所であり、1519 年頃（尚真王代）に造られた。琉球石灰岩で造られた石門はオヤケアカハチの乱（1500 年）の際、王府軍に見込まれて連れて来られた石工「西塘」（にしとう）によって創建された。1833 年に国宝に指定されたが、沖縄戦の戦禍で荒廃し指定解除された。1957 年には旧石門の残欠を再利用して修復作業が行われた。園比屋武御嶽石門は 1972 年に改めて国の重要文化財に指定され、2000 年には首里城跡などとともにユネスコの世界遺産（文化遺産）にも登録された。

⑤ Sunuhyan-*utaki*, Sunuhyan-*utaki* Stone Gate

Behind the stone gate is the Sunuhyan-*utaki*. This *utaki* was the sacred place where the King prayed for safety whenever he went out, and was also the national sanctuary where was prayed first for Kikoe Okimi when she took office. This *utaki* enshrines Sonohiyabu, a deity from Iheya Island, an island related to the Sho royal lineage. The Sunuhyan-*utaki* Stone Gate, located between the main gate of Shuri Castle, the Kankai-*mon* and the Shurei-*mon*, is the place of worship for the *utaki* and was built around 1519 (during the reign of King Sho Shin). The stone

園比屋武御嶽の石門（那覇市首里）
Sunuhyan-*utaki* Stone Gate(Shuri,Naha City)

gate, made of Ryukyu limestone, was built by a stonemason named Nishitou, who was brought in by the royal army because of his skills during the Oyake Akahachi Rebellion (1500). It was designated as a national treasure in 1833, but the designation was lifted after it was devastated by the Battle of Okinawa. Restoration work began in 1957, reusing the remnants of the old stone gate. The Sunuhyan-*utaki* Stone Gate was redesignated as a national important cultural property in 1972, and in 2000, it was registered as a UNESCO World Heritage Site (cultural heritage) along with the ruins of Shuri Castle.

⑥弁ヶ嶽（べんがだけ）

首里城の東方約 1km の場所に位置し、嶺全体が御神体になっており俗に「ビンヌウタキ」とも呼ばれ、那覇市内で最も高い場所（海抜約 165m）にある。沖縄戦の前までは松などの大木が茂り、航海の目印にもなっていたという。琉球王国時代には国家的な祭祀を行う聖地であり、国王自らも参拝した。弁ヶ嶽には大小 2 つの御嶽があり、東西に走る参拝道を挟んで北側の小高い杜が「大嶽」で、南側の低い方は「小嶽」と呼ばれる。大嶽は久高島への遙拝所で、小嶽は斎場御嶽への遙拝所であったといわれる。大嶽前の石門は、1519 年頃に園比屋武御嶽の石門とともに石工・西塘

弁ガ嶽の大嶽（那覇市首里鳥堀町）
Uhu'taki in Benga-*dake*(Shuri Torihori-*cho*)

（にしとう）によって築かれたといわれ構造や工法がよく似ている。この石門は 1938 年に国宝に指定されたが、沖縄戦で破壊され、現在のコンクリート造りに建て替えられている。

⑥ Benga-*dake* (Bin'nu-*utaki*)

It is located about 1km to the east of Shuri Castle, and the entire ridge is the sacred body of the deity, also known as Bin'nu-*utaki*, and is the highest point in Naha City (about 165m above sea level). Before the Battle of Okinawa, the area was covered with large pine trees and is said to have served as a landmark for navigation. During the time of the Ryukyu Kingdom, it was a sacred place where national rituals were held, and the king himself visited here. Benga-*dake* has two *utaki,* a large and a small one. The higher forest on the north side of the path running east to west is called *Uhu'taki*, and the lower one on the south side is called *Kuu'taki*. It is said that *Uhu'taki* was a place of worship that enshrines Kudaka Island from afar, and *Kuu'taki* was a place of worship that enshrines Seifa-*utaki* from afar. The stone gate in front of the *Uhu'taki* is said to have been built by a stonemason named Nishitou along with the stone gate of Sunuhyan-*utaki* around 1519, and the structure and construction method are very similar. The stone gate was designated as a national treasure in 1938, but it was destroyed during the Battle of Okinawa and was rebuilt with the current concrete structure.

⑦御茶屋御殿跡（うちゃやうどぅんあと）

首里崎山町にあった旧王家の別邸で、1677 年に造られた。1683 年に来琉した冊封使の汪楫（おうしゅう）が、首里城の東にありこの付近を景勝の地と讃えて「東苑」と名付けた。東苑は、国王が薩摩の在藩奉行や冊封使など国賓を歓待するところで主に迎賓館のような役割を果たしていた。文化人を集めて、歌三線や琉球舞踊、組踊り、能、茶道、和歌、琉歌、空手などさまざまな芸能が披露され、文化の殿堂でもあった。俗に崎山御殿とも呼ばれ、後には王家の産殿や隠居殿に当てられたが、

1898 年（明治 31）に払い下げら
れた。沖縄戦で苑内の建造物は全
て破壊された。激戦地だったため
に土地を購入する者がなく、カト
リック教会が敷地を購入した。現
在は跡地に首里カトリック教会
や附属幼稚園が建っている。2006
年 12 月、那覇市議会において「御
茶屋御殿跡の早期復元・整備を求
める意見書」が議決され、早期復
元の機運が高まっている。

戦前の御茶屋御殿（那覇市首里崎山町）
Pre-war Uchaya-*udun* (Shuri,Naha City)

⑦ Site of Uchaya-*udun*

This was the former royal residence in Shuri Sakiyama-*cho*, built in 1677 and named *Tou-en* (East Garden) by the royal envoy to the Ryukyu, Wang Hsiu, who came to Ryukyu in 1683 and praised the area to the east of Shuri Castle as a place of scenic beauty. The *Tou-en* was the place where the king hosted state guests such as the Satsuma Magistrate and the *sappuu-shi* (envoys from China), and mainly served as a guest house. It was also a temple of culture, where cultural figures were invited to perform various arts such as *sanshin* playing, singing, *ryubu* (Ryukyuan dance), *kumi-odori* (Ryukyuan Opera), *noh*, tea ceremony, *waka* (Japanese poetry), *ryuka* (Ryukyuan poetry), and karate. Commonly called Sakiyama-*udun*, it was later used as a royal maternity and retreat hall, but was sold in 1898. All buildings in the garden were destroyed during the Battle of Okinawa. Because the area was the site of a fierce battle, there was no one to purchase the land, so the Catholic Church purchased the site. Today, Shuri Catholic Church and its attached kindergarten stand on the site. In December 2006, the Naha City Assembly voted on an "Opinion for the Early Restoration and Maintenance of the Uchaya-*udun*," and momentum is building for its early restoration.

⑧万国津梁の鐘（ばんこくしんりょうのかね）

1458 年、尚泰久王の命により鋳造された重量約 720kg の青
銅製で、かつて首里城正殿に掛けられた梵鐘。鐘に刻まれた
有名な銘文の一部から、「万国津梁の鐘」という呼称が一般的
である。この鐘は、仏教の加護によって国内を安定させる目
的で作られたものだが、銘文は 15 世紀中頃における琉球の海
外貿易の隆盛や制海の気概を的確に表現している。その部分
を表した最も有名な銘文の大意は「琉球は南海の良い場所に
あり、中国と日本の間にある蓬莱島（ユートピア）で、船で
『万国の津梁＝世界の架け橋』となって貿易を行い、宝物が国
中に満ちている」というもの。

2022 年 5 月、南城市玉城冨里にある風葬墓「神座原古墳群」
（かんざばるこふんぐん）から出土した人骨（1,400 〜 1,600
年前）のうち、2 体が西ヨーロッパ・中央アジア由来と、朝鮮
半島由来であることが発表された。当時の琉球人が外国人を
排除せずに受け入れ、多様性ある社会を形成していたことが
明らかになった。当時から沖縄は「万国津梁の邦」だったのであ

万国津梁の鐘（沖縄県立博物館・美術館）
Bankoku-shinryo-no-kane(Bridge of Nations Bell)

る。資源が乏しい琉球王国は交易国として成り立っており、「万国津梁の鐘」はまさにその象徴である。現在、この鐘は沖縄県が所有し、県立博物館・美術館に展示されている。

⑧ *Bankoku-shinryo-no-kane* (Bell of the *Bankoku-shinryo*)

Made of bronze and weighing about 720kg, this bell was cast in 1458 by order of King Sho Taikyu, and once the bell that hung in the main hall of Shuri Castle. From some of the famous inscriptions on the bell, it is commonly referred to as the *Bankoku-shinryo-no-kane*. This bell was made to stabilize the country with the blessings of Buddhism, but the inscription accurately expresses the prosperity of Ryukyu's overseas trade and the spirit of sea control in the middle of the 15th century. The main meaning of the most famous inscription is: "Ryukyu is located in a good place in the South Sea, it is a utopia between China and Japan, it trades by ship as a 'bridge of all nations,' and the country is full of treasures".

In May 2022, it was announced that two of the human bones (1,400 to 1,600 years old) excavated from the Kanzabaru-*kofun-gun* (wind burial tombs) at Tamagusuku Husato, Nanjyo City, are of Western European/ Central Asian origin and Korean Peninsula origin. It became clear that Ryukyuans at that time did not exclude foreigners but accepted them, forming a diverse society. Even at that time, Okinawa was a "country of the *Bankoku-shinryo*". The Ryukyu Kingdom, with its lack of natural resources, has been a trading nation, and the *Bankoku-shinryo-no-kane* is a perfect symbol of this. The bell is now owned by Okinawa Prefecture and is on display at the Prefectural Museum/Art Museum.

⑨天山陵跡（てんざんりょうあと）

「天山ようどれ」または単に「天山」とも呼ばれ、那覇市首里池端町にある第一尚氏王統の陵墓跡である。天山陵は南向きの崖面に造営された掘り込み墓で、東室、中室、西室の３室が存在していたといわれる。首里王府の外交文書である『歴代宝案』には尚巴志王の死去（1439 年）と彼が天山陵に葬られたことが記されており、1439 年には既に造営されていたことになる。1469 年の金丸（後の尚円王）による政変で焼き討ちに遭ったが、その前に尚徳王の近親者らによって王たちの遺骨は運び出された。天山陵と命名したのは国相・懐機で、長虹堤の完成後、彼は天山陵の近くに住んだ。死後、天山陵の脇に作られた懐機の墓は「坊主の墓」（ボウジヌハカ）とも称された。天山陵は第一尚氏王統の滅亡後、第二尚氏の尚清王の五男・北谷王子に下賜され、北谷家の墓として使用された。墓庭は沖縄戦で破壊され、戦後は宅地造成のため東室と中室は破壊され私有地となっている。今日、天山陵跡には西室の近くにあった尚巴志の石棺台のみが残っている。

天山陵跡（那覇市首里池端町）
Site of Tenzan-*ryo*(royal tomb of the kings of the First Sho Dynasty),(Shuri Ikehata-*cho*,Naha City)

⑨ Site of Tenzan-*ryo* (royal tomb of the kings of the First Sho Dynasty)

This is the site of the mausoleum of the First Sho Dynasty, located in Ikehata-*cho*, Shuri, Naha City, is also known as Tenzan-*youdore* or simply Tenzan. Tenzan-*ryo* was one of *horikomi-baka* (dug-in tomb) built on a south-facing cliff face, and is said to have had three chambers: an east chamber, a middle chamber, and a west chamber.

The diplomatic document of the Shuri royal government, Rekidai-houan, mentions the death of King Sho Hashi (1439) and his burial in Tenzan-*ryo*, which means that it was already built in 1439. The tomb was burned down in 1469 during a political uprising by Kanamaru (later King Sho En), but the remains of the kings were removed by King Sho Toku's relatives before the uprising. It was Minister of State, Kaiki who named the tomb of the First Sho Dynasty Tenzan-*ryo*, and he lived near Tenzan-*ryo* after the completion of *Chokou-tei* (an artificial road built into the sea). After his death, Kaiki's tomb, built beside the Tenzan-*ryo,* was also called the *Boujinu-haka* (Tomb of the Monk). After the fall of the First Sho Dynasty, the Tenzan-*ryo* was given to Prince Chatan, the fifth son of King Sho Sei of the Second Sho Dynasty, and used as the tomb of the Chatan family. The tomb garden was destroyed during the Battle of Okinawa, and after the war, the east and middle chambers were destroyed to make way for a housing development and became private property. Today, only the sarcophagus stand of Sho Hashi, which was located near the west chamber, remains at the site of the Tenzan-*ryo*.

⑩玉陵（たまうどぅん）

　尚真王が 1501 年、父・尚円王の遺骨を再葬するために建造した第二尚氏王統の歴代国王と家族の陵墓。当時の宮殿の形を模して作られた石造りで、沖縄県最大の破風墓である。沖縄戦で大きな被害を受けたが、1974 年から 3 年以上の歳月をかけて修復が行われ、現在はほぼ往時の姿に戻った。建造物の外は外庭と中庭が石壁で仕切られ、中庭には珊瑚の破片が敷き詰められている。中庭左手に石碑があり、玉陵に埋葬される資格者の名前が記されている。この碑文は尚円王妃・オギヤカの意向が刻まれているといわれ、王位継承を巡る一族内の争いがあったことを示唆している。墓室は 3 つあり、洗骨までの遺体を安置する中室、王・王妃・世子・世子妃の遺骨を安置する東室、その他の王子・王女などの遺骨を安置する西室で構成されている。葬儀後に遺体は中室に運ばれ、遺骸が骨になるまでそこに放置された。数年後に骨を取り出し、洗骨した遺骨は骨壺に納められ東室または西室に納められた。「玉陵」と名が付く墓所は他に「伊是名玉陵」、「山川の玉陵」、「末吉の玉陵」があり、いずれも第二尚氏王統の陵墓である。

玉陵（那覇市首里）
Tama-*udun*(royal tomb of the Second Sho Dynasty successive kings and their families)(Shuri, Naha City)

⑩ Tama-*udun* (royal tomb of the Second Sho Dynasty successive kings and their families)

The mausoleum of the kings of the Second Sho Dynasty and their families, built by King Sho Shin in 1501 to reinter the remains of his father, King Sho En. It is the largest *hahuu-baka* in Okinawa Prefecture, built of stone in the shape of a palace of the time. It was severely damaged during the Battle of Okinawa, but after more than three years of restoration since 1974, it is now almost back to its original state. The outer and inner courtyards are separated by a stone wall, and the inner courtyard is covered with coral fragments. There is a stone monument on the left side of the courtyard with the names of those who are to be buried in this tomb. This inscription is said to be inscribed with the intentions of Ogiyaka, queen of King Sho En, suggesting that there was a family dispute over the succession to the throne. There are three tomb chambers: the middle chamber for the remains until the bones are washed, the east chamber for the remains of the king, queen, the king-elect and his wife, and the west chamber for the remains of other princes and princesses. After the funeral, the body was taken to the middle chamber and left there until the remains were reduced to bones. After a few years, the bones were removed and washed, and the remains were placed in an urn and placed in the east or west chamber. The other tombs named Tama-*udun* are Izena-tama-*udun*, Yamagawa-tama-*udun*, and Sueyoshi-tama-*udun*, all of which are the mausoleums of the Second Sho Dynasty.

⑪守礼門（しゅれいもん）

「守礼」とは「礼節を守る」という意味で、門に掲げられている扁額には「守禮之邦」と書かれている。これは「琉球は礼節を重んずる国である」という意味である。首里城は石垣と城門の多い城だが、中でもエレガントな雰囲気のある代表的な門が首里城のシンボルともいえる守礼門である。尚清王代（1527 〜 55）に建立された当時は「待賢（たいけん）」、その次は「首里」の扁額が掲げられたので、それに合わせて「待賢門」、「首里門」と呼び名が変化した。「守禮之邦」の扁額は、尚永王代（1573 〜 88）に作られ、尚質王代（1648 〜 68）からは常に掲げられるようになったが、庶民は愛称として「上の綾門」（上の方にある美しい門）と呼んだ。一見中国風に見えるが、琉球独特の手法で造られた王朝時代の建築文化の代表作の一つで、1933 年には国宝に指定されたが沖縄戦で破壊された。現在の守礼門は 1958 年に復元されたもので、戦後沖縄の平和主義を象徴する観光施設となっている。

守礼門（那覇市首里）
Shurei-*mon* Gate(Shuri,Naha City)

⑪ Shurei-*mon* Gate

The word *Shurei* means observing civility, and the tablet on the gate reads *Shurei-no-kuni*. This means that Ryukyu is a country that respects civility. Shuri Castle is a castle with many stone walls and gates, and one of the most elegant and representative gates is Shurei-*mon*, the symbol of Shuri Castle. When it was first erected in the reign of King Sho Sei (1527-55), a tablet with the word *taiken* written on it was displayed, followed by Shuri, the name of the gate was changed to Taiken-*mon* and Shuri-*mon* accordingly. The tablet with the words *Shurei-no-kuni* was made during the reign of King Sho Ei (1573-88), and from the reign of King Sho Shitsu (1648-68), it was always displayed, but the common people affectionately called it *Uwii-nu-ayajou* (the beautiful gate in the upper part). At first glance, it looks Chinese, but it was built using a unique Ryukyu method and is one of the representative works of the architectural culture of the dynasty period. It was designated as a national treasure in 1933, but was destroyed during the Battle of Okinawa. The current Shurei-*mon* was restored in 1958, and has become a tourist facility that symbolizes the pacifism of post-war Okinawa.

(31) 識名園（しきなえん）

　那覇市真地の高台にある琉球王家最大の別邸で、国王一家の保養所や外国使臣の接待などに利用された。御茶屋御殿を「東苑」と呼ぶのに対して「南苑」や「識名の御殿」ともいう。造園は第二尚氏王朝 14 代目・尚穆王の時代に始まったといわれるが定かではない。1799 年に完成し、1800 年に尚温王の冊封のために来琉した冊封使一行（正史：趙文楷、副使：李鼎元）を当園に招いている。識名園の造園形式は、池のまわりを楽しむことを目的とした「回遊式庭園」。「心」の字を崩した池の形（心字池）を中心に、池に浮かぶ島には中国風あずま屋の六角堂や大小のアーチが配されている。池の周囲には琉球石灰岩を積みまわすなど、随所に琉球独特の工夫が見られる。美しい曲線で石積みされた湧泉「育徳泉」（いくとくせん）は池の水源の一つで、井戸口の上には 1800 年と 1838 年に来琉した 2 人の冊封使が題した石碑が建っている。この泉に自生していた紅藻類「シマチスジノリ」は国の天然記念物だが、1970 年には泉の枯渇により死滅した。1941 年には「国の名勝」に指定されたが、沖縄戦では一時陸軍病院として使用され、砲撃などで壊滅的被害を受けた。識名園は 1975 年〜95 年に約 20 年かけて復元整備され 1976 年には国の名勝に再指定。2000 年にはユネスコ世界遺産の一つに登録された。

識名園（那覇市真地）
Shikina-*en* Garden(Maaji, Naha City)

(31) Shikina-*en* Garden

　It was the largest villa of the Ryukyu royal family, located on a hill in Maaji, Naha City, and was used as a recreational facility for the royal family and as a reception center for foreign envoys. While Uchaya-*udun* is called *Tou-en* (East Garden), Shikina-*en* Garden is also called *Nan-en* (South Garden) or Shikina'nu-*udun*. It is said that the landscaping began during the reign of King Sho Kou, the 14th king of the Second Sho Dynasty, but it is not certain. It was completed in 1799, and in 1800, a group of *sappuu-shi* (official envoys: Zhao Wen Kai, deputy envoy: Li Ding Yuan) who came to Ryukyu to appoint King Sho On were invited to this garden. The landscaping style of Shikina-*en* Garden is a "circular garden" designed for people to enjoy strolling around the pond. The pond, *shinji-ike,* is shaped like a corrupted version of the kanji character for heart, and on an island floating in the pond, there is a Chinese-style pavilion called *Rokkaku-dou* and "large and small arches". Around the pond, Ryukyu limestone is piled up, and other unique Ryukyu innovations can be seen everywhere. The beautifully curved stone piled spring Ikutoku-*sen* is one of the sources of water in the pond, and above the well are two stone monuments written by two *sappuu-shi* who came to Ryukyu in 1800 and 1838. The red algae that used to grow naturally in this spring, the *shima-chisuji-nori*, is a national natural monument, but it died out in 1970 when the spring dried up. In 1941, the park was designated as a "national scenic beauty," but during the Battle of Okinawa, it was temporarily used as an army hospital and was devastated by shelling. Shikina-*en* Garden was restored and maintained over a period of about 20 years from 1975 to 1995, and was re-designated as a national scenic beauty in 1976. It registered as a UNESCO World Heritage Site in 2000.

(32) 崇元寺跡（そうげんじあと）

　16世紀初めに建造された臨済宗の仏教寺院。初代・舜天王から最後の尚泰王までの歴代琉球国王の霊が祀られていた国廟で、1945年の沖縄戦で焼失した。正廟を中心に、中国風の伽藍が立ち並び、正廟や石門などが旧国宝に指定されていた。現在は修復された石門だけが残っているが、沖縄を代表する石造建築で1972年には国の重要文化財に指定された。中国皇帝からの冊封使は、首里城で挙行される新王の冊封儀式に先立って、当寺院で先王の霊を慰める儀式「諭祭」（ゆさい）が行われた。冊封を受ける新国王は、宿舎・天使館を出発した冊封使の一行を門外の崇元寺橋で出迎え、冊封使らを歴代王の位牌の前に案内。冊封使は新王とともに先王を供養した。崇元寺は、尚円王が第一尚氏王統の祟りを鎮めるために建造したともいわれる。

戦前の崇元寺（那覇市泊）
Pre-war Sougenji Temple(Tomari, Naha City)

(32) Sougenji Temple Ruins

A Buddhist temple of the Rinzai sect built in the early 16th century. The national temple enshrined the spirits of the successive kings of Ryukyu, from the first King Syunten to the last King Sho Tai, and was destroyed by fire during the Battle of Okinawa in 1945. The Chinese-style temple complex was lined up around the main temple, and the main temple and stone gate were designated as former national treasures. Today, only the restored stone gate remains, but it is one of Okinawa's representative stone structures and was designated a national important cultural property in 1972. Prior to the *sappuu-gishiki* (appointment ceremony for the new king) at Shuri Castle, the *sappuu-shi* (royal envoys from the Chinese emperor) went to the temple for the *Yusai* ceremony to console the spirit of the previous king. The new king who was to receive the title of "King of Ryukyu" welcomed the envoys who departed from Tenshi-*kan,* their dormitory, at Sougenji bridge outside the temple gate, and led them to the tablets of the successive kings. The envoys and the new king made offerings to the previous king. The temple is said to have been built by King Sho En to appease the haunting of the First Sho royal line.

(33) 屋良座森城跡（やらざむいぐすくあと）

　那覇港を守るために、南口に尚清王の命によって築かれた台場が屋良座森城である。1554年に建立された「やらさもりくすくの碑」には、有事の際に南風原、島添大里、知念、佐敷、など南部の軍隊を当グスクの守備に充てることが記されている。長方形の石垣の壁は厚く、16カ所の銃眼が設けられていた。1609年の薩摩侵攻時には約3000の王府軍が集結し、対岸（北側）の三重城との間に鉄鎖を張って港口を封鎖した。両グスクからの砲撃で撃退を余儀なくされた薩摩軍は予定を変更して、今帰仁間切運天港と読谷山間切海岸から上陸した。その後もグスクは海賊対策として引き続き使用

されたが、一般的には住民が船を見送るため
に利用された。戦後、米国は那覇港南岸を海
軍基地として整備・拡張したため当グスクは
1950 年、徹底的に破壊された。

戦前の屋良座森グスク（那覇市那覇港）
Pre-war Yarazamui-*gusuku(in Naha Port, Naha City)*

(33) Yarazamui-*gusuku* Ruins

Yarazamui-*gusuku* is a fort with a battery built
at the southern entrance of Naha Port by order of
King Sho Sei to protect the port. The "Yarasamori-
Kusuku Monument," erected in 1554, stated
that in the event of an emergency, troops from
Haebaru, Shimasoe-Ozato, Chinen, Sashiki, and
other southern areas would be assigned to defend
this *gusuku*. The walls of the rectangular stone wall were thick and had 16 gun sights. During the invasion
of Satsuma in 1609 a royal army of about 3,000 soldiers gathered and blocked the entrance to the harbor by
stretching an iron chain between the *gusuku,* and Mii-*gusuku* on the opposite (north) side of the sea. Forced
to retreat by the bombardment from both *gusuku*, the Satsuma forces changed their plans and landed from
Unten Port in Nakijin *magiri* and from the coast of Yomitan *magiri*. Later, the *gusuku* continued to be used
for anti-piracy purposes, but was generally used by residents to see off ships. After the Battle of Okinawa, the
U.S. developed and expanded the southern coast of Naha Port as a naval base, and the *gusuku* was thoroughly
destroyed in 1950.

(34) 三重城跡（みーぐすくあと）

戦前の三重城（那覇市西町）
Pre-war Mii-*gusuku(Nishi-machi, Naha City)*

　沖縄方言では「ミーグスク」と
呼び、「新しい城」という意味であ
る。対岸の「屋良座森城」（ヤラザ
ムイグスク）が 1554 年（尚清王代）
に築城されており、三重城はそれ
より遅れて築城されたのでそう呼
称されているといわれる。伝承に
よると、奥武山に住んでいた汪之
大親（南山・他魯毎王の曾孫）は
三重城に別荘を持っており、海賊
（倭寇）の侵攻を恐れて高く城壁を
築き、さらに長堤を造って備えた
という。そのため三重城は「汪之
大親グスク」とも称される。その
後、屋良座森城と三重城には砲台が置かれ、それぞれ南砲台、北砲台と呼ばれた。長堤の中ほどに臨
海寺を抱え、4 つの橋で連なっていた。1609 年の薩摩侵攻以降は砦としての存在理由を失い、城壁だ
けが空しく残っている。「西の海」と呼ばれていた海の部分が明治から大正時代にかけて埋め立てられ、
現在のような地勢となった。今では旅先や県外で亡くなった人の慰霊や、離島の御先祖様への遥拝所
として多くの人々が訪れる。

(34) Mii-*gusuku* Ruins

In Okinawan dialect, it is called Mii-*gusuku*, meaning "new castle". It is said that Mii-*gusuku* is so called because it was built later than Yarazamui-*gusuku* on the other side of the sea, which was built in 1554 (during the reign of King Sho Sei). According to legend, *Ohnu-uhuya* (great-grandson of King Tarumii of Nanzan), who lived in Ohnoyama island, had a villa in Mii-*gusuku* and built high walls and a long embankment to protect it from invading pirates(*wakou*). That's why Mii-*gusuku* is also called *Ohnu-uhuya-gusuku*. Later, Yarazamui-*gusuku* and Mii-*gusuku* were equipped with gun batteries, called the South Battery and North Battery, respectively. It was connected by four bridges, with the Rinkaiji Temple in the middle of the long bank. After the invasion of Satsuma in 1609, it lost its reason to exist as a fort and only the walls remain empty. The part of the sea known as the "Sea of the West" was reclaimed during the Meiji and Taisho eras, and the terrain became what it is today. Nowadays, it is visited by many people as a memorial for those who have passed away while traveling or out of the prefecture, and as a place of worship for the ancestors of the remote islands.

(35) 御物城跡（おものぐすくあと）

那覇港内の小島にある首里王府の倉庫で、中国や東南アジア等との交易品が収蔵されていた。築城年や築城者は不明だが、15世紀前半に築かれたと考えられている。このグスクを管理していた王府役人は御物城御鎖之側（おものぐすく・うさしぬすば）と呼ばれ、1459年（尚泰久王代）には、金丸（後の尚円王）がその役職に任じられていた。廃藩置県後に建物が解体されて、1884年（明治17）には物産展示場となった。その後、大正、昭和にかけて跡地に高級料亭

戦前の風月楼（那覇市那覇港内）
Pre-war Fuugetsurou(Omono-*gusuku* Ruins)(in Naha Port, Naha City)

「風月楼」（ふうげつろう）が建てられた。風月楼は料理も芸奴も日本風で、政治家や官僚、実業家などが利用した。料亭は1944年の米軍による空襲（十・十空襲）で焼失したが、戦後は米軍施設内に取り込まれ、現在では城郭の一部とアーチ門が残っている。御物城は、屋良座森城と三重城によって守られ、海外と盛んに交易していたことを物語る貴重な遺跡である。

(35) Omono-*gusuku* Ruins

This was a warehouse of the Shuri royal government located on a small island in Naha Port, where trade goods with China and Southeast Asia were stored. The date of construction and who built it are unknown, but it is thought to have been built in the first half of the 15th century. The royal official who managed this *gusuku* was called Omono-*gusuku-usashinusuba*, and Kanamaru (later King Sho En) was appointed to this position in 1459 (during the reign of King Sho Taikyu). After the abolition of the feudal domain, the building was dismantled and turned into an exhibition hall for products in 1884 (Meiji 17). Later, during the Taisho and Showa periods, the high-class *ryotei* restaurant Fuugetsurou was built on the site. Fuugetsurou, with its Japanese style cuisine and geisha, was used by politicians, bureaucrats, and businessmen. The *ryotei* was destroyed by fire in an air raid by the U.S. military in 1944 (*Juu-juu-kuushuu*), but after the war it was incorporated into the U.S. military facilities, and today only part of the *gusuku* and the archway gate remain. The Omono-*gusuku* was protected by the Yarazamui-*gusuku* and the Mii-*gusuku*, and is a valuable remnant of the active trading with foreign countries.

(36) 浦添ようどれ（うらそえようどれ）

浦添グスクの北側崖の中腹に設けられた琉球王国初期の王陵で、極楽陵の別名がある。「ようどれ」とは琉球の言語で「夕凪」を意味し、静かで穏やかなイメージから「墓」の意としても用いられる。「浦添ようどれ」は最初、13世紀（1274年が有力）に英祖王によって築かれ、その後、尚寧王が1620年に修築し自身もここに葬られた。向かって右側（西室）が英祖王陵で、左側（東室）は尚寧王一族陵である。西室には、中国産の閃緑岩製の石棺が3基あり、最も大きいのが英祖王の石厨子と見なされている。東室には閃緑

浦添ようどれ（浦添市仲間）
Urasoe-*youdore*(Nakama, Urasoe City)

岩製1基、微粒子砂岩（ニービヌフニ）製1基、石灰岩製1基の計3基の石厨子がある。近接している「浦添グスク・ようどれ館」には、浦添グスクと浦添ようどれの発掘調査での出土品などが展示されている。また、石厨子のレプリカなどを実物大で復元し、英祖王陵内部を再現している。

(36) Urasoe-*youdore*

This is the royal mausoleum in the early days of Ryukyu Kingdom, built in the middle of the cliff on the north side of Urasoe-*gusuku*, and is also known as *Gokuraku-ryo*. *Youdore* means "evening calm" in Ryukyu language, and it is also used to mean "tomb" because of its quiet and peaceful image. It was first built by King Eiso in the 13th century (most likely in 1274), and was later renovated by King Sho Nei in 1620, who himself was buried here. The tomb on our right side (West Room) is the tomb of King Eiso, and the one on our left side (East Room) is the tomb of King Sho Nei's family. In the west room, there are three sarcophagi made of Chinese diorite, the largest of which is believed to be that of King Eiso. In the east room, there are a total of three sarcophagi made of diorite, fine sandstone (*niibinu-huni*) and limestone. In the nearby Urasoe-*gusuku-youdore* Museum, artifacts from the excavation of Urasoe-*gusuku* and Urasoe-*youdore* are displayed. The museum also has a full-scale replica of the sarcophagi to recreate the interior of King Eiso's tomb.

(37) 佐敷ようどれ（さしきようどれ）

尚巴志の父で、第一尚氏王統初代王・尚思紹夫妻ら家族7人の遺骨が安置されている（尚巴志王の墓は、読谷村伊良皆の東北約1kmにあるサシジャー森の山中にある）。当初は南城市佐敷の南崖を掘って造られた横穴造りの墓であったが、崩れやすく使用できなくなったため、1764年に現在地に移された。墓は籠型をした独特の形式で、横から見ると半月形の屋根形をしている。現在は、自衛隊の知念分屯基地（管理地区）内にあり、南城市教育委員会が管理している。自衛隊の知念分屯基地のゲートで受付すれば予約なしで見学が可能である。

(37) Sashiki-*youdore*

The tomb contains the remains of seven family members, including Sho Hashi's father, the first king of the First Sho Dynasty, Sho Shisho and his wife (the tomb of King Sho Hashi is located in the mountains of Sashijaa Forest, about 1 km northeast of Iramina, Yomitan Village). Initially, it was a side-cave tomb dug into the southern cliff of Sashiki, Nanjo City, but it was moved to the present location in 1764 because it was prone to collapse and could no longer be used. The tomb has a unique shape like an old vehicle basket, and when viewed from the side, it has a half-moon shaped roof. Sashiki-

佐敷ようどれ（南城市佐敷）
Sashiki-*youdore*(Sashiki, Nanjo City)

youdore is now located in the Chinen sub-base of the Self-Defense Forces (management area) and is managed by the Nanjo City Board of Education. Visitors can visit without reservations if they are accepted at the gate of the Chinen Sub-base of the Self-Defense Forces.

(38) 命どぅ宝（ぬちどぅたから）

　沖縄語で、「何をおいても命こそが大切である」という意味の言葉。この言葉は、1950年代に伊江島での土地闘争のスローガンとして用いられ、さらに1980年代の反戦平和運動の中でも広く普及し、沖縄の非暴力による抵抗運動の基幹となっていった。沖縄出身の画家で作家の山里永吉（1902～1989）が、1932年に書いた戯曲「那覇四町気質」が原典とされる。戯曲の幕切れに、人質となった国王が上京する際に「みるく世んやがてぃ　嘆くなよ臣下　命どぅ宝」（争いの世が終わり、やがて平和の世が訪れる。臣よ、嘆かないでくれ。命あっての物種だ）という琉歌を詠む。「お金やどんな所有物よりも大事なものは命である。失うと二度と手に入らない」という意味を持つこの格言は、明治政府による琉球処分や沖縄戦を経て現在に至るまで、沖縄の人々の心に刻み込まれている。

(38) *Nuchi-du-takara* (Above all else, human life is treasure)

In Okinawan, it means "Life is the most important thing, no matter what". The term was used as a slogan for the land struggle on Ie Island in the 1950s, and then became widespread in the anti-war peace movement of the 1980s, becoming the backbone of the nonviolent resistance movement in Okinawa. This phrase is said to have originated from the play *Naha-yumachi-kishitsu* (the temperament of a four-township town in Naha) written in 1932 by Yamasato Eikichi (1902-1989), a painter and writer from Okinawa. At the end of the play, when the King of Ryukyu, who has been taken hostage, on his way to Tokyo, the king composes a *ryuka* poem, "The age of strife will soon end, and the age of peace will soon be upon us," "Don't

平和祈念公園内にある「命どぅ宝」の碑（糸満市摩文仁）
Monument of "*Nuchi-du-takara*" in the Peace Memorial Park(Mabuni, Itoman City)

be sad, my retainers, *nuchi-du-takara*". The saying *nuchi-du-takara*, which means "Life is more important than money or any other possessions, and if you lose it, you will never get it again," has been engraved in the hearts of Okinawans to this day after the disposal of Ryukyu by the Meiji government and the Battle of Okinawa.

(39) しまくとぅば（島言葉）

　「しまくとぅば」は漢字で「島言葉」と表記される。島（しま）とは、島々という意味があるが、「地域」または「集落」という意味で用いられることが多い。「しまくとぅば」は、沖縄の各地域で伝えられてきた言葉で「琉球語」または「琉球方言」とも称される言語である。本土の日本語と系統を同じくするが、口頭では互いに全く通じ合わない程の違いがあるため、日本語とは別の言語（琉球語）と見なす主張や、日本語内部の一方言（琉球方言）と見なす意見がある。沖縄では日本への併合（1879 年）とともに、強力な標準語励行運動が県当局や教育界を中心に展開され、伝統的な言葉が衰退した。その結果、高齢者以外の日常会話は「しまくとぅば」と日本語が混ざった方言「ウチナーヤマトゥグチ」が主流となった。2050 年頃には、流暢な「しまくとぅば」を話す人がいなくなるともいわれている。郷土文化を見直す機運が高まる中、「しまくとぅば」の現状を危惧する声も強くなった。「しまくとぅば」の次世代への継承等の趣旨で 2006 年、毎年 9 月 18 日を「しまくとぅばの日」とすることが沖縄県条例によって定められ、各地で「しまくとぅば」に親しむイベントや「しまくとぅば」の今後を考えるシンポジウムなどが開催される。「く」で 9、「とぅ」で 10、「ば」で 8 という語呂合わせで、地域の言葉を奨励する条例の制定は国内では初めてである。

(39) *Shima-kutuba* (Ryukyu language)

崇元寺下馬碑（そうげんじげばひ）「あんしもけすもくまにてむまからおれるへし」（按司も下衆もここからは馬から降りるべし）と島言葉入りで記されている
Monument to the order to get off one's horse at Sougenji Temple, reads "Both *aji* and the low-ranking official should get off their horses from here" in Ryukyu language

　Shima-kutuba is written in Chinese characters as "island language". The word *shima* means islands, but it is often used to mean region or village. *Shima-kutuba* is a language that has been handed down from region to region in Okinawa, and is also called "Ryukyu language" or "Ryukyu dialect". Although it shares a system with the Japanese language of the mainland, there are some who argue that it is a different language from Japanese (Ryukyu language) or a dialect of the Japanese language (Ryukyu dialect) because there are so many differences between the two languages that they cannot be understood orally. In Okinawa, with the annexation of the island to Japan in 1879, a strong campaign to encourage the use of the standard language was launched by the prefectural authorities and the educational community, and the traditional language declined. As a result, daily conversation among non-elderly people became dominated by *uchina-yamatu-guchi*, a mixture of *shima-kutuba* and Japanese. It is said that by the year 2050, there will be no one left who can speak *shima-kutuba* fluently. As the momentum to reevaluate the local culture grows, people are becoming increasingly concerned about the current state of *shima-kutuba*. In 2006, an Okinawa Prefecture ordinance designated September 18 as "*Shima-kutuba* Day" in order to pass on *shima-kutuba* to the next generation. Events to familiarize people with *shima-kutuba* and symposiums to discuss the future of *shima-kutuba* are held in various places. This is the first time in Japan that an ordinance has been enacted to encourage a local word, based on the combination of the words *ku* for 9, *tu* for 10, and *ba* for 8.

第４章　沖縄県民の日常生活

沖縄は、三山時代に察度王が明国皇帝の冊封を受けてその配下となり（1372 年）琉球王国時代の薩摩侵攻（1609 年）、明治政府による琉球処分（1879 年）、沖縄戦後の米軍統治（1945 年～ 1972 年）、そして日本復帰（1972 年）と、幾度も「世替わり」を経験。日本の他地域とは異質の歴史を持っているという背景から、他府県とは違う県民意識を持っている。それは、時には本土に対する劣等感となり、ある時は強烈な郷土意識として表れ「郷土愛」が強い県民と言われている。「ナンクルナイサ」、「テーゲー」や「イチャリバ チョーデー」などのキーワードに沖縄の県民気質が凝縮されている。清明祭、ハーリーや盆旧など、伝統行事のほとんどには今日でも旧暦が使用されており、本土では消滅したアジアの文化が脈々と沖縄の日常生活の中には息づいている。

第一牧志公設市場 (2019 年 5 月、那覇市牧志)。1951 年に「牧志公設市場」として開設され、「市民の台所」として戦後の沖縄を支えてきた。沖縄県の珍しい食材を安価で購入でき、食堂では家庭料理が安く味わえることから、観光客も多く訪れる。老朽化のため 2019 年 6 月に仮設市場に移転されたが、2023 年春には元の場所に新築移転される予定である。
Daiichi Makishi Public Market (Makishi, Naha City).Established in 1951 as "Makishi Public Market," it has supported postwar Okinawa as "Citizens' Kitchen".Many tourists visit the market because they can purchase rare Okinawan foodstuffs at low prices and enjoy home-cooked food at the cafeteria at a reasonable price. Due to aging, the market was relocated to a hypothetical market in June 2019, but is scheduled to be newly built and relocated to its original location in the spring of 2023.

Chapter 4 Daily Life of Okinawans

Okinawa has experienced several *Yogawari* (drastic changes of regimes) in its history, from the Sanzan period when King Satto became a member of China under the Ming emperor (1372), to the invasion of Satsuma Domain during the Ryukyu Kingdom (1609), the disposal of Ryukyu by the Meiji government (1879), the U.S. military rule after the Battle of Okinawa (1945-1972), and the reversion to Japan (1972). Due to its background of having a history that is different from that of other regions in Japan, the prefecture has a different prefectural consciousness than other prefectures. Sometimes this is a sense of inferiority to the mainland, and at other times it is a strong sense of hometown, and the Okinawans are said to have a strong "love for their hometown". Key words such as *"nankuru-naisa," "tee-gee,"* and *"ichariba-chodee"* sum up the Okinawan character. The lunar calendar is still used for most traditional events such as the *seimei-sai, haarii,* and *kyu-bon,* and Asian culture, which has disappeared on the mainland, is still alive in Okinawa's daily life.

（1）ウチナーンチュ気質（うちなーんちゅきしつ）

　明治新政府による 1879 年（明治 12）の琉球併合までは琉球王国という独立国であった沖縄は、本土とは異なる独自の文化や県民性を有する。温暖な気候がもたらす夜型社会で飲酒を好む県民性や車社会という風土がその背景にあるといわれる。各市町村には「私たちは、きまりと時間を守りましょう」という住民憲章が今でも盛り込まれているのが多い。南国・沖縄でゆっくりと流れる時間は「ウチナータイム」と称され、県民性は「テーゲー」または「ナンクル ナイサ」などとも表現される。「幸せな人は、曖昧な状況を楽観的に捉える傾向がある」という研究結果がある。「なぜ沖縄の人は悲壮感がないのか」「なぜ沖縄は長寿県なのか」などの沖縄に対する質問があるが、その研究結果が的確に答えている。

（1）The temperament of *Uchinanchu*

　Until the annexation of Ryukyu by the new Meiji government in 1879, Okinawa was an independent country called the Kingdom of Ryukyu, and thus has its own unique culture and character that is different from that of the mainland. It is said that this is due to the warm climate of Okinawa, the nocturnal lifestyle, the preference for drinking, and the car-oriented culture. Many cities, towns, and villages still include a residents' charter that says, "Let's observe rules and time". The time that passes slowly in the tropical island of Okinawa is called *uchina*-time, and the prefectural character is also expressed as *tee-gee* or *nankuru-naisa*. Studies have shown that "happy people tend to be optimistic about ambiguous situations". The result of the study answers aptly such questions about Okinawa as, "Why are Okinawans so free of sadness?" and "Why is Okinawa a prefecture of longevity?"

①ウチナータイム

　沖縄県に存在する日本本土とは異なる独特の時間感覚をいう。飲み会など私的な集まりにおいて約束の時間に間に合わせるという意識が希薄である。その背景として「大らかな県民性」「以前は電車がなかったので、時間に縛られる習慣がない」「細かい時間という概念がない旧暦の名残が今でも根強い」などが挙げられる。待つ側に怒りや苛立ちはなく、待たせる側にも罪悪感はない。逆に、遅刻ぐらいで文句を言う人間は嫌われる場合もある。しかし、ウチナータイムには使い分けがある。宴会など私的でハッピーな会合の場合は間に合わせる必要はないが、葬式やビジネスなどアンハッピーな出来事には時間を守る。楽しいことは、時間を守るという拘束からも解放されるべきであるという考え方が根底にある。日本人は世界で唯一、何事もきっちりと時間通りに行う民族ではないだろうか。欧米やアジア各国を旅行するとそのことを実感する。そう考えると、むしろ「ウチナータイムの方がグローバルスタンダード」といえる。

① *Uchina*-time

　This refers to the unique sense of time that exists in Okinawa Prefecture that differs from that of mainland Japan. In private gatherings such as drinking parties, there is little sense of being on time for the appointment. The reason for this is that the people of the prefecture are very open-minded, there used to be no trains in the past, so there was no habit of being bound by time, and there are still strong vestiges of the lunar calendar, which has no concept of detailed time. There is no anger or frustration on the part of those who wait, and no guilt on the part of those who makes to wait. On the contrary, a person who complains about a person for being late may be disliked. However, there are different ways to use *uchina*-time. For private, happy meetings such as banquets, there is no need to be on time, but for unhappy events such as funerals and business, is punctual. The underlying idea is that fun things should be free from the constraints of punctuality. I think the Japanese are the only people in the world who do everything exactly on time. I realize this when I travel to Western and Asian countries. In this light, it can be rather said that "*uchina*-time is the global standard".

②ナンクルナイサ

　挫けずに正しい道を歩むべく努力すれば、いつか良い日が来るという意味。この言葉は「マクトゥソーケー　ナンクルナイサ」という定型句からきたもので、「マクトゥソーケー」（人として正しい行いをして努力していれば）というのが言外に含まれている。努力もせずに、単に「何とかなる」という楽天的な見通しを意味するものではない。「人事を尽くして天命を待つ」と同様に、「ナンクルナイサ精神」には単に物事を楽観的に捉えるということに加え、「しっかりと準備をしているからこそ良い未来が待っている」という視点が含まれる。主に、落ち込んだ人に対して「やるだけやったのだから、きっと何とかなる」という前向きな気持ちにさせて励ます時などに使われる。ナンクルナイサという楽観的でプラス思考的な言葉には、南国・沖縄人の大らかさ、優しさ、自信の表れが込められている。

ナンクルナイサ（Tシャツ）
Nankuru-naisa T-shirt

② *Nankuru-naisa*

　Nankuru-naisa means that if you work hard to stay on the right path, one day a good day will come. This phrase is derived from a fixed phrase "*Makutu-soukee nankuru-naisa*," which is included the wording that *makutu-soukee* (if you do the right thing as a human being and makes an effort). It does not simply an optimistic outlook that one can simply "get by" without effort. Like the phrase "do your best in all circumstances and wait for your destiny," the "*nankuru-naisa* spirit" includes not only an optimistic view of things, but also the perspective that "a good future awaits us because we are well prepared". It is mainly used to encourage people who are depressed by making them feel positive, saying, "You've done all you can, so you'll get through this. The optimistic and positive thinking phrase *nankuru-naisa* expresses the generosity, kindness, and confidence of the people of Okinawa, a tropical country.

③テーゲーとテーゲー主義（てーげーしゅぎ）

　「大概」「おおよそ」「おおよそその程度」を意味する沖縄方言。程度の意や相手の力量を認める場合などにも用いられるが、物事を否定的に、あるいは軽くみる時にも使われる。そこから、問題を突き詰めて考えずに大まかに受け止め、のんびりと気楽に過ごす悠長で楽天的な態度が生まれる。このような時間的感覚を示す用語として「ウチナータイム」がある。それらが転じてウチナーンチュの人生観や性格などを指して「テーゲー」や「テーゲー主義」と言われ、内外からしばしば批判されることがある。決められたルールや約束を遵守できない、言動が無責任で業務も雑で信用できないという否定的なニュアンスで捉えられることが多い。一方で「細かいことや過ぎたことは気にしない」「規則に縛られず融通が利く」「大らかで寛容である」などの意味で、沖縄県の良き文化としても評価されている。根底には、ウチナータイムと同様に「許し合う精神」があるとみる考え方である。一時期は「テーゲー」はネガティブな意味で認知されていたが、近年は沖縄の「スローライフ」的な、ゆったりとした部分が注目され「テーゲー」も再評価されつつある。骨と骨が直に当たってギスギスしない役目を軟骨が果たしているように、狭い島社会の中で調和して生きていくためにウチナーンチュは、

テーゲーの精神を育んできた。テーゲー主義は、馴染めない人には「単なるいいかげん」としか捉えられないかも知れないが、実は奥が深いのである。ウチナーンチュの性格を表現している「テーゲー」は沖縄の代表的な方言の一つであり、人生観である。

③ *Tee-gee* and *Tee-geeism*

An Okinawan dialect word meaning "approximately," "about," or "about that much. It can be used to indicate degree or to acknowledge someone's ability, but it can also be used to negatively or lightly evaluate something. From this comes the attitude of taking a broad view of the problem without thinking it through, and a carefree, easy-going, optimistic attitude. The term *uchina*-time is used to describe this sense of time, and is often used to refer to *uchinanchu's* outlook on life and character as *tee-gee* or *tee-geeism,* which is often criticized from within and without. It is often perceived as a negative nuance, as an inability to comply with set rules and promises, irresponsible in words and actions, and unreliable because of messy work. On the other hand, it is also regarded as a good cultural trait of Okinawa, as it means "not caring about details and things that have gone," "flexible without being bound by rules," and "generous and tolerant. The idea is that there is a "spirit of forgiveness" at the root, just as there is in *uchina*-time. At one time, *tee-gee* was perceived in a negative way, but in recent years, "*tee-gee*" is being reevaluated as the "slow life" of Okinawa is gaining attention. Just as cartilage plays the role of preventing bones from becoming misshapen when they come into direct contact with each other, *uchinanchu* has developed the spirit of *tee-gee* in order to live in harmony with the narrow island society. *Tee-geeism* may be viewed as "just, simply loose" by those who are not familiar with it, but it is actually profound. *Tee-gee*, which describes the character of *uchinanchu*, is one of the typical Okinawan dialects and outlook on life.

④イチャリバ チョーデー

　沖縄の諺で、単独でも使われるが続けて「ぬーふぃだてぃぬあが」とよく用いられる。「いったん出会ったら兄弟のように、何の隔てがあるか」という一期一会のような意味である。「ゆきずりの人と道ですれ違うのも前世からの因縁である」という仏教の教えにも共通する。イチャリバ チョーデーの精神は、沖縄の歴史の悲惨な経験や苛酷な体験を経て助け合いの精神が生まれ、根付いたものといわれる。人と人との繋がりを大切にし、出会った相手のことを家族のように思うウチナーンチュの深い人情の表れともいえる。イチャリバ チョーデーの例文として有名なのが、沖縄民謡の「兄弟小節」（ちょうでぇーぐゎーぶし）の一節。曲の中で繰り返される歌詞「いちゃりばちょーで

兄弟小節の歌碑（与那原町東浜）
Monument of Okinawan folk song "*Chodee-gwaa-bushi*"
(Agarihama, Yonabaru Town)

ー　ぬーふぃだてぃぬ　あが　かたれー　あしば」の歌意は「出会えば兄弟、何の隔たりもない、酒を飲んで語りあい、歌い、踊ろう」というものである。大らかで明るく、人と人との出会いを大切にするウチナーンチュの県民性がこの歌にも表現されている。

④ *Ichariba-chodee*

This is an Okinawan proverb that is often used alone or in combination with the phrase *"Nuu fidatinu aga"*. It means, "Once you meet, you are like brothers, what is the distance between us?" It is also common to the Buddhist teaching that "passing by a stranger on the street is a cause from a previous life". The spirit of *ichariba-chodee* is said to have been born and rooted in the spirit of mutual help through the tragic and harsh experiences of Okinawa's history. It can be said to be an expression of the deep human feelings of *uchinanchu*, who value human relationships and consider the people they meet to be like family. One of the most famous examples of *ichariba-chodee* is a passage from the Okinawan folk song *Chodee-gwaa-bushi*. The lyrics repeated in the song, *"Ichariba chodee nuu fidatinu aga katare ashiiba,"* mean: "When we meet, we are brothers, there is no gap between us, let's drink, talk, sing, and dance". The song also expresses the *uchinanchu* Prefectural Characteristics, which is generous, cheerful, and values encounters with other people.

（２）チャンプルー文化（ちゃんぷるーぶんか）

　沖縄県民の日常や文化を語る時、「チャンプルー」という言葉はキーワードの１つである。「ゴーヤーチャンプルー」や「そうめんチャンプルー」などの沖縄料理は今や完全に全国区になっており、チャンプルーという言葉も全国区になりつつある。チャンプルー料理は、沖縄の家庭料理の代表で野菜や肉、豆腐などいろんな食材を炒め合わせた料理で、単なる「ごちゃ混ぜ」と思うかも知れないが、「他の土地からいいものを取り入れ、ウチナーンチュの好みに合うように手を加え、改良を重ね、独自のものに仕上げた沖縄オリジナル料理」である。チャンプルーは料理に限らず、沖縄文化の基本をなす。例えば首里城の別邸・識名園には室町時代の数寄屋様式の中に中国的な様式や、石材を用いた沖縄様式がミックスされている。ユネスコの無形文化遺産に登録されている「組踊」は日本の能と歌舞伎を取り入れた沖縄版オペラで、世界に認められたチャンプルー芸能である。首里城跡、座喜味城跡、勝連城跡などの世界遺産も「中国にも日本にもない沖縄独特の産物」である。県民の日常生活で生き続ける清明祭、ハーリー、エイサーや盆行事など、今日でも旧暦を使用する伝統行事は多く、本土では消滅したアジアの文化が脈々と沖縄に息づいている。チャンプルー文化は、小国が諸国との争いを避け生き延びる知恵であり、沖縄文化の根幹を成している。

(2) *Champuruu* Culture

The word *champuruu* is one of the key words when talking about the daily life and culture of Okinawans. Okinawan dishes such as *gouyaa-champuruu* and *soumen-champuruu* are now completely nation-wide, and the word *champuruu* is also becoming nation-wide. *Champuruu* cuisine is a typical Okinawan home-style dish made by stir-frying various ingredients such as vegetables, meat, tofu, etc. You may think it is just a jumble of ingredients, but it is an "original Okinawan dish made by taking good things from other places and modifying and improving them to suit the tastes of *uchinanchu*, and it is an Okinawan original dish. *Champuruu* is not limited to cooking, but forms the basis of Okinawan culture. For example, the Shuri Castle's villa, Shikina-*en* Garden, is a mix of *Muromachi*-era Sukiya style, Chinese style, and Okinawan style using stone. *Kumi-odori*, which is registered as an intangible cultural heritage by UNESCO, is an Okinawan version of opera that incorporates Japanese *noh* and *kabuki,* and is a world-recognized *champuruu* performing art. World heritage sites such as the ruins of Shuri Castle, Zakimi Castle, and Katsuren Castle are also "unique products of Okinawa, not found in China or Japan". Even today, there are many traditional events that use the lunar calendar, such as the *seimei* festival, *haarii*, *eisaa*, and *bon* festivals that continue to live on in the daily lives of the people of the prefecture, and Asian cultures that have disappeared in the mainland are still alive and well in Okinawa. The *champuruu* culture is also a wisdom for small countries to survive and avoid conflicts with other countries, and is the basis of Okinawan culture.

（３）旧正月（きゅうしょうぐゎち）

　太陰暦の正月のことで、太陰暦を使っていた中国文化圏や、中国人や華僑の多い国や地域で祝われる。日本はアジア圏の国の中で、旧正月を祝わない数少ない国の一つである。今日の沖縄本島では新暦の１月１日に正月を行うところが殆どだが、漁業が盛んな海人の町・糸満市やうるま市では、旧正月を祝う風習が現在でも残っている。大晦日には「沖縄そば」を食べて年を越し、年が明けると各家庭には年賀状が届き、子供たちは「お年玉」をもらう。沖縄には正月が３回あると言われている。新暦の１月１日、旧正月、そして旧暦の１月16日である。旧暦１月16日は、「ジュールクニチー」と呼ばれ、あの世の正月（ご先祖様の正月）といわれる。今では新暦使用が主流だが、古くからの風習や文化を大切にする沖縄では、今でも各地に残る年中行事は殆どが旧暦によるものである。

旧正月の仏壇（糸満市）
Buddhist altar(*Butsu'dan*) on Lunar New Year's Day (Itoman City)

（３）*Kyu-shogwachi* (Lunar New Year)

　Kyu-shogwachi is the lunar New Year and is celebrated in the Chinese cultural sphere where the lunar calendar was used and in countries and regions where there are many Chinese and overseas Chinese. Japan is one of the few countries in Asia that does not celebrate the Lunar New Year. Today, most of the main island of Okinawa celebrates New Year's Day on the first day of the first month of the new calendar year, but in Itoman City and Uruma City, where the fishing industry is thriving, the custom of celebrating the Lunar New Year still remains. On New Year's Eve, we eat Okinawa-*soba* to pass the year, and at the beginning of the year, each family receives a New Year's greeting card, and the children get "New Year's gifts". It is said that there are three New Year's days in Okinawa: January 1 of the new calendar, the Lunar New Year, and January 16 of the Lunar calendar. The 16th of January in the lunar calendar is called *juuruku-nichii* and is said to be the "New Year's Day for ancestors". Nowadays, the new calendar is the mainstream, but in Okinawa, where customs and culture from long ago are important, most of the annual events that still remain in many places are based on the lunar calendar.

（４）初起し（はちうくし）

　旧正月２日または３日に行う仕事始めの儀礼である。農家では「初畑（ハチバル）」と称し、鍬で３度畑を掘り起こしたり、畑の見回りをして朝のうちに切り上げる。漁師は漁船にお供え物をして、大漁旗を掲げる。年間の安全や豊漁を祈願した後は船上で酒と料理を用意して祝宴を行う。大工は鋸（のこぎり）の目立てをする。どの職業も本格的な仕事始めは「初起し」の翌日である。

(4) *Hachi-ukushi*

It takes place on the second or third day of the Lunar New Year, and is a ritual for starting work. Farmers call it *hachi-baru*, digging up the field three times with a hoe or making rounds of the field to cut off work in the morning. Fishermen make offerings to the fishing boats and raise the big fishing flag. After praying for safety and a good catch during the year, a feast is held on board with sake and food prepared. Carpenters sharpen their saws. The first day of work for all professions is the day after *hachi-ukushi*.

糸満漁港の大漁旗（初起し）
Hachi-ukushi, Big Fishing Flag at Itoman Fishing Port
(Itoman City)

（5）十六日（じゅうるくにちー）

旧暦1月16日は「グソーの正月」とも称されるように、亡くなった祖先のための正月を祝う概念であり、供物を献じて故人の霊を偲び供養する。ほとんどの地域で、かつてはお墓参りをして墓前祭を営むのが当たり前とされていたが、現在は、三年忌を過ぎると墓の掃除のみ済ませ、供物は仏壇だけとする家庭が増えている。その一方で、沖縄本島北部や宮古・八重山などの離島では、正月に帰郷できない人たちも十六日祭に合わせて里帰りするほど重要な行事である。過去1年間に亡くなった人は「ミーサ」（新霊）と呼ばれ、ミーサのある家のジュールクニチーは「ミージュルクニチー」と称し、通常のジュールクニチーより盛大に営まれる。

(5) *Juuruku-nichii* (January 16th of lunar calendar)

The 16th day of the first lunar month, also known as the "New Year of *gusou*," is the concept of celebrating the New Year for deceased ancestors, and offerings are made to endure and memorialize the spirits of the deceased. In the past, it was considered normal to visit the grave and hold a graveside service, but now, after the third anniversary of the death of the deceased, more and more families seem to only clean the grave and make offerings at the Buddhist altar. On the other hand, in the northern part of the main island of Okinawa and in remote islands such as Miyako and Yaeyama, this event is so important that people who are unable to return home for the New Year's Day also return home for *Juuruku-nichii*. People who have died in the past year are called *miisa* (new spirits), and the *Juuruku-nichii* of a house with a *miisa* is called *mii-Juuruku-nichii*, and is held more grandly than the usual *Juuruku-nichii*.

宮古島の十六日
Visitting to the grave on *Juuruku-nichii* (January 16th of lunar calendar) (Miyako Island)

（6）二十日正月（はちかしょうぐゎち）

　古来の習わしでは、1 月 20 日をもって正月行事がすべて終了するとされており、餅や正月料理を食べ尽くしたり飾り物を納めたりする。沖縄で「ハチカ・ショウグヮチ」と呼ばれるこの伝統は、日本各地でもまだ息づいている。正月料理として残った魚の骨や頭を、大根や団子などと一緒に煮て食べたので本土では「骨正月」や「団子正月」ともいわれる。かつて沖縄ではこの日、那覇市辻の遊郭では華やかに着飾った「ジュリ（尾類・遊女・芸奴）」たちが郭内を踊り歩く「尾類馬祭り」が催された。これは、かつて辻の遊郭で働いた女性たちに祈りを捧げ、商売繁盛と豊年を願う奉納演舞。ジュリウマ祭りは、那覇ハーリー、那覇大綱挽と並ぶ那覇の 3 大行事で、300 年以上の歴史があるといわれる。

ジュリ馬祭り（2019 年）
Juri'uma-matsuri on *Hachika-shogwachi* (January 20th of the lunar calendar)(Naminoue, Naha City)

（6）*Hachika-shogwachi* (January 20th of the lunar calendar)

　According to ancient custom, January 20th marks the end of all New Year's events, with all rice cakes and New Year's dishes eaten and decorations put away. This tradition, known as *hachika-shogwachi* in Okinawa, is still alive and well in many parts of Japan. The bones and heads of fish left over from New Year's cooking were boiled with *daikon* (Japanese radish), dumplings and eaten, so the day is also called *hone-shougatsu* or *dango-shougatsu* in the mainland. In Okinawa, the *juri'uma-matsuri* used to be held on this day at the Tsuji brothel in Naha City, where gaily dressed *juri* (prostitutes, geisha) dancing around the brothel. This is a dedication performance to the women who once worked at Tsuji's brothel, praying for prosperity and a good harvest. The *juri'uma-matsuri* is one of the three major events in Naha, along with Naha-*haarii* (Dragon Boat Race) and Naha-*oh-tsunahiki* (Great Tug of War) and is said to have a history of over 300 years.

（7）ウマチー

　沖縄の御願行事としてのウマチー（お祭り）は、もともと首里王府が積極的に行っていた稲と麦の豊穣祈願と収穫祭である。本来は、旧暦 2 月から 6 月にかけて麦 2 回、稲 2 回の合計 4 回行われた。2 月 15 日は「ニングゥチウマチー」と称する麦の穂祭、3 月 15 日の「サングゥチウマチー」は麦の収穫祭。5 月 15 日の「グングゥチウマチー」は稲の穂祭で、6 月 15 日の「ルクグゥチウマチー」は稲の収穫祭である。八重山諸島では麦稲よりも粟の栽培が盛んだったため「プーリィー」など様々な呼び名がある。ウマチーが最も盛んな時期は琉球王朝時代で、ノロを中心として各集落の拝所で儀礼が行われた。現在では都市部ではすっかり見られないが、集落単位や門中単位で行うところが本島南部など地方に残っている。門中単位の場合は、宗家（ムートゥヤー）の神棚に神酒（みき）や菓子・果物の盛り合わせをお供えし、子孫繁栄を願う。

（7）*Umachii* (fertility rites)

　Umachii, a prayer event in Okinawa, was originally a prayer for a good harvest of rice and wheat and a harvest festival, actively conducted by the Shuri royal government. Originally, four festivals were held every year from February to June of the lunar calendar, twice for wheat and twice for rice: on February 15 for the Festival of the Ears of Wheat, *ningwachi-umachii*; on March 15 for the Festival of the Harvest of Wheat, *sangwachi-umachiii*; on May 15 for the Festival of the Ears of Rice, *gungwachi-umachii*; and on June 15 for the Festival of the Harvest of Rice, *rukugwachi-umachii*. In the Yaeyama Islands, millet cultivation has been more popular than wheat or rice cultivation, so it is called by various names such as *puurii*. *Umachii* was most popular during the Ryukyu dynasty, when rituals were performed at worship sites in each village, led by *noro*. Nowadays, it is no longer seen in urban areas, but there are still some places in the southern part of the main island where it is performed at the village unit or at the *munchu* unit. If the ceremony is held on a *munchu* basis, sacred *sake*, sweets and fruits are offered at the altar of the *souke* (the representative of the *munchu* also known as *muutu-yaa*) to pray for the prosperity of their descendants.

（8）浜下り（はまうり）

　旧暦3月3日に浜辺に下りて災厄を払い清める民間信仰による風俗。沖縄では昔から女性たちは皆で塩水に手足を浸して汚れを落とす儀礼を行ってきた。以前は、男性は一緒に参加しなかったが、今ではビーチでの行楽としての意味合いが強くなり、家族行事となっている。

　旧暦3月3日は1年間で干満の差が最も大きい大潮になり、この日の干潮時には海浜や干瀬が最も広がる。奄美諸島では、餅を作り先祖に供え、老若男女が浜辺に下りて潮干狩りをする。沖縄では、重箱にご馳走を盛り祖霊に供えたあと浜辺に下り、潮に手足を浸して不浄を清め健康を祈願す

三月菓子（浜下りの行事菓子）
Sangwachi-gwaashi (confectionery eaten on March 3rd of the lunar calendar for the *Hamauri* event)

る。今日の沖縄では、集落の老若男女が総出して浜辺で過ごす地域や、女性だけが浜に下りて一日を過ごす地域がある。宮古諸島では、「サニツ」と称して血族集団ごとに浜下りする古風な行事がある。美男に化けた蛇に犯された娘が浜に下りて身を清めたという伝説が沖縄の「浜下り」行事の由来である。3月に農事との関わりで禊（みそぎ）をするため、イソアソビやイソマツリと称して潮干狩りや飲食をする習俗は、かつて日本各地でみられた。

(8) *Hamauri*

　A custom based on folk belief that on the 3rd day of the 3rd month of the lunar calendar, people go down to the beach to purify themselves from bad luck. In Okinawa, women have long performed the ritual of soaking their hands and feet in salt water to remove dirt. In the past, men did not participate together, but now it has become more of a picnic on the beach and a family event.

　The third day of the third lunar month is the highest tide of the year with the greatest difference in ebb and flow, and at low tide on this day, the beaches and ebb currents are at their widest. On that day in the Amami Islands, people make *mochi* (rice cakes) and offer them to their ancestors, and then men and women of all ages go down to the beach for Clam digging. In Okinawa, after offering a stacked box filled with food to the spirits of the ancestors, people go down to the beach and dip their hands and feet in the tide to purify themselves of impurities and pray for good health. In Okinawa today, there are areas where all the people in the village, young and old, men and women, spend the day at the beach, and areas where only the women go down to the beach to spend the day, and in the Miyako islands, it is called *sanitsu*, an old-fashioned event in which each group of people of the same bloodline goes down to the beach. The legend of a girl who was raped by a snake disguised as a beautiful man and went down to the beach to purify herself is the origin of the *hamauri* event in Okinawa. In March, people in many parts of Japan used to purify themselves by eating and drinking at the tide, called *iso-asobi* or *iso-matsuri*, in order to purify themselves in connection with agricultural work.

（9）ユタ

　沖縄県と鹿児島県奄美諸島の民間霊媒師（シャーマン）であり、霊的問題のアドバイスや、解釈を生業とする霊能者である。東北地方の「イタコ」等と同様に、呪術・宗教職能者は奄美・沖縄諸島では「ユタ」、「ムヌシリ」または「トキ」などと呼ばれ、宮古諸島では「カンカカリヤ」、八重山諸島では「カンピトゥ」などと呼ばれる。沖縄で民衆の宗教的機能を担う職能者は、祝女（ノロ）・根神（ニーガン）・司（ツカサ）等の神人（カミンチュ）と、シャーマンとしての「ユタ」に大別される。前者は、主として御嶽やグスク等の拝所において集落の公的祭祀や共同体の祈

三重城で祈るユタ
Yuta praying at Mii-*gusuku*(Nishi-*machi*, Naha City)

願行事の司祭をする。後者は、個人や家族に関する運勢、吉凶の判断、禍厄の除災、病気の平癒祈願など私的な呪術信仰的領域に関与している。ユタの多くは女性で、サーダカウマリ（生まれつき霊能が高い）とされ、ユタになる過程でカミダーリという特異な心身の異常を体験し、苦しみながら長年の修行を経る。ユタは迷信で人々を惑わすものとして、かつては厳しく弾圧されてきた歴史がある。ユタに対する取り締まりは、「羽地仕置」（1673 年）など王府によるものばかりでなく、内法でもユタ禁止政策が貫かれてきた。近代でもユタが警察に拘留されたり、戦時体制下でも「ユタ狩り」が実施された。他方、沖縄では「医者半分、ユタ半分？」ともいわれ、原因不明の病や精神的な病の場合は、医師が「ユタに診てもらったら」と助言する場合もあるほど、今日でも県民生活に根付いている。ユタからの助言は、心身の不調や災凶の原因を祖先祭祀のあり方や屋敷・聖地との関わりを説明することが多い。

(9) *Yuta*

　A folk medium (shaman) in Okinawa Prefecture and the Amami Islands in Kagoshima Prefecture, a spiritualist who makes a living advising on and interpreting spiritual matters. Like *itako* in the Tohoku region, witchcraft religious practitioners are called *yuta*, *munu-shiri* or *toki* in the Amami and Okinawa islands, *kan-kakariya* in the Miyako islands, and *kam-pitu* in the Yaeyama islands. In Okinawa, the professionals who perform religious functions for the people can be roughly divided into two groups: *Kaminchu*, such as *noro*, *nii-gan*, and *tsukasa*, and *yuta*, who are shamans. The former mainly preside over public rituals of the village and prayer events for the community at worship sites such as *utaki* and *gusuku*. The latter is involved in the realm of private magical beliefs, such as personal and family fortune, good and bad fortune, the elimination of disasters, and prayers for healing of illness. Most of *yuta* are women and are considered to be *saadaka-umari* (highly psychic by nature), and in the process of becoming a *yuta*, they experience a peculiar physical and mental abnormality called *kami-daari* and go through years of suffering and training. *Yuta* has a history of being severely suppressed in the past as something that misled people with superstition. Crackdowns on *yuta* have not only been imposed by the royal government, such as the *Haneji-shioki* (1673), but also by internal laws. Even in modern times, *yuta* was detained by the police, and *yuta* hunting was carried out during the war. On the other hand, in Okinawa, it is said that "*isha-hambun yuta-hambun*" (the doctor and the *yuta* play a half and half role in curing illness), and *yuta* is so ingrained in the lives of the people of the prefecture even today that doctors sometimes advise people to consult with *yuta* in cases of unexplained illness or mental illness. Advice from *yuta* often explains the cause of physical and mental illnesses and disasters to be the ancestral rituals and the relationship with the house or sacred place.

(10) 門中 (むんちゅう)・門中墓（むんちゅうばか）

①門中

　門中とは父方血縁によって結びつく一族であり、同一の墓を有し祭祀を一緒に行う。日本の同族や中国の宗族などは門中に似た血縁集団の概念である。門中の本家筋にあたる宗家（むーとぅやー）と分家筋が一緒に共通の祖先祭祀を行い、本家が中心的な役割を果たす。本土の「同族」と比較すると、集団の結合が村落の枠を超えて機能している点も特徴である。門中の代表的な年中祭祀として、門中の祖先に関わる墓に詣でる清明祭、旧暦４月・５月のウマチー（御祭り）、東御廻り（あがりうまーい）や今帰仁御廻り（なきじんうまーい）といわれる聖地巡拝などがある。士族の家譜編集（1689年）を機に17世紀末以降、王府時代の士族を中心に生成、発達してきたとされ、時代とともに平民層、農耕社会に模倣されてきた。主として沖縄本島南部を中心に発達し、後には本島北部や離島にも広がったが、その活動形態や組織の結合の度合いは地域によって大きく異なる。家の継承において、本土では婿養子による継承も許されるが、沖縄の門中では父系血縁による継承を守ろうという強い指向があり、養子を取る場合にも養子同門中制の原則に固執する。かつては門中の結束は固く、奨学金を出したり託児所を作ったりもしたが、現在は門中意識も次第に薄まってきている。

　（例）幸地腹（こうちばら）門中、大屋（うふや）門中、山口門中、平田門中、世理（しりー）門中、照屋腹門中、与谷腹門中

(10) *Munchu, Munchu-baka* (*Munchu* tombs)

① *Munchu*

Munchu is a clan that is related by blood on the father's side, and share the same tomb and perform rituals together. The Japanese *douzoku* (relative) and Chinese *souzoku* (sect) are similar concepts of *munchu*. The head family (*muutu-yaa*) and the branch families perform the rituals for their common ancestors together, with the head family playing the central role. Compared to the clan system on the mainland, the Okinawan *munchu* is unique in that the group is organized beyond the geographical limits of a village. The typical annual rituals include *seimei-sai* in which the clan members visit their clan tombs to offer prayers, *umachii* (fertility rites) held in April and May of the lunar calendar, and pilgrimage to the sacred sites called *agari-umaai* and *nakijin-umaai*. It is said to have been created and developed mainly among the samurai during the Royal period since the end of the 17th century with the compilation of the family tree of the samurai (1689), and has been imitated by the commoners and agricultural society with time. It developed mainly in the southern part of the main island of Okinawa and later spread to the northern part of the main island and the outlying islands, but the form of its activities and the degree of organization vary greatly from region to region. In the past, there was a strong sense of unity among the members, and they even offered scholarships and built day-care centers, but nowadays the sense of unity among the members is gradually fading.

examples: Kouchi-*bara-munchu*, Uhuya-*munchu*, Yamaguchi-*munchu*, Hirata-*munchu*, Shirii-*munchu*, Tiira-*bara-munchu*, Yuutan-*bara-munchu*

②門中墓

　門中によって所有、使用される共同墓である。本島北部や周辺離島でも門中組織の発達に伴い、門中墓がみられるようになった。沖縄本島南部に比較的多く分布しており、宮古や八重山などでは門中墓がみられないところもある。清明祭や七夕、十六日（ジュウルクニチー）などでは門中墓を前に一族が集まりお墓参りを行う。幼くして亡くなった子どもや事故死、自殺など「天寿を全うしていない」と判断された遺骨は中に入れない門中も多い。このような場合は「子ども墓」や「納骨堂」を敷地内に造り弔うことがある。県内最大級の門中墓は、糸満市にある幸地腹（こうちばら）・赤比儀腹（あかひぎばら）の共同墓で約 1600 坪もの敷地面積を持ち、両門中の子孫は現在約 5000 人ともいわれる。

幸地腹・赤比儀腹門中の共同墓 (糸満市)
Communal tomb of Kochi-bara and Akahigi-*bara-Munchu* (Itoman City)

② *Munchu-baka*

　A *munchu-baka* is a communal tomb owned and used by the *munchu*. In the northern part of the main island and in the surrounding islands, as the organization of *munchu* developed, *munchu* tombs began to be found. They are relatively common in the southern part of the main island of Okinawa, and in some places such as Miyako and Yaeyama, there are no *munchu* tombs. During the *seimei-sai, tanabata* (Star Festival), and *Juuruku-nichii* (January 16th of the lunar calendar), clan members gather in front of the tombs and visit the tombs. In many cases, the remains of children who died at an early age, in accidents, suicides, etc., are not allowed inside. In such cases, a children's grave or ossuary may be built on the premises for mourning. One of the largest *munchu-baka* in the prefecture is the Kouchi-*bara* and Akahigi-*bara* communal tombs in Itoman City, which cover a land area of about 1,600 *tsubo* (about 5,300 ㎡), and the descendants of both *munchu* are said to number about 5,000 at present.

(11) 屋号 (やごう)

　屋号は、各戸が持つ「姓」以外の通称で、日本だけでなくヨーロッパ諸国においても使われており、家の称号のようなものであった。日本では、士農工商の身分制度によって分類されていたため、武士以外の一般庶民は名字を持つことが許されなかった。人口があまり多くない頃は名前だけで十分個人が特定できたが、人口増加に伴い、特に商人の場合は個人が特定できなければ不都合が生じた。そこで、武士が使用する名字の代わりに、庶民は「屋号」で個人を特定し、各家で代々引き継がれた。商家独特のものと考えられているが、祖先名、職業名の他に、家の本家・分家、その家の立地条件に添

う形で名付けられる。

　沖縄では、「仏壇を継ぐ＝家を継ぐ」という考えが根強く、家の継承者は一族の長男というケースが多い。屋号は長男が代々引き継ぐので、長男以外の分家する者は本家の屋号が使えなくなり新たに作ることになる。特に田舎の場合、同じ姓が多く、屋号を付けて区別する必要があった。沖縄では「ヤーンナー」（家名）と呼ばれ、村落など地域社会において家族や個人の識別に大きな機能をはたしてきた。他集落や県外からの移

屋号「御殿」の門中墓（糸満市与座）
Munchu-baka with the house name "Udun" (Yoza, Itoman City)

住者が多い都心部では、屋号を持たない世帯も増えているが、都心部から離れた地域では今でも屋号が人々のコミュニケーションに欠かせない大切なものとされている。今日でも告別式の新聞広告に、故人の名前と合わせて屋号を掲載することが一般的である。

　（例）御殿（うどぅん）、宮城小（なーぐすくぐゎー）、親国（えーぐん）、百次（門南）（むんなん）、新屋（みーや）、比嘉門（ひがじょう）、上外間（うぃーふかま）

(11) *Yagou* (*Yaan'naa*)

　Yagou is a common name other than surname that each household has, and was used not only in Japan but also in European countries, and was a kind of family title. In Japan, there was a status system of samurai-farmers-artisans-merchants, and ordinary people other than samurai were not allowed to have surnames. When the population was not so large, the name alone was sufficient to identify an individual, but as the population grew, it became inconvenient if the individual could not be identified, especially in the case of merchants. Therefore, instead of the surname used by the samurai, the common people identified themselves personally by their *yagou*, and it passed down from generation to generation in each family. *Yagou* is considered to be unique to the merchant family, but in addition to the name of the ancestor and the name of the occupation, the *yagou* is given in accordance with the main or branch family of the family, and the location conditions of the house.

　In Okinawa, the idea that "inheriting a Buddhist altar = inheriting a family" is deeply rooted, and in many cases, the family's eldest son is the inheritor of the family. Since the *yagou* is passed down from generation to generation by the eldest son, those who branch out other than the eldest son can no longer use the family name and must create a new one. Especially in the countryside, there are many people with the same surname, so it was necessary to distinguish them by adding *yagou*. In Okinawa, it is also called *yaan'naa*, and it has played a major role in identifying families and individuals in local communities such as villages. In urban centers, where many people move from other villages or from outside the prefecture, an increasing number of households do not have *yagou*, but in areas far from the city center, *yagou* are still considered important and indispensable for communication among people. Even today, it is common for newspaper advertisements regarding farewell ceremonies to include *yagou* along with the name of the deceased.

　examples: Udun, Naagusuku-gwaa, Eegun, Mun'nan, Miiya, Higajoh, Uwii-Hukama

(12) 清明祭（シーミー）

賑やかな清明祭（那覇市、識名霊園）
Lively Seimei Festival
(Shikina Cemetery, Naha City)

　旧暦３月の「清明の節」に行う祖先供養の墓参り行事であり、中国より伝わったこの習俗は久米村では古くから行われていた。親族が墓の前に集まり、墓前に供えた「ウサンミ」といわれる重箱料理を頂く（ウサンデーと呼ばれる）。首里王府が編纂した『球陽』に、1768 年に初めて玉陵で行われたことが記されている。首里士族を中心に普及し、しだいに地方へも伝播していった。先祖祭祀とはいえ、時期的に好天の多い時期に行われる清明祭は行楽的要素も強く、中国の清明祭の面影を色濃く残している。沖縄本島北部や宮古・八重山ではシーミーより「ジュールクニチー」の方が盛大である。清明祭は神御清明（カミウシーミー）と清明祭（シーミー）に分かれる。神御清明は、門中の構成員が費用を出し合って宗家（ムートゥヤー）が料理や飲み物を準備。各家の代表が集まって、一族に繋がりの深い祖先の墓「神墓」（アジシー墓）を清明入りの早い時期に巡拝する。各家庭の清明祭はカミウシーミーが終わった後、日を改めて「トーシー墓」（当世墓）で行う。

(12) *Shiimii-sai* (*Seimei* Festival)

　This is an event to visit tombs to make offerings to ancestors during the *seimei* season in March of the lunar calendar, and this custom, which was introduced from China, had been practiced in Kume Village (*Kuninda*) for a long time. The relatives gather in front of the grave and eat a stacked box dish called *usanmi* offered in front of the grave, and eating *usanmi* is called *usandee*. In the history book Kyuyou compiled by the Shuri royal government, it is written that the ceremony was first held in 1768 at Tama-*udun* (the royal tomb). It spread mainly among the Shuri warriors, and gradually spread to other regions as well. Even though it is an ancestral ritual, the *seimei* festival is held in a time when the weather is often fine, and it has a strong recreational element, and it still retains many aspects of the *seimei* festival in China. In the northern part of the main island of Okinawa, and in Miyako and Yaeyama, the *juuruku-nichii* event is more grandiose than *shiimii*. The *simei* festival is divided into *kami-ushiimii* and *shiimii*. In the case of *kami-ushiimii*, the members of the *munchu* share the expenses and the *muutu-yaa* (head of the *munchu*) prepares the food and drinks, and representatives from each family gather to visit the "divine graves," (*kami-baka* or *ajishii-baka*) the graves of an ancestors with close ties to the *munchu*, early in the season of the *seimei* festival. The *shiimii*, which is held by each family, is held on a different day after the *kami-ushiimii* is over, at *toushii-baka*.

(13) トートーメー（位牌）

　沖縄諸島では、「お月様」と「御先祖様」のことをトートーメーと称する。今日ではもっぱら後者の意味で用いられ、先祖の位牌の別称となっている。沖縄の位牌は本土とは形状が異なる衝立状の屏位式（びょういしき）が一般的で、これに祖先の男女複数が祀られている。トートーメーは「尊御前」（とうといウメー）が訛ったもので、王府が重要視した儒教思想に基づいているといわれる。

　沖縄では父系・男系重視の門中の形成に伴って、女性の位牌継承禁止など独特の禁忌が作られた。したがって家や祖先祭祀の象徴でもある位牌（トートーメー）の祭祀権は、基本的に長男が排他的に

相続継承していく。位牌を継承することは財産相続とセットという考えがあり、家の後継者に男子がいない場合、娘に他系の婿養子をとることはなく、同じ門中内から男子を迎えることになる。これらのルールはユタ（霊能者）がもたらした規則といわれている。1980年代には「トートーメー問題」が起こり、女性が位牌祭祀の相続継承できない現実に様々な問題点が浮き彫りにされ、大きな反響を巻き起こした。男女同権思想が強まった現在でも、沖縄ではしばしばトートーメーの相続を巡る問題が起きている。

尚巴志王（左）と尚思紹王（右）の位牌（南城市佐敷）
Buddhist mortuary tablets of King Sho Hashi（left）and King Sho Shisho(right) (Sashiki, Nanjo City)

(13) *Tou-tou-mee* (memorial tablets)

In the Okinawa islands, moon and ancestors are referred to as *tou-tou-mee*. Nowadays, it is used in the latter sense, and is another name for memorial tablets. Unlike the Japanese memorial tablets, the Okinawan variation has a screen-like form, and several ancestors, both male and female, are commemorated on it. *Tou-tou-mee* is an accent on *"toutoi umee"* (the noble one), and it is said to be based on Confucianism, which was considered important by the royal government.

In Okinawa, with the formation of the patrilineal and male lineage oriented *munchu*, unique taboos were created, such as the prohibition of female from inheriting the *tou-tou-mee*. Therefore, the right to enshrine the tablets *(tou-tou-mee)*, which are the symbol of the house and ancestral rituals, is basically inherited exclusively by the eldest son. There is a belief that inheriting a memorial tablet is like inheriting property, if there are no sons in the family, it is customary to adopt a boy from the same clan, instead of adopting a husband from another lineage. These rules are said to have been brought about by *yuta* (spiritualists). In the 1980s, *"tou-tou-mee-mondai"* (inheritance rights problem) became a big issue, drawing the attention of many Okinawan women. Their main concern was that female heir inheritance of *tou-tou-mee* is still denied in modern day Okinawa, causing many problems for women. Even today, when the idea of equal rights for men and women has been strengthened, the issue over the inheritance of *tou-tou-mee* often arises in Okinawa.

(14) ハーリー

旧暦5月4日（ユッカヌヒー）に、航海の安全や豊漁を祈願して沖縄各地の漁港で行われる競漕行事。八重山では、船を沖合に出して、沖から海岸に向かって競漕するが、これも海の彼方からユー

（豊穣・幸福・富貴）を迎える儀礼といえる。「ハーリー」は「爬竜」の中国音で、竜のことである。競漕に用いるサバニと呼ばれる伝統漁船は舳先（へさき）に竜頭、艫（とも）を竜尾の彫りもので飾る。首里王府の歴史書『球陽』によると、沖縄のハーリーは 1400 年頃、南山王の弟・汪応祖（ヤフス）が中国の南京に留学し、帰国後に豊見城城の城主となり、中国で見た竜舟を作って城下の江（漫湖）で競わせたのが始まりといわれている。那覇ハーリーでは競技の前に豊見城城内の拝所を城下から参拝する。

　その他にも、久米三十六姓や那覇・西村の長浜大夫（ながはまたいふ）という人物がもたらしたなどの説がある。本来は神事だが、那覇や糸満のハーリーは大規模・観光化しているのが現状である。沖縄では例年、ゴールデンウィークが過ぎた頃に梅雨入りし「ハーリー鉦が響き渡ると梅雨が明け、本格的な夏が訪れる」といわれる。

ハーリー発祥の地（豊見城城跡内）
Stone monument at the "Birthplace of *Haarii*" (inside the ruins of Tomigusuku Castle)

(14) *Haarii* (Okinawan dragon boat race)

　The event of the rowing boats race held on the 4th day of the 5th month of the lunar calendar (*yukkanu-hii*) at fishing ports throughout Okinawa to pray for safe voyages and good catches. In Yaeyama Islands, boats are taken offshore and the race starts from there, and people row the boats toward the seashore. This can also be interpreted as a ritual to welcome *yuu* (fertility, happiness, and wealth) beyond the sea. The word *haarii* is the Chinese sound of *haryu*, meaning a dragon. The traditional fishing boats called *sabani* used for the race are decorated with a carved dragon head on the bow and a carved dragon tail on the stern. According to Kyuyo, a history book written by the Shuri royal government, it is said that Okinawa's *haarii* started around 1400 when Yafusu, the younger brother of King Nanzan, returned to Ryukyu after studying in Nanjing, China to become the lord of Tomigusuku Castle, and made dragon boats that he had seen in China to race on the river (Lake Manko) below the castle. In Naha-*haarii*, the representatives worship to the *utaki* in Tomigusuku Castle from below the castle before the competition.

　Other theories include that it was brought by Kume-*sanjuroku-sei* and a man named Nagahama Taihu of Nishimura, Naha. Originally it was a Shinto ritual, but the *haariies* of Naha and Itoman have become large scale and tourist oriented. In Okinawa, the rainy season usually begins around the time the Golden Week holidays have passed, and it is said that "the rainy season ends when the *haarii-gane* (gong) echoes through the air, and the full-blown summer arrives.

①那覇ハーリー（なははーりー）

　王府時代には国王の観覧があり、冊封使が来琉の時は首里の龍潭池でも催された。古代の那覇ハーリーは琉球王国の国家的行事として栄えたが、廃藩置県（1879 年）で琉球王国が消滅したことにより廃止された。その後、年中行事としては長らく途絶えていたが、1975 年に復活した。古くは久米、那覇、若狭町、垣花、泉崎、上泊、下泊などが参加したが、現在の競漕は泊・久米・那覇の 3 組で競われゴールデンウィーク期間中に那覇新港内

那覇ハーリー（那覇新港埠頭）
Naha-*haarii*
(Naha New Port Whart, Naha City)

で行われる。各チームともそれぞれハーリー歌があり、久米には中国語のハーリー歌もある。他地域のハーリーでは 1 つの船に 10 人程度が乗る小型のサバニ（手漕ぎ漁船）を使用するが、那覇ハーリーでは 42 人が乗る大型の爬龍船を使用する。

① Naha-*haarii*

The Naha-*haarii* is a festival that was also held at the Ryutan Pond in Shuri when envoys from China came to the Ryukyu kingdom, and there was a viewing by the king. In ancient times, the Naha-*harii* flourished as a national event of the Ryukyu Kingdom, but was abolished when the Ryukyu Kingdom ceased to exist due to the abolition of feudal domains (1879). After that, it was discontinued as an annual event for a long time, but was revived in 1975. In the past, Kume, Naha, Wakasa-*machi*, Kakinohana, Izumizaki, *Uwii*-Tomari and *Shicha*-Tomari participated in this event, but the current rowing race is competed by three groups, Tomari, Kume and Naha, and is held in Naha New Port during the Golden Week holidays. Each team has its own *haarii* song, and Kume has a Chinese *haarii* song. While other regions use small *sabani* (rowing fishing boats) with a capacity of about 10 people per boat, the Naha-*haarii* uses a large dragon boat with a capacity of 42 people.

②糸満ハーレー（いとまんはーれー）

　中国から伝来した当初は豊見城城下（漫湖）で行われた。1429 年の南山滅亡、豊見城城廃城の時点で豊見城ハーリーは糸満に移されたといわれ、糸満ハーレーの方が那覇ハーリーより歴史が古い。糸満ハーレーでは、競漕に先立って当日、市内の小高い丘「山巓毛」（サンティンモー）でノロが航海安全や豊漁を祈願する。出発の合図として「デーフイ」（旗振り）の役割をするのは、南山王から役目と屋号を授かったと伝わる「徳屋」の子孫である。競漕は西村・中村・新島の 3 チームで競

糸満ハーレー（糸満市糸満漁港）
Itoman-*Haaree* (Itoman Fishing Port, Itoman City)

われ、勝った順に集落北側にある白銀堂に詣でて 1 年間の大漁と航海安全を祈願する。現在では港内を数回廻る競漕だが、かつては沖までの折り返し競漕で、ユーをもたらす意味があった。アトラクションとしてアヒル取り競争があるが、福建省の伝統行事に因んでいるといわれる。ハーレーの翌日は「グソー（後生）バーレー」と呼ばれ、その日は水没者が海上でハーレーをするので漁師は漁に出ない。他の地域ではハーリーと呼ばれるが、糸満では「ハーレー」と呼ばれ、県内では最も壮大に行われる。漁業の町・糸満では今日でも旧暦 5 月 4 日に実施されるので市内の小中学校は休校となる。

② Itoman-*haaree*

Itoman-*haaree* was first introduced from China, and was held below the castle of Tomigusuku (Lake Manko). It is said that Tomigusuku-*haarii* was moved to Itoman at the time of the destruction of Nanzan and the abandonment of Tomigusuku Castle in 1429, and Itoman-*haaree* has a longer history than Naha-*haarii*. In the Itoman-*haaree*, *noro* prays for safe voyage and good catch at Santinmou, a small hill in the city, prior to the race. The role of *deehui* (flag-waving) as a signal for departure is played by the descendants of Tokuya, who is said to have been given the role and *yagou* by the King of Nanzan. The three teams of Nishimura, Nakamura, and Niijima compete in the *haaree* race, and in the order of victory, the winners pay a visit to Hakugindo, located on the north side of the village, to report their victories and pray for a good catch of fish and safe voyages throughout the year. Nowadays, it is a rowing race that goes around in the harbor several times, but in the past, it was a turn-around rowing race to the sea, which was meant to bring *yuu* (fertility, happiness, and wealth). The duck catching competition, which is held as an attraction, is said to be associated with a traditional event in Fujian Province. The day after the *haaree* event is called *gusou-baaree* and fishermen do not fish because it is said that the submerged will have a *haaree* race at sea. In other parts of the country, it is called a *haarii*, but in Itoman it is called a *haaree* and is the most grandiose in the prefecture. In the fishing town of Itoman, the event is still held on the fourth day of the fifth lunar month, so elementary and junior high schools in the city are closed on the day.

(15) トゥシビー（生年祝い）

　奄美・沖縄では、自分の生まれ年と同じ十二支の年を「生まれ年」といい、その新年始めの同じ十二支の日に無病息災を先祖や火の神に願い、祝宴を開く。この祝いを一般に「トゥシビー」という。生まれ年は 12 年ごとに廻ってくるから数え年 13 歳、25 歳、37 歳、49 歳、61 歳、73 歳、85 歳、97 歳にトゥシビーを催す。その中で 13 歳の祝いと 73 歳以降の祝いは特に盛大に行われる。沖縄では本土で行われる 70 歳（古希）の祝いはないが、88 歳（米寿）にも年祝いが行われる。88 歳と 97 歳

カジマヤーのパレード（カジマヤーとは「風回し」からきた方言。カジマヤーを迎える人は生まれ変わり子供に戻るという言い伝えがあり、赤い着物を着て風車を持って祝う）
Kajimayaa's Celebration Parade (*Kajimayaa* is a dialect word derived from "wind turning". There is a legend that the person who welcomes *Kajimayaa* will be reborn and become a child again, and is celebrated wearing a red kimono and holding a windmill.

のトゥシビー祝いは、語呂合わせでそれぞれ旧暦 8 月 8 日と 9 月 7 日に実施される。数え 88 歳の祝いは「トーカチ」と言われ、本土の「米寿の祝い」と同じだが、沖縄では米寿より斗掻（トカキ＝トーカチ）と呼ぶのが一般的。「カジマヤー」と呼ばれる 97 歳の祝いは、カラフルな風車を飾ったオープンカーに乗せ、風車を持たせて集落内をパレードして祝う。明治時代までのカジマヤーは、模擬葬礼だったといわれる。カジマヤーを迎えた人に死装束を着せて、模擬葬式の儀式として村の四辻（十字路）を回り、墓まで連れて行ったという記録もある。生まれ年は「厄年」といい、地域によっては今でも家や墓の新築または結婚を忌む遺習がある。13 歳に行われる生年祝いは、最初の「トゥシビー」。女子は、24 歳までに結婚するものと考えられ、実家でやる唯一の生年祝いで、次回（25 歳）以降は嫁ぎ先で行うものとされていた。

(15) *Tushibii* (Celebration of birth year)

　In Amami and Okinawa, the year of the twelve signs of the Chinese zodiac, which is the same as the year of one's birth, is called the *umare-doshi* (year of birth), and at the beginning of the New Year, a feast is held on the day of the Chinese zodiac that corresponds to one's own zodiac sign to pray to ancestors and *hinukan* (God of Fire) for good health. This celebration is generally called *tushibii*. The year of birth rotates every 12 years, so *tushibii* is held when the counting years are 13, 25, 37, 49, 61, 73, 85, and 97. Among them, the *tushibii* for 13-year-olds and 73-year-olds and beyond is a grand event. In Okinawa, people do not celebrate for 70 years of age (*Koki*), which is celebrated in mainland Japan. Rather, people celebrate for 88 years of age (*toukachi*). To play on words, the *tushibii* celebrations for the 88-year-olds and 97-year-olds are held on August 8 and September 7 of the lunar calendar, respectively. The celebration of 88 years of age is called *toukachi*, which is the same as the "celebration of *beiju*" of the mainland, but in Okinawa it is more common to call it *toukachi* (*togaki*) than *beiju*. The 97th birthyear celebration is called *kajimayaa*, and is celebrated by all the villagers with a parade through the village in an open car decorated with colorful windmills. Until the Meiji era (1868-1912), *kajimayaa* was said to be a mock funeral service. There is also a record of a mock funeral rite that the person of *kajmayaa* were dressed in death garb with a windmill and taken around the village crossroads to the grave. The year of birth is said to be a "bad year," and in some areas there is still a custom to avoid building a new house or tomb or getting married. The first *tushibii* is held at the age of 13 for everyone. However, girls were expected to be married by the age of 24, and this was the only celebration of their *tushibii* held at their parents' home, while the next one (at the age of 25) and onward was to be held at their place of marriage.

(16) 旧盆行事 (きゅうぼんぎょうじ)

　沖縄の旧盆は、清明祭（シーミー）と並び、大きな行事の一つで、旧暦 7 月 13 日から 16 日未明にわたって各家で「精霊（祖先）」を祀る行事である。その約 1 週間前の 7 月 7 日は「七夕」と呼び、精霊を家へ案内するため墓を掃除し焼香する。13 日は「ウンケー」と呼ばれ、精霊を家に迎え入れ、「ウンケージューシー」を仏壇に供えて家族と一緒に食する。14 日は「ナカヌヒー」といい、3 度の食事を仏壇に供える。15 ～ 16 日の「ウークイ」は盆行事の中心となる「精霊送り」の儀式によって、ウンケーでお迎えしたご祖先を

旧盆の仏壇 (南風原町)
Buddihist altar during *Kyu-bon* (*Obon* Festival)
(Haebaru Town)

あの世に送る日である。ウークイの夜には「ウサンミ」（御三味）と呼ばれる重箱料理をお供えする。「精霊送り」の儀式の最後は、拝みを捧げた後、「ウチカビ」（打ち紙）を燃やし、ご先祖様を見送る。ウチカビとは、「あの世のお金」のことで、ご先祖様があの世でお金に困らないように、ウチカビを燃やして見送るのである。盆行事の期間中にエイサーや獅子舞、綱引きなどの行事が地域の広場で演じられる。

(16) *Kyu-bon* (*Obon* Festival)

　The Lunar *bon* Festival in Okinawa is one of the major events, along with the *Seimei* Festival(*shiimii*), in which the "spirits (ancestors)" are worshipped in each family from July 13th to the early morning of July 16th in the lunar calendar. About a week before, on July 7, people clean the graves and burn incense to welcome the spirits into the house. The 13th is called *unkee*, when the spirits are welcomed into the house and *unkee-juushii* is offered on the altar and eaten with the family. The 14th is called *nakanu-hii* to offer three meals to the altar, and the 15-16th *uhkui* is the day to send the ancestors who were welcomed at *unkee* to the other world by the "Spirit Sending" ceremony, which is the center of the *bon* Festival. On the night of *uhkui*, a stacked box of food called *usanmi* is offered to the people. At the end of the spirit-sending ceremony, after offering prayers, *uchikabi* is burned to send off the ancestors. *Uchikabi* means "money in the afterlife," and people burn *uchikabi* to see off their ancestors so that they will not have to worry about money in the afterlife. *Eisaa* (Okinawan bon dance), *shishi-mai* (lion dances), *tsuna-hiki* (tug of war), and other events are performed in the community square during the *Obon* festival.

(17) エイサー（えいさー）

　エイサーは本土の盆踊りにあたる沖縄の伝統芸能の一つで、旧盆の時期に沖縄本島や周辺の離島および奄美群島で踊られる。囃子詞の「エイサー」が語源で、1603 年に来琉したいわき市（現在の福島県）出身の袋中上人が、仏典を踊りながら唱える「念仏踊り」を伝えたのが始まりといわれている。エイサーは従来の集団舞踊に念仏形式が加わったものと言われ、旧盆の時期に現世に戻ってくる祖先の霊を送迎するため、若者たちが歌と囃子に合わせ踊りながら地域内を練り歩く。従って、

全島エイサー祭り（コザ運動公園）
All Island *Eisaa* Festival (Koza Athletic Park, Okinawa City)

本来は単なる娯楽としてではなく、集落の重要な宗教行事であり、お盆には欠かせない魂祭として演じられた。当初は念仏歌などに合わせて踊っていたが、明治以降になって各地にエイサーが普及するようになると民謡を取り込む例が増えてきた。戦前のエイサーでは太鼓を使う例は少なく、浴衣などの普段着姿で手拭を頭に巻くスタイルが主流であったが、戦後は本島中部を中心に大きく変わった。近年では太鼓を持つスタイルが多くなり、踊り自体を鑑賞するために「全島エイサー祭り」をはじめとする各地域のエイサーを集めたイベント等も開催されている。古い伝統に新しい要素が加わり、年々盛んになっているエイサー。現在では沖縄の夏の風物詩の一つで、重要な観光イベントにもなっている。近年、沖縄では独自の文化を発展させようとする青年達の取り組みによって特に 1990 年代以降、沖縄県出身者が中心となってエイサー団体が全国的に増えている。この波は沖縄県人の移住地である北米や南米、フランスなどのヨーロッパまで広がっている。

(17) *Eisaa*

Eisaa is one of Okinawa's traditional performing arts, similar to *bon-odori* on the mainland, and is danced on the main island of Okinawa, the surrounding islands, and the Amami Islands during the Lunar *Bon* Festival. The word *eisaa* is derived from a *hayashi-kotoba* (meaningless words added a song for rhythmical effect), *eisaa*, and is said to have originated when the Buddhist priest, Taichu-*Shonin* from Iwaki City (present-day Fukushima Prefecture), who came to the Ryukyus in 1603, introduced the *nenbutsu-odori*, a dance in which Buddhist scriptures are chanted while dancing. *Eisaa* is said to be a traditional group dance with the addition of a Buddhist nembutsu style, and is performed by young people who dance to songs and music as they parade through the community to welcome and send off the spirits of ancestors who return to this world during the lunar *bon* festival. Therefore, it was originally performed not as a mere entertainment, but as an important religious event of the village, and as an indispensable soul festival for *obon*. In the beginning, people danced to Buddhist songs, but after the Meiji era (1868-1912), when *eisaa* became popular in many areas, more and more people began to incorporate folk songs. In the pre-war period, there were few examples of *eisaa* performances using drums, and the mainstream style was to wear *yukata* (summer kimono) and wrap a *tenugui* towel around one's head, but after the war, this style changed dramatically, especially in the central part of the main island. In recent years, more and more people have started to carry drums, and to appreciate the dance itself, events such as the "All Island *Eisaa* Festival" have been held to gather *eisaa* from various regions. With the addition of new elements to the old traditions, *eisaa* is becoming more and more popular every year, and is now one of the most popular summer traditions in Okinawa and an important tourist event. In recent years, especially since the

1990s, the number of *eisaa* groups mainly composed of people from Okinawa, has increased nationwide, due to the efforts of young people from Okinawa to develop their own unique culture. This wave is spreading to North and South America, where Okinawans have settled, and to Europe, including France.

(18) 綱引き (つなひき)

　豊年を祈る神事として、東西に分かれた雌雄 2 本の綱の結合によって実りを予視し、勝負の結果で豊凶を占う行事。稲作が盛んな頃は、各村落単位の「年中行事」として沖縄のほぼ全域で行われた。首里では「綾門大綱」（あいじょううーんな）と呼ばれた綱引きが、世継ぎの誕生や御冠船（冊封船）の来航時などに国家的祝賀行事として催された。近年は大衆娯楽行事としての傾向が強く、那覇・与那原・糸満（ 3 大大綱引き）のように観光化されているのが現状である。

　「那覇三大祭り」の一つである那覇大綱挽は、毎年、10 月の「体育の日」の連休に国道 58 号線の「久茂地交差点」で行われ、400 年以上の歴史と伝統を持っている。那覇大綱挽の起源は琉球王国時代にさかのぼり、本来、仲島と辻の遊女たちが引き合ったのが始まりとされる。勝負は、雌綱が勝つと翌年は豊年になるとされた。その後、国際交流都市として繁栄するのに伴い、国王即位の祝賀行事として曳かれるなど、琉球王国独特の大綱挽に成長した。沖縄戦で一時中断したが、1971 年（昭和 46 年）に那覇市制施行 50 周年を記念して復活した。「農村の稲作儀礼としての綱引きとは異なり、都市型のイベント綱挽」が特徴といわれ、1995 年には「世界一の藁綱」としてギネスブックに認定された。

那覇大綱挽（国道 58 号線、久茂地交差点）
Naha Great Tug-of War (Route 58, Kumoji intersection, Naha City)

(18) *Tsuna-hiki* (tug of war)

　As a Shinto ritual to pray for a good harvest, and an event to predict the harvest by the union of two ropes, one male and one female, divided into east and west. The result of the game is used to predict the fertility of the harvest. When rice cultivation was flourishing, it was held as an "annual event" in each village in almost all areas of Okinawa. In Shuri, a tug-of-war called *Aijo-uun'na* was held as a national celebration for the birth of an heir or the arrival of *ukansen* (tributary ships from China). In recent years, the tug-of-war has tended to be a mass entertainment event, and has become a tourist attraction, as in the case of Naha, Yonabaru, and Itoman (the three major tug-of-war events).

　The Naha Great Tug-of-War, one of the "Three Biggest Festivals of Naha City," is held every year in October during the "Sports Day" holidays at the Kumoji intersection on Route 58, and has a history and tradition of over 400 years. The origin of the Great Tug-of-War of Naha dates back to the Ryukyu Kingdom era, is said to have been started by courtesans from Nakajima and Tsuji, the pleasure quarters in Naha. It was thought that if the female rope won, there would be a good harvest the following year.　Later, as the city prospered as a city of international exchange, it grew into the great tug-of-war unique to the Ryukyu Kingdom, being held as a celebration of the enthronement of the king. The event was temporarily suspended during the Battle of Okinawa, but was revived in 1971 to commemorate the 50th anniversary of Naha City's establishment. Unlike the tug of war as a ritual of rice cultivation in rural areas, the tug of war is said to be an urban event, and in 1995, it was recognized by the Guinness Book of World Records as the "world's largest rope made of straw".

(19) ユイマールとモアイ

　ユイマールとは、賃金の支払いをともなわない労働交換の慣行で、単にユイ（結）とも言う。「ゆい」は「結」（共同、協労）で、「まーる」は「回る」の訛りで順番を表す。従って「ユイマール」とは「相互扶助」を順番にかつ平等に行うことを意味する。主に、地縁や血縁で結ばれた数戸の農家同士で行われ、共同体の最も原始的な相互助け合いである。農村に資本主義経済が浸透し、労働力が賃金で評価されるようになるとユイマールは崩壊していった。沖縄では、サトウキビの刈り取り、田植え、稲刈りの他、家や墓の建築時のユイマールもあった。

　沖縄にはユイマールの精神から生まれた「模合」（モアイ）という文化がある。簡単に言うと「金融機関を通さない、仲間内での金の貸し借り」のこと。模合発祥の詳細は明らかではないが、18世紀以前から行われていたようである。形態としては、親族模合、職場などで行われる友人模合や、事業経営者同士で行われる高額模合などがある。模合は今ではメンバーが顔を合わせ、飲食しながら近況を報告するコミュニケーションの一つという要素が強いが、メンバー同士の信頼が不可欠で、人間関係をはかるバロメーターとしての側面もある。

(19) *Yuimaaru, Moai*

　Yuimaaru is the practice of exchanging labor without payment of wages, also known as *yui*. The word *yui* means "cooperation or collaboration," and *maaru* is a corruption of "turn," indicating order. Therefore, *yuimaaru* means "mutual aid" in turn and equally. This is the most primitive form of mutual help in a community, mainly among a few farmers who are related by land or blood. As the capitalist economy penetrated the rural areas and labor became valued by wages, *yuimaaru* gradually collapsed. In Okinawa, in addition to sugar cane harvesting, rice planting, and rice harvesting, there was also *yuimaaru* during the construction of houses and tombs.

　In Okinawa, there is a culture called *moai*, which was born from the spirit of *yuimaaru*. In simple terms, it means "lending and borrowing money among friends without going through a financial institution. The details of the origin of *moai* are not clear, but it seems to have been practiced before the 18th century. The forms of *moai* include those between relatives, those between friends at work, and those between business owners who handle large sums of money. *Moai* is now more of a communication tool where members gather to eat and drink together and report on each other's progress, but it also serves as a barometer of human relations, as trust among members is essential.

(20) 泡盛 (あわもり)、古酒 （クース）、ハブ酒

　泡盛の名前の由来は、かつて酒精度を測るのに「泡を盛る」方法がありそのことに起因すると言われる。沖縄では「サキ」と呼ばれ、「焼酎」と書くのが普通だったので、泡盛の命名は薩摩といわれる。泡盛のルーツはタイ国の「ラオ・ロン」といわれ、殆どの泡盛が原料にタイ米を使用している。泡盛を3年以上、保存熟成したものが「クース」（古酒）で、このクースによって泡盛が天下の名酒と言われている所以である。沖縄の伝統的な酒に泡盛をベースにした「ハブ酒」がある。中国では古来より「蛇酒」として蛇を酒に漬け込む文化があり、沖縄のハブ酒の製法も16世紀に中国から伝わったといわれる。昔から良薬として重宝されていた沖縄名物のハブ酒は、沖縄旅行のお土産としても人気がある。

(20) *Awamori, Kuusu* and *Habu-shu*

The name *awamori* is said to have originated from the method of "heaping bubbles" used in the past to measure the accuracy of sake. The name *awamori* is said to have originated in Satsuma, as it was called *saki* in Okinawa, and it was common to write *shochu*. The origin of *awamori* is said to be *Lao Long* in Thailand, and most *awamori* is made from Thai rice. When *awamori* is stored and matured for more than three years, it is called *kuusu* (well-cured sake), and this is the reason why *awamori* is considered to be one of the best sake in the

グラスに注がれた泡盛とスクガラス豆腐 (おつまみ)
Awamori poured into a glass and *sukugarasu-tofu* (side dish)

world. One of the traditional Okinawan drinks is *habu-shu*, which is based on *awamori*. In China, there has been a culture of soaking snakes in alcohol as "snake liquor" since ancient times, and the process of making Okinawan *habu-shu* is said to have been introduced from China in the 16th century. *Habu-shu*, a specialty of Okinawa, has been valued as a good medicine since ancient times, and is popular as a gift of a trip to Okinawa.

(21) オリオンビール

アメリカ合衆国統治下の 1957 年 5 月 18 日に、戦後沖縄の経済復興のために第 2 次産業（製造業）を興す必要から、当時、名水が湧出していた名護町（現在の名護市）で「沖縄ビール株式会社」が設立された。ビールブランド名を県民に公募し、同年 11 月 1 日に「オリオンビール」と命名し、その後、社名も「オリオンビール」に変更した。1959 年に生産を開始したが、当初は他の日本の大手ビールの勢力が強く苦戦した。それまでのドイツ風ビールから、沖縄の気候を考慮したアメリカ風ビールに切り替えると共に、県内全域で営業活動を行った結果、県内でのシェアが 1 位となった。1972 年の本土復帰の際、期限付きで沖縄県内のみ酒税が減免された優遇措置はオリオンビールに有利に働いた。優遇措置は 5 年ごとに延長が繰り返され、ビールの税率は本土に比べて軽減された。販路拡大には本土

や海外への進出が不可欠だが、拡大戦略はなかなか進まなかった。そのような中、2002 年、優遇措置の延長廃止が政府内で議論された。優遇措置廃止は価格競争力の低下を意味するため、2002 年、大株主でもあるアサヒビールと提携関係を結んだ。その結果、本土でも沖縄料理店を中心にオリオンビールが提供されることも多くなった。本土復帰直前の最盛期には県内市場の 90% ないし 80% を占めていたため、県内では「県民ビール」と定着している。沖縄本島北部の名護市に唯一の生産工場を持つので、県民からは「名護ぬミジグヮー」（名護の水）という愛称でも親しまれている。

オリオンビール （キラキラビーチ、西原町）
Orion beer (Kira Kira Beach, Nishihara Town)

(21) Orion Beer

On May 18, 1957, during the U.S. occupation, "Okinawa Beer Company" was established in Nago Town (present-day Nago City), where famous water was gushing at the time, in response to the need to start a secondary industry (manufacturing) for the economic recovery of postwar Okinawa. The name of the beer brand was publicly solicited from the people of the prefecture, and on November 1 of the same year, it was named "Orion Beer," after which the company name was also changed to "Orion Beer". The company began production in 1959, but initially struggled due to the strong presence of other major Japanese beers. As a result of switching from the German-style beer to an American-style beer that took into account the climate of Okinawa and marketing activities throughout the prefecture, Orion Beer's market share in the prefecture became the highest. When Okinawa reverted to mainland Japan in 1972, the preferential treatment of reducing and exempting liquor tax only in Okinawa Prefecture for a limited period worked in Orion Beer's favor. The preferential treatment was repeatedly extended every five years, and the tax rate on beer was reduced compared to the mainland. In order to expand sales channels, it was essential to expand into the mainland and overseas, but the expansion strategy did not go very far. In such a situation, the extension of the preferential treatment was discussed within the government in 2002, and the decision was effectively made to abolish it. Since the abolition of preferential treatment would mean a decline in price competitiveness, in 2002 the company entered into a partnership with Asahi Breweries, which is also a major shareholder. As a result, Orion Beer is now often served on the mainland, especially in Okinawan restaurants. At the height of its popularity just prior to its return to the mainland, it accounted for 90% or 80% of the prefecture's market, and has become firmly established as the "prefectural beer" of Okinawa. Since the only production plant is located in Nago City in the northern part of the main island of Okinawa, it is nicknamed *Nago-nu-mijigwa* (Nago's delicious water) by the residents of the prefecture.

(22) 三線（さんしん）

　三線（サンシン）は、中国から移入された 3 本の弦を持つ楽器である。沖縄県や鹿児島県の奄美諸島では「サンシン」と呼ばれるが、日本本土では「サミセン」と言う。沖縄サンシンが蛇皮を使用するのに対して、本土のサミセンには猫皮が用いられ、両者間には音色の違いがある。特に、王朝時代の琉球サンシンの名器は「ケージョー」と称される。ケージョー（開鐘）とは夜明けにつく寺院の鐘のことで、その音は遠くまで響き渡るので、それに因んでサンシンの名器にもつけられた。

　（例）アマダンジャーケージョー、盛嶋ケージョー

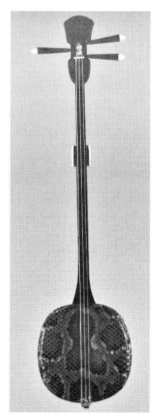

三線（盛嶋ケージョー）
Sanshin(Murishima-*Keejou*), (Okinawa Prefectural Museum & Art Museum)

(22) *Sanshin*

Sanshin is a three-stringed musical instrument that has been handed down in Ryukyu from China. In Okinawa Prefecture and Amami Islands of Kagoshima Prefecture, it is called *sanshin*, but in mainland Japan it is called *samisen*. While the Okinawan *sanshin* uses snakeskin, the mainland *samisen* uses catskin, and there is a difference in tone between the two. In particular, the best Ryukyu *sanshin* instruments from the dynastic period are called *keejou*. *Keejou* is the temple bell that is rung at dawn, and the sound resonates far and wide, hence the name of the famous *sanshin* instrument.

　Examples: Amadanjaa-*keejou*, Murishima-*keejou*

(23) カチャーシー

　祝いの座、あるいは昔日の「毛遊び」（モーアシビ）でも踊られるアップテンポな大衆の踊りで、見ているだけでも楽しくなる。両手を頭上に上げ、手首を回しながら左右に振って踊る。女性はしなやかに、男性は力強く、そして足はリズムに合わせて動かす。カチャーシーというと、「こねり手」がとかく重視されるが、手はどちらかというと副次的で、しっかり落とした腰（ガマク）と、リズムに乗り切る足の動きが重要とされる。カチャーシー音楽は「ソービチ」とも称される、自風の早弾き奏法による即興の乱舞曲である。「カチャースン」という沖縄語はすべてのものを「かき混ぜる」という意味で、島人の喜怒哀楽を歌や踊りに「かきまぜて」即興の歌舞に興ずることに由来する。カチャーシーは宴会や座興の最後に踊られ、代表的な曲に「トーシンドーイ」や「アッチャメーグヮー」、「多幸山」、「天川」などがある。

(23) *Kacha-shii*

　Kacha-shii is an up-tempo popular dance performed by the masses at celebratory ceremonies or at the *mou-ashibi* of bygone days, and is a joy to watch. Raise both hands above your head and dance, turning your wrists and swinging them from side to side. Women should be supple, men should be strong, and the feet should move to the rhythm. In *Kacha-shii*, the emphasis is often placed on the "kneading hands," but the hands are more secondary, and the importance is placed on the firmly slumped hips (*gamaku*) and the foot movements to keep up with the rhythm. *Kacha-shii* music is an improvisational dance piece with a rapid-fire, self-playing style, also known as *sou-bichi*. The Okinawan word *Kacha-sun* means "to stir" everything together, and is derived from the islanders' improvised singing and dancing, "stiring" their joy, anger, sorrow, and happiness into songs and dances. *Kacha-shii* is danced at the end of a banquet or entertainment, and typical *Kacha-shii* songs include *Tousin-doui* (It's a ship from China!), *Acchamee-gwa, Takou-yama,* and *Amakawa.*

(24) 琉球（沖縄）料理（りゅうきゅう・おきなわりょうり）

　琉球料理は、琉球王国時代に中国や日本、東南アジア諸国との交易により、さまざまな文化の影響を受けてきた。沖縄県は本土と異なり、年中温暖で四季が比較的不明瞭な気候であるため亜熱帯性の食材が多く用いられる。反面、冷涼な気候に適した食材は栽培や入手が難しい土地柄であり、使用される野菜類が本土とは異なる。亜熱帯に属するが香辛料はあまり使用されず、伝統的な味付けは塩、味噌、鰹節、昆布を多用し、日本料理の範疇に収まる。しかし、食材に豚肉を多用する点で本土とは大きな違いがある。四方を海に囲まれている沖縄にしては、意外にも魚料理はあまり豊富ではない。亜熱帯の気候的条件で魚の鮮度が長く保てないからだといわれる。中国との交流に負うところが大きく、料理内容では豚肉料理が多いのが特徴とされる。

　琉球料理には宮廷料理と一般庶民の料理がある。宮廷料理は、琉球王国時代に接待や儀式、年中行事などで供された料理で、約150種類あると言われている。接待料理で重要だったものは、国王が交代する度に中国から派遣された冊封使を迎える行事や薩摩の在藩役人をもてなす料理であった。首里王府は、これらの接待のための料理人を修業させるため、中国や日本へも派遣した。宮廷料理の伝統は、首里の士族層で受け継がれ、結婚式や正月などに儀式料理として振る舞われた。一般庶民の料理は、南方的な気候風土を反映して、大まかで、多量的で、素朴さにあふれているが、滋養に富み、理にかなった調理法である。現在、琉球料理店で提供される料理は、ほとんどが家庭料理である。琉球王国時代から続く伝統的な琉球料理は、2019年に日本遺産として認定された。
【東道盆（口絵4-24、P5参照）】

(24) Ryukyuan (Okinawan) Cuisine

Ryukyuan cuisine was influenced by many different cultures through its trade with China, Japan and Southeast Asian countries during the Ryukyu Kingdom period. Unlike the mainland, Okinawa Prefecture has a warm climate all year round with four relatively indistinct seasons, so many subtropical foods are used. On the other hand, ingredients suitable for cooler climates are difficult to grow and obtain, and the vegetables used in Okinawa differ from those used in mainland Japan. Although Okinawa belongs to the subtropical zone, spices are not often used, and traditional seasonings fall within the category of Japanese cuisine, with extensive use of salt, *miso*, *katsuobushi* (dried bonito flakes), and *kombu* seaweed. However, there is a major difference from the mainland in the extensive use of pork as an ingredient. Surrounded by the sea on all sides, Okinawa has surprisingly few fish dishes. It is said that this is because the subtropical climate does not allow the fish to stay fresh for long. The cuisine is characterized by a large number of pork dishes, largely due to exchanges with China.

Ryukyuan cuisine includes both court cuisine and common people's cookery. Court cuisine was served for entertainment, ceremonies, and annual events during the Kingdom of the Ryukyus, and it is said that there are approximately 150 types of court cuisine. The most important entertainment dishes were those that greeted the envoys (*sappuu-shi*) sent from China each time the king changed kings, and those that entertained the officials of Satsuma's clans. The Shuri royal government also sent cooks to China and Japan to train cooks for these receptions. The tradition of court cuisine was passed down among the samurai class in Shuri and was served as ceremonial food at weddings, New Year's, and other occasions. Reflecting the southern climate, common people's cookery is rough, plentiful, and simple, but nourishing and a reasonable cooking method. Currently, most of the dishes served in Ryukyuan restaurants are home-cooked. Traditional Ryukyuan cuisine, which has continued since the days of the Ryukyu Kingdom, was recognized as a Japanese Heritage in 2019.
【*Tundaa-Bun*(Frontispiece 4-24, See page 5)】

①沖縄そば（おきなわそば）

　沖縄における麺料理の起源は、琉球王国時代に中国南部から伝来し、中国からの使者をもてなす接待料理に取り入れられたという説がある。明治後期に本土出身者が連れてきた中国人コックが那覇の辻遊郭近くに開いた「支那そば屋」が、今日の沖縄そばの直接のルーツと考えられている。町中にそば屋が増え、一般庶民が気軽に食べられるようになったのは大正に入ってからで、当初は、豚のだしをベースにした醤油味のスープで、具材も豚肉とネギのみで本土の支那そばと変わらないものだった。その後、沖縄県民の味覚に合わせて改良が重ねられ現在の沖縄そば独自のスタイルが形成されたが、当時は支那そばと並んで「琉球そば」と呼称された。沖縄そばは、中華麺に由来する製法の麺を使用し、そば粉を使用していないが、日本政府から商標として「そば」と名乗ることが許可されている。

　沖縄そばは、麺・つゆ・具とも本土のそばとは違い、沖縄独特で、沖縄を代表する軽食として普及している。スタンダードな沖縄そばは豚骨・鶏骨・カツオ節で出汁を取った汁を麺にたっぷりかけ、具は豚三枚肉の煮付け・カマボコ・ネギなどをのせる。この代表的なスタイルに豚の骨付きあばら肉（ソーキ＝スペアリブ）をトッピングした「ソーキそば」は、1972 年の復帰前後から広く出回り、沖縄料理の定番となった。復帰以降、沖縄でも本土由来の「大晦日の年越し蕎麦」の風習が広まったが、食されるのは蕎麦粉を用いた「日本蕎麦」ではなく、沖縄そばである。
【沖縄そば（口絵 4-24-1、P5 参照）】

① Okinawa-*soba*

There is a theory that noodle dishes in Okinawa originated from southern China during the Ryukyu Kingdom period and were added into the cuisine for entertaining emissaries from China. The "*Shina-soba* restaurant" opened near Tsuji-*yuukaku*(red light district) in Naha by a Chinese cook brought by a mainland Japan native in the late Meiji period is considered to be the direct root of today's Okinawa-*soba*. It was not until the Taisho era that the number of *soba* restaurants in town increased and ordinary people were able to enjoy eating *soba* easily. In the beginning, *soba* had a soy sauce-flavored soup based on pork broth, with only pork and green onions as ingredients, no different from *Shina-soba* in the mainland. Later, it was modified to suit the tastes of Okinawans, forming the unique style of Okinawa-*soba* as we know it today, but at the time it was called Ryukyu-*soba* along with *Shina-soba*. Okinawa-*soba* is made from noodles derived from the Chinese noodle manufacturing process and does not contain buckwheat flour, but is permitted by the Japanese government to use the name "*soba*" as a trademark.

Okinawa-*soba* is different from mainland-*soba* in terms of rice noodles, dipping sauce, and ingredients, and is unique to Okinawa, and it is popular as a typical Okinawan light meal. Standard Okinawa-*soba* is made with a broth made from pork bones, chicken bones, and *katsuobushi* (dried bonito flakes), poured over noodles, and topped with braised pork tripe, *kamaboko* (fish paste), and green onions. *Souki-soba*, a standard Okinawa-*soba* topped with *souki* (bone-in pork ribs), became widely popular around 1972, when Okinawa was returned to Japan, and became a staple of Okinawan cuisine. After Okinawa's reversion to Japan, the custom of *toshikoshi-soba* (New Year's Eve *Soba*) derived from mainland Japan became widespread in Okinawa, but it is not Japanese-*soba* made from buckwheat flour but Okinawa-*soba* that is eaten.

【Okinawa-*soba*(Frontispiece 4-24-1, See page 5)】

②チャンプルー料理（ちゃんぷるーりょうり）

　豆腐と野菜などの油炒めで、沖縄で最も親しまれている家庭料理である。現在ではポーク・ベーコン・ツナ・卵なども使用されるが、木綿豆腐と野菜を主材料にして炒めるだけの簡単な料理だが、手早くできて美味しい。経済的・栄養的にも優れており、よく作られる代表的な琉球料理である。ゴーヤーチャンプルー・マーミナチャンプルー・ソーミンチャンプルー・フーチャンプルーなど、食材名を付ける。多種類の野菜を用いるのは「野菜チャンプルー」と称する。元々は、あり合わせの野菜に安価で毎日手に入る豆腐、保存食である塩漬けの豚肉などを加えた沖縄の家庭料理だが、近年はテレビ番組で紹介されるなどして、沖縄県以外の日本各地でも食べられるようになった。さまざまなチャンプルー料理があるが、チャンプルーの定義は「豆腐と野菜の炒め物」で、豆腐が入っていない炒め物は、「タシヤー」と呼ぶ。チャンプルーの語源は諸説あるが、インドネシア語・マレー語のチャンプール（campur）説が有力。沖縄と同様、「混ぜる」「混ぜたもの」という意味を持つ。沖縄のチャンプルーが日本本土に渡り、長崎の「ちゃんぽん」になり、更に江戸の「ちゃんこ」になったといわれる。【ゴーヤーチャンプルー（口絵 4-24-2、P5 参照）】

② *Champuruu* Cuisine

Champuruu is a stir-fried dish of tofu and vegetables, and is one of the most popular home cooking in Okinawa. Nowadays, pork, bacon, tuna, eggs, etc. are also used, but it is a simple dish of tofu and vegetables stir-fried as the main ingredients, but it is quick to make and delicious. It is economical and nutritious, and is a typical Ryukyuan cuisine that is often prepared. Add the names of the ingredient at the beginning of the dish name, such as *gouyaa-champuruu*, *maamina-champuruu*, *soumin-champuruu*, and *huu-champuruu*. When many kinds of vegetables are used, it is called *yasai-champuruu*.

Originally, it is an Okinawan home-style dish consisting of ready-made vegetables, tofu, which is inexpensive and available every day, and salted pork, which is a preserved food, however, in recent years, it has been introduced on TV programs and is now eaten in many parts of Japan outside of Okinawa Prefecture. There

are various *champuru* dishes, but the definition of *champuru* is "stir-fried tofu and vegetables in oil," and stir-fried dishes that do not contain tofu are called "*tashiyaa*". There are many theories about the origin of the word *champuruu*, but the most popular is the Indonesian (Malay) word *campur*. As in Okinawa, it means "to mix" or "mixed thing". It is said that Okinawan-*champuruu* made its way to mainland Japan and became Nagasaki's *champon*, and then Edo's *chanko*.
【*Gouyaa-Champuruu*(Frontispiece 4-24-2, See page 5)】

③イナムドゥチ (イナムルチ)

　豚三枚肉、椎茸、かまぼこ、コンニャク、揚げ豆腐など５～６種の材料を短冊切りにして甘い白味噌でとろりと煮込んだ味噌汁。沖縄では正月や盆など、祝料理には欠かせない郷土料理で、「イナムルチ」とも称される。昔は猪の肉を使っていたが後に豚肉を使用するようになり、「イノシシもどき」が訛って「イナムドゥチ」と呼ばれるようになった。「ムドゥチ」とは模造品という意味で、名称から、「琉球料理がいろいろな形で日本料理の影響を受けていることを示している。琉球料理は中国料理のこってりした味を基調としながら、日本料理のあっさりした風味も取り入れているところに特徴があるといえる。【イナムドゥチ （口絵 4-24-3、P5 参照）】

③ *Ina-muduchi (Ina-muruchi)*

A miso soup made with five to six ingredients such as pork, *shiitake* mushrooms, *kamaboko* (fish paste), kon'nyaku, and fried tofu, cut into strips and simmered in sweet white *miso*. In Okinawa, it is a local dish that is indispensable for celebratory dishes such as New Year's Day and *Bon* Festival, and is also known as *ina-muruchi*. In the past, wild boar meat was used for this dish, but later pork was used, and the name *ina-muduchi* was derived from "wild boar *modoki*". *Muduchi* (*modoki*) means imitation, and the name suggests that Ryukyuan cuisine has been influenced by Japanese cuisine in many ways. Ryukyuan cuisine is based on the rich flavors of Chinese cuisine, but also incorporates the lighter flavors of Japanese cuisine.【*Ina-muduchi*(Frontispiece 4-24-3, See page 5)】

④ジューシー （硬・柔）

　ジューシーには、炊き込みご飯と雑炊の２種類がある。前者は「クファジューシー」、後者は「ボロボロジューシー」または「ヤファラジューシー」という。両者とも豚のだし汁でこってりした味に仕上げ、単に「ジューシー」と呼ぶのが一般的である。ジューシーは家庭料理であるため、基本的には飲食店のメニューでよく見かけるものではないが、「クファジューシー」はしばしば「沖縄そば」とセットで提供される。温かい「ボロボロジューシー」は、豚肉をはじめ、人参、椎茸、こんにゃくなどの具材がふんだんに入っており栄養豊富で、沖縄語で「フーチバー」と呼ばれる「よもぎ」が添えられる。冷たい北風が吹く頃に食べる「ボロボロジューシー」は心身にやさしく、消化が良くて胃腸にも優しい「おふくろの味」である。沖縄では旧盆の初日 （ウンケー）に「ウンケージューシー」を仏壇に供え、冬至には「トゥンジージューシー」が行事食として作られるが、両者とも「クファジューシー」である。【ジューシー （口絵 4-24-4、P5 参照）】

④ *Juushii* (hard/soft)

There are two types of *juusii*:*Takikomi-gohan*(cooked rice) and *zousui* (porridge). The former is called *kufa-juushii* and the latter *boro-boro-juushii* or *yafara-juushii*. Both are made with pork broth to give them a rich taste and are commonly referred to simply as *juushii*. Since *juushii* is a home-style dish, it is not usually found on restaurant menus, but *kufa-juushii* is often served with Okinawa-soba. The hot *boro-boro-juushii* is rich in nutrients with plenty of pork, carrots, *shiitake* mushrooms, *kon'nyaku* and other ingredients, and is served with

yomogi (Japanese mugwort called *huuchi-baa* in Okinawan language). *Boro-boro-juushii*, eaten when the cold north wind blows, is gentle on the body and mind, and is a "mother's taste" that is easy to digest and gentle on the stomach. On the first day of the Lunar *Bon* Festival (*unkee*), *unkee-juushii* is offered to the Buddhist altar, and on the Winter Solstice, *tunjii-juushii* is made as an event food, both of which are *kufa-juushii*.
【*Juushii*(Frontispiece 4-24-4, See page 5)】

⑤中味汁（なかみじる）

　沖縄では「鳴き声以外は全部食べる」といわれるほど「豚」は利用度が高い。かつて沖縄では正月に備えて年末に豚を潰す習慣があり、その新鮮な臓物を用いた中味汁は本土の雑煮に相当するご馳走であった。中味汁は豚の旨味と鰹ダシ、椎茸のダシが合わさった旨味成分の詰まった料理。現在でも正月やお盆には欠かせない郷土料理として県民に親しまれており、ほとんどの大衆食堂でも味わうことができる。中味（ナカミ）とは豚の大腸、小腸、胃袋を意味し、中味汁は臓物料理の代表的な汁物で滋養食でもある。「見た目がちょっと・・・」と少し尻込みする人もいるかも知れないが、とても美味しい料理である。中味は、良質な蛋白質が豊富で脂肪分が少なく、鉄分、ビタミンＡ・Ｄ、ミネラル類の宝庫といわれる。【中味汁（口絵 4-24-5、P6 参照）】

⑤ *Nakami-jiru*

In Okinawa, pigs are so highly used that people say they eat everything but pig squealers. In the past, Okinawa had a custom of killing pigs to obtain pork at the end of the year in preparation for the New Year's holiday, and *nakami-jiru*, made with fresh pork offal (*nakami*), was a feast equivalent to *zouni* on the mainland. *Nakami-jiru* is a dish full of *umami* ingredients, combining the flavor of pork, bonito broth, and *shiitake* mushroom broth. Even today, it is an indispensable local dish for New Year's Day and *Obon*, and is well known by the people of the prefecture, and can also be tasted in most popular restaurants. Some may shy away from this dish, saying, "It looks a little..." but it is very tasty. *Nakami* means the large intestine, small intestine, or stomach of a pig, and *nakami-jiru* is a typical soup of "internal organs" cuisine, and is also a nourishing dish. *Nakami* is rich in high quality protein, low in fat, iron, vitamins A and D, and minerals. 【*Nakami-jiru*(Frontispiece 4-24-5, See page 6)】

⑥山羊汁（やぎじる）

　古くから「ヒージャーグスイ」（山羊薬）といわれる沖縄のスタミナ料理の一つで、「ヒージャー汁」の呼称が一般的である。山羊特有の強い臭いを消すためフーチバー（よもぎ）や生姜など、香りの強い薬草が薬味として加えられる。味付けには主として塩を用いるが地域によっては味噌味で仕上げるところもある。山羊汁には鉄、亜鉛などのミネラルが多く含まれており、疲労回復や脂肪燃焼効果、滋養強壮などの優れた効能があり、低カロリーで高タンパク。沖縄の伝統料理の一つでもあり、新築祝いやユイマールなどの席でふるまわれる高級料理である。クセの強い料理だけに、ウチナーンチュでも苦手な人がいるが、好きな人にとっては猛烈に食欲をそそられる香りとなり「世界一旨い料理」と称える声も聞かれる。【山羊汁（口絵 4-24-6、P6 参照）】

⑥ *Yagi-jiru (Hiijaa-jiru)*

It is one of the stamina dishes of Okinawa, which has been known as *hiijaa-gusui* since ancient times, and is commonly called *hiijaa-jiru*. In order to eliminate the strong odor characteristic of goats, herbs with strong aroma such as *huuchibaa* (mugwort) and ginger are added as condiments. Salt is used for seasoning mainly, but in some regions it is flavored with *miso* (soybean paste). *Yagi-jiru* is high in iron, zinc, and other minerals, and has excellent benefits such as relieving fatigue, burning fat, and tonicity, and is low in calories and high in protein. It is also one of the traditional Okinawan dishes, and is a high-class dish served at housewarming celebrations and *yuimaaru*. Some *uchinanchu* don't like it because of its strong smell, but for those who love it, the aroma is so appetizing that some call it "the best food in the world".

【*Yagi-jiru*(Frontispiece 4-24-6, See page 6)】

⑦豆腐餻（とうふよう）

　島豆腐を米麹、紅麹、泡盛によって発酵・熟成させた発酵食品で、沖縄の珍味といわれる。発酵の効果で、泡盛とエダムチーズを合わせたような味わいが特徴である。交易国家として栄えていた琉球王国時代に明（中国）から伝来し、琉球の宮廷料理人によって現在の豆腐餻の製法に改良され宮廷料理として確立され、上流階級で珍重された。中国や台湾では雑菌の繁殖を抑えるために製造中に塩漬けにするが、豆腐餻は沖縄で一般的であった泡盛漬けにすることが製法上の大きな違いである。作り方は熟練を要し手作りに頼っていたが、現在は観光みやげ用に大量生産され食通に好まれている。主に酒の肴に使われ、泡盛と共に食するのが最高の組み合わせといわれるが、ビールや焼酎などともよく合う。栄養価も高く、琉球王朝時代には高貴な人々の間で病後の滋養食としても重宝されたという。

【豆腐餻（口絵 4-24-7、P6 参照）】

⑦ *Toufu-yoh*

　It is a fermented food made by fermenting and maturing *shima-doufu* (Okinawan cotton overstuffed tofu) with rice malt, red malt, and Awamori, and is considered a delicacy of Okinawa. The effect of fermentation gives it a taste like a combination of Awamori and Edam cheese. It was introduced from Ming China during the Ryukyu Kingdom, which flourished as a trading nation, and was refined by Ryukyu court chefs into the current *toufu-yoh* method and established as a court dish, which was highly prized by the upper class. The main difference in the production method is that *toufu-yoh* is pickled in Awamori, which was common in Okinawa, while in China and Taiwan it is pickled in salt during production to prevent the growth of bacteria. It used to be made by hand and required a lot of skill, but now it is mass-produced as a tourist souvenir and is favored by gourmets. It is mainly used as a snack with sake, and is said to be best served with Awamori, but also goes well with beer and *shochu*. It is also highly nutritious, and during the Ryukyu Dynasty, it was valued by the nobility as a nourishing food after illness. 【*Toufu-yoh*(Frontispiece 4-24-7, See page 6)】

⑧ゴーヤー

　ウリ科に属する熱帯アジア原産のゴーヤー（ニガウリ）は宮古で「ゴーラ」、八重山では「ゴーヤ」と呼ばれ、時代は不明だが沖縄へは中国を経て渡来した。ヘチマや冬瓜（シブイ）と並ぶ夏野菜の中心で、沖縄県外で食用とする地域は九州にみられる。ゴーヤーチャンプルーやゴーヤージュースなどの調理法が知られており、夏バテ防止になくてはならない野菜である。さわやかな苦みと豊富なビタミンＣ、解熱作用、利尿効果などの健康野菜や薬用野菜としての知名度が高まり、近年は本土でも需要が伸びている。日本各地で、日除けの目的でも栽培されるようになった。ゴーヤーは夏野菜だが、最近ではビニールハウスによる周年栽培も盛んに行われている。沖縄では、5月8日を語呂合わせで「ゴーヤーの日」と定めている。【ゴーヤー（口絵 4-24-8、P6 参照）】

⑧ *Gouyaa* (Bitter melon)

　Native to tropical Asia, *gouyaa* (bitter melon) belongs to the Cucurbitaceae family and is called *goura* in Miyako and *gouya* in Yaeyama, and was brought to Okinawa via China, although its age is unknown. It is one of the main summer vegetables along with loofah and winter melon(*shibui*), and the areas outside Okinawa where it is eaten are found in Kyushu. It is known for its preparation of *gouyaa-champuruu* and *gouyaa*-juice, and is an indispensable vegetable for preventing summer fatigue. With its refreshing bitterness, abundant vitamin C, antipyretic effect, and diuretic effect, it is becoming increasingly well known as a healthy and medicinal vegetable, and in recent years, demand for it has been growing in the mainland. In many parts of Japan, it is also grown for the purpose of shading from the sun. *Gouyaa* is a summer vegetable, but recently it has become popular for year-round cultivation in plastic greenhouses. In Okinawa, May 8 has been designated as *gouyaa*-day to coincide with the word *gouyaa*. 【*Gouyaa*(Frontispiece 4-24-8, See page 6)】

⑨島豆腐

　安くて栄養価に富む豆腐は健康食品で、沖縄県の消費量は日本一である。長寿の島といわれる沖縄は「豆腐の島」といわれるくらい、昔から豆腐を普段の食事に取り入れてきた。県内長寿者の三大好物は「豆腐、ゴーヤー、芋」という調査結果もある。沖縄の豆腐は「島豆腐」や「沖縄豆腐」とも呼ばれ、かつては大豆からおからを分離し豆乳だけを煮て温かい状態で販売されるという、他府県で作られる豆腐と違う特徴があった。程良く堅くて大きいアツアツの島豆腐は、チャンプルー料理（季節野菜と島豆腐の炒め物）や珍味・豆腐餻（豆腐の発酵食品）などに適している。本土での豆腐は冷水に浸かった状態で販売されているが、沖縄県内のスーパーの店頭では、島豆腐を入れた袋は口を開けたままの状態で、アツアツのまま販売されている。これは、豆腐が各家庭で作られていた頃の名残で、「豆腐はアツアツ」という沖縄県民の食習慣がその理由とされる。水に晒さないことで、栄養分や旨味を逃がさず、美味しさが保たれるのである。【島豆腐（口絵 4-24-9、P6 参照）】

⑨ *Shima-doufu* (Okinawan tofu)

　Inexpensive and nutritious, tofu is a health food, and Okinawa Prefecture is the largest consumer of tofu in Japan. Okinawa, known as the island of longevity, has been incorporating tofu into its daily meal since ancient times, so much so that it is called the "island of tofu". A survey has shown that the three favorite foods of people with longevity in Okinawa are "tofu, *gouyaa* (bitter melon), and imo (sweet potato). Tofu in Okinawa, also called *shima-doufu* or Okinawa-tofu, in the past, the *okara* (bean curd) was separated from the soybeans, and only the soy milk was boiled, heated and sold, making it different from tofu in other prefectures. The moderately hard, large, and hot *shima-doufu* is suitable for *champuruu* dishes (stir-fried *shima-doufu* with seasonal vegetables) and the delicacy *toufu-yoh* (fermented tofu). On the mainland, tofu is sold soaked in cold water, but in supermarkets in Okinawa Prefecture, the bags containing hot *shima-doufu* are sold with the mouths open. This is a remnant from the days when each household made its own tofu, and the reason for this is said to be the Okinawans' food custom of "tofu is hot". By not exposing them to water, nutrients and flavor are not lost, and the flavor is preserved. 【*Shima-doufu*(Frontispiece 4-24-9, See page 6)】

⑩昆布（こんぶ）、クーブイリチー

　沖縄料理では豚肉や豆腐がよく使用されるが、県内では採れない昆布も必須の食材になっており消費量は全国でもトップクラスである。高温多湿で食品の保存が難しい沖縄では、保存の効く昆布は以前から重宝された。酸性食品の豚肉とアルカリ食品の昆布の組み合わせは栄養学的にもバランスが取れていると言われる。代表的な昆布料理である「クーブイリチー」は細切りにした昆布を豚肉や蒟蒻、カマボコなどと一緒に鰹だしで煮る。元々はお祝い事などハレの日に欠かせない縁起の良い郷土料理である。

　昆布は、1609 年の薩摩藩の侵攻後、琉球から中国への進貢品に加わり、蝦夷地（北海道）から薩摩藩を通して琉球へ運ばれ定着した。薩摩は大阪や下関で琉球の砂糖を昆布に換え、その昆布が琉球を通して中国に運ばれた。かなりの量が琉球に集められ、貿易品として扱えない不良品や、余った昆

布が一般庶民の手に渡った。琉球から中国への輸出品は昆布の他にもフカヒレなどがあり、逆に中国からは薬品、茶、磁器などが入ってきた。この貿易は昆布と薬品の交換といえる状況で、日本から琉球への昆布導入への筋道ができた。【クーブイリチー（口絵 4-24-10、P6 参照）】

⑩ *Kombu* (kelp),*Kuubu-irichii*

Pork and tofu are often used in Okinawan cuisine, but *kombu* (kelp), which cannot be harvested in the prefecture, is also an essential ingredient, and its consumption is one of the highest in Japan. In Okinawa, where it is difficult to preserve food due to the high temperature and humidity, kelp has long been valued for its ability to be preserved. The combination of pork, an acidic food, and kelp, an alkaline food, is said to be nutritionally balanced. A typical kelp dish, *kuubu-irichii*, is made by boiling shredded kelp with pork, *kon'nyaku*, and fish paste(*kamaboko*) in bonito broth. Originally, it was an auspicious local dish that was indispensable for celebrations and other special occasions.

After the invasion of the Satsuma domain in 1609, kelp was added to the tribute paid by Ryukyu to China, and was transported from *Ezo-chi* (Hokkaido) to Ryukyu through the Satsuma clan, where it took root. Satsuma exchanged Ryukyu sugar for kelp in Osaka and Shimonoseki, and the kelp was transported to China through Ryukyu. A considerable amount was collected in Ryukyu, and defective products that could not be handled as trade goods and surplus kelp were handed over to the general public. In addition to kelp, shark fins were exported from Ryukyu to China, and conversely, medicine, tea, and porcelain came from China. This trade can be said to be an exchange of kelp and medicine, and the path to the introduction of kelp from Japan to Ryukyu was established. 【*Kuubu-irichii*(Frontispiece 4-24-10, See page 6)】

⑪タコライス

　メキシコ風アメリカ料理の「タコス」の具材を米飯の上に乗せた沖縄県の料理である。タコライスは金武町にある米海兵隊基地・キャンプハンセンのゲート前に広がる飲食店街にあった「パーラー千里」（せんり）の創業者・儀保松三の考案によって 1984 年（昭和 59 年）に誕生した。もともと彼はバーを経営していたが、ドルの変動相場制への移行による海兵隊員たちの緊縮傾向をみて、安価でボリュームある食事を提供する事業へ鞍替えした。バーで人気のあったタコスをご飯に乗せたメニュー（タコライス）は、たちまち「パーラー千里」で好評を博した。「パーラー千里」は 2015 年 6 月に閉店したが、系列店の「キングタコス」を通して沖縄本島各地にチェーン展開していった。沖縄県内では 1990 年代から学校給食に採用されるなどポピュラーな料理となっている。
【タコライス（口絵 4-24-11、P6 参照）】

⑪ Taco-rice

It is an Okinawan dish made of rice topped with ingredients from the Mexican-style American dish Tacos. Taco-rice was invented in 1984 by Gibo Matsuzo, the founder of "Parlor Senri," which was located in the restaurant district in front of the gate of Camp Hansen, a U.S. Marine base in Kin Town. Originally, he ran a bar, but seeing the austerity trend among Marines due to the transition to a floating exchange rate system for the dollar, he switched his business to providing inexpensive, hearty meals. The "Taco-rice" menu, which featured rice topped with tacos that were popular in bars, quickly became a hit at Parlor Senri. Parlor Senri closed in June 2015, but the Taco-rice chain expanded to the entire main island of Okinawa through its affiliate "King Tacos". It has been a popular dish in Okinawa Prefecture since the 1990s, and has been used in school lunches. 【Taco-rice(Frontispiece 4-24-11, See page 6)】

(25) ポークランチョンミート（ポーク缶詰）

元々は戦後、米軍から配給され、その後定番化したデンマーク産の豚肉加工缶詰だが、いろんなメーカーがあり味が濃いのにケチャップをかけて食する県民も多い。本土では「スパム」という米国産の豚肉加工缶詰が知られているが、沖縄では以前から食べ慣れているデンマークやオランダ産のポークランチョンミートが今でも根強い人気である。以前の缶詰は、缶の底に付いているカギを使ってクルクルと巻き取って開けていく缶の開け方が独特であった。缶詰自体に味が付いているので味付けは不要。

ポークランチョンミート
Pork luncheon meat

切って入れるだけでタンパク質たっぷりの料理が簡単に完成してしまう。チャンプルー料理（炒め物）はもちろん、おにぎり、味噌汁、サンドイッチなど、いろんな料理に使われる身近な食材である。ウチナーンチュが「ポーク」と呼び、きわめて日常的なこの缶詰は沖縄県民のソウルフードといっても過言ではない。

(25) Pork luncheon meat (canned pork)

Originally rationed by the U.S. military after the Battle of Okinawa, these canned processed pork products from Denmark have become a standard item. There are many manufacturers and many prefectural residents eat them with ketchup, even though the taste is strong. In the mainland, processed canned pork from the U.S. called "Spam" is well known, but in Okinawa, pork luncheon meat from Denmark and the Netherlands, which people have been accustomed to eating for a long time, is still very popular. In the past, cans were opened in a unique way, using a key attached to the bottom of the can and rolled it along the side of the can. The canned pork itself is flavorful, so no seasoning is needed. Just cut it up and put it in, and we have an easy protein-rich dish. It is a familiar ingredient used in various dishes such as *champuruu* (stir-fry), *onigiri*, *miso*-soup, and sandwiches. It is no exaggeration to say that this canned food, which *uchinanchu* call "pork" and which is very common, is the soul food of Okinawans.

(26) カメーカメー攻撃（かめーかめーこうげき）

沖縄の特に「オバァ」達が、何か食べ物があると「カメー、カメー（方言で『食べなさい、食べなさい』という意味）と、やたら来客に勧めること。もてなすのが好きな県民性からくる愛情表現の一つであるが、来客はかなり無理して食べることになる。「もうお腹いっぱいで食べられない」と断っても、「大丈夫！たくさん食べなさい」と次から次へと食べ物や飲み物が運ばれてくる。しかし、その行為は「もっと食べたいけど食べ物がなかった」という食糧難時代を生き抜いた沖縄のオバァ達のやさしさ、おもてなしの気持ちの表れである。カメーカメー攻撃には、第二次世界大戦で悲惨な地上戦による「飢え」を体験した県民生活がその背景にある。

(26) *Kamee! Kamee!* Attacks

In Okinawa, especially the *obaa* (elderly women in Okinawan language), when there is something to eat, they always recommend *"kamee! kamee!"* (meaning "eat! eat!" in dialect) to their guests. This is one of the expressions of affection that comes from the prefectural character of being hospitable, but the visitors will be forced to eat quite a bit. Even if you say no, "I'm too full to eat," she says, "Don't worry! Eat lots of food". She brings you food and drinks one after the other. However, this act is an expression of the kindness and hospitality of the Okinawan old ladies (*obaa*) who survived the food shortage era, when they wanted to eat more but there was no food. The background to the "*kamee! kamee!* Attacks" is the lives of the Okinawan people who experienced the "hunger" caused by the tragic ground battles of World War II.

(27) 代表的な沖縄の菓子（だいひょうてきなおきなわのかし）

本土とは異なる独特の歴史や文化が根付いている南国の島・沖縄には琉球王朝時代から県民に愛されてきた伝統菓子がある。一口に沖縄菓子といっても種類が多く、宮廷菓子や旧暦行事や祝い事などで食される郷土菓子があり時代とともに変化している。琉球王国時代（1429 〜 1879）に国王や、貿易をしていた中国や海外の使節団をもてなす際に作られた宮廷菓子は琉球菓子とも呼ばれる。当時、宮廷専任の菓子職人たちは中国の菓子製法技術を習い、限られた材料を用いて製法を工夫し約 160 種類もの菓子を作ったといわれる。その一方で、チンビン、ポーポー、タンナファクルー、ムーチーなど、素朴で安価な庶民向けの郷土菓子も作られた。

沖縄ぜんざい (黒糖で甘く炊いた金時豆の上に、タップリのかき氷をのせた冷たいスイーツで、暑い夏には欠かせない)
Okinawa-*zenzai* (A cold treat of *kintoki-mame* beans sweetened with brown sugar and topped with a generous amount of shaved ice, a must for hot summers)

(27) Typical Okinawan sweets

Okinawa, a tropical island with a unique history and culture different from that of the mainland, has traditional sweets that have been loved by the people of Okinawa since the days of the Ryukyu Dynasty. There are many kinds of Okinawan confections, including court confections and local confections eaten at lunar calendar events and celebrations, which have changed with the times. During the period of the Ryukyu Kingdom (1429-1879), court confectionaries were made to entertain the king and delegations from China and other countries that traded with Ryukyu, also known as Ryukyu confectionaries. At that time, the court confectioners learned the techniques of Chinese confectionery production, and it is said that they made about 160 kinds of confectioneries by devising methods using limited ingredients. On the other hand, simple and inexpensive local snacks for the common people were also made, such as *chimbin, poh-poh, muuchii* and Tan'nafa-*kuruu.*

①ムーチー

ムーチーとは「餅」の沖縄方言であり、カーサ（月桃の葉）で包むことから「カーサムーチー」とも呼ばれる行事料理の一種である。作り方は糯米粉に水を加えてこね、白糖や黒糖、紅芋などで味付けし、平たく長方形に形を整え、月桃（サンニン）の葉で包んで蒸す。旧暦 12 月 8 日に厄払い・健康・長寿祈願のための縁起物としてムーチーを食する習慣がある。子どもがいる家庭では、その年齢の数だけ紐で結んで天井から吊し、男の子には「力餅」（チカラムーチー）と呼ばれる特別に大きなものを作る。この季節は、沖縄では最も寒い時期で「ムーチービーサ」と呼んでいる。ムーチーは「鬼餅」

とも称されるが、内金城御嶽（首里金城町）に住んで鬼と化した兄に妹が金属入りのムーチーを食べさせて 12 月 8 日に退治したという民話に由来する。一方で、「稲作文化社会であった当時の琉球に、製鉄技術文化を持った武士団（鬼）が流入し、両文化の衝突を暗示しているのが鬼餅伝説の本質で、金城の"金"は金属（鉄）の意である」ともいわれる。

ムーチー（3・5・7個、子どもたちの年齢の数だけ天井から吊されている）
Muuchii (Hanging from the ceiling as many times as the ages of the children: 3, 5, and 7 years old)

① *Muuchii*

Muuchii is an Okinawan word for *mochi* (rice cake) and is also called *kaasa-muuchii* because it is wrapped in *kaasa* (leaves of shell ginger), and is a type of event dish. To make it, add water to glutinous rice flour, knead, season with white sugar, brown sugar, or red sweet potato, shape it into a flat rectangle, wrap it in *san-nin* leaves (leaves of shell ginger), and steam it. It is customary to eat *muuchii* on the 8th day of the 12th lunar month as a good luck charm to ward off bad luck and pray for good health and long life. In households with children, they are tied with string and hung from the ceiling in the number of children's ages, and for boys, they are called *chikara-muuchii*, are made especially large. This is the coldest season of the year in Okinawa, and is called *muuchii biisa*. *Muuchii*, also called *Oni-mochi* (demon-*muuchii*), originates from a folk tale about an elder brother who lived in Uchikanagusuku-*utaki* (Shuri Kinjou-*cho*) and turned into a demon, which was exterminated on December 8 by his younger sister who fed him the *muuchii* containing metal. On the other hand, it is said that "the essence of the legend of *Oni-mochi* is that the warrior group (demons) with iron-making technology culture flowed into Ryukyu, which was a rice farming culture society at that time, and the clash between the two cultures is implied in the legend, and *kin* in Kinjou means metal (iron)."

②タンナファクルー

作り方は、水で煮溶かした黒糖液に小麦粉と重曹を混ぜてこね、1 cm くらいの厚さに伸ばして丸く型抜きして焼き上げる（現在、市販されているものには鶏卵や牛乳などが加えられている）。黒糖風味を生かし、保存のきく素朴で安価な沖縄の郷土菓子で、お茶菓子として根強い人気がある。明治 20 年頃、首里で菓子商を営む玉那覇二郎（タンナファ・ジルー）さんによって考案された。元来、琉球王家には「光餅」（クンペン）という胡麻餡入りの宮廷菓子があったが、庶民には高嶺の花で手が届かなかった。餡を用いてないタンナファクルーはその代用品で、庶民に親しまれ、今では沖縄の伝統的な焼き菓子として愛されている。「タンナファクルー」という菓子名は、二郎さんが色黒であり「クルー」と綽名（あだな）されていたことに由来するといわれるが、「黒」（クルー）は菓子のこんがり焼けた色を表すという異説もある。【タンナファクルー（口絵 4-27-2、P7 参照）】

② Tan'nafa-*kuruu*

To make Tan'nafa-*kuruu*, mix flour and baking soda into the brown sugar solution that has been boiled and dissolved in water, knead it, roll out to about 1cm thick, mold into a round shape and bake (currently, eggs and milk are added to commercially available products). These simple and inexpensive local sweets with a brown sugar flavor that can be preserved are very popular as tea cakes. It was invented around 1887(Meiji 20) by Mr. Tamanaha Jiruu, a confectioner in Shuri. Originally, the royal family of Ryukyu had a court snack called *kumpen* with sesame bean paste, but it was too expensive for the common people to have access to. Tan'nafa-*kuruu*, which does not contain red bean paste, is a substitute for *kumpen* and was popular among the common people in those days, and is now loved as a traditional Okinawan baked sweet. The name of the pastry, Tan'nafa-*kuruu* is said to have come from Jiruu's nickname *Kuruu* because he was dark-skinned, but there is another theory that *kuruu* (black)represents the color of the baked sweets.【Tan'nafa-*kuruu*(Frontispiece 4-27-2, See page 7)】

③チンスコウ

　中国由来の焼き菓子で代表的な琉球銘菓の一つ。琉球王朝時代の後期に、冊封使の食事を賄うために料理座の料理人が中国（福州）で学んだ「中国菓子」と、薩摩役人への接遇のために学んだ「日本菓子」。双方の技術の融合によって琉球独自の菓子として誕生したのが「チンスコウ」の始まりといわれる。元来は、琉球王朝の王族や貴族の祝いの席で振る舞われ、庶民の食べ物ではなかった。名前の由来は2つある。「ちん」は「珍」で「すこう」は「お菓子」で「とても珍しいお菓子」と、「ちん」は「金」を意味し「とても高価なお菓子」という2説である。元々は、米の粉を用いた蒸し菓子だったが、大正時代に現在のような焼き菓子になった。特に、本土復帰や沖縄海洋博覧会により、沖縄土産としての知名度が高まった。近年はプレーンの他に黒糖、紅芋、パイナップル、チョコレート、宮古島産の雪塩など、味の種類が豊富になっている。ラードをたっぷり使うのが特徴で、保存がきく。【ちんすこう（口絵 4-27-3、P7 参照）】

③ *Chinsukou*

　Chinsukou is a baked cake of Chinese origin and one of the most famous confections of Ryukyu. It is said that the origin of *chinsukou* is the fusion of "Chinese confectionery" techniques learned in China (Fuzhou) by the chefs of the Shuri royal government in the late Ryukyu Dynasty to prepare meals for the *sappuu-shi* (envoys from China), and "Japanese confectionery" techniques learned to entertain officials of Satsuma, and the creation of a unique Ryukyu confectionery. Originally, it was served at celebrations of the royalty and nobility of the Ryukyu Dynasty and was not a food for the common people.

　There are two theories about the origin of the name: "*Chin* means rare" and "*sukou* means sweets," making it "very rare sweets," and "*Chin* means gold," making it "very expensive sweets. Originally, it was a steamed confection made of rice flour, but in the Taisho era (1912-1926), it became the baked confection we know today. In particular, the return of Okinawa to the mainland (1972) and the Okinawa Ocean Expo (July 1975-January 1976) increased its popularity as a souvenir of Okinawa. In recent years, in addition to plain, a wide variety of flavors have been added, including brown sugar, red sweet potato, pineapple, chocolate, and *Yukishio* (salt) from Miyako Island. It is characterized by the use of a lot of lard and can be stored well.
【*Chinsukou*(Frontispiece 4-27-3, See page 7)】

④サーター アンダギー

　中国から伝わったとされる沖縄の代表的な揚げ菓子で、縁起の良い菓子とされ結婚式など祝いの席には欠かせない。沖縄方言で「サーター」は砂糖、アンダ（油）、アギー（揚げる）で、「油で揚げた丸いドーナツ」という意味である。主材料は小麦粉、卵、砂糖で、ボール状に丸めた生地（タネ）を揚げると、チューリップ型の割れ目ができる。その様子が破顔して笑っているように、あるいは花が咲いているように見えることから縁起の良い菓子とされている。サーター アンダギーは表面に割れ目を生じるその形状から、沖縄では「女性」を象徴する菓子とされている。結納では同じく「男性」を象徴する菓子である「カタハランブー」と対になって多量に盛られる習慣があり、子孫繁栄などの願いが込められている。同じ生地を四角に揚げたものは、サングヮチグヮーシ（三月菓子）と呼ばれ、旧暦3月3日の「浜下り」の行事で振る舞われる。沖縄の家庭では定番のおやつで、日持ちするので観光客のお土産としても人気がある。【サーターアンダギー（口絵 4-27-4、P7 参照）】

④ *Sataa-andagii*

  This is a typical Okinawan deep-fried sweet that is said to have come from China, considered an auspicious sweet and is indispensable for weddings and other celebratory occasions. In Okinawan dialect, *saataa* means sugar, *anda* (oil), and *agii* (to fry), which means "a round donut fried in oil". The main ingredients are flour, eggs, and sugar, and when the dough is rolled into a ball and fried, it forms a tulip-shaped crack. It is considered a confectionery of good luck because its appearance looks like a broken face smiling or a flower blooming. Because of its shape, which makes crack on its surface, *saataa-andagii* is considered a pastry symbolizing "women" in Okinawa. At the betrothal ceremony, it is customary to be served a large amount of *saataa-andagii*, paired with *katahara-nbuu*, a confectionary that also symbolizes "men," to express the wish for the prosperity of offspring. The same dough, fried into squares, is called *sangwachi-gwaashi*, and is served at the *hamauri* event on the third day of the third month of the lunar calendar. *Saataa-andagii* is a standard snack in Okinawan households, and since it lasts for a long time, it is a popular souvenir for tourists.

【*Saataa-andagii*(Frontispiece 4-27-4, See page 7)】

⑤沖縄（那覇）の三大饅頭「山城まんじゅう」「天妃前饅頭」「ぎぼまんじゅう」

　沖縄県民に永きにわたり愛されている「山城まんじゅう」、「天妃前饅頭」、「ぎぼまんじゅう」は「沖縄の三大饅頭」または「那覇の三大饅頭」と呼ばれ、いずれも那覇市内でつくられている。

　「山城まんじゅう」（やまぐすくまんじゅう）は創業160年といわれる首里の老舗饅頭で、龍潭池から少し下った場所にある。伝統の味を守り続け、地元民のおやつとして今でも愛されている。粒餡（つぶあん）とこし餡を合わせた自家製の餡が透けて見えるほどの薄い皮で包まれており、絶品である。甘さ控えめで素朴な味は甘いものが苦手な男性にも好評で、女性客よりも男性客が多いという。材料がすべて無添加無農薬だから日持ちがせず、お土産には不向きかもしれない。

　「天妃前饅頭」（てんぴぬめーまんじゅう）は、かつて久米村の天妃宮（現・天妃小学校）前の市場で販売されていた饅頭が名前の由来。戦前の天妃前饅頭は様々な店があったが、戦後はこのうちの一つである「ぺーちん屋」（那覇市泉崎）が唯一の専門店になっている。「ユーヌク」と呼ばれる「はったい粉」（小麦を炒って挽いた粉）と黒糖で作る独特の餡を薄い皮で包んで蒸し上げる。冷めても硬くならないので、冷やして食べても美味しい饅頭である。多少、日持ちするのでお土産にも適している。

　「ぎぼまんじゅう」は創業100年を誇る首里名物である。「のまんじゅう」とも呼ばれ大きく食紅で書かれた「の」の字は熨斗（のし）の「の」で縁起を担いでおり、本来はお祝い菓子である。近年では、バレンタインシーズンには「の」の代わりに客の注文に応じて「♡」を描いてくれたりする。店名のとおり、当初はユイレール儀保駅近くにある盛光寺の境内を間借りして営業していたが、寺の再建工事のため2004年に現在の場所（石嶺駅近く）に移転した。夕方前には売り切れてしまうほどの人気で、今や沖縄を代表する饅頭である。　【山城まんじゅう・天妃前まんじゅう・のまんじゅう（口絵4-27-5、P7参照）】

⑤ Okinawa's(Naha's) three major *manjuu* (buns)

  Yamagusuku-*manjuu*, Tempinumee-*manjuu*, and Gibo-*manjuu*. which have long been loved by Okinawans, are called "Okinawa's three major *manjuu*," or "Naha's three major *manjuu*," and all of them are made in Naha City.

  Yamagusuku-*manjuu* is a long-established bun in Shuri, said to have been in business for 160 years, and is located a short distance down the road from Ryutan Pond. They have kept their traditional taste and are still loved as a snack by the locals. The homemade red bean paste mixed with *tsubu-an* (mashed sweet bean paste) and *koshi-an* (strained sweet bean paste), is wrapped in a thin skin that is so thin you can see through it, making it an exquisite treat. The mildly sweet and simple taste is popular even among men who do not have a sweet tooth, and there are more male customers than female customers. Because all ingredients are additive-free and pesticide-free, Yamagusuku-*manjuu* does not last long and may not be suitable as a souvenir.

The name Tempinumee-*manjuu* comes from the *manjuu* that used to be sold at the market in front of the Tempiguu Temple (now Tempi Elementary School) in Kume Village. Before the war, there were various stores selling Tempinumee-*manju*, but after the war, one of them, *Peechin-ya* (Izumizaki, Naha City), became the only store specializing in the product. The bun is made by steaming a unique red bean paste called *yuu'nuku* which made of *hattai* flour (roasted and ground wheat flour) and brown sugar, wrapped in a thin skin. It is a delicious bun that does not become hard even when cooled. It lasts for a while, so it is suitable as a souvenir.

Gibo-*manjuu* is a Shuri specialty that has been in business for 100 years. It is also called *Noh-manjuu*, the character "の" written in large red letters with food coloring is "の" for "*noshi*," bringing good luck, and was originally a congratulatory confectionery. In recent years, they have even drawn "♡" instead of the letter "の" during the Valentine's season according to customer orders. As the name suggests, the store was originally located in a rented space in the precincts of Seikouji Temple near Yui-Rail Gibo Station, but due to the reconstruction of the temple, it was moved to its current location (near Ishimine Station) in 2004. It is so popular that it is sold out before evening, and is now Okinawa's representative bun.

【Yamagusuku-*manjuu*/Tempinumee-*manjuu*/Noh-manjuu(Frontispiece 4-27-5, See page 7)】

⑥桔餅（きっぱん）

　300 年ほど前に中国から伝わり、琉球王朝時代には王府や冊封使へ提供された沖縄の伝統的なスイーツ。仄かに柑橘の香りがして、甘さ控えめで上品な味は濃いお茶と合う。王朝時代から受け継がれてきた伝統菓子で「ちっぱん」とも呼ばれ、一般の人も食べるようになったのは明治以降のことである。沖縄本島北部産のカーブチーなどの柑橘類を砂糖煮にし、砂糖衣をかけて仕上げるが、作るには技術と手間を要する。今では那覇市内に専門店が 1 店舗あり、食通な観光客などにも人気がある。

【きっぱん（口絵 4-27-6、P7 参照）】

⑥ *Kippan*

This traditional Okinawan sweet was introduced from China about 300 years ago, and during the Ryukyu Dynasty, it was served to the royal government and *sappuu-shi* (envoys from China). It has a subtle citrus aroma, and its elegant taste with a moderate sweetness goes well with strong tea. Also called *chippan*, this traditional confectionery has been handed down since the dynastic period, and it was not until the Meiji period that the general public began to eat it. Citrus fruits such as *kaabuchii* from the northern part of Okinawa's main island are boiled in sugar and covered with a sugar batter to finish, but it requires skill and effort to make. Nowadays, there is one specialty store in Naha City, which is popular among foodie tourists and others.

【*Kippan*(Frontispiece 4-27-6, See page 8)】

⑦チンビン

　甘みのある巻菓子で、本来は旧暦 5 月 4 日の「ユッカヌヒー」（本土の端午の節句）に作られた行事食である。かつては子供の健康・成長を祈って神々や仏壇に捧げられたが、現在では普通の菓子としてスーパーなどでも買い求めることができる。黒糖入りの沖縄風クレープで、中国の影響を受けている。名前の由来は中国語の「煎餅」によると思われ、北京語の「チエンビン」(jianbing) もしくは他の方言音に基づくものと考えられている。中国の「煎餅」は必ずしも小麦粉で作られないが、華北、西北部では小麦粉を使った料理が発達しており、そこから琉球に伝わったとも推測されている。作り方は、黒砂糖、卵白、小麦粉を水に混ぜ、少量の油で薄く焼いて、くるくる巻く。表面にブツブツ穴の空いたものが上出来とされる。　【チンビン（口絵 4-27-7、P8 参照）】

⑦ *Chimbin*

This is a sweetened event food, rolled pancake, originally made for *yukka-nu-hii* (Boy's Day celebration in the mainland) on the 4th day of the 5th month of the lunar calendar. In the past, it was offered to gods and altars to pray for the health and growth of children, but today they can be got in supermarkets as ordinary sweets. It is an Okinawan-style crepe with brown sugar, and Chinese influences. The name is thought to be derived from the Chinese word for "cracker" and is thought to be based on the Beijing word *jianbing* or other dialectal sounds. Although Chinese crackers are not necessarily made with wheat flour, it is speculated that they were introduced to the Ryukyus from North China and Northwest China, where flour-based dishes were well developed. To make it, mix brown sugar, egg white, and flour in water, cook it thinly in a little oil, and roll it up. A piece with several holes on the surface is considered good. 【*Chimbin*(Frontispiece 4-27-7, See page 8)】

⑧ポーポー

漢字では「炮炮」の文字をあて、名前は中国に由来するといわれているが、「ポーポー」とカタカナ表記が多い。作り方は、小麦粉を少量の水で溶き、フライパンなど平たい鍋で焼いた薄焼きの皮に油味噌を芯に入れ、くるくる巻く。現在ではおやつとして食べられるが、昔は旧暦5月4日の「ユッカヌヒー」に子どもの成長を願い、行事食としてチンビンとともに各家庭で作られた。本来のポーポーは甘みのない白い生地で油味噌を巻き込んだものだが、チンビンをポーポーの一種とみなし「黒ポーポー」と呼ぶこともあるため、地域や世代によっては両者が混同されることも多い。素朴で庶民的な軽食だが、今日では伝統的な沖縄料理の一つで、地元のスーパーやパーラーなどでも販売されている。【ポーポー（口絵 4-27-8、P8 参照）】

⑧ *Poh-poh*

In Chinese characters, the word "炮炮" is applied to it, and the name is said to be of Chinese origin, but it is often written in *katakana* as *poh-poh*. It is made by dissolving flour in a small amount of water, wrapping the oil *miso* in a thin pancake baked in a frying pan or other flat pan, and rolling it up. Nowadays, it is eaten as a snack, but in the old days, it was made in each household along with *chimbin* as an event food on *yukka-nu-hii* (the fourth day of the fifth lunar month), to wish for the growth of the child. The original *poh-poh* is made of unsweetened white dough rolled with oil *miso*, but since *chimbin* is sometimes considered a type of *poh-poh* and called "black *poh-poh*," the two are often confused in some regions or generations. It is a simple, commonplace snack, but today it is one of the traditional Okinawan dishes and is sold in local supermarkets and parlors. 【*Poh-poh*(Frontispiece 4-27-8, See page 8)】

(28) 沖縄の墓（おきなわのはか）

①歴史と特徴

沖縄の代表的な墓には亀甲墓や破風墓が有名だが、そのような墓が造られるようになったのは16世紀以降である。かつて庶民は、森や洞窟の中に遺体を安置・埋葬する「風葬」が一般的で、亀甲墓や破風墓を造ることは王族や士族にしか許されなかった。廃藩置県後の明治時代にようやく一般の人々は墓を造ることが許された。聖地・久高島では、1960年代まで風葬が行われていた。沖縄の墓の最大の特徴に父系親族の遺骨を埋葬する伝統的な門中墓がある。門中墓は儒教の影響を受けているため「先祖を敬う」という強い意識に基づいており、必然的に多くの遺骨を納骨することになる。沖縄の墓は、長方形の石を積み重ねた本土の一般的な墓の形式とは異なり、独特の文化や風習を併せ持っている。その形や大きさが最大の特徴である沖縄の墓には、屋根や扉もあり、温かみのある小さ

な家のような印象を与える。故人を供養するための行事である「清明祭」という宴会が墓の前で行われるため、広いスペースが必要とされるのである。沖縄には「神墓」とよばれる現在は使用されていない墓があり「アジシー墓」または「アジ墓」と称する。沖縄の人は、古い墓にも魂がまだ残っており、長い年月を経て神化した「祖霊」が宿っていると考える。門中と繋がる墓であれば清明祭などにお参りする。対して現在使用している墓は「トーシー墓」（当世墓）と呼ばれる。沖縄の墓には、墓地特有の怖いイメージはない。清明祭などで一族が墓に集い、先祖を身近に感じながら供養する沖縄の人々の生死観が表れている。沖縄の墓の種類で最も代表的なのが掘り込み墓・破風墓・亀甲墓である。

風葬跡（久高島）
Ruins of a wind burial
(Kudaka Island)

(28) Graves in Okinawa

① History and Characteristics

  Typical Okinawan graves are known as *kamekou-baka* (tortoise-shell tombs) and *hahuu-baka* (gable tombs), but it was not until the 16th century that such tombs began to be built. In the past, the common people used *huu-sou* (wind burial), in which the body was laid to rest and buried in a forest or cave, and only royalty and warriors were allowed to build *kamekou-baka* or *hahuu-baka*. It was not until the Meiji era (1868-1912), after the abolition of the feudal domain, that ordinary people were finally allowed to build their own tombs. In the sacred island of Kudaka Island, wind burials were practiced until the 1960s. One of the most distinctive features of Okinawan graves is the traditional *munchu-baka*, where the remains of paternal relatives are buried. *Munchu-baka* is influenced by Confucianism and are based on a strong sense of "respect for ancestors," which inevitably leads to the burial of a large number of remains. The graves in Okinawa are different from the common grave forms on the mainland, which are made of rectangular stones stacked on top of each other, and have both unique culture and customs. Okinawan tombs, whose shape and size are their most distinctive features, also have roofs and doors, giving the impression of a warm, small house. A large space is needed for the *seimei-sai*, a banquet held in front of the tomb to honor the deceased. In Okinawa, there is a tomb that is no longer in use called *kami-baka* and is called *ajishii-baka* or *aji-baka*. Okinawans believe that even in old tombs, the soul still remains, and that the "ancestral spirit" that have been deified over the years still reside there. If the tomb is connected to the *munchu*, we visit it during the *seimei-sai* or other times. In contrast, the tombs in use today are called *toushii-baka* (contemporary tombs). Tombs in Okinawa do not have the scary image typical of cemeteries. This shows the Okinawan people's view of life and death, where descendants gather at the graves during the *seimei-sai* and other events to memorialize their ancestors while feeling close to them. The most typical types of tombs in Okinawa are *horikomi-baka*, *hahuu-baka*, and *kamekou-baka*.

②掘り込み墓（横穴墓）（ほりこみばか・よこあなばか）

　以前は、故人の遺体は山や崖などの人目に付かない場所へ移動して、数年間放置して白骨化するのを待った。白骨化すると一族の女性が洗骨を行い、骨壺に入れた。さらにその後になると、山や崖を

掘り込んで遺体をその中に安置し、それを取り囲むようにして石を積み上げた。これが掘り込み墓の始まりだが、現在では入り口を石や漆喰などで塞ぐ。シンプルな掘り込み墓は方言で「フィンチャー」とも呼ばれ、かつては仮の墓としても使用されていた。特に砂岩層地域に多く見られ、現代でも沖縄全域に分布している墓である。英祖王や尚寧王が眠る「浦添ようどれ」も掘り込み墓である。

掘り込み墓（尚泰久王の墓、南城市冨里）
Horikomi-baka of King Sho Taikyu (Husato, Nanjo City)

② *Horikomi-baka*
(Dug-in grave /side-hole grave)

In the past, the bodies of the deceased were moved to a secluded place such as a mountain or cliff and left there for several years to wait for the bones to turn white. When the bones turned white, the women of the dead man's clan washed them and placed them in an urn. In later times, mountains and cliffs were dug into which the bodies were placed, and stones were piled up to surround them. This was the beginning of the dug-in grave, but nowadays the entrance is sealed with stone or plaster. The simple, dug-in grave, also known as *finchaa* in the dialect, was once used as temporary tomb. This type of tomb is especially common in sandstone strata areas and is still distributed throughout Okinawa today. The Urasoe-*youdore*, where King Eiso and King Sho Nei are buried, is also a dug-in grave.

③破風墓（はふうばか）

掘り込み墓の周囲の壁や屋根を装飾し、発展した家型の墓が破風墓である。琉球王国時代には王室だけしか造ることを許されなかったが、1879年以降は解禁され一般にも普及した。屋根部分が三角形になっているのが特徴である。屋根の側面につけられている山形の板は「破風」と呼ばれ、雨や風の吹き込みを防ぐ役割を担っている。1501年に尚真王によって造られた第二尚氏王統の墓「玉陵」は、沖縄で最古かつ最大の破風墓である。

宮城小門中の破風墓（糸満市武富）
Hahuu-baka of Naagusukugwaa-*munchu*(Taketomi, Itoman City)

③ *Hahuu-baka*(Gable tomb)

A house-shaped tomb that developed by decorating the walls and roof of "Dug-in tombs" is *hahuu-baka* (Gable tombs). In the days of the Ryukyu Kingdom, only the royal family was allowed to build these tombs, but the ban was lifted after 1879 and they became popular among the general public. It is characterized by the triangular shape of the roof. The mountain-shaped boards on the sides of the roof are called *hahuu*, and serve to prevent rain and wind from blowing in. Tama-*udun*, the tomb of the Second Sho Dynasty, built by King Sho Shin in 1501, is the oldest and largest *hahuu-baka* in Okinawa.

④亀甲墓（かめこうばか・きっこうばか）

　破風墓に続いて登場した墓で、屋根部分が亀の甲羅に似ているので「亀甲墓」（カメコウバカ・キッコウバカ）と称され、沖縄方言で「カーミヌクーバカ」と言われる。人間は死後、母の胎内に戻るとして「女性の子宮」をイメージした墓である。17世紀に中国南部から伝来したといわれ、中国福建省や台湾でも似たような墓が見られる。沖縄戦では墓の大きさから防空壕としても使用されたが、米軍に狙われる対象にもなった。もともと琉球王朝時代に造られたが、廃藩置県以降に庶民に広がったことで沖縄本島の中南部を中心に普及した。亀甲墓の前には清明祭が行われる広い前庭があるのが特徴である。沖縄では伝統的に個人墓は稀で、亀甲墓も殆どが家族墓か門中墓のいずれかである。本土の墓に比べて著しく異なる亀甲墓は近年、沖縄を愛する他府県からの移住者にも人気がある。1687年に建造された那覇市石嶺町にある琉球王族・伊江御殿の墓は県内最古の亀甲墓といわれる。

④ *Kamekou-baka/Kikkou-baka* (Turtleback tomb)

　Turtleback tomb appeared after the *hahuu-baka* (gable tomb), and are called *Kamekou-baka* or *Kikkou-baka* (turtle shell tomb) because the roof part resembles a turtle shell, and are called *Kaaminukuu-baka* in Okinawan dialect. This type of tomb is based on the image of a "woman's womb," as humans are supposed to return to their mother's womb after death. It is said to have been introduced from southern China in the 17th century, and similar tombs can be found in Fujian Province, China and Taiwan. During the Battle of Okinawa, it was used as an air-raid shelter due to its size, but it also became a target for the US military. It was originally made during the Ryukyu Dynasty, but spread to the common people after the Haihan-chiken (abolition of the domain system), and became popular mainly in the central and southern parts of Okinawa Island. In front of the turtleback tomb, there is a large forecourt where the *seimei-sai* is held. Traditionally, individual tombs are rare in Okinawa, and most of the turtle shell tombs are either family tombs or *munchu* tombs. The Turtleback tombs, which are remarkably different from those in the mainland, have recently become popular among immigrants from other prefectures who love Okinawa. Built in 1687, the tomb of Ryukyu royalty Ie-*udun* in Ishmine-*cho*, Naha City is said to be the oldest turtleback tomb in Okinawa Prefecture.

伊江御殿の亀甲墓（那覇市首里石嶺町）
Kamekou-baka of Ie-*udun* (Shuri Ishimine-*cho*, Naha City)

第 5 章　沖縄の貴重生物

（1）沖縄の貴重動物、東洋のガラパゴス（おきなわのきちょうどうぶつ、とうようのがらぱごす）

　世界遺産は文化財、景観、自然など、人類が共有すべき「顕著な普遍的価値」を持つものである。「奄美大島、徳之島、沖縄本島北部および西表島」が 2021 年 7 月、世界自然遺産に登録された。かつて中国大陸と繋がっていたこれらの地域は、海面上昇で島となり、アマミノクロウサギ、ヤンバルクイナ、イリオモテヤマネコなど、多くの希少な固有種がそれぞれの島で独自の進化を遂げている。周囲が海に囲まれたことによって移動が妨げられ、動物たちは島の中で独自の進化を遂げてきた。そのことが「東洋のガラパゴス」と呼ばれるほどの固有種の多さにつながっている。これらの地域は全て、かつての琉球王国の領内にあり、今後は学術的な価値のみならず観光資源としての活用も期待されている。その一方で本来、人類の宝として保護していかなければならない貴重な固有種が林道建設やダム建設などの公共事業、米軍演習によって絶滅の危機に瀕しているのも事実である。

やんばるの森（比地大滝、国頭村）
Yambaru Forest (Hiji-Ohtaki Waterfall, Kunigami Village)

Chapter 5 Precious Species of Okinawa

(1) Precious animals in Okinawa, the Galapagos of the Orient

　World Heritage sites are cultural assets, landscapes, and natural features that have "outstanding universal value" that should be shared by all humankind. In July 2021, "Amami Oshima, Tokunoshima, the northern part of Okinawa Island and Iriomote Island" were registered as World Natural Heritage sites. These areas, once connected to mainland China, have become islands due to rising sea levels, and many rare endemic species such as the Amami'*no-kurousagi* (black rabbits in Amami Island), the Yambaru-*kuina* (flightless wild birds in northern Okinawa Island), and the Iriomote *yamaneko* (wild cats in Iriomote Island) have evolved independently on each island. Surrounded by the sea, migration was hindered, and animals evolved independently within the islands. This has led to a large number of endemic species that have earned the island the nickname "Galapagos of the Orient". All of these areas are within the territory of the former Ryukyu Kingdom, and are expected to be used not only for their academic value but also as tourism resources in the future. On the other hand, it is also true that valuable endemic species, which should be protected as treasures of humankind, are in danger of extinction due to public works projects such as forest road construction and dam construction, and U.S. military exercises.

①ハブ

　ハブはクサリヘビ科に属する毒蛇であり、体長は 2 m にも達する。日本産の毒ヘビ中、最大で最も攻撃的で危険である。黄色または灰白色の基色に不規則な黒色の斑紋を有するのが一般的。主に哺乳類（ネズミ、ウサギ）、鳥類、爬虫類、両生類、魚類などを捕食する。繁殖は、 4 月に交尾を行い、 7 月に 4 〜 15 個の卵を産み、約 40 日で孵化する。成長にともない、毎年数回、脱皮を行う。夜行性で日中は自然の洞穴や石垣の穴、墓穴などに潜み、主に夕方から活動する。咬傷された場合は循環不全によるショック状態に陥るため、血清の使用などによる迅速な治療が必要になる。咬傷例は 1970 年代には約 300 人だったが、減少傾向にあり、血清の普及により死亡例はほとんどなくなった。一方、沖縄・奄美の農家にとっては、害獣であるネズミを退治する益獣としての側面も持つ。南西諸島の島々は、大きく分けて隆起石灰岩からなる標高の低い島と、火成岩からなる標高の高い島があり、ハブが生息する島々と生息しない島々が存在する。その理由として、氷河期に伴う間氷期の海進の影響（海水面の上昇と降下）が考えられている。ハブにかかわる迷信や民話も多く、人間生活に及ぼす影響は大きい。例えば、琉球絣の柄模様はハブの模様に酷似しており、沖縄空手のティー（手）はハブの攻撃姿勢と似ている。「ハブ酒」は薬酒の一種で、老化防止作用や精力剤として効果があるとされている。かつては沖縄や奄美の各地で観光客向けに「ハブとマングースの決闘ショー」が行われていたが、2000 年の動物愛護法改正により禁止された。ちなみに、ハブとマングースの対決では 1 対 20 くらいの割合でマングースが勝つといわれる。【ハブ（口絵 5-1-1、P8 参照)】

① *Habu*

　The *habu* is a poisonous snake belonging to the viper family, and can grow up to 2 meters in length. It is the largest, most aggressive and most dangerous of all Japanese vipers. It usually has a yellow or grayish-white base color with irregular black spots. Feeds primarily on mammals (mice, rabbits), birds, reptiles, amphibians, and fish. Breeding takes place in April for mating, followed by the laying of 4-15 eggs in July, which hatch in about 40 days. As it grows, it molts several times each year. They are nocturnal, hiding in natural caves, holes in stone walls, graves, etc. during the day, and are mainly active in the evening. Bite victims go into shock due to circulatory failure and require prompt treatment, including the use of serum. The number of bites was about 300 in the 1970s, but has been declining and deaths have virtually disappeared due to the widespread use of sera. On the other hand, for farmers in Okinawa and Amami, *habu* also has the aspect of a beneficial animal that exterminates rats, which are vermin. The islands of the Nansei Islands can be roughly divided into two groups: lower elevation islands composed of uplifted limestone and higher elevation islands composed of igneous rock, with some islands inhabited by *habu* and others not. The reason for this is thought to be the effect of interglacial sea advance (rise and fall of sea level) associated with glacial periods. There are many superstitions and folk tales about *habu*, and their influence on human life is great. For example, the patterns on Ryukyu-*kasuri* patterns closely resemble those of *habu*, and the *tii* (hands) in Okinawan *karate* resemble the attacking posture of *habu*. *Habu-shu* is a type of medicinal wine that is believed to have anti-aging and energizing properties. In the past, "dueling shows between *habu* and mongoose" were held for tourists in various places in Okinawa and Amami, but were banned due to the revision of the Animal Protection Law in 2000. Incidentally, in a duel between a *habu* and a mongoose, the mongoose is said to win by a ratio of about 1 to 20.
【*Habu* (Frontispiece 5-1-1, See page 8)】

②マングース

　マングースは西アジアから東南アジアにかけて分布する雑食性の哺乳類で、日本では沖縄諸島と奄美大島に定着している。かつて沖縄島民にとってネズミは重要な収入源であるサトウキビに大きな被

害をもたらし、そのネズミを餌として畑に侵入するハブは恐ろしい動物であった。それらを駆除するための天敵としてマングースの導入を提案したのは東京大学・渡瀬庄三郎名誉教授で、1910 年、沖縄島に最初に持ち込まれた。1970 年代までマングース神話は続き、1979 年には奄美大島にも導入された。ところが、その後の調査では、マングースによるハブの駆除効果はほとんどなかったことが明らかになった。胃の内容物や糞の分析から、マングースは昆虫類、鳥類、爬虫類、哺乳類から果実まで食べる雑食性で、昆虫類が主な食べ物であることがわかった。昼行性のマングースが猛毒を持つ夜行性のハブをわざわざ捕食する必要はなく、沖縄島のヤンバルクイナや奄美のアマミノクロウサギなどの希少種は天敵から逃げる能力が低く、ハンティングの名手・マングースの犠牲となっていたのである。西インド諸島やフィジー諸島などの島では、マングースによる爬虫類の絶滅も起きているといわれる。2000 年から環境省によって奄美・沖縄の両島でマングースの駆除事業が行われ、奄美諸島では 2019 年度から捕獲数ゼロの状態が続いている。【マングース（口絵 5-1-2、P8 参照）】

② Mongoose

The mongoose is an omnivorous mammal that is distributed from West Asia to Southeast Asia, and is found in Okinawa Islands and Amami Oshima Island in Japan. In the past, rats caused serious damage to sugarcane, an important source of income for the Okinawans, and *habu*, which fed on rats and invaded the fields, was a fearsome animal. It was Professor Emeritus Watase Shozaburo of the University of Tokyo who proposed the introduction of the mongoose as a natural enemy to exterminate them, and it was first introduced to Okinawa Island in 1910. The myth of the mongoose continued until the 1970s, and was also introduced to Amami Islands in 1979. Subsequent research, however, showed that the mongoose was not useful in killing *habu*. Analysis of stomach contents and feces revealed that mongooses are omnivorous, eating everything from insects, birds, reptiles, and mammals to fruit, with insects being their primary food. Diurnal mongooses did not bother to prey on nocturnal *habu*, which are highly poisonous. Rare species such as the Yambaru-*kuina* in Okinawa Island and the Amami'*no-kurousagi* (black rabbits in Amami Island) were victims of the mongoose, a master hunter, because of their poor ability to escape from their natural enemies. The extinction of reptiles by mongoose is also said to have occurred on islands such as the West Indies and Fiji Islands. Since 2000, a mongoose extermination project has been conducted by the Ministry of the Environment in both Amami and Okinawa Islands, and the Amami Islands have had zero captures since FY 2019.
【Mongoose (Frontispiece 5-1-2, See page 8)】

③イリオモテヤマネコ

　西表島民からは「ヤマピカリャー」、「ピカリャー」、「ヤママヤー」と呼ばれ、以前からその存在は知られていた。沖縄がアメリカの占領下にあった頃、アメリカの大学による調査も行われたが発見には至らず、飼い猫が野生化したものではないかという考えもあった。学術上の発見は 1965 年で、1977 年には国の天然記念物に指定された。イリオモテヤマネコは西表島の固有種で、現存するヤマネコ類の中で最も原始的で「生きた化石」といわれている。琉球列島がアジア大陸と陸続きだった頃、イリオモテヤマネコはアジア大陸の東縁部に異動し、その後の海面上昇や地殻変動によって琉球列島が成立していくなかで西表島に取り残されたものと考えられている。世界の野生ネコはネズミやウサギなどの小型哺乳類を餌としているが、西表島のような小さい島ではそのような小型哺乳類は少なく、イリオモテヤマネコはコオロギなどの昆虫や川エビなどの小動物も食べ、島の食物連鎖の頂点に君臨する。様々な生物を餌資源として利用することは世界中でもイリオモテヤマネコだけが持つ特徴である。遺伝的にはピューマに近い種で、全身に斑点模様があり耳が丸く、尻尾が太く長いのが外見的な特徴。寿命は、他のネコ科の動物に比べるとやや短く、10 年ほどである。開発による生息地の破壊、

イヌによる捕食、交通事故などで生息数は減少している。2007 年には絶滅危惧種の「レッドリスト」に分類され、現存種の中でもっとも絶滅の危機が高い種とされている。
【イリオモテヤマネコ（口絵 5-1-3、P9 参照）】

③ Iriomote *yamaneko* (wildcat)

Iriomote Islanders call it *yama-pikariyaa*, *pikariyaa,* or *yama-mayaa*, and its existence has been known for a long time. When Okinawa was under the U.S. occupation, a survey was conducted by an American university but failed to discover the cat, and some thought it might be a domesticated cat that had become feral. Its academic discovery was made in 1965, and it was designated as a national natural monument in 1977. The Iriomote *yamaneko* (wildcat) is endemic to Iriomote Island, and is considered the most primitive and "living fossil" of all wildcat species in existence. When the Ryukyu Archipelago was connected to the Asian continent by land, the Iriomote wildcat was transferred to the eastern edge of the Asian continent and is thought to have been left behind on Iriomote Island as the Ryukyu Archipelago was established by subsequent sea level rise and tectonic movement. Wild cats in the world feed on small mammals such as rats and rabbits, but such small mammals are scarce on small islands like Iriomote Island, and the Iriomote wildcat also feeds on insects such as crickets and small animals such as river shrimp, reigning at the top of the island food chain. The use of various living things as food resources is a characteristic that only the Iriomote wildcat has in the world. Genetically similar to the puma, the species is characterized by its spotted pattern all over its body, rounded ears, and thick, long tail in appearance. Their lifespan is somewhat shorter than that of other felines, about 10 years. Their population is declining due to habitat destruction caused by development, predation by canines, and traffic accidents. In 2007, the Iriomote *yamaneko* was classified on the "Red List" of endangered species and is considered the most endangered species in existence.【Iriomote *yamaneko* (Frontispiece 5-1-3, See page 9)】

④ヤンバルクイナ

「慌て者」という意の「アガチ」「アガチャー」や、「ヤマドゥイ」（やまどり）という呼称で以前から地元住民には知られていた。1981 年、研究者による調査の結果、沖縄島北部（ヤンバル）の森だけに生息し未知の新種であることが判明。日本で唯一の飛べないこの鳥は「ヤンバルクイナ」と名付けられ、1982 年に国の天然記念物に指定された。飛べない代わりに足が太く大きく発達し、地上をすばしっこく走る。夜行性で警戒心が強くなかなか見ることができない。主に、平地から標高 500 メートル以下にある常緑広葉樹林に生息するが、海岸付近の民家周辺などで見られることもある。夜間になると樹上で休むが、これはヘビ類を避けるためだと考えられている。

ヤンバルクイナを捕食するマングースやネコなどが外部から持ち込まれたことや、道路やダム建設による生息地の破壊や分断、交通事故の被害、米軍演習などによって個体数が減少し 2006 年には絶滅危惧種に指定された。2000 年度から沖縄県による罠を用いたマングースやネコの駆除・捕獲が進められているが、完全駆除の目途はたっていない。1999 年には「やんばる野生生物保護センター」が設置され、2005 年には「ヤンバルクイナ救急救命センター」の運営が開始され、保護対策が行われている。ヤンバルの森は世界的にも希少な亜熱帯雨林で、多くの固有種を含む豊かな生態系が築かれている。【ヤンバルクイナ（口絵 5-1-4、P9 参照）】

④ Yambaru-*kuina*

This bird had long been known to local residents by the names *agachi* or *agachaa* (meaning panicky), and *yamadui* (meaning "mountain bird"). In 1981, as a result of a survey conducted by researchers, it was discovered that it was a new, unknown species living only in the forests of northern Okinawa Island (Yambaru). And the only flightless bird in Japan was named Yambaru-*kuina* and designated as a national natural monument in 1982. Instead of being flightless, it has large, thick legs and runs swiftly on the ground. It is nocturnal, cautious, and difficult to see. It is mainly found in evergreen broad-leaved forests from the plains to altitudes below 500 meters, but can also be found around houses near the coast. At night, they rest in the trees, thought to be to avoid snakes. The population had declined due to the introduction of mongooses and cats, which prey on the Yambaru-*kuina*, were brought in from the outside as well as habitat destruction and fragmentation caused by road and dam construction, damage from traffic accidents, and U.S. military exercises, and was designated as an endangered species in 2006. Okinawa Prefecture has been exterminating and capturing mongooses and cats using traps since 2000, but there is no prospect of complete extermination. In 1999, the "Yambaru Wildlife Conservation Center" was established, and in 2005, the "Yambaru-*kuina* Emergency Rescue Center" began operations, and protection measures are being taken. The Yambaru forest is a rare subtropical rainforest in the world, and a rich ecosystem including many endemic species has been established.

【Yambaru-*kuina* (Frontispiece 5-1-4, See page 9)】

（2）沖縄県の植物、県花・県木・県鳥・県魚・県蝶（おきなわけんのしょくぶつ）

　沖縄には亜熱帯気候特有の多種多様な植物が数多く、約 2,000 種以上が見られるといわれる。代表的なものとしては、県花に指定されているデイゴがあげられる。特に沖縄島北部や八重山の島々、南・北大東島などでは、他府県にはない珍しい植物も多く見ることができる。西表島では、アフリカや南アメリカにある熱帯のジャングルのような森が島全体を包み込んでいる。西表島でよく目にする植物はマングローブである。マングローブとは単一の植物の名前ではなく、海に近い海岸や河口に多く見られる「ヒルギ」を主体とした林のことである。海水に浸かって広がるマングローブは、魚やカニなどの小さな生物を育み、周囲の環境を整える重要な役割も担っている。沖縄全域に分布するハイビスカスやブーゲンビレアなどは、一年中南国らしい鮮やかな花を咲かせ、地元の人々や観光客の目を楽しませてくれる。

西表島のマングローブ
Mangroves in Iriomote Island

(2) Plants in Okinawa, prefectural flower, tree, bird, fish, and butterfly

Okinawa has a wide variety of plants unique to its subtropical climate, and it is said that more than 2,000 species can be found here. A typical example is *deigo*, which is designated as the prefectural flower. Especially in the northern part of Okinawa Island, the islands of Yaeyama, and South and North Daito Islands, many rare plants can be seen that are not found in other prefectures. In Iriomote Island, a forest like a tropical jungle in Africa or South America envelops the entire island. The plants we often see in Iriomote Island are mangroves. Mangrove is not the name of a single plant, but rather a forest of mainly *hirugi* (an evergreen tree of the *hirugi* family distributed in tropical and subtropical regions) that are often found along the coast and at river mouths near the ocean. The mangroves, which spread out as they are submerged in seawater, also help to nurture small organisms such as fish and crabs, and play an important role in regulating the surrounding environment. Hibiscus and Bougainvillea, which are distributed all over Okinawa, bloom in vivid tropical colors all year round, delighting the eyes of locals and tourists alike.

①県木（琉球松）

　琉球松は、高さ 25m 以上になるマツ科の常緑高木で、沖縄方言で「マーチ」と呼ばれ、九州および沖縄（奄美大島から与那国島）に自生する。美しい枝振りや台風に強い性質を活かして防潮林・防風林・街路樹などに、木材は造船用材やパルプ材などに利用される。美しい木目を生かしたテーブル・椅子などの家具や、お盆・食器などの工芸品の材料としても使われている。「伊平屋島の念頭平松」（伊平屋村）と「久米の五枝の松」（久米島町）は沖縄県の 2 大名松と評価されている。両者とも国の天然記念物に指定されており、「新日本名木 100 選」にも選定されている。琉球松は「デイゴ」と同様、1967 年に県民投票によって「沖縄県の木」に選ばれた。【久米の五枝の松（口絵 5-2-1、P9 参照）】

① Ryukyu-*matsu* (Prefectural tree)

　The Ryukyu-*matsu* is a tall evergreen tree of the pine family, reaching a height of 25 meters or more. It is called *maachi* in Okinawan dialect grows wild in Kyushu and Okinawa (from Amami Oshima to Yonaguni Island). The beautiful branching and typhoon-resistant nature of the tree make it ideal for use as a tide-break forest, windbreak forest, and roadside tree, while the wood is used for shipbuilding and pulpwood. The beautiful grain of the wood is also used for furniture such as tables and chairs, and for handicrafts such as trays and tableware. The two most famous pine trees in Okinawa are the *"Nentou-hiramatsu* of Iheyajima" (Iheya Village) and the *"Goeda-no-matsu* Kume'no-Goeda'no-Matsu" (Kumejima Town). Both are designated as national natural monuments and selected as one of the "New Japan's 100 Best Trees. The Ryukyu-*matsu,* like the *deigo*, was selected as the "Okinawa Prefectural Tree" by a prefectural referendum in 1967. 【Kume'no-*Goeda'no-Matsu* (Frontispiece 5-2-1, See page 9)】

②県花（デイゴ）

　マメ科の落葉高木で高さは 15m に達し、樹皮には多数の鋭い棘がある。インドやマレー半島原産で日本では沖縄が北限とされている。3 月から 5 月にかけて咲く深紅で燃え立つような美しい花は、毎年満開になる保証はなく年ごとの差が大きい。根の力が強く、家の近くに植えると根が伸びて家を傾けてしまうことから、沖縄では「ヤシチクーサー」（屋敷壊し）とも呼ばれる。有名な沖縄ソング「島唄」の歌詞にも登場するデイゴの花言葉は「夢・活力・生命力」で、古くからウチナーンチュの心に根ざして愛されてきた。その一方で、デイゴの花が満開に咲くと、その年は台風の当たり年で、干魃に見舞われるという不吉な迷信がある。木は観賞用として街路樹や公園樹に植栽され、幹材は琉球漆器の材料に用いられる。1967 年に県民投票によって「沖縄県の花」に選定された。
【デイゴ（口絵 5-2-2、P9 参照）】

② *Deigo* (Indian coral tree),(Prefectural flower)

　A deciduous tree of the Fabaceae family, reaching a height of 15 meters, with many sharp thorns on its bark. It is native to India and the Malay Peninsula, and Okinawa is considered to be the northern limit in Japan. The beautiful, deep red, flaming flowers, which bloom from March to May, are not guaranteed to be in full bloom every year, and vary greatly from year to year. In Okinawa, it is also called *yashichi-kuusaa* (house destroyer) because its roots are so strong that if planted near a house, the roots will grow and cause the house to tip over. The flower language of the *deigo*, which appears in the lyrics of the famous Okinawan song *Shima-uta*, is "dream, vitality, and life force," and it has been rooted in the hearts of *uchinanchu* and loved by them since ancient times. On the other hand, there is an ominous superstition that when the *deigo* flowers are in full bloom, it is a year with many typhoons and a drought. The tree is planted as an ornamental tree along streets and in parks, and the trunk wood is used to make Ryukyu lacquer ware. It was selected as the "Flower of Okinawa Prefecture" by a prefectural referendum in 1967.【*Deigo* (Frontispiece 5-2-2, See page 9)】

③ハイビスカス

　沖縄では島津氏の琉球侵略時（1609 年）には自生しており、島津家久が戦利品として徳川家康に献上したのが日本本土への最初の渡来と言われる。原産地は中国南部やインドといわれ、マレーシアでは国花とされ硬貨にも刻まれている。ハワイでは州の花で、明るく輝く太陽の光に映えて咲く真っ赤なハイビスカスは、観光客を迎える「歓迎の花」としても使われる。一方、沖縄では生け垣として利用され年中咲くが、特に沖縄戦での激戦地・沖縄南部では死者の慰霊として墓の周辺にも植えられた。そのため、沖縄では「後生花」（ぐそーばな）や「仏桑花」（ぶっそうげ）という別名を持つ。「仏様に供える花」という意味である。

ハイビスカス (温暖な気候の沖縄では、年中どこでも咲く)
Hibiscus (blooms everywhere year-round in the warm climate of Okinawa)

③ **Hibiscus**

　In Okinawa, it grew wild during the Shimazu clan's invasion of Ryukyu (1609), and is said to have first come to mainland Japan when Shimazu Iehisa presented it to Tokugawa Ieyasu as a trophy of war.Said to originate in southern China and India, it is considered the national flower of Malaysia and is inscribed on coins.In Hawaii, the bright red hibiscus, the state flower, shining in the bright sunshine and is used as a "welcoming flower" to greet tourists.On the other hand, in Okinawa, it is used as a hedge and blooms year-round. Especially in southern Okinawa, the site of the fierce Battle of Okinawa, it was also planted around graves as a memorial to the dead. Therefore, in Okinawa, it has another name, *Gusou-bana* or *Bussouge*, meaning "flower offered to the dead".

④県鳥（ノグチゲラ）

　沖縄島北部の山林、通称「ヤンバルの森」だけに生息するキツツキの仲間で、体長は約 30cm。食性は、動物食性の傾向が強い雑食で、昆虫、クモ、多足類、果実などを食べる。繁殖期になると縄張りを形成し、直径 20cm 以上の枯れ木に穴を開けた巣に、4 〜 5 月に 1 度に 2 〜 4 個の卵を産む。雌雄交代で抱卵し、育雛も雌雄共に行う。ノグチゲラが新種として発見されたのは 1887 年で、この発見に関わった「野口氏」が名前の由来となっている。世界でも珍しい 1 属 1 種の日本固有種で、1970 年には「沖縄県の鳥」に、1977 年には国の特別天然記念物に指定された。沖縄が誇る幻の鳥・ノグチゲラだが、今、絶滅の危機にある。人間が持ち込んだネコやマングースがその原因とされている。
【ノグチゲラ（口絵 5-2-4、P9 参照）】

④ **Noguchi-*gera* (Prefectural bird)**

　The noguchi-*gera* is a species of woodpecker that lives only in the mountain forests of northern Okinawa Island, commonly known as "Yambaru Forest," and is about 30 cm long. Dietary habits are omnivorous with a strong tendency toward zoophagy, feeding on insects, spiders, polypods, and fruit. During the breeding season, they form territories and lay two to four eggs at a time in nests drilled into dead trees with a diameter of 20 cm or more in April and May. Males and females take turns warming the eggs and raising chicks together. The noguchi-*gera* was discovered as a new species in 1887, and its name is derived from Mr. Noguchi who was involved in the discovery. It is a rare species in the world, belonging to one genus and one species, endemic to Japan, and was designated as the "Bird of Okinawa Prefecture" in 1970, and as a special natural monument of Japan in 1977. The noguchi-*gera*, a fantastic bird that Okinawa is proud of, is now in danger of extinction. It is believed that cats and mongooses brought in by humans are the cause. 【Noguchi-*gera* (Frontispiece 5-2-4, See page 9)】

⑤県魚（タカサゴ・グルクン）

　色鮮やかで、体長 25cm 前後まで成長する。和名は「タカサゴ」だが、県民には「グルクン」の別称で呼ばれ「沖縄県の魚」に指定されている。熱帯性の魚で、西太平洋からインド洋にかけて分布している。珊瑚礁の海に暮らすグルクンは、昼間はリーフの外を群れて遊泳して餌を探し、夜は群れを解消してサンゴの下に隠れて眠る。沖縄では重要な食用魚として釣りや追い込み、網など沿岸漁業で漁獲される。唐揚げや刺身の料理のほか、カマボコの材料としても用いられる。
【グルクン（口絵 5-2-5、P9 参照）】

⑤ *Gurukun* **(Double-lined fusilier),(Prefectural fish)**

　A brightly colored fish that grows up to about 25 cm in length. Its Japanese name is *takasago*, but people in Okinawa call it *gurukun*, another name, and it is designated as the "fish of Okinawa Prefecture." It is a tropical fish distributed from the western Pacific to the Indian Ocean. *Gurukun* live in coral reef waters, and during the day they swim in groups outside the reef to search for food, and at night they dissolve their groups and hide under the coral to sleep. In Okinawa, it is an important food fish and is caught by coastal fisheries such as fishing, chasing, and netting. *Gurukun* is used for deep frying and sashimi dishes as well as an ingredient in *kamaboko*.【*Gurukun* (Frontispiece 5-2-5, See page 9)】

⑥県蝶（オオゴマダラ）

　オオゴマダラは日本の蝶としては最大種であり、羽を広げると 13cm~15cm にも及ぶ。東南アジアに広く分布し、国内では鹿児島県喜界島以南の南西諸島にしか生息しておらず、全国的には「沖縄の蝶」として知られている。白黒のまだら模様が特徴的な大型のマダラチョウで、蛹（さなぎ）が金色になることでも知られている。オスは人間の頭に群がることがあるが、これは整髪料や香水にフェロモンの原料となるパラベンが含まれているためである。ゆっくりと羽ばたき優雅に飛ぶ姿から「南国の貴婦人」とも呼ばれ、飛び方や羽の模様が、新聞紙が風に舞い飛んでいるようにも見えるので「新聞蝶」という別称もある。糸満市の平和祈念公園では毎年、6 月 23 日の「慰霊の日」に沖縄戦で亡くなられた人々の慰霊のためオオゴマダラが放蝶される。2020 年 4 月 1 日、「沖縄県の蝶」に指定された。
【オオゴマダラ（口絵 5-2-6、P9 参照）】

⑥ *Ohgomadara* **(tree nymph butterfly),(Prefectural butterfly)**

　The *ohgomadara* (tree nymph butterfly) is the largest species of butterfly in Japan, with wings that are 13cm to 15cm long. It is widely distributed in Southeast Asia, and in Japan, it is found only in the southwestern islands south of Kikai Island in Kagoshima Prefecture, and is known nationwide as the "butterfly of Okinawa". It is a large butterfly with a distinctive black-and-white speckled pattern, and is also known for its golden chrysalis. Males sometimes flock to human heads because hairdressing products and perfumes contain parabens, which are the source of pheromones. It is also called the "lady of the tropics" because of the way it slowly flaps its wings and flies gracefully, and is known as the "newspaper butterfly" too, because the way it flies and the pattern of its wings looks like a newspaper flying in the wind. Every year, on June 23, Memorial Day, tree nymph butterflies are released at Peace Memorial Park in Itoman City to commemorate those who died in the Battle of Okinawa. The butterfly was designated as the "Butterfly of Okinawa Prefecture" on April 1, 2020.
【*Ohgomadara* (Frontispiece 5-2-6, See page 9)】

第6章　沖縄戦

（1）沖縄戦の特徴

　沖縄戦とは、太平洋戦争末期の 1945 年 3 月 26 日、慶良間諸島に上陸したアメリカ軍を主体とする連合軍と日本軍との間で行われた戦闘。この戦いを連合軍側は「アイスバーグ作戦」と命名し、沖縄では「ウチナーイクサ」と呼んでいる。沖縄戦の特徴は①沖縄守備軍（第 32 軍）の任務は住民を守ることではなく、本土戦を避けるための持久戦であった②戦闘員よりも一般住民の戦死者が多い③軍人と住民が混在する場所で地上戦が行われ、住民の集団自決があった、などである。当時の兵役法では、17 歳以上の男子に兵役の義務が課された。しかし沖縄戦では、軍・県・警察が主導し、市町村長や学校に義勇隊の結成を指示した。法的根拠のない 17 歳未満の若者（男女）の動員が進められ、義勇隊、救護班、炊事班として戦場に配属された。それは、皇民化教育に染まった住民にとっては断ることの出来ない「強制」だった。「軍官民共生共死」という日本軍の方針によって、住民にも軍人同様に死ぬことが求められた。悲惨な地上戦では砲弾が大嵐のように降り注いだので、「鉄の暴風」とも言われ、米軍は「ありったけの地獄を集めた戦場」と表現した。沖縄戦の教訓として「命どぅ宝」、「軍隊は住民を守らなかった」と語り継がれている。

捕虜になった民間兵（左から 75 歳、16 歳、15 歳）（沖縄県公文書館所蔵）
Civilian soldiers taken prisoner(from the left, 75,16 and15 years old)

Chapter 6 Battle of Okinawa

（1）Features of the Battle of Okinawa

　The Battle of Okinawa was fought on March 26, 1945, at the end of the Pacific War, between Allied forces, mainly American, and Japanese forces that landed on the Kerama Islands. The Allied forces named this battle "Operation Iceberg," while the Okinawans called it *Uchina-ikusa*. The Battle of Okinawa was characterized by (1) the mission of the Okinawa defensive forces (the 32nd Army) was not to protect the residents, but to fight an enduring war to avoid a battle on the mainland, (2) more ordinary residents died in the battle than combatants, (3) the ground battle was fought in a place where military personnel and residents were mixed, and there was mass suicide by the residents. According to the Military Service Law of the time, all males over the age of 17 were required to perform military service. However, in the Battle of Okinawa, the military, prefectural government, and police took the lead in instructing the mayors of municipalities and schools to form volunteer units. Young people (boys and girls) under the age of 17, who had no legal basis, were mobilized and assigned to the battlefield as volunteer troops, relief workers, and cooks. Because the shells rained down like a huge storm, it was also called the "Iron Storm" and the U.S. military described it as "a battlefield that collected all the hell it could". The lessons of the Battle of Okinawa have been passed down as *Nuchi-du-takara* (Life is the greatest treasure of all) and "The military did not protect the population".

（2）対馬丸遭難事件（つしままるそうなんじけん）

　沖縄戦前年の1944年8月22日、沖縄から長崎へ向かう学童疎開船（対馬丸）が悪石島（あくせきじま）付近で撃沈された事件。1944年7月、サイパン島では兵隊、住民もろとも「玉砕」するという悲惨な結果を招き、次は沖縄での決戦とみられた。政府は7月19日、沖縄県知事に「本土決戦に備え、非戦闘員である老人や婦女、児童10万人を本土または台湾へ疎開させよ」という命令を出した。対馬丸による学童疎開もそれに基づく国の施策であった。対馬丸は元貨物船で8月21日、那覇港を出港。

翌22日、奄美大島十島村悪石島の西海上で米海軍潜水艦の魚雷を3発受けて沈没した。学童約800人を含む約1,700人の乗客のうち生存者はわずか280人程度で、児童の90％以上が犠牲となった。対馬丸事件によって、疎開が進まなくなることを恐れた政府は、厳重な箝口令を敷き、憲兵などによる生存者への監視が行われた。1953年、遭難学童慰霊碑「小桜の塔」が那覇市波の上に建立され、2004年には犠牲者の鎮魂や、子供たちに平和と命の尊さを教える場として「対馬丸記念館」が那覇市若狭に開館した。対馬丸を沈めた潜水艦「ボーフィン号」は現在、ハワイ真珠湾に係留され、内部を見学できる。

小桜の塔　1953年5月5日のこどもの日に除幕式が行われた慰霊塔は、那覇港を向いている（那覇市波の上）
Kozakura-no-tou, unveiled on Children's Day, May 5, 1953, faces Naha Port (Naminoue, Naha City)

（2）Tsushima Maru Distress Incident

　On August 22, 1944, the year before the Battle of Okinawa, the Tsushima Maru, a ship for evacuating school children from Okinawa to Nagasaki, was sunk near Akuseki-jima Island. In July 1944, a tragedy occurred on the island of Saipan where all the soldiers and residents died rather than surrender, and the next battle was expected to be a decisive one in Okinawa. On July 19, the government issued an order to the governor of Okinawa to evacuate 100,000 non-combatants, including the elderly, women and children, to the mainland or Taiwan in preparation for a decisive battle on the mainland. The evacuation of school children by the Tsushima Maru was also a government policy based on this order. The Tsushima Maru, a former cargo ship, left Naha Port on August 21. On the following day, August 22, it was hit by three torpedoes from a U.S. Navy submarine and sank in the sea west of Akuseki-jima Island, Toshima Village in Amami Oshima. Of the approximately 1,700 passengers on board, including about 800 school children, only about 280 survived, and more than 90% of the children were killed. Fearing that the Tsushima Maru incident would interfere with the evacuation measures, the government imposed a strict gag order and survivors were monitored by the military police. In 1953, the *Kozakura-no-tou*, a cenotaph for schoolchildren, was erected at Naminoue in Naha City, and in 2004, the "Tsushima Maru Memorial Museum" was opened in Wakasa, Naha City, as a place to repose the souls of the victims and teach children about peace and the preciousness of life. The submarine that sank the Tsushima Maru, the Bowfin, is now moored at Pearl Harbor, Hawaii, and visitors can tour its interior.

（3）十・十空襲（じゅうじゅうくうしゅう）

　沖縄の地上戦が始まる前年の 1944 年 10 月 10 日に、南西諸島の広い範囲で米海軍機動部隊が行った大規模な空襲。米軍の攻撃目標は飛行場と船舶や軍施設で、この空爆には、沖縄戦に臨む米軍の情報収集という側面もあったといわれる。午前 6 時 40 分の第一次攻撃から午後 3 時 45 分までの第 5 次攻撃まで 9 時間にわたる波状的空爆が行われ、のべ 1,396 機の米軍艦載機が爆弾や焼夷弾を縦横無尽に投下した。日本軍の防衛体制は不十分で、空襲に対する有効な反撃も行えなかった。日本軍艦船なども甚大な損害を受け、県都・那覇市では市街地の大半が焼失し民間人にも大きな被害が出た。

十・十空襲（沖縄県公文書館所蔵）
Naha City being bombed by U.S. fighter planes
(October 10, 1944)

　第 32 軍（沖縄守備隊）は 10 月 10 日に首脳部を集めての大がかりな演習を予定しており、前日は各地の司令官たちは那覇市内の料亭に集められて宴会を開いていた。そのため、指揮官不在の各部隊は有効に対処することができなかった。10 日予定の演習は、兵士には単に「演習」としか知らされておらず、空襲は「本格的な演習」と受け止めた者が多かった。せっかくのレーダーによる攻撃隊の探知も、レーダーの故障と思われて有効に活用されなかった。

（3）*Juu-juu-kuushuu*（10.10 Air Raids）

　On October 10, 1944, the year before the ground war in Okinawa began, the U.S. Navy's task force conducted a large-scale air raid over a wide area of the Nansei Islands. The targets of the U.S. forces were airfields, ships, and military facilities, and it is said that this airstrike had the aspect of gathering information for the U.S. forces in the Battle of Okinawa. From the first attack at 6:40 a.m. to the fifth attack at 3:45 p.m., nine hours of aerial bombardment took place in waves, with a total of 1,396 aircraft dropping bombs and incendiary bombs in all directions. The Japanese defense system was inadequate, and they were unable to mount an effective counterattack against the air raids. Japanese warships and other vessels were severely damaged, and in Naha City, the capital of the prefecture, most of the urban area was burned down, and civilians were also badly affected.

　On October 10, a major exercise was scheduled to gather and assemble the leaders of the 32nd Army (Okinawa Defense Force), and the day before that, a banquet was held at a *ryotei* restaurant in Naha City for the commanders of the various regions. Soldiers were informed that the exercise scheduled for the 10th was merely an "exercise," and many of them took the air raids as a "full-scale exercise by the Japanese forces". Even the radar detection of the attacking force was not used effectively because it was thought to be a malfunction of the radar.

（4）第 32 軍司令部壕跡（だいさんじゅうにぐんしれいぶごうあと）

　第 32 軍司令部壕は、アメリカ軍が上陸する 4 ヶ月前の 1944 年（昭和 19）12 月から首里城地下に突貫工事で作られた。全長は 1 km 余りで、首里城の地下約 30m を南北に縦断するように掘られた。この場所が司令部に選ばれた主な理由は「アメリカ軍の 1 トン爆弾や艦砲射撃に耐えられる琉球石灰岩の硬い地層を備えている」「高台に位置し周囲の戦況も把握できる展望の良さ」などであった。入り口は

５カ所あり、正面入り口にあたる北側には３カ所が設けられている。守礼門からわずか数十メートル北側の斜面に入り口があるが、今では埋もれて入れない。壕の中には参謀室や作戦室、多数の居室があり、7000余人の将兵を収容し、一大地下ホテルの観があったといわれる。アメリカ軍は第32軍の激しい攻撃を受けながらも、5月半ばには首里を包囲した。5月22日、司令官の牛島満中将は南部へ撤退。糸満市摩文仁の洞窟に司令部を移し、持久戦を繰り広げた。しかし、その作戦は住民を戦場に巻き込み、多くの命が失われる悲劇となった。負の遺産であるこの司令部壕跡は、沖縄戦を知る上で最も重要な戦跡として保存、公開を求める気運が高まっている。

第 32 軍司令部壕入リ口（那覇市首里）
Entrance to the 32nd Army Headquarters bunker
(Shuri, Naha City)

(4) Ruins of the 32nd Army Headquarters bunker

The bunker for the 32nd Army Headquarters was built in a rush underneath Shuri Castle in December 1944, four months before the landing of American troops. The total length of the bunker was about one kilometer, and it was dug about 30 meters beneath Shuri Castle in a north-south traverse. The main reasons for choosing this location for the headquarters were that it had hard strata of Ryukyu limestone that could withstand the one-ton bombs and artillery fire of the U.S. forces, and that it was located on high ground with a good view of the surrounding battlefield. There are five entrances, three of which are located on the north side, the main entrance. There is an entrance on the northern slope just a few dozen meters from the *Shurei-mon*, but it is currently buried and cannot be entered. The bunker is said to have housed more than 7,000 generals, with a general staff room, an operations room, and many other rooms, giving it the appearance of a large underground hotel. American forces surrounded Shuri in mid-May, despite heavy attacks by the 32nd Army. On May 22, Lieutenant General Ushijima Mitsuru, the commander of the 32nd Army, withdrew to the south, moved his headquarters to a cave in Mabuni, Itoman City, and fought an endurance battle. However, the operation turned out to be a tragedy, involving the local residents in the battlefield and resulting in the loss of many lives. There is a growing momentum to preserve and open the site of the command bunker, which is a negative legacy, as the most important battle site for understanding the Battle of Okinawa.

(5) 旧海軍司令部壕（きゅうかいぐんしれいぶごう）

　当時の小禄海軍飛行場を守るため、1944年（昭和19年）に日本海軍設営隊によって構築された司令部壕で、当時は450mあったといわれている。カマボコ型に掘り抜いた横穴をコンクリートと坑木で固め、米軍の艦砲射撃に耐え、持久戦を続けるための地下陣地で、約4,000人の兵が収容されていた。戦後はしばらく放置されていたが、数回にわたる遺骨収集の後、1970年（昭和45年）、司令官室を中心に約300mが整備されて現在、公開されている。

　1945年6月13日夜半、海軍司令部壕の司令官・大田實中将ら幹部6名が壕内で拳銃自殺を遂げ、日本海軍は組織的戦闘を終えた。1945年1月に赴任した大田司令官は、当時の島田叡沖縄県知事から戦争で苦しむ県民の実情を詳しく聞いていた。自身も県内各地を視察して実態をよく知っていた。

そうしたことから、大田司令官が自決する前に海軍次官に宛てた電文では、沖縄戦の悲惨さと沖縄県民の献身的な協力について記し、「後世特別の配慮を」と訴えた。一方、陸軍の牛島満司令官は「最後まで敢戦するように」と部下に命令し、6月23日に本島南部で自決した。その命令のため、組織的戦闘が終わった後も多くの住民らが犠牲となった。日本の中で唯一、住民を巻き込んだ地上戦となった沖縄戦における両司令官の最後の行動は実に対照的である。

旧海軍司令部壕跡（豊見城市豊見城）
Ruins of the former Naval Headquarters bunker
(Tomigusuku, Tomigusuku City)

(5) Former naval command bunker

This command bunker was built in 1944 by the Japanese Navy's construction team to protect the Oroku Naval Air Station, and is said to have been 450 meters long at the time. It was an underground position where about 4,000 soldiers were housed in a horizontal hole dug out in the shape of a semi-cylinder and hardened with concrete and pit wood in order to withstand the U.S. artillery fire and continue the endurance battle. It was abandoned for a while after the war, but after collecting the remains several times, an area of about 300 meters of the bunker, mainly the commander's office, was reconstructed in 1970, and is now open to the public.

In the middle of the night of June 13, 1945, the commander of the bunker, Lieutenant General Ota Minoru and six other senior officers committed suicide by shooting themselves in the bunker, ending organized combat for the Japanese Navy. Commander Ota, who was assigned to the post in January 1945, had heard in detail from then Okinawa Governor Shimada Akira about the realities of the people of the prefecture suffering from the war. He himself had visited various parts of the prefecture and was well aware of the actual situation. For this reason, Commander Ota sent a telegram to the Vice Minister of the Navy before he committed suicide, in which he described the tragedy of the Battle of Okinawa and the devoted cooperation of the Okinawans, and appealed for "special consideration for the future". On the other hand, Army Commander Ushijima Mitsuru ordered his men to "fight bravely until the end" in the southern part of the main island, and committed suicide in the command bunker on June 23. Because of this order, many residents were killed even after the organized fighting was over. The final actions of the two commanders in the Battle of Okinawa, the only ground battle in Japan that involved the local population, are a stark contrast.

(6) 地上戦（ちじょうせん）

　沖縄戦は 1945 年 3 月 26 日の慶良間諸島への米軍上陸から始まり、主要な戦闘は沖縄本島で行われた。第 32 軍の任務は南西諸島を日本の一部として守ることではなく、沖縄を「捨て石」にした消耗戦を展開して米軍を沖縄に釘付けし、国体護持や本土上陸を遅らせる時間稼ぎの作戦であった。米軍は、4 月 1 日に本島中部西海岸から日本軍の抵抗をほとんど受けることなく無血上陸し、本島を南北に二分する作戦に出た。本島分断に成功した米軍は、主力を司令部壕がある首里方面へ向けて進軍した。日本軍は、首里陣地本部を死守しようと反撃。首里北方の浦添村前田や宜野湾村嘉数高地を中心に、日米両軍による一進一退の激しい攻防は 40 日間も展開された。この戦いで日本軍は主戦力の 80％を失い、5 月下旬、首里を放棄して本島南部の摩文仁へ撤退した。その決定によって軍人と住民が混在することになり、更に悲劇を拡大させた。各部隊を南部に再配置したため、各地で日本軍による住民

の壕追い出しや食料強奪などが相次いだ。日本軍は撤退したものの組織的抵抗はほとんどなくなり、6 月 23 日未明、牛島満・総司令官と長勇・参謀長は摩文仁丘中腹の司令部壕内で自決した。牛島司令官は部下に対して「最後まで敢戦するように」と命令したのでその後も戦闘は続いた。日本政府は 8 月 14 日にポツダム宣言を受諾し、東京湾のミズーリ号上で公式に降伏調印したが、沖縄だけがその後も戦闘状態が続いたのである。沖縄戦の降伏調印式は 1945 年 9 月 7 日、旧越来村森根（現・嘉手納飛行場内）で行われた。戦前の沖縄県の人口は約 49 万人で、戦没者が約 12 万人。県民の約 25％が亡くなった。

ハクソー・リッジ(1945 年 5 月 4 日、浦添市前田高地)(沖縄県公文書館所蔵)
Hacksaw Ridge(May 4,1945,Maeda Highlands, Urasoe City)

(6) The ground battle

The Battle of Okinawa began with the landing of U.S. troops on the Kerama Islands on March 26, 1945, and the main fighting took place on the main island of Okinawa. The mission of the 32nd Army was not to defend the Southwestern Islands as part of Japan, but to wage a war of attrition, using Okinawa as an "abandoned stone," to keep the U.S. forces glued to Okinawa and buy time to protect the national identity and delay the mainland landings. On April 1, the U.S. forces made a bloodless landing from the west coast of the central part of the main island with little resistance from the Japanese forces, and launched an operation to divide the main island into north and south. Having succeeded in dividing the main island, the U.S. forces marched their main force toward Shuri, where the Japanese command bunker was located. The Japanese forces launched a counterattack to defend their underground headquarters in Shuri. The fierce, back-and-forth battle between the Japanese and U.S. forces unfolded for 40 days, centering on Maeda in Urasoe Village and Kakazu Highlands in Ginowan Village, north of Shuri. In this battle, the Japanese lost 80% of their main forces, and in late May, they abandoned Shuri and withdrew to Mabuni in the southern part of the main island. But this decision led to a mixture of soldiers and residents, which further escalating the tragedy. As troops were redeployed to the south, there were a series of incidents in which Japanese solders drove residents out of their shelters and robbed them of food. Although the Japanese forces withdrew, organized resistance was almost non-existent, and in the early hours of June 23, General Ushijima Mitsuru and Chief of Staff Cho Isamu committed suicide in their command bunker on the hillside of Mabuni Hill. Commandant Ushijima ordered his men to "fight bravely until the end," and so the battle continued. The Japanese government accepted the Potsdam Declaration on August 14 and officially signed the surrender on the USS Missouri in Tokyo Bay, but Okinawa was the only island that continued to be fought. The signing ceremony for the surrender of the Battle of Okinawa was held on September 7, 1945 at Morine (now located in Kadena Airfield) in the former village of Goeku. The pre-war population of Okinawa Prefecture was about 490,000, and the number of war dead was about 120,000. About 25% of the prefecture's population died.

(7) 鉄の暴風（てつのぼうふう）

第二次世界大戦末期の沖縄戦は米軍によって「アイスバーグ作戦」（氷山作戦）と命名され、悲惨な地上戦は約 3 ヶ月に及び、民間人も含めた日米約 20 万人（日本人 188,000、米軍人 12,500）の尊い命が失われた。米軍の激しい空襲や艦砲射撃を受け、無差別に多量の砲弾が撃ち込まれる様は暴風にたとえられた。「鉄の暴風」という言葉は、1950 年に沖縄タイムス社（新聞社）が刊行した同名の書

籍タイトルにちなんでいる。これまでの沖縄戦記は日本軍兵士たちの戦記だけであったが、『鉄の暴風』は住民の動きに重点をおいて沖縄戦全体の様相を記録したもので、沖縄の人による最初の戦争記録である。『鉄の暴風』の原稿は全て英訳され、GHQ（連合国軍最高司令部）の検閲を受けた。従って当時は、「日本は残虐、アメリカは救世主」としか書くことが許されなかった。

バクナー中将の慰霊碑（米軍総司令官が戦死した場所）
（糸満市真栄里）
Where the Commander-in-Chief of the U.S. Army Simon Bolivar
Buckner,Jr was killed in action(Maezato, Itoman City)

(7) *Tetsu-no-bouhuu* (Iron Storm)

The Battle of Okinawa at the end of World War II was named "Operation Iceberg" by the U.S. military and the tragic ground war lasted about three months, during which approximately 200,000 Japanese and Americans, including civilians (188,000 Japanese and 12,500 U.S. military personnel), lost their precious lives. It was subjected to fierce air raids and artillery fire by the U.S. military, and the indiscriminate firing of large numbers of shells was likened to a storm. The term *Tetsu-no-bouhuu* (Iron Storm) is derived from the title of a book of the same title published by the Okinawa Times (a newspaper company) in 1950. While previous accounts of the Battle of Okinawa were limited to the war stories of the Japanese soldiers, but the *Tetsu-no-bouhuu* is the first war record written by Okinawans and records the entire battle of Okinawa with emphasis on the movements of the residents. All the manuscripts of the *Tetsu-no-bouhuu* were translated into English and censored by the GHQ (Supreme Headquarters of the Allied Powers). Therefore, at the time, people were only allowed to write "Japan is cruel, America is the savior".

(8) 集団自決（しゅうだんじけつ）

　沖縄戦において発生した集団自決は、主に慶良間諸島、伊江島、沖縄本島の中南部など、殆どの激戦地域で多発した。自決者の実数は調査が困難のため不明のままであるが、米軍が最初に上陸した慶良間諸島の場合、座間味村で 358 人、渡嘉敷村で 329 人と報告されている。自決未遂で米軍に保護された事例も多く、敵前で逃げ場を失った避難民のあいだで集団自決を決行するのが一般的だった。自決の手段は、防衛隊や義勇隊らが持ち込んだ手榴弾や爆雷などで一瞬のうちに爆死するのが普通であったが、それらが入手できない場合は剃刀（カミソリ）・鎌（かま）・鍬（くわ）・棍棒（こんぼう）・毒薬・縄などが用いられた。自決は多くの場合、家族単位または壕単位で同時一斉に行われた。

　日本軍が、避難場所や食料を奪って住民を危険地帯へ追い出したり、軍の意向に従わない住民を「スパイ」の嫌疑で拷問・虐殺したり、「集団自決」を強制・誘導したり、ガマの中で泣き叫ぶ赤ん坊を口封じのために殺害した事例も多く報告されている。住民たちは、米軍の無差別攻撃（鉄の暴風）を避けなければならない一方で、「友軍」と信じていた日本軍の暴力行為からも身を守らなければならなかった。

　当時の国際法では、捕虜になるのは軍人だけで民間人は保護されることになっていたが、「生きて虜囚の辱めを受けず」という軍陣訓などが民間人の集団心理にも大きな影響を与え、集団自決へつながったと指摘する研究者も多い。日本軍は沖縄戦を、「国体護持や本土防衛のための捨て石であり、消耗戦」と位置づけ、作戦遂行にあたって非戦闘員を安全地帯に避難させる処置が不徹底であった。

集団自決は、日本軍の強制や命令があったかどうかについては未だに論争があるが、数十万の一般住民が前線に放置されたことによって発生した惨劇であることに疑う余地はない。

(8) Mass suicide

The mass suicides that occurred in the Battle of Okinawa were mainly in the Kerama Islands, Ie Island, the south-central part of Okinawa Island, and most other heavily fought areas. The actual number of people who committed suicide remains unknown due to the difficulty of conducting surveys, in the case of the Kerama Islands, where the U.S. forces first landed, 358 people were reported to have committed suicide in Zamami village and 329 in Tokashiki village. There were many cases of people who attempted to commit suicide and were protected by the U.S. military, and it was common for displaced people

米軍が撮影した、集団自決と思われる写真 (慶良間諸島)
Photo taken by the U.S. military of what appears to be a mass suicide (Tokashiki Island).

who had nowhere to run in front of the enemy to commit mass suicide. The usual means of committing suicide was to die in an instant by bombing with grenades and explosive mines brought in by the garrison or volunteer soldiers, but if these were not available, razors, sickles, hoes, sticks, poison, and ropes were used. Mass suicides were often carried out simultaneously in family units or air-raid shelters.

Moving residents to dangerous places by depriving them of air-raid shelters and food, torturing and massacring residents suspected of being "spies" who did not comply with the military's wishes, forcing and inducing "mass suicides," and killing crying babies in air-raid shelters to keep them from talking. While avoiding the indiscriminate attacks of the U.S. military (Iron Storm), the residents also had to protect themselves from the violent acts of the Japanese military, which they believed to be "the army that protects them". According to international law at the time, only military personnel were supposed to be taken prisoner, while civilians were protected. However, many researchers have pointed out that the education on military precepts such as "Do not be humiliated as a prisoner of war alive" had a great impact on the collective psychology of civilians, leading to mass suicide. The Japanese military positioned the Battle of Okinawa as a "war of attrition," "an abandoned stone" for the protection of the national identity and the defense of the mainland, and took inadequate measures to evacuate non-combatants to safe zones during operations. There is still controversy over whether mass suicide was forced or ordered by the Japanese military, however, there is no doubt that mass suicide was a tragedy caused by the hundreds of thousands of civilians left on the front lines.

(9) ひめゆりの塔 (ひめゆりのとう)

　米軍の沖縄上陸が確実になったため、第32軍司令部は県下の女子学徒を軍看護要員として動員を要請した。沖縄師範学校女子部と沖縄県立第一高等学校の女生徒たちによって構成された看護隊は通称「ひめゆり学徒隊」と呼ばれた。「ひめゆり」の名称は、両校の校歌や校友会雑誌の「白百合」と「乙姫」からとられた。ひめゆりの塔は、沖縄戦で犠牲となったひめゆり学徒隊と職員の計 210 名を合祀する慰霊塔である。学徒隊は軍とともに沖縄本島南部に追いつめられ、「ガマ」と呼ばれる天然の洞窟を利用した第 1・第 2・第 3 外科壕などで必死の看護活動にあたった。6 月 18 日の学徒隊の解散後、

第1・第2外科壕にいた学徒隊たちは脱出を
はかって壕を出るが、途中で砲弾に倒れたり、
捕虜になることを恐れて自決した。第3外科
壕では脱出できず、ガス弾を投下され一挙に
40人が最期を遂げた。沖縄戦の実相を示すひ
めゆり学徒隊の悲劇は幾度も映画化され、世
論を喚起した。

ひめゆりの塔（糸満市伊原）
Himeyuri-no-tou(Ihara, Itoman City)

(9) *Himeyuri-no-tou* (*Himeyuri* Monument)

As the U.S. military was certain to land in Okinawa, the 32nd Military Command (Okinawa Defense Force) requested that female students in the prefecture be mobilized as military nursing factors. The nursing corps, consisting of female students from the Women's Division of *Okinawa-shihan-gakkou* (teacher's training school) and "Okinawa Prefectural Daiichi High School," was commonly known as the *Himeyuri-gakutotai*. The name *Himeyuri* was taken from the school songs of the two schools and the words *Shirayuri* and *Otohime* in the alumni magazine. *Himeyuri-no-tou* (*Himeyuri* Monument) is a cenotaph enshrining a total of 210 *Himeyuri* students and staff who lost their lives in the Battle of Okinawa. The students, along with the Japanese military, were driven to the southern part of the main island of Okinawa by the U.S. military, and carried out nursing activities desperately in the first, second, and third surgical bunkers, which were made of natural caves called *gama*. After the disbanding of the *Himeyuri-gakutotai* on June 18, the students in the 1st and 2nd surgical bunkers left the bunkers to escape, but they were hit by shells on the way or committed suicide for fear of being taken prisoner. In the third surgical bunker, where they could not escape, 40 people died at once due to gas bombs dropped on them. The tragedy of the *Himeyuri-gakutotai,* which shows the reality of the Battle of Okinawa, has been made into movies many times and has aroused public opinion.

(10) 健児之塔（けんじのとう）

健児之塔（糸満市摩文仁）
Kenji-no-tou(Mabuni, Itoman City)

米軍が上陸する直前の沖縄には師範学
校1校、実業学校を含め県・私立の中学校
が11校あった。時局の戦時体制への移行
に伴い、男子生徒たちは軍に動員され、学
業を捨てて飛行場建設や地下陣地構築など
に従事させられた。米軍の沖縄上陸が必至
となった1945年3月になると、第32軍
（沖縄守備隊）司令部は、男子生徒たちを
戦時要員として徴用した。人数等は各学校
によってそれぞれ異なったが、沖縄師範学
校のように全男子生徒が動員された学校も
あった。4月1日、米軍が上陸すると同時
に戦列に加わり、戦場におけるあらゆる戦
闘任務を兵隊同様に果たした。従軍した男子生徒1,780人中、半数の890人が戦死した。戦後は各学
校の同窓会が中心となって、それぞれゆかりの地に「健児之塔」が建立された。

(10) *Kenji-no-tou* (*Kenji* Monument)

　Just before the U.S. forces landed in Okinawa, there was one teacher's training school and 11 prefectural and private junior high schools, including a business school. With the transition to a wartime regime, male students were mobilized by the military and forced to abandon their studies to work on the construction of airfields and underground camps. In March 1945, when it became inevitable that the U.S. military would land on Okinawa, the 32nd Army headquarters commandeered the boys as a wartime factor. The number of students differed from school to school, but there were some schools, such as *Okinawa-shihan-gakkou* (teacher's training school), where all male students were mobilized. As soon as the U.S. troops landed on April 1, they joined the battle line and performed every combat duty on the battlefield as well as the soldiers. Of the 1,780 boys who served, 890, or half of them, were killed in the war. After the war, the alumni associations of each school took the lead in erecting *Kenji-no-tou* at the sites associated with their respective schools.

(11) 魂魄の塔（こんぱくのとう）

　糸満市米須にある慰霊塔で、1946 年 2 月、島尻郡真和志村（現在の那覇市の一部）の住民によって建立された。周辺に散乱していた遺骨 35,000 余柱の遺骨を納めたとされ、終戦後、最も早い時期に建てられた慰霊碑でもある。真和志村の住民は米軍の都合によって帰村が認められず、米須でのテント仮住まいを余儀なくされた。金城和信（きんじょう・わしん）村長を中心に、散乱している遺骨の収集を米軍に申し入れたが「敵である日本兵を祀り称える」動きにならないかと難色を示した。折衝を重ねて許可を貰い、収骨隊を組織

魂魄の塔（糸満市米須）
Kompaku-no-tou(komesu, Itoman City)

して野ざらしになっていた遺骨の収集を始めた。納骨場所は当初、海岸近くの自然洞窟を利用していたが、予想以上に遺骨が集まったため、現在のような饅頭形のような納骨所になった。1957 年、琉球政府は那覇市識名に「戦没者中央納骨堂」を建設し、各地の納骨所にある遺骨の集約を開始した。魂魄の塔でも 1975 年 1 月に遺骨を戦没者中央納骨堂へ移した。現在でも毎年、慰霊の日には県内外から多くの参拝者が魂魄の塔を訪れる。

(11) *Kompaku-no-tou* (*Kompaku* Monument)

　This is a memorial tower located in Komesu, Itoman City, and was built in February 1946 by the residents of Mawashi Village, Shimajiri County (now part of Naha City). It is said that the remains of more than 35,000 scattered around the area were placed here, and it is also the earliest cenotaph built after the end of the war. The residents of Mawashi Village were not allowed to return to their village due to the U.S. military, and were forced to live temporarily in tents in Komesu. The mayor of the village, Kinjou Washin, and others asked the U.S. military for permission to collect the scattered remains, but the U.S. military balked at the idea, saying it would be a move to "enshrine and honor Japanese soldiers who were our enemies". After repeated negotiations, he received permission and organized an ossuary team to begin collecting the remains that had been left out in the open. Initially, a natural cave near the beach was used for the ossuary, but the number of remains gathered exceeded expectations, so the current ossuary, shaped like a bun, was built. In 1957, the Ryukyu government built the "Central Ossuary for the War Dead" in Shikina, Naha City, and began to collect the remains from various ossuaries. In January 1975, the *Kompaku-no-tou* also moved the remains to the "Central Ossuary for the War Dead". Even today, many people from inside and outside of the prefecture visit *Kompaku-no-tou* every year on Memorial Day.

(12) 南北の塔 （なんぼくのとう）

南北の塔 （糸満市真栄平）
Namboku-no-tou(Maehira, Itoman City)

　糸満市真栄平地区は、沖縄戦の激戦地で住民の約3分の2が戦死し、終戦当時は集落内に遺骨が散らばっていた。地域住民は遺骨を収集してガマ（自然洞窟）に安置し、そこを納骨堂とした。その後も遺骨が発見され、納骨堂は改修・整備された。1957年、那覇市内に中央納骨堂が造られ、そこに各地の遺骨を納めるように呼びかけられたが、真栄平住民はそれに反対し、恒久的な慰霊塔を建立することを決議。その後、集落内外からの寄付545ドル60セントが集まり、1966年に慰霊塔が設置された。慰霊碑の名称の由来は、南の沖縄から北の北海道まで、ここで眠っている戦争で命を落とした人たちを弔いたいということに由来する。沖縄戦では北海道出身の兵士が多数戦死しており、その中にアイヌ民族も含まれていることから、北海道アイヌ協会が南北の塔でほぼ5年おきにイチャルパ（供養祭）を実施している。

(12) *Namboku-no-tou* (*Namboku* Monument)

　The Maehira district of Itoman City was a fierce battleground in the Battle of Okinawa, where about two-thirds of the residents were killed in the war, and their remains were scattered throughout the village when the war ended. The local residents collected the remains and placed them in *gama* (natural cave), which was used as an ossuary. Since then, more remains have been found, and the ossuary has been renovated and maintained. In 1957, a central ossuary was built in Naha City, and it was called for to store the remains from all over the country there, but Maehira residents opposed it and resolved to build a permanent memorial tower. Later, donations of $545.60 were collected from inside and outside the village, and a memorial tower was established in 1966. The origin of the name of the cenotaph comes from the desire to mourn those who lost their lives in the war, who lie here from Okinawa in the south to Hokkaido in the north. Since many soldiers from Hokkaido were killed in the Battle of Okinawa, including the *Ainu* people, the Hokkaido *Ainu* Association holds an *Icharupa* (memorial service) almost every five years at *Namboku-no-tou*.

(13) カンカラサンシン

　戦争ですべてを失った沖縄の人々は終戦直後、捕虜収容所での生活を強いられた。そんな中でもウチナーンチュは唄と三線を忘れなかった。収容所では物資不足の中で、胴として米軍支給の粉ミルクや食料の空き缶（カンカラ）を、棹は米軍が使ったベッドの木部を銃剣で削って利用、不要になったパラシュートの紐を弦に使った三線は「カンカラサンシン」と呼ばれた。米軍の統治下での物資不足や精神的にも不安な時に、県民の心の支えとなったのが唄とサンシンの音色だった。世界の民族楽器は、子供の頃から自分の手で作り壊れると修理して演奏された。音楽は特別なものではなく日常生

活の一部で、カンカラサンシンもそのような楽器かも知れない。日本にはそのような楽器が少ないため、音楽を特別なものと捉える人が多いといわれる。1945 年、金武村屋嘉の捕虜収容所で生まれた「屋嘉節」は、捕虜たちの屈辱とやるせなさをカンカラサンシンで歌った反戦哀歌。カンカラサンシンは戦後復興のシンボルであり、悲惨な戦争から生まれた平和の象徴でもある。

屋嘉の捕虜収容所（沖縄県公文書館所蔵）
POW camp at Yaka(Yaka, Kin Village)

(13) *Kankara-sanshin*

The people of Okinawa who lost everything in the war were forced to live in POW (prisoner of war) camps immediately after the war. Even under such circumstances, *uchinanchu* never forgot their songs and *sanshin*. *Sanshin* made in the midst of a shortage of supplies were called *kankara-sanshin*, in the POW camp, the body of the instrument was made from empty cans(*kankara*) of powdered milk and food provided by the U.S. military, the neck was made from the wood of a bed used by the U.S. military and shaved with a bayonet, and unneeded parachute strings were used for the strings. During the time of material shortages and mental unrest under the U.S. military rule, the people of the prefecture found emotional support in the songs and the sounds of *kankara-sansin*. Folk instruments from all over the world were made and played with their own hands from childhood and repaired when they were broken. Music is not something special, but a part of daily life, and the *kankara-sanshin* may be one of such instruments. Since there are few such instruments in Japan, it is said that many people consider music as something special. The Okinawan folk song *Yaka-bushi,* born in 1945 at the POW camp in Yaka, Kin Village, is an anti-war lament sung with *kankara-sanshin* about the humiliation and frustration of the POWs. The *kankara-sanshin* is a symbol of post-war reconstruction and also a symbol of peace born out of the tragic war.

(14) 艦砲ぬ喰ぇー残さー（かんぽうぬくぇーぬくさー）

　悲惨な地上戦が繰り広げられた沖縄では、県民の約 25％が犠牲になった。艦砲射撃などから運良く生き残った人たちは沖縄の方言で「艦砲ぬ喰ぇー残さー」と表現された。戦中・戦後の体験を歌った同名の沖縄民謡がある。読谷村楚辺出身の比嘉恒敏氏（ひがこうびん）が 1971 年に自らの体験をもとに作ったもので、戦争で家族を失った憎しみや平和を願う庶民の気持ちを素直に表現している。自身の 4 人娘「でいご娘」が歌い、多くの人々の共感を呼んだ。曲の完成から数年後の 1973 年、作者の比嘉さんは酔っぱらった米兵の運転する車に衝突され 56 歳で亡くなった。2013 年、比嘉さんの故郷である読谷村楚辺の「ユーバンタ浜」に歌碑が建立された。

「艦砲ぬ喰ぇー残さー」歌碑（読谷村楚辺）
Song monument of "*Kampou-nu-kwee-nukusaa*" (Sobe, Yomitan Village)

(14) *Kampou-nu-kwee-nukusaa*

In Okinawa, where the tragic ground war unfolded, about 25% of the prefecture's population was killed. Those who were fortunate enough to survive the bombardment were described in Okinawan dialect as *Kampou-nu-kwee-nukusaa*. There is an Okinawan folk song of the same title that sings about the experiences during and after the war. This folk song was written in 1971 by Mr. Higa Koubin, a native of Sobe, Yomitan Village, based on his own experiences, and it honestly expresses the hatred of ordinary people who lost their families in the war and their desire for peace. The song was sung by his own four daughters, the *Deigo-Musume*, and drew the sympathy of many people. In 1973, a few years after the song was completed, Mr. Higa, who wrote the song, was struck by a car driven by a drunken American soldier and died at the age of 56. In 2013, a monument to the song was erected at Yuubanta Beach in Sobe, Yomitan Village, Higa's hometown.

(15) 慰霊の日（いれいのひ）

6月23日の「慰霊の日」は沖縄県が独自に制定している記念日で、沖縄全域では正午に1分間の黙祷を行う。沖縄県および県内市町村の公的機関は休日となり、沖縄戦などの戦没者を追悼する日と定められている。第32軍司令官（牛島満中将）と参謀長（長勇）が自決した1945年6月23日は、日本軍による組織的な戦闘が終結した日とされる。慰霊の日は、アメリカ統治下の1961年に設定された。当初、6月22日と定められていたが、自決した日の再調査が行われ、4年後に6月23日に変更された。慰霊の日には県内各地でさまざまな行事が行われるが、沖縄戦の激戦地となった糸満市摩文仁にある「平和祈念公園」で毎年行われる沖縄県主催の「沖縄全戦没者追悼式」はその代表。総理大臣らも参加し、沖縄戦の犠牲者を偲び、世界平和への祈りを捧げる式典である。

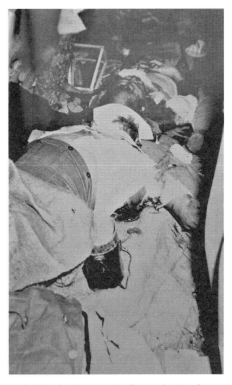

牛島満司令官、長勇参謀長の自決写真
（糸満市摩文仁）、（沖縄県公文書館所蔵）
Photo of Commander Ushijima Mitsuru and Chief of Staff Cho Isamu committing suicide(Mabuni, Itoman City)

(15) Memorial Day of the Victims of the Battle of Okinawa (*Irei-no-hi*)

The "Memorial Day" on June 23 is a commemorative day established independently by Okinawa Prefecture, and all of Okinawa observes a minute of silence at noon. This day is designated as a day of mourning for all war dead of the Battle of Okinawa and other battles, and is a holiday for public organizations in Okinawa Prefecture and municipalities. June 23, 1945, when the commander of the 32nd Army (Lieutenant General Ushijima Mitsuru) and the Chief of Staff (Cho Isamu) committed suicide, is considered to be the day when the systematic fighting by the Japanese forces came to an end. The Memorial Day was established in 1961 during the American occupation. Initially, the date was set for June 22, but later the suicide date was reviewed and four years later it was changed to June 23. On Memorial Day, various events are held in various parts of the prefecture, including the Okinawa Prefectural Government's annual "Okinawa All War Dead Memorial Ceremony" held at the Peace Memorial Park in Mabuni, Itoman City, where was the site of the fierce battle of Okinawa. The Prime Minister and others participate in this ceremony to remember the victims of the Battle of Okinawa and offer prayers for world peace.

(16) 平和の礎（へいわのいしじ）

　「礎」（いしじ）とは、建物などの基礎「いしずえ」を沖縄方言で「いしじ」と発することに由来する。「平和の礎」は、沖縄戦終結 50 周年記念事業の一環として、国籍を問わず、また、軍人、民間人の別なく全ての戦没者の氏名を刻んで、永久に残すために 1995 年 6 月 23 日に建設した（刻銘者数は約 23 万人で、刻銘は毎年、慰霊の日に合わせて追加・修正される）。その趣旨は、沖縄戦などで亡くなられた全ての戦没者を追悼し、恒久平和の希求と悲惨な戦争の教訓を正しく継承するとともに、平和学習の拠点とするためである。「平和の礎」のデザインコンセプトは、「平和の波永遠なれ」(Everlasting waves of peace）で、屏風状に並んだ刻銘碑は世界に向けて平和の波が広がるようにという願いをデザインしている。平和祈念公園から「平和の広場」に通ずるメイン通路は、その中心線が 6 月 23 日の日の出の方位に合わせて設定されている。平和の広場の中央には「平和の火」が灯されている。この火は、沖縄戦最初の米軍上陸地である座間味村阿嘉島で採取した火と、広島市の「平和の灯」、長崎市の「誓いの火」からいただいた火を合わせたもの。1991 年から灯し続けた火を、1995 年 6 月 23 日の「平和の礎」除幕式典においてここに移した。

(16) *Heiwa-no-ishiji* (the peace monument)

　The word *ishiji* is derived from the Okinawan dialect word for the foundation of a building, *ishizue*. The peace monument called *Heiwa-no-ishiji* was built on June 23, 1995 as part of the commemoration of the 50th anniversary of the end of the Battle of Okinawa, to eternally preserve the names of all the war dead, regardless of nationality, military or civilian by inscribing them (the number of inscriptions is about 230,000, and inscriptions are added and revised every year on Memorial Day). The purpose is to memorialize all the war dead who died in the Battle of Okinawa and other battles, to pass on the desire for lasting peace and the lessons of the tragic war, and to serve as a base for peace education. The design concept of the Cornerstone of Peace is "Everlasting waves of peace," and the monuments lined up in the shape of folding screens are designed to express the wish that the waves of peace will spread to the world. The main walkway leading from the Peace Memorial Park to the "Peace Plaza" has its centerline aligned with the direction of the sunrise on June 23. In the center of the Peace Plaza, the "Fire of Peace" is lit. This fire is a combination of fire collected from Aka Island in Zamami Village, the first U.S. landing site during the Battle of Okinawa, and fire from the Hiroshima City "Peace Light" and Nagasaki City "Fire of Oath". The fire, which had been lit since 1991, was moved here at the unveiling ceremony of the *Heiwa-no-ishiji* on June 23, 1995.

平和の礎（1995 年、糸満市摩文仁）
Heiwa-no-Ishiji (in1995,Mabuni, Itoman City)

第 7 章　米軍統治時代

（1）アメリカ世（あめりかゆー）

　アメリカ合衆国による沖縄統治は、1945 年の米軍による沖縄占領から 1972 年 5 月 15 日の本土復帰に至るまでの 27 年間に及ぶ。「アメリカ世」とはこの時代をいう。敗戦後に待っていたのは昔のような「平和な島・沖縄」ではなく、米軍による統治という屈辱的な異民族支配だった。本土へ渡るのもパスポートが必要で、通貨は「B 円」と呼ばれた軍票（1945-1958）や US ドル（1958-1972）が使用された。アメリカ合衆国の地域として扱われたこの期間を、沖縄では「アメリカ世」（アメリカユー）とも呼んでいる。

降伏調印式
(1945 年 9 月 7 日、嘉手納飛行場) (沖縄県公文書館所蔵)
Surrender signing ceremony,
(September 7, 1945 at Kadena Air Base)

　米軍支配のもとでは全てが軍事優先で人権は侵害され、住民の生活は常に危険と隣り合わせだった。アメリカ軍人の無謀な行為によって、何の罪もない善良な住民が尊い命を奪われたり傷つけられたりしたが、加害者である米兵に対する処遇にも問題があった。事件・事故を起こした米兵の多くが無罪になり、有罪になっても刑の執行が行われたかどうかは不明であった。被害を受けた沖縄住民の多くが、満足な補償を得ることができず、泣き寝入りさせられたのが実情であった。アメリカ軍人による事件や事故は米軍が占領者として沖縄住民を見下し、住民の生活よりも、すべてに軍事を優先させたことに大きな要因があった。沖縄住民が、平和で豊かな沖縄を築くために、基地の撤去と平和憲法を持った日本への復帰を願うようになったのは当然の成り行きであった。

　アメリカは 1945 年 9 月、民主主義の基礎として市町村長・市町村議会の選挙を捕虜収容所内でも実施した。1947 年には幾つかの政党が結成されたが、米軍政府は「政党の行動制限」を設け、軍政府の政策に批判的な政党には厳しい罰則が加えられた。1949 年には、東西冷戦の激化や朝鮮半島の軍事的緊張が高まってきた。アメリカによる極東地域戦略のため、沖縄には大規模な軍事基地や施設が建設された。その結果、沖縄本島は極東最大の米軍基地へと変わり、米軍からは「太平洋の要石（Keystone of the Pacific）」とも称された。

Chapter 7 The Era of U.S. Military Rule

（1）America-*yuu*（Governed by the U.S. military）

　The United States occupation of Okinawa spanned 27 years from the 1945 U.S. military occupation of Okinawa to the reversion of Okinawa to mainland Japan on May 15, 1972. The term America-*yuu* refers to this era. What awaited Okinawa after World War II was not the "peaceful island" of the past, but the humiliating domination by the U.S. military. A passport was also required to cross over to the mainland, and the currency used was the military voucher called "B-*yen*" (1945-1958) and the U.S. dollar (1958-1972). During this period, when Okinawa was treated as a U.S. territory, is also referred to as the America-*yuu* in Okinawa.

　Under the U.S. military rule, everything took priority over the military, human rights were violated, and the lives of the residents were always in danger. Due to the reckless actions of American soldiers, innocent and good residents lost their precious lives or were injured, but there were also problems with the treatment of the perpetrators, the American soldiers. Many U.S. soldiers who had made the incidents or accidents were found not guilty, and even if convicted, it was unclear whether their sentences had been carried out. Many of the affected Okinawans were unable to obtain satisfactory guarantees and were forced to cry themselves to sleep. Incidents and accidents caused by U.S. military personnel were largely due to the fact that the U.S. military looked down on the residents of Okinawa as occupiers and prioritized the military in everything over the lives of the residents. It was only natural that Okinawans began to wish for the removal of the bases and the return to Japan with a peaceful constitution, in order to build a peaceful and prosperous Okinawa.

In September 1945, the U.S. held elections for municipal mayors and municipal councils as a basis for democracy, even in POW camps. In 1947, several political parties were formed, but the U.S. military government imposed "restrictions on the conduct of political parties," and severe penalties were imposed on parties that were critical of the military government's policies. In 1949, the Cold War between East and West intensified and military tensions on the Korean Peninsula increased. The Far East regional strategy by the U.S. led to the construction of large-scale military bases and facilities in Okinawa. As a result, the main island of Okinawa was transformed into the largest U.S. military base in the Far East, and was called the "Keystone of the Pacific" by the U.S. military.

（2）サンフランシスコ講和条約（さんふらんしすここうわじょうやく）

　第二次世界大戦で戦争関係にあった連合国 49 カ国と日本との間で締結された講和条約。1951 年 9 月 8 日にサンフランシスコで調印され、翌年 4 月 28 日に発効した。前文と 7 章 27 条で構成され、対日講和条約とも呼ばれる。この条約の締結によって戦争状態は終了し、終戦後に連合国軍に占領されていた日本は独立国として国際社会に復帰したが、北緯 29 度以南の奄美群島や小笠原諸島、沖縄県などは事実上、アメリカの軍事植民地下に置かれることになった。これらが返還されたのは、奄美群島が 1953 年 12 月、小笠原諸島が 1968 年 6 月、沖縄県は 1972 年 5 月である。

　ただ、この条約は日本とすべての連合国（55 カ国）との合意の上に締結された全面講和ではなく、ソ連やポーランドなどは講和会議には参加したが条約には調印しなかった。1950 年には朝鮮戦争が勃発し、その背景にはアメリカとソ連の冷戦があった。中国は、中国共産党政府と台湾の国民党政府のいずれを代表として認めるかをめぐって連合国内で意見が対立し、招請されなかった。当条約は西側諸国という片方の陣営だけとの講和で「片面講和条約」ともいわれ、「講和条約を結ぶなら、西側だけでなく東側諸国とも結ぶべきである」という反対を押し切って、当時の吉田茂首相が日本代表として調印した。ソ連との関係が悪化する中で、アメリカをはじめとする西側諸国は、第二次世界大戦後に東アジアで台頭してきた中国や北朝鮮などの共産主義国家への防波堤としての日本の必要性からこの条約を結んだのである。日本を西側陣営に取り込もうという考えは、主権の回復を悲願とする日本政府にとっても好都合であった。

サンフランシスコ講和条約に調印する吉田茂
（1951 年 9 月 8 日）
Yoshida Shigeru signs the San Francisco Peace Treaty
(September 8, 1951)

戦後の日本の領域を定める条項によって日本は朝鮮の独立を承認し、台湾や千島列島および樺太の一部、日本が統治していた太平洋諸島などの領土を放棄した。この条項の文言を巡って、北方領土問題の他、竹島問題や尖閣諸島問題など、当該国間で今でも解釈が分かれている。

(2) San Francisco Peace Treaty

A peace treaty signed between Japan and the 49 Allied nations that were at war in World War II. The treaty was signed in San Francisco on September 8, 1951, and entered into force on April 28 of the following year. It consists of a preamble and seven chapters and 27 articles, and is also called the Peace Treaty with Japan. With the conclusion of this treaty, the state of war ended, and Japan, which had been occupied by the Allied forces after the end of the war, returned to the international community as an independent country, but the Amami Islands south of 29 degrees north latitude, the Ogasawara Islands, and Okinawa Prefecture were effectively placed under the U.S. military colony. These were returned in December 1953 for the Amami Islands, June 1968 for the Ogasawara Islands, and May 1972 for Okinawa Prefecture.

However, this treaty was not a full-fledged peace agreement between Japan and all 55 Allied nations, and although the Soviet Union and Poland, among others, participated in the peace conference, they did not sign the treaty. In 1950, the Korean War broke out, and the Cold War between the United States and the Soviet Union was behind it. China was not invited because of disagreements within the coalition over whether to recognize the Chinese Communist government or the Nationalist government of Taiwan as its representative. This treaty was also called a "one-sided peace treaty" because it was signed with only one side, the Western countries. Yoshida Shigeru, the Prime Minister of Japan at the time, signed the treaty as the representative of Japan, overcoming the objection that "if a peace treaty was to be concluded, it should be with the East as well as the West". As relations with the Soviet Union worsened, the United States and other Western nations concluded this treaty out of the need for Japan to serve as a bulwark against communist states such as China and North Korea, which had emerged in East Asia after World War II. The idea of bringing Japan into the Western camp was also convenient for the Japanese government, which longed to regain its sovereignty.

In a post-war clause defining Japan's territories, Japan recognized Korea's independence and renounced territories that had been under Japanese control, including Taiwan, parts of the Karahuto Island, Chishima Islands, and the Pacific Islands. The wording of this clause is still being interpreted differently among the countries concerned, not only over the Northern Territories issue, but also over the Takeshima and Senkaku Islands issues.

(3) 高等弁務官（こうとうべんむかん）

1957年6月5日、アメリカのアイゼンハワー大統領は、「琉球列島の管理に関する行政命令」と題する大統領行政命令10713号を発令した。これにより高等弁務官制が導入され、高等弁務官が沖縄における最高責任者となった。高等弁務官はアメリカ合衆国大統領の承認を得て、国防長官が現役アメリカ陸軍将官から任命した。1959年には、沖縄住民の歓心を得るために高等弁務官資金が新設され、水道・道路・港などのインフラ、公民館や学校施設の建設整備に使われた。この資金は米軍の統治に好意的であるかどうかが支給の対象となり、高等弁務官の裁量で決定された。高等弁務官は行政主席や裁判官の任命権、琉球政府全職員の罷免権、立法院が制定する立法の拒否権などの職務権限を持っていた。琉球政府の政策にも介入するなど、その権限は絶対的で「沖縄の帝王」とも称され、それが沖縄住民の反発を買い祖国復帰運動が激化していった。1972年5月15日に施政権が日本に返還されるまでの15年間に、6人の高等弁務官が任命された。初代高等弁務官はジェームズ・ムーア陸軍中将で、最後はジェームズ・ランパート中将が就任した。

(3) High Commissioner

On June 5, 1957, U.S. President Eisenhower issued Presidential Executive Order No. 10713, entitled "Executive Order on the Administration of the Ryukyu Islands". This led to the introduction of the High Commissioner system, and the High Commissioner became the chief executive in Okinawa. The High Commissioner was appointed by the Secretary of Defense, with the approval of the President of the United States, from active duty U.S. Army generals. In 1959, a new High Commissioner's Fund was established to win the hearts and minds of Okinawans and was used to build and maintain infrastructure such as water supply, roads, and ports, as well as community centers and school facilities. The funds were awarded on the basis of favorability to U.S. military rule and were determined at the discretion of the High Commissioner. The High Commissioner had the authority to appoint the administrative head of the Ryukyu government and judges, to dismiss all Ryukyu government officials, and to veto legislation enacted by the Legislative Yuan in Okinawa and other duties. The High Commissioner also intervened in the policies of the Ryukyu government, and his authority was so absolute that he was called the "Emperor of Okinawa," and this led to protests from the Okinawan people, and the movement to return to the motherland intensified. Six High Commissioners were appointed in the 15 years before Okinawa's administration was returned to Japan on May 15, 1972. The first High Commissioner was Lieutenant General James Moore, and the last was Lieutenant General James Lampert.

初代高等弁務官（ジェームズ・ムーア陸軍中将）
First High Commissioner (Lieutenant General James Moore, Army)

（4）米軍関連の主な事件・事故 (べいぐんかんれんのおもなじけん・じこ)

①由美子ちゃん事件（ゆみこちゃんじけん）

　1955 年 9 月 3 日、石川市（現・うるま市）に住む永山由美子ちゃん（6 歳）が米兵に暴行・殺害され、嘉手納海岸に死体で発見された事件である。逮捕発表の翌日の 9 月 10 日には具志川村（現・うるま市）の農家に米兵が押し入って小学 2 年生の少女を拉致・強姦するという事件も発生した。これら連続する事件を受けて沖縄では全沖縄組織「子どもを守る会」が結成され、住民大会を開いて抗議し公正な裁判を求めた。米軍の軍法会議は 1955 年 12 月、由美子ちゃん事件の加害者・空軍軍曹に対して死刑判決を言い渡した。その後、米本国で行われた第 2 審では無期懲役に減刑され、最終的には懲役 45 年が確定した。当時は米軍による軍用地接収をめぐる「島ぐるみ闘争」が高まっており、激しい抗議運動が展開された。由美子ちゃん事件は米軍人・軍属の犯罪が大きく取り上げられ、米軍当局に抗議の矛先が向けられた最初の事件である。

(4) Major incidents and accidents related to the U.S. military

① Yumiko-*chan* incident

On September 3, 1955, Nagayama Yumiko (Yumiko-*chan*, age 6), a resident of Ishikawa City (now Uruma City), was assaulted, killed and dumped by American soldiers and found dead on the beach at Kadena. On September 10, the day after the arrest was announced, U.S. soldiers broke into a farmhouse in Gushikawa Village (now Uruma City) and abducted and raped a second-grade girl. In response to these successive incidents, an all-Okinawa organization, "*Kodomo-*

軍法会議に向かう加害者のアイザック・ハート軍曹（沖縄県公文書館所蔵）
Sergeant Isaac Hart, the assailant, on his way to court-martial

wo-Mamoru-Kai" (Association to Protect Children), was formed in Okinawa, and held a residents' convention to protest, and demand a fair trial. In December 1955, a U.S. military court sentenced the perpetrator of the "Yumiko-*chan* incident," an Air Force sergeant, to death. The sentence was later commuted to life imprisonment in the second trial held in the U.S. home country, and was finally confirmed at 45 years in prison. At the time, the *shimagurumi-tousou* (Island-wide Struggle) over the confiscation of military land by the U.S. military was gaining momentum, and a fierce protest movement developed. The Yumiko-*chan* incident was the first case in which the crimes of U.S. servicemen and servicewomen were widely reported and protests were directed at the U.S. military authorities.

②宮森小学校ジェット機墜落事故（みやもりしょうがっこう　じぇっときついらくじこ）

　1959 年 6 月 30 日、米空軍の F100 ジェット戦闘機が操縦不能に陥り、パイロットは空中で脱出したが、機体は民家 35 棟をなぎ倒し、石川市にある宮森小学校を直撃し炎上した。事故当時、学校には児童・教職員ら約 1,000 人がおり、ミルク給食の時間でほぼ全児童が校舎内にいた。火災は 1 時間後に鎮火したが、死者 17 人（小学生 11 人、一般人 6 人）、重軽傷者 210 人が発生するという大惨事となった（火傷による後遺症で事故の 17 年後に 1 人が 23 歳で亡くなっている）。米軍は事故原因を「エンジン故障による不可抗力の事故」と発表したが、最大の原因は「整備ミス」で、本来なら飛行してはいけなかった。当時としては世界の航空機史上まれな大事故として内外に報道された。事故後 63 年経って、明らかになった当時の米軍の内部文書によると、「石川の悲劇は何も目新しい要素があるわけではない。不慮の事故は有史以来、普通に起きている出来事」と事故を矮小化し、犠牲者を冒瀆した内容であった。事故直後から全沖縄で反米感情が高まり、折しも米軍による土地接収が強行されていた時期と重なって、激しい抗議行動や補償要求が行われた。この事故に対する米軍の補償額は死者が 4,500 ドル、重傷者は障害に応じて 2,300-5,900 ドルが支払われたが、この額は被害者側要求の 10% 程度であった。一方、当時の市長は、賠償交渉を円滑に進め事故の復旧に貢献したとして米軍に感謝状を贈っている。宮森小学校の中庭には、犠牲となった児童らを慰霊する「仲良し地蔵」が設置されており、毎年 6 月 30 日に児童らによる追悼式が行われている。

石川市と学校側が米軍施設内に出向き、補償金の小切手が手渡された。皆の表情が暗いとは思えない（沖縄県公文書館所蔵）
Ishikawa City and the school officials went to the U.S. military facility and was handed over a check for compensation.It is hard to believe that everyone's fares are gloomy.

② **Jet fighter crash at Miyamori Elementary School**

　On June 30, 1959, a U.S. Air Force F100 jet fighter plane lost control and the pilot escaped in midair, but the plane knocked down 35 private houses, hit Miyamori Elementary School in Ishikawa City, and burst into flames. At the time of the accident, there were about 1,000 children and faculty members at the school, and almost all of them were inside the school building during the milk lunch time. The fire was extinguished an hour later, but it turned out to be a catastrophe with 17 dead (11 elementary school students and 6 civilians) and 210 seriously or lightly injured (one of the victims died at the age of 23, 17 years after the accident from the after-effects of the burns). The U.S. military announced that the cause of the accident was "force majeure accident due to engine failure," but the primary cause was "maintenance error" and the aircraft should not have flown. At the time, it was reported in Japan and abroad as a major accident, a rare occurrence in the history of aviation in the world. According to an internal U.S. military document from that time revealed 63 years after the accident, "There is nothing new about the tragedy of Ishikawa. Unforeseen accidents have been a common occurrence since the dawn of history," trivializing the accident and blaspheming the victims. Immediately after the accident, anti-American sentiment rose in all of Okinawa, and coinciding with the period when the U.S. military was forcibly seizing land, there were violent protests and demands for compensation. The U.S. military's compensation for the accident was $4,500 for the dead and $2,300 to $5,900 for the seriously injured, depending on the degree of their disability, which was only about 10% of the amount demanded by the victims. On the other hand, the mayor at the time presented the U.S. military with a letter of appreciation for their contribution to the smooth negotiation of compensation and recovery from the accident. In the courtyard of Miyamori Elementary School, there is a *Nakayoshi-jizou* to memorialize the children who lost their lives, and a memorial ceremony is held every year on June 30 by the children.

③国場君轢殺事件（こくばくんれきさつじけん）

　1963 年 2 月 28 日午後 4 時過ぎ、那覇市内の泉崎橋前の軍用道路 1 号線（現・国道 58 号線）で発生した男子中学生轢殺事件。上山中学校 1 年生・国場秀夫君ら中学生 14 〜 15 人が「青信号を確認して横断歩道を横断中、米海兵隊員が運転する大型トラックが信号を無視して猛スピードで突っ込み、帰宅途中の同君を轢殺した。沖縄教職員会や PTA など 12 団体による対策協議会が結成され、加害者への厳罰や裁判の公開、捜査権・裁判権の民移管などを米軍側に要請した。同年 5 月 1 日に開かれた軍法会議では「無罪」の判決が下された。裁判は傍聴を許さず、「背後からの太陽の反射で信号が見えなかった」と発表されただけで、判決文も明示されなかった。当時の軍事裁判は、判事・検事役の全員が加害者と同じ部隊の人間で構成され、非公開で記録も開示しないという一方的なものだった。米国の施政権下にあり、米軍人・軍属などへの裁判権が及ばない当時の沖縄においては、このような事故処理が数多くなされ、同事件はその典型でもあった。この事件は、沖縄の日本復帰の際、第一次裁判権の保有を求める大きなきっかけとなった。

国場くん轢殺事件現場（那覇市泉崎交差点付近）
The scene where Kokuba-*kun* was run over and killed
(near the Izumisaki intersection in Naha City)

③ A junior high school boy (Kokuba-*kun*) was run over and killed

　A junior high school boy was run over and killed on February 28, 1963, just after 4:00 p.m. on military road No. 1 (now Route 58) in front of Izumizaki Bridge in Naha City. Kokuba Hideo, a first-year student at Uenoyama Junior High School, and 14 or 15 other junior high school students were crossing a "crosswalk after checking for a green light" when a large truck driven by a U.S. Marine ignored the light and drove into them at high speed, running over and killing Kokuba Hideo on his way home. A countermeasure council was formed by 12 organizations, including the Okinawa Teachers Association and the PTA, and requested the U.S. military to severely punish the perpetrators, open the trial to the public, and transfer the investigation and trial rights to the private sector. A court-martial held on May 1 of the same year ruled that he was "not guilty". The trial was not allowed to be heard, and it was simply announced that the traffic lights could not be seen due to the reflection of the sun from behind, and the sentence of decision was not explicitly stated. Military tribunals at that time were one-sided, with all of the judge and prosecutor officers being from the same unit as the perpetrators, and were closed to the public and records were not disclosed. At that time, Okinawa was under the control of the United States, and jurisdiction was not applied to U.S. military personnel and U.S. civilian employees, so many accidents related to the U.S. military were often handled in this way, and this case was a typical example. This incident was a major impetus for the Japanese side to seek the retention of primary jurisdiction when Okinawa was returned to Japan.

④ B52 墜落事故（B52 ついらくじこ）

　1968 年 11 月 19 日未明、嘉手納基地内で戦略爆撃機（B52）が離陸に失敗し、爆発・炎上した事故。住民 316 人が重軽傷を負い、周辺の住宅や学校などの窓ガラスが割れるなどの被害が出た。核兵器や毒ガスが貯蔵されているといわれた知花弾薬庫近くで起きたこの事故は県民に大きな衝撃を与えた。B52 は 1968 年 2 月から嘉手納基地に常駐。ベトナム戦争では広範囲を破壊するじゅうたん爆撃を行い、ベトナム人から「死の鳥」として恐れられた。当時、沖縄の米軍基地は補給基地から出撃基地に変化しており、ベトナム戦争に直結する「黒い殺し屋」として、B52 撤去運動が全県下に拡大した。沖縄返還が近づく 1970 年 9 月、米軍は屋良朝苗行政主席に「B52 を数日以内に撤去する。ただし作戦上で必要とあれば再配備する」と表明し、常駐体制は消えた。しかし B52 は復帰後も数回、嘉手納基地に飛来している。

B52 撤去抗議集会（写真：沖縄タイムス社）
Protest rally to demand removal of B-52s
(in front of Kadena Air Base gate)

④ B-52 crash

　In the early morning of November 19, 1968, a strategic bomber (B-52) failed to take off and exploded and burst into flames inside Kadena Air Base. Three hundred and sixteen residents were seriously injured, and windows of nearby houses and schools were broken. The accident, which occurred near the Chibana ammunition depot where nuclear weapons and poisonous gas were said to be stored, had a great impact on the people of Okinawa. The B-52s had been stationed at Kadena Air Base since February 1968, and during the Vietnam War they were feared by the Vietnamese as "birds of death" for their carpet bombing that destroyed large areas. At the time, the U.S. bases in Okinawa were changing from supply to sortie bases, and the movement to remove the B-52s as "black killers" directly linked to the Vietnam War expanded throughout Okinawa. In September 1970, as the reversion of Okinawa to Japan approached, the U.S. military announced to Yara Chobyo, the chief administrative officer of Okinawa, that the B-52s would be removed within a few days, but would be reassigned if operationally necessary, and the resident system disappeared. However, the B-52s have continued to fly to Kadena Air Base several times since its return.

⑤ 主婦轢殺事件（しゅふれきさつじけん）

　1970 年 9 月 18 日夜、糸満町（現・糸満市）の糸満ロータリー付近で、酒気運転かつスピード違反の米兵（海軍 2 等軍曹）が車を歩道に乗り上げて、歩行中の主婦（54 歳）を轢殺する事故を起こした。

歩道を歩行中の彼女に過失は全く無く、速度制限（24 キロ）を大きく超過する「暴走運転」（80 キロ）だった。地元の青年たちは事故直後から十分な現場検証と捜査を求め、現場保存のため1週間にわたってMP（Military Police）のレッカー車を包囲し、事故車の移動を阻止した。沖縄側は事故対策協議会を発足させ、琉球警察を通じて米軍に対し謝罪、軍法会議の公開、遺族に対する完全賠償を要求した。

主婦轢殺事件現場（糸満市、糸満ロータリー付近）
The scene where a housewife was run over and killed (near Itoman Rotary, Itoman City)

しかし、同年 12 月 11 日に開かれた米軍法会議では、被害者への賠償は認めたものの、加害者に対しては証拠不十分として無罪判決を下した。無罪判決に対する反発は全県に広がり、裁判のやり直しを求める県民大会が糸満町で開催されたが、再審は実現しなかった。米軍に対する住民の強い反発の背景には、ベトナム戦争の激化による米兵犯罪の増加と、裁判権を米側に握られているという事実があった。この事件は、3 ヶ月後に起こるコザ反米暴動の引き金になった。

⑤ A housewife was run over and killed
(in Itoman Town)

　On the night of September 18, 1970, a drunk and speeding U.S. soldier (Navy Staff Sergeant 2nd Class) drove his car onto the sidewalk near the Itoman Rotary in Itoman Town (now Itoman City) and ran over and killed a 54-year-old housewife who was walking. She was walking on the sidewalk and was not at fault at all, but the assailant was a "runaway driver" (80km/h), far exceeding the speed limit (24km/h). Immediately after the accident, local youths demanded a thorough site inspection and investigation, and surrounded the MP (Military Police) tow truck for a week to preserve the scene and prevent the accident vehicle from moving. The Okinawan side set up an accident countermeasure council and, through the Ryukyu Police, demanded an apology from the U.S. military, disclosure of the court-martial, and full compensation to the bereaved families. However, a U.S. court-martial held on December 11 of the same year approved compensation for the victims, but acquitted the perpetrators for lack of evidence. The outcry against the acquittal spread throughout the prefecture, and a prefectural assembly was held in Itoman Town to demand a new trial, but there was no new trial. Behind the residents' strong opposition to the U.S. military was the increase in crimes committed by U.S. soldiers due to the escalation of the Vietnam War and the fact that the U.S. held the right to trial. This incident triggered the Koza Anti-American Riots that would occur three months later.

（5）島ぐるみ闘争（しまぐるみとうそう）

　島ぐるみ闘争とは、アメリカの施政権下にある沖縄で、1956 年に起きた軍用地をめぐる住民と米国民政府間の大規模な闘争をいう。住民側の「土地を守る4原則」を踏みにじった米側の「プライス勧告」の発表をきっかけに、沖縄全域に爆発的な勢いで広がった大衆運動である。1956 年6月20日、「軍用地料の一括払い反対」や「土地を守る4原則の貫徹」を求めるための第1回住民大会が沖縄全島で一斉に開かれ、約30万人が参加した。この要求は①軍用地料の大幅引き上げ②使用料は原則毎年払いとするが、希望者には 10 年分の前払いを可能とする、などで一応決着した。島ぐるみ闘争の背景には、沖縄における恒久的基地建設を本格化し軍用地を確保するために、後に「銃剣とブルドーザーによる強制的な土地接収」と言われた米軍の圧政に対する民衆の強い不満や怒りがあった。次第に闘争は単なる軍用地問題から、米軍政全体に対する批判・抵抗運動としての性格を帯びていった。強力

な米国を相手にしたこの闘争は、日本本
土および全世界に沖縄問題の存在を知ら
せることになった。この闘いによって沖
縄の人々は、絶対的な権力者であるアメ
リカの政策を部分的にでも修正すること
ができたという大きな自信を得ることが
でき、その後の祖国復帰運動の原動力と
なった。

(5) *Shimagurumi-tousou* (Island-wide Struggle)

The *Shimagurumi-tousou* (island-wide struggle) refers to the large-scale struggle between residents and the U.S. national government over military land in Okinawa,

「金は 1 年、土地は万年」と書かれた旗の下で、銃剣とブルドーザー
で奪われた美田を見る伊佐浜住民 (現在の北谷町ハンビータウン辺り)
Residents of Isahama look at the beautiful rice fields stolen by bayonets
and bulldozers under the banner, "Money is only worth a year, but the land
is worth 10,000 years"(around present-day Hanby Town, Chatan Town)

which was under U.S. control in 1956. It was a mass movement that spread with explosive force throughout Okinawa, triggered by the announcement of the U.S. "Price-Recommendations," which trampled on the residents' "Four Principles for Protecting Land". On June 20, 1956, the first residents' convention was held simultaneously on all islands of Okinawa to demand "opposition to the lump-sum payment of military land fees" and "adherence to the four principles of land protection," with about 300,000 people participating. This demand was settled on the following points. (1) that the military land fee be increased substantially; (2) that the military land fee be paid annually in principle, but that those who wished to pay for ten years could do so in advance. The background of the *Shimagurumi-tousou* was the strong dissatisfaction and anger of the people against the oppressive policies of the U.S. military, later described as "forcible land seizure with bayonets and bulldozers," in order to secure military land for full-scale construction of permanent bases in Okinawa. Gradually, the struggle shifted from a mere military land issue to one of criticism and resistance against the U.S. military government as a whole. This struggle against the powerful United States made the existence of the Okinawa problem known not only to mainland Japan but also to the entire world. The people of Okinawa gained a great deal of confidence from this struggle in that they were able to modify, even partially, the policies of an absolute power, the United States, and it became the driving force behind the subsequent movement to return to the homeland.

(6) 祖国復帰運動 (そこくふっきうんどう)

　第二次世界大戦の沖縄戦で米軍に占領され、日本から分離された沖縄において日本への復帰を求めて展開された社会運動。戦後の沖縄では、帰属問題について①日本への復帰②独立③国際連合の信託統治下など多様な議論が交わされた。サンフランシスコ講話条約 (1952 年 4 月 28 日発効) によって、北緯 29 度以南の奄美や沖縄は日本の行政から分離された。それによって沖縄の住民が日本本土へ渡航する際にはパスポートを要することとなった。アメリカ合衆国による長期支配が行われ、米軍による軍事優先策が明らかになっていくと、沖縄の世論は独立や信託統治ではなく日本への復帰を望んだ。米軍兵士や米軍基地から派生する事件・事故が相次ぎ、住民からも多くの犠牲者が出たため、住民運動を中心とする日本復帰運動が展開された。

　当初、アメリカは沖縄に対する施政権の維持と米軍基地の機能維持の目的から、運動を厳しく弾圧した。

しかし、米軍が強権的な政策を行うほど、復帰を求める声は逆に高まっていった。1950 年代後半に軍用地問題に端を発した「島ぐるみ闘争」が起こると運動が再燃した。1960 年 4 月 28 日、教職員組合を中心とする「復帰協」が結成された以後は、毎年 4 月 28 日にはデモ行進が行われ、辺戸岬沖では海上集会が開かれた。1960 年代後半のベトナム戦争激化によって沖縄が最前線基地になると、沖縄住民の反米・反戦色が激しさを増した。1969 年の日米首脳会談で 1972 年の沖縄返還が約束されたが、奄美諸島は 1953 年には既に日本復帰していた。

祖国復帰運動行進
Homeland Reversion Movement March

(6) *Sokoku-hukki-undou* (Return to the Motherland Movement)

It is a social movement in Okinawa, which was occupied by the U.S. military during the Battle of Okinawa in World War II and separated from Japan, to seek the return of Okinawa to Japan. In post-war Okinawa, there were various debates on the issue of belonging, including (1) reversion to Japan, (2) independence, and (3) under the trusteeship of the United Nations. Under the Treaty of San Francisco (effective April 28, 1952), Amami and Okinawa south of 29 degrees north latitude were separated from the Japanese administration. This meant that residents of Okinawa were required to have a passport when traveling to mainland Japan. As the long-term rule by the United States took place and the U.S. military priority policy became apparent, public opinion in Okinawa wanted not independence or trusteeship, but a return to Japan. A series of incidents and accidents stemming from U.S. soldiers and U.S. military bases resulted in many casualties among the local residents, and a movement to return to Japan centered on the residents' movement developed.

Initially, the U.S. severely suppressed this movement in order to maintain U.S. administrative authority over Okinawa and to keep the U.S. military bases functioning. However, the more forceful the U.S. military's policies were, the more the calls for their return grew in reverse. In the late 1950s, the *Shimagurumi-tousou* (Island-wide Struggle) triggered by the military land issue reignited the movement. On April 28, 1960, the *Hukki-kyo* (Okinawa Reversion Association) was formed mainly by the teachers' union, and every year since then, a demonstration march was held on April 28, and a marine rally was held off Cape Hedo. As the Vietnam War intensified in the late 1960s and Okinawa became a frontline base, the anti-American and anti-war sentiment of the Okinawans intensified. At the Japan-U.S. summit meeting in 1969, the return of Okinawa in 1972 was promised, but the Amami Islands had already been returned to Japan in 1953.

(7) コザ反米暴動（こざはんべいぼうどう）

1970 年 12 月 20 日午前 0 時 15 分頃、コザ市（現沖縄市）中の町でアメリカ人の運転する車両が横断中の男性を引っかけて怪我を負わせるという交通事故が発端となった。3 ヶ月前に糸満町で起きた米兵による主婦轢殺事件で、軍事法廷が無罪判決を出した直後とあって、事故処理する MP を群衆が取り囲み、「糸満の二の舞にするな！！」と騒いだ。MP 隊が威嚇発砲したことから群衆の怒りが爆発し、駐車中の MP カー、米人の車両に次々と放火した。琉球警察は全警官を非常招集し、米軍はカービン銃で武装した MP 約 300 人を出動させた。約 5,000 人の群衆とにらみ合うなど、騒ぎは朝

まで続いた。この騒動では住民、警官ら23人が重軽傷を負い、19人が逮捕された。1972年5月15日の復帰を目前に起きたこの騒動は、日米両政府に衝撃を与えた。

コザ反米暴動（沖縄市中の町）（沖縄タイムス社）
Koza Anti-American Riots (Nakamachi, Okinawa City)

(7) Koza Anti-American Riot

It all started with a traffic accident that occurred in Nakanomachi, Koza City (now Okinawa City) at about 0:15 a.m. on December 20, 1970, when a vehicle driven by an American hit and injured a man crossing the street. On that day, a crowd surrounded the MP (Military Police) handling the accident because it was right after a military court had acquitted him of the murder of a housewife by a U.S. soldier in Itoman Town three months earlier, and shouted, "Don't repeat what happened in Itoman!! The MP unit fired warning shots, which caused the crowd to explode in anger and set fire to a series of parked MP cars and American vehicles. The Ryukyu Police Department called an emergency call for all police officers, and the U.S. military dispatched about 300 MPs armed with carbine rifles. The commotion continued until morning, including a standoff with a crowd of about 5,000 people. Twenty-three residents and police officers were seriously injured and 19 were arrested in the riot. The riot, which occurred just before the May 15, 1972 reversion to Japan, shocked the Japanese and U.S. governments.

(8) 屋良朝苗（やらちょうびょう）

1902年、読谷村字瀬名波で生まれた沖縄県の政治家、教育者。1930年に広島高等師範学校（現・広島大学）を卒業後、沖縄県女子師範学校、沖縄県立第一高等女学校、台北第一師範学校などで教職を勤めた。戦後は、沖縄教職委員会長などを歴任後、1968年の行政主席選挙では革新共同候補として立候補した。これまでは米軍による任命者しかなれなかった沖縄の行政主席だったが、大衆運動の高まりによって住民の直接選挙による制度が実現したのである。選挙は保守系の西銘順治氏を相手に行われたが、本土への早期復帰を訴えた屋良氏が当選し、第5代行政主席に就任した。この選挙では、西銘氏の当選のために日米両政府が裏で動いていたことが2010年12月に公開された外交文書によって明らかになったが、屋良氏は、裏工作を撥ね除けての当選だった。

屋良朝苗の銅像（読谷村役場中庭）
Bronze statue of Yara Chobyo (Yomitan Village Hall courtyard)

　行政主席在任中は、復帰を円滑に進めるために日米両政府の折衝などで苦渋に満ちた表情をすることが多く、いつしか「縦しわの屋良」と呼ばれるようになった。復帰の年（1972年）の沖縄県知事選挙で再選され、その後は沖縄県知事を2期務めた。知事在任中の1975年、糸満市の「ひめゆりの塔」で皇族に対する火焔瓶によるテロ事件が発生した。事前の地下壕の安全確認を主張した警備陣に対して、屋良知事は「聖域に土足で入るのは県民感情を逆なでする」

として実施させなかった。事前調査しておれば未然に防げた事件であったことは、警備担当者が明らかにしている。

　知事を退いた後も、沖縄の伝統的な保革対立の中で、革新陣営のシンボル的存在として革新共闘会議を主導した。1997 年 2 月 14 日、心不全のため 94 歳で死去した。

(8) Yara Chobyo

He was born in 1902 in Senaha, Yomitan Village, and was a politician and educator in Okinawa Prefecture. After graduating from Hiroshima Higher Teacher's Training School (now Hiroshima University) in 1930, He held teaching positions at Okinawa Prefectural Women's Teacher's Training School, Okinawa Prefectural Daiichi Higher School for Girls, and Taipei Daiichi Teacher's Training School. After the war, he served as head of the Okinawa Teachers' Association, and then ran as an innovative joint candidate in the 1968 election for the Chief Executive of the Government of the Ryukyu Islands. In the past, only U.S. military appointees had been allowed to serve as Okinawa's chief of government, but with the rise of the mass movement, a system of direct election by the local people was realized that year. The election was held against the conservative Nishime Junji, but Yara, who appealed for an early return to the mainland, won the election and became the fifth Okinawa's Chief Executive. In this election, diplomatic documents released in December 2010 revealed that the Japanese and U.S. governments had been working behind the scenes to help Mr. Nishime win the election, but Mr. Yara won the election by overcoming the backroom manipulation.

During his tenure as the Okinawa's Chief Executive, he often wore a pained expression as he negotiated with the Japanese and U.S. governments to ensure the smooth return of the mainland to Japan, and he came to be known as "Mr. Yara with vertical wrinkles". He was re-elected in 1972, the year of Okinawa's reversion to Japan, and subsequently served two terms as governor of Okinawa Prefecture. In 1975, during his tenure as governor, a terrorist attack with flaming bottles against the royal family occurred at Himeyuri Monument in Itoman City. When the security team insisted on checking the safety of the underground bunker beforehand, Governor Yara refused to allow them to do so, saying that it would offend the people of the prefecture to enter the sanctuary with their feet on the ground. The security officer made it clear that the incident could have been prevented if there had been a prior investigation.

After leaving office as governor, he continued to lead the *Kakushin-Kyoutou-Kaigi* as a symbolic figure for innovative groups in the traditional conflict between conservative and innovative groups in Okinawa. He died of heart failure on February 14, 1997, at the age of 94.

(9) 瀬長亀次郎（せながかめじろう）

　1907 年、現在の豊見城市我那覇に生まれ、現・鹿児島大学在学中に社会主義運動に加わったことが理由で退学処分となった。2 年間の兵役を経て、1932 年に丹那トンネル労働争議を指導したため治安維持法違反で検挙され、懲役 3 年の刑で横浜刑務所に投獄される。戦後は名護町（現・名護市）助役、沖縄朝日新聞記者、毎日新聞沖縄支局記者を経て、1946 年に「うるま新報」（現・琉球新報）の社長に就任した。在任中、沖縄人民党の結成に参加したことで米軍の圧力により同社長を辞任した。その後、雑貨店を経営しながら沖縄人民党書記長となり、沖縄群島知事選挙に立候補するが、落選。1952 年の第 1 回立法院議員選挙ではトップ当選を果たしたものの、選挙後の琉球政府創立式典で宣誓拒否をしたことで米軍から睨まれることとなる。

　1954 年 10 月、米軍は、沖縄から撤去命令を受けた人民党員をかくまった容疑（出入国管理令違反）で瀬長を逮捕。弁護士なしの裁判にかけ、懲役 2 年の判決で投獄された。1956 年 4 月の出獄後、

同年 12 月に行われた那覇市長選挙に出馬。対立候補からの妨害を受けながらも、大方の予想を覆して当選する。彼の市政運営に対して米軍と沖縄自民党は 7 度に渡る不信任決議案を提出するが、いずれも不発に終わった。高等弁務官は布令を改定して 1957 年、瀬長を追放して被選挙権を剥奪した（通称、瀬長布令）。市長在任期間は 1 年足らずであったが、那覇市政を巡る米軍との攻防は、瀬長に対する沖縄住民の絶大なる支持を得た。1967 年 12 月に瀬長布令が廃止され、被選挙権を回復した。1970 年の沖縄初の国政選挙で衆議院議員に当選し、以降 7 期連続当選を果たした。日本共産党に所属し共産党副委員長などを歴任し、1990 年に政治活動を引退した。

出獄時、市民に手を振る瀬長亀次郎氏
（沖縄県公文書館所蔵）
Senaga Kamejiro, waving to the public
upon his release from prison

　1998 年には映画「カメジロー沖縄の青春」が制作され、瀬長亀次郎が残した資料を中心に、沖縄の民衆の闘いを後世に伝える目的で、「不屈館」が 2013 年 3 月、那覇市に開館した。施設名は占領軍の弾圧を受けながらも抵抗運動の先頭に立って闘い続けた瀬長が、生前好んで書いた「不屈」に因んでいる。2001 年 10 月 5 日、肺炎のため 94 歳で死去した。

(9) Senaga Kamejiro

　He was born in 1907 in Ganaha, present-day Tomigusuku City, and was expelled from school for joining the socialist movement while a student at what is now Kagoshima University. After serving two years in the military, he was arrested in 1932 for violating the Public Security Law for leading the Tanna Tunnel labor dispute and was imprisoned in Yokohama Prison for three years. After the war, he worked as an assistant director of Nago Town（now Nago City）, a reporter for the Okinawa Asahi Shimbun, and a reporter for the Okinawa branch of the Mainichi Shimbun before becoming the president of the Uruma Shimpo (now the Ryukyu Shimpo) in 1946. During his tenure, he resigned as president of the newspaper due to pressure from the U.S. military for his participation in the formation of the Okinawa People's Party. Later, while running a general store, he became the general secretary of the Okinawa People's Party and ran for governor of the Okinawa archipelago, but was not elected. Although he was the top elected official in the first Legislative Assembly election in 1952, after the election, he refused to take the oath of office at the founding ceremony of the Ryukyu government, and the U.S. military stared at him.

　In October 1954, the U.S. military arrested Senaga on suspicion of harboring a People's Party member who had been ordered removed from Okinawa (a violation of the Immigration Control Order). He was tried without a lawyer and sentenced to two years in prison. After his release from prison in April 1956, he ran in the Naha mayoral election held in December of the same year, and despite interference from opposing candidates, defied most expectations and won the election. The U.S. military and the Okinawa Liberal Democratic Party submitted seven resolutions of no confidence in his management of the city, but each was unsuccessful. The High Commissioner revised the Proclamation and in 1957, expelled Senaga and deprived his eligibility for election (commonly known as the Senaga Proclamation). His tenure as mayor lasted less than a year, but his battles with the U.S. military over Naha's city government earned him the tremendous support of Okinawans. In December 1967, the Senaga Proclamation was repealed and his eligibility for election was restored. In 1970, he was elected to the House of Representatives in Okinawa's first national election, and since then he had been elected to seven consecutive terms. He was a member of the Communist Party of Japan and served as Vice Chairman of the Communist Party, before retiring from politics in 1990.

In 1998, the film "Kamejiro-Okinawa's Youth" was produced, and the *Hukutsu-kan* was opened in Naha City in March 2013 with the aim of conveying the struggles of the Okinawan people to future generations, focusing on the materials left behind by Senaga Kamejiro. The name of the facility is derived from "Fortitude," a phrase that Senaga liked to write before his death, as he continued to fight at the head of the resistance movement despite the oppression of the occupying forces. He died of pneumonia on October 5, 2001, at the age of 94.

（10）阿波根昌鴻（あはごんしょうこう）

反戦平和資料館「ヌチドゥタカラの家」の入リロに立つ阿波根昌鴻氏（沖縄タイムス社）
Mr. Ahagon Syokou standing at the entrance of the "House of the *Nuchi-du-takara*" (Anti-War Peace Museum)

　阿波根昌鴻（1901 ～ 2002）は沖縄の平和運動家で、戦後、アメリカ施政権下の沖縄で米軍による土地の強制接収に反対する反基地運動を主導した。沖縄本島北部の本部町に生まれ、17 歳でクリスチャンとなり、無教会主義に強い影響を受けた。成人後は伊江島へ渡り結婚し、1925 年にキューバに移住した。その後、ペルーへ移り 1934 年に日本へ帰国。京都や沼津で学んだ後は伊江島に帰り、デンマーク式農民学校建設を志して奔走したが、建設中の学校は沖縄戦で失われ、一人息子も戦死した。

　戦後、伊江島の土地の約 60% が米軍に強制接収された際、反対運動の先頭に立った。「全沖縄土地を守る協議会」の事務局長や「伊江島土地を守る会」の会長を務め、1955 年 7 月から 1956 年 2 月にかけて沖縄本島で非暴力による「乞食行進」を行って、米軍による土地強奪の不当性を訴えた。この行動は、1956 年夏の「島ぐるみ土地闘争」に大きな影響を与えた。米軍の伊江島補助飛行場内に土地を所有し、1972 年の沖縄返還後も日本政府との賃貸借を拒否し続けた。

　基地撤去闘争や反戦平和の思いを伝えるため 1984 年、自宅敷地内に反戦平和資料館「ヌチドゥタカラの家」を自費で建設。県内外から訪れる人々に戦争の愚かさと平和の尊さを説き続けた。1998 年には彼の活動を取り上げたドキュメンタリー映画が制作された。2002 年 3 月 21 日、肺炎のため 101 歳で死去した。

（10）Ahagon Syokou

　Ahagon Shokou (1901-2002) was an Okinawan peace activist who led the anti-base movement against the forced land seizure by the U.S. military in postwar Okinawa. Born in Motobu Town in the northern part of Okinawa Island, he became a Christian at the age of 17, and was strongly influenced by non-churchism. After coming of age, he moved to Ie Island (Iejima), got married, and immigrated to Cuba in 1925. He then moved to Peru and returned to Japan in 1934. After studying in Kyoto and Numazu, he returned to Ie Island and worked hard to build a Danish-style peasant school, but the school under construction was lost in the Battle of Okinawa, and his only son was killed in the war.

　After the war, when about 60% of the land on Ie Island was forcibly seized by the U.S. military, he led the opposition movement. He served as secretary general of the "All Okinawa Land Protection Council" and president of the "Iejima Land Protection Association," and from July 1955 to February 1956, he held a non-violent *Kojiki-koshin* (beggar's march) on the main island of Okinawa to call out the injustice of land grabbing by the U.S. military. This action had a great impact on the *Shimagurumi-tochi-tousou* (island-wide land struggle) in the summer of 1956. He owned land within the U.S. military's Iejima auxiliary airfield and continued to refuse to lease it to the Japanese government even after Okinawa was returned to Japan in 1972.

In 1984, in order to convey his thoughts on the struggle for the removal of the base and anti-war peace, he built the anti-war peace museum the "House of the *Nuchi-du-takara*" on the premises of his home at his own expense, and had continued to lecture visitors from inside and outside of the prefecture on the folly of war and the preciousness of peace. In 1998, a documentary film was produced on his activities. He died of pneumonia on March 21, 2002, at the age of 101.

(11) アメラジアン

アメラジアンスクール沖縄 (宜野湾市志真志)
AmerAsian School in Okinawa(Shimashi, Ginowan City)

　アメラジアン（Amerasian）とは、アメリカン（American）とアジアン（Asian）を組み合わせた造語で 1970 年代からアメリカで用いられてきた。日本、韓国、フィリピン、ベトナムなど、アジアに駐留した米軍人と地元の女性との間に生まれた子どもを指す。終戦後の沖縄では「合いの子」、「アメリカーグヮー」「ヒージャーミー」などの差別語で呼ばれ、日常生活のさまざまな場面で、理由すら理解できないままいじめを体験し、心に深く傷を負った。沖縄の祖母らに養育され、アメリカンスクールに通えず英語を話せないアメラジアンは「島ハーフ」と呼ばれることもあり、父親に棄てられた「基地の落とし子」というレッテルを貼られた。彼らは、中途半端ゆえに小さい頃から周囲に過剰に反応し、沖縄人、日本人、アメリカ人を不自然なほど演じた。容姿からくる「内なる人種・人権侵害」はハーフを生んだ母親にも及び、トラウマとして残るケースも少なくない。

　戦後 77 年を過ぎた今日の沖縄でも毎年、約 300 人のアメラジアンが生まれ続けている。1945 年の悲惨な沖縄戦や、今なお広大な米軍基地を抱えている沖縄の人々の心の奥には反米感情が根深く潜んでいる。その結果、米軍基地の象徴的存在としてのアメラジアンに対する差別や偏見が生まれた。子供たちには自分の父親を知る権利があり、その権利はアメリカの裁判所では認められている。アメリカはフランスやドイツなどとは既に養育費相互協定を結び、父親が養育費を送っているが、日本とはまだ未締結である。

　軍人である父親が一度姿をくらますと、「軍事作戦上の秘密」などと言われて、なかなか居場所が確認できなくなる場合が多いといわれる。1960 年～ 80 年代の沖縄では、無国籍児のハーフの子ども達の養子縁組が多く行われた。アメラジアンの国籍取得や教育問題、国民健康保険問題などの沖縄からの声が国会でも取り上げられた。1985 年の国籍法改正では父親だけでなく、母親からも国籍が取得できるようになった。日本では二重国籍を持つアメラジアンの子どもたちは、将来どちらかの国籍を選ばなければならないが、その後も彼らは「自分は人種的、言語的、文化的に日本人なのかアメリカ人なのか」というジレンマを絶えず抱える運命を背負わされることになる。

　1998 年 6 月にアメラジアンを持つ 5 人の母親たちの出資によって「2 つの言語・文化のどちらか 1 つを選択させるのではなく、2 つとも教える環境の中で子供たちを育てていく」という教育理念で「アメラジアン・スクール・イン・オキナワ（AASO）」が宜野湾市に誕生した。均質性、同一性を重視する日本の教育界にあって、AASO の教育はダブル・アイデンティーを目指す教育、異なる 2 つの言語・文化を身につけさせる教育目標である。国や県からの経済的補助や宜野湾市からの施設提供、授業料などによって学校が運営されているが、教室不足のため複式学級を余儀なくされ、体育の授業は近くの公園を利用しているのが現状である。この学校を卒業すると日本の小中学校の卒業資格が得られるが、民間の教育施設のため公的支援や援助はまだ十分とは言えない。

エリザベス・サンダースホーム。1953 年に厚生省が行った調査によると国内には 4972 人の GI ベビー（アメラジアン）がいたとされるが、実際には 2-3 万人といわれる。彼らは教育・経済困難などの理由で孤児になり「混血孤児」と呼ばれた。この孤児院は沢田美喜という日本人女性によって開設され、700 人以上の孤児を世話したが、アメリカ人の父親の訪問や支援はなかった

Elizabeth Saunders Home. A survey conducted by the Ministry of Health and Welfare in 1953 indicated that there were 4,972 GI babies (Amerasians) in the country, but the actual number is said to be 20-30,000. They were called "mixed orphans" because they became orphans due to educational and economic difficulties. The orphanage was opened by a Japanese woman named Sawada Miki, who cared for more than 700 orphans, but without the visitation or support of their American fathers

(11) Amerasian

Amerasian is a term coined by combining the words "American" and "Asian," and has been used in the United States since the 1970s. The term refers to children born to U.S. military personnel stationed in Asia, including Japan, Korea, the Philippines, and Vietnam, and to local women. In Okinawa after the war, they were referred to by discriminatory terms such as *Ainoko* or *Americaa-gwaa*, and experienced bullying in various aspects of their daily lives without even understanding the reasons, which deeply traumatized them. Raised by their grandmother and others in Okinawa, Amerasians, who could not attend American school and did not speak English, were sometimes called *Shima-half*, and labeled a "bastard child of the base" who was abandoned by their fathers. Because of their half-heartedness, Amerasians overreacted to their surroundings from a young age, playing Okinawan, Japanese, and American to an unnatural degree. It is an "inner racial and human rights violation" that stems from their appearance, and in many cases, it is also traumatic for the mothers who gave birth to the half-breeds.

Even today, 77 years after the war, about 300 Amerasians continue to be born every year in Okinawa. Anti-U.S. sentiment lies deep in the hearts of the Okinawan people, who are still burdened by the tragic Battle of Okinawa in 1945 and the vast U.S. military bases that still exist there. As a result, discrimination and prejudice against Amerasians as a symbol of the U.S. military base developed. Children have the right to know their fathers, and that right is recognized in American courts. The U.S. already has reciprocal child support agreements with France and Germany, where the father sends child support, but has not yet signed one with Japan.

It is said that once a military father disappears, it is often difficult to ascertain his whereabouts because of "military and operational secrecy" and other reasons. From the 1960s to the 1980s, many adoptions of stateless half-breed children (Amerasian) took place in Okinawa. Voices from Okinawa regarding the acquisition of Amerasian nationality, educational issues, and national health insurance issues were taken up in the Diet, and in 1985 the Nationality Law was revised so that nationality could be acquired not only from the father but also from the mother. In Japan, children of Amerasians with dual citizenship must choose one of the two nationalities in the future, but even after that, they are doomed to constantly face the dilemma of whether they are racially, linguistically, or culturally Japanese or American.

In June 1998, the AmerAsian School in Okinawa (AASO) was established in Ginowan City, funded by five mothers with Amerasian, with the educational philosophy of "raising children in an environment where both languages and cultures are taught, rather than having them choose one or the other". In a Japanese educational world that emphasizes homogeneity and sameness, AASO's educational goal is to educate students toward a double identity, to help them acquire two different languages and cultures. Currently, the school operates on tuition, government and prefectural subsidies, and facilities provided by Ginowan City, but due to a lack of classrooms, the school is forced to offer double classes, and physical education classes are held in a nearby park. Graduates of this school receive a Japanese elementary and junior high school diploma, but because it is a private educational facility, public name support and assistance are not yet sufficient.

第 8 章　日本（祖国）復帰

　1972 年 5 月 15 日、悲願であった日本復帰（祖国復帰）を果たしたが、以後も米軍基地が固定化されるなど、沖縄住民が手放しで喜べる復帰ではなかった。復帰に際して「即時・無条件・全面返還」を掲げ、「基地のない平和な島」を描いていた沖縄県民の思いとは大きくかけ離れていたからである。1969 年 11 月に発表された日米共同宣言では「核抜き、米軍基地の本土並み負担、1972 年返還」を基本方針に掲げていた。ところが日米両政府は、従来どおり沖縄を「太平洋の要石」と位置づけ、米軍基地の安定保持を条件とした施政権返還を考えていたのである。

　全国民が沖縄の施政権返還を祝い、沖縄に対する理解を深めるとともに、遅れている沖縄の社会基盤を整備する目的で「復帰記念植樹祭（1972 年 11 月）」、沖縄特別国民体育大会（若夏国体、1973 年 5 月）」、「沖縄国際海洋博覧会（1975 年 7 月〜 76 年 1 月）」の三大事業が行われた。

　沖縄の日本復帰に伴い、ドルから円への通貨切り替えが行われた。ところが、1 ドル＝ 360 円だった固定相場が変動相場制へ移行されたため、復帰時の為替レートは 1 ドル＝ 305 円となった。県民が保持するドルを確認して差額分が保証されたが、法人は除外された。通貨切り替えに伴うトラブルで、消費者物価は 1 ヶ月間で 14.5 ％も上昇した。米軍占領から続いていた交通方法の変更（ナナサンマル）は、復帰の総仕上げとして、1978 年 7 月 30 日に行われた。

祖国復帰闘争碑（国頭村辺戸岬）
Monument commemorating the struggle
to return to the motherland (Cape Hedo,
Kunigami Village)

Chapter 8 Returning to Japan (reversion to our homeland)

　On May 15, 1972, Okinawa achieved its long-cherished dream of returning to Japan (reversion to our homeland), but it was not a return that the residents of Okinawa could enjoy with open arms, as U.S. military bases remained fixed in place. The reason for this was that it was a far cry from the aspirations of the people of Okinawa, who had envisioned a "peaceful island without bases," and had called for the "immediate, unconditional, and total return of Okinawa to Japan. The Japan-U.S. Joint Declaration announced in November 1969 stated the basic policy of "no nuclear weapons, US military base burden on par with mainland, and the return of Okinawa in 1972". However, as in the past, both the Japanese and U.S. governments continued to regard Okinawa as the "keystone of the Pacific Ocean," and were considering returning control of the island on the condition that the U.S. military bases would remain stable.

　In order for all the people to celebrate the return of Okinawa's sovereignty, deepen the understanding of Okinawa, and improve Okinawa's lagging social infrastructure, three major projects were held: the Reversion Commemorative Tree Planting Festival (November 1972), the Okinawa Special National Sports Festival (*Wakanatsu Kokutai,* May 1973), and the Okinawa International Ocean Expo (July 1975-January 1976).

　With the reversion of Okinawa to Japan, a currency switch from the dollar to the yen took place. However, since the fixed exchange rate of 360 yen to one dollar was shifted to a floating exchange rate system, the exchange rate was 305 yen to one dollar when Okinawa returned. The dollars held by residents of the prefecture were checked and the difference was guaranteed, but corporations were excluded. Consumer prices rose by 14.5% in one month due to the troubles associated with the currency change. As finishing touch to the reversion, right-lane driving, introduced by the U.S. occupation army 27 years previously, was changed into left-lane driving on July 30th, 1978.

（1）復帰後の米軍関連事件・事故（ふっきごのべいぐんかんれんじけん・じこ）

　1952年4月28日に発効したサンフランシスコ講和条約によって日本は独立したが、同時に発効した日米安保条約によってアメリカは日本全土に米軍基地を置く権利を獲得した。その時点では、沖縄の在日米軍専用施設は10%だったのに対し、沖縄以外の日本では90%を占めていた。しかし、それは日本国民の反米感情を刺激したため、日米両政府は日本から米地上部隊を撤退させ安保条約を改定した。こうして在日米軍は約4分の1に削減されたが、日本から撤退した米海兵隊などが沖縄に移駐したため、沖縄の米軍基地は約2倍に増えた。その後、日本政府は1972年の沖縄返還を機に在日米軍基地の整理統合を図り、日本本土の米軍基地は更に減った。沖縄の米軍基地はほとんど減らさなかったので、現在のように沖縄だけに米軍基地が集中するようになった。国土面積の0.6%に過ぎない沖縄に、全国の米軍専用施設面積の約70%が今も集中しており、米軍機の騒音被害や米軍基地由来の事件・事故、環境汚染は後を絶たない。沖縄に米軍専用施設を過大に押し付けている現状は明らかに不平等であり、沖縄県民はそれを「構造的な差別」と捉えている。

　沖縄県警察本部の統計によると、1972年の復帰から2007年までに米軍人等による刑法犯罪は5,514件にのぼり、そのうち殺人・強盗・婦女暴行などの凶悪事件が552件、粗暴犯が1,008件も発生するなど、復帰後も県民の生命、生活や財産に大きな影響を及ぼしている。沖縄が日本に返還された以降は、公務中の米軍関連事件についてはアメリカ側が、公務外の事件の場合は日本側に裁判権が移った。しかし、公務中であったか否かはその米兵の指揮官が決め、指揮官が「公務証明書」を発行すれば、日本側は一切、口出しできない。これらの不条理な状況は日米地位協定が根拠となっており、その改定を求める沖縄県民の声は大きいが、日本政府は聞く耳を持たない。

　2022年は祖国復帰から50年の節目だが、ハワイを凌ぐほどの観光客が来沖して観光産業が発展しているにもかかわらず完全失業率は全国最悪レベル。県民所得も全国平均の約7割で全国最下位が続いており、子供の貧困率は全国の2倍近い。県民所得に占める基地関連収入の割合は1965年には30.4%、復帰時には15.5%だったが、現在ではわずか5%程度しかなく、「米軍基地は県経済の最大の阻害要因」となっている。

米海兵隊基地・キャンプハンセン、ゲート1（金武町金武）
U.S. Marine Corps Base, Camp Hansen, Gate 1 (Kin, Kin Town)

(1) Incidents and accidents related to U.S. military bases after the reversion to Japan

　The San Francisco Peace Treaty, which went into effect on April 28, 1952, gave Japan independence, but the Japan-U.S. Security Treaty, which went into effect at the same time, gave the United States the right to establish U.S. military bases throughout Japan. At that point, dedicated U.S. military facilities in Japan accounted for 90% of the total in Japan outside of Okinawa, compared to 10% in Okinawa. However, this provoked anti-American sentiment among the Japanese people, so the U.S. and Japanese governments withdrew U.S. ground troops from

Japan and revised the Security Treaty. Thus, the U.S. forces in Japan were reduced by about a quarter, but the U.S. Marines and other U.S. forces that withdrew from Japan were relocated to Okinawa, and the U.S. military bases in Okinawa doubled in size. Subsequently, the Japanese government used the reversion of Okinawa in 1972 to consolidate U.S. military bases in Japan, further reducing the number of U.S. military bases on the Japanese mainland. Since the number of U.S. military bases in Okinawa was hardly reduced, the U.S. military bases became concentrated only in Okinawa, as they are today. About 70% of the total area of facilities dedicated to the U.S. military in Japan is still concentrated in Okinawa, which accounts for only 0.6% of the country's land area, and there is no end to the noise damage caused by U.S. military aircraft, incidents and accidents originating from U.S. military bases, and environmental pollution. The current situation of overburdening Okinawa with dedicated U.S. military facilities is clearly unequal, and the Okinawans view it as "structural discrimination".

According to statistics from the Okinawa Prefectural Police Headquarters, there were 5,514 criminal offenses committed by U.S. military personnel and others from the time of Okinawa's reversion to Japan in 1972 to 2007, of which 552 were violent crimes such as murder, robbery, and assault on women, and 1,008 were violent crimes. Even after the reversion, it has had a great impact on the lives, livelihoods and property of the people of Okinawa. Since the reversion, jurisdiction has shifted to the U.S. side for U.S. military-related cases during official duties, and to the Japanese side for cases outside of official duties. However, the commander of the U.S. soldier decides whether or not he was on official business, and once the commander issues an "official business certificate," the Japanese side has no say in the matter. These absurd situations are based on the Status of Forces Agreement between the U.S. and Japan, and although the Okinawan people have voiced strong demands for its revision, the Japanese government refuses to listen.

The year 2022 will mark the 50th anniversary of the return to Japan, but even though the tourism industry is growing with more visitors than Hawaii, the unemployment rate is at the worst level in the nation. The prefectural income is about 70% of the national average and continues to be the lowest in the country, and the child poverty rate is almost double the national rate. The share of base related income in the prefectural income was 30.4% in 1965 and 15.5% at the time of the return to Japan, but now it is only about 5%, making the "U.S. military bases the biggest impediment to the prefectural economy".

①米兵による少女暴行事件 （1995 年 9 月 4 日）

　1995 年 9 月 4 日、沖縄に駐留するアメリカ海兵隊員 2 人とアメリカ海軍軍人 1 人の計 3 人が、12 歳の女子小学生を拉致し集団強姦した事件。この事件は日本国内のみならず海外においても関心を集めた。この事件に関して当時のアメリカ太平洋軍司令官（海軍大将）が「レンタカーを借りる金で女が買えた」という旨の発言をしたため、女性差別発言として問題となり同年 11 月に更迭された。「起訴に至

少女暴行事件を糾弾する県民大会（1995 年 10 月 21 日、宜野湾市）
Prefectural assembly denouncing the assault of a young girl by U.S. soldiers (Ginowan City, October 21, 1995)

らなければ、関与が明らかでもアメリカ兵の身柄を日本側に引き渡すことが出来ない」という日米地位協定によって、実行犯の 3 人が引き渡されなかったことが大きな問題になった。これを受けて沖縄県民の反基地感情や反米感情が一気に爆発し、事件を糾弾する県民集会が開かれた。8 万 5 千人が参加したこの集会では同協定の見直しのみならず米軍基地の縮小・撤廃も求めた。1996 年 3 月、那覇地方裁判所は 3 人に対して懲役 6 年 6 ヶ月や 7 年の実刑判決を言い渡し、その後 2 人が控訴したが、控訴は棄却され刑が確定した。

① Assault of a young girl by an American soldier (September 4, 1995)

　On September 4, 1995, two U.S. Marines and one U.S. Navy serviceman stationed in Okinawa abducted and gang-raped a 12-year-old elementary school girl, an incident that attracted attention not only in Japan but also overseas. The commander of the U.S. Pacific Command (a navy general) at the time made a comment about the incident, saying that they could have bought a woman with the money from renting a car, which became a problem as a discriminatory remark against women, and was removed from office in November of the same year. It became a major issue that three of the perpetrators were not handed over due to the Japan-U.S. Status of Forces Agreement, which states that American soldiers cannot be extradited to Japan unless they are indicted, even if their involvement is clear. In response, anti-base and anti-U.S. sentiment among the Okinawans exploded, and a prefectural assembly was held to denounce the incident. The rally, attended by 85,000 people, called not only for a review of the agreement but also for the reduction or elimination of U.S. military bases. In March 1996, the Naha District Court sentenced three of them to six years and six months or seven years in prison, and two of them appealed, but the appeals were dismissed and the sentences were finalized.

② 沖国大米軍ヘリ墜落事件（2004 年 8 月 13 日）（おきこくだいべいぐんへりついらくじけん）

　2004 年 8 月 13 日午後 2 時過ぎ、普天間海兵隊基地所属の大型輸送ヘリコプター（CH-53）が訓練中にコントロールを失い、沖縄国際大学に墜落し炎上した事件。沖縄県で住宅地に米軍ヘリが墜落したのは 1972 年の復帰後初めてであり、事故原因は機体の整備ミスであった。幸いにも夏休み期間中であったため、学生や職員など民間人に負傷者は出なかったが、搭乗していた乗員 3 人が負傷した。この墜落事故により同大学は電話・インターネット回線等を切断され、近くの民家やガソリンスタンド・保育所などにヘリコプターの部品が落下した。事故直後、消火作業の終了後にアメリカ軍が現場を封鎖し、事故機を撤去するまで日本の警察・消防・行政・大学関係者の立ち入りを禁止した。この事故は、日本の施政権や大学の自治を侵害する事件であるとして県民の反発を招き、同年 9 月 12 日には抗議集会が開かれ 3 万人が参加した。2007 年、沖縄警察は乗員のアメリカ海兵隊軍曹ら、4 人を氏名不詳のまま書類送検したが、那覇地方検察庁は地位協定の壁に阻まれて全員を不起訴処分とした。現在、墜落現場には事故で焼けたアカギの木がモニュメントとして保存されている。

沖国大米軍ヘリ墜落事故（宮里秀雄氏撮影）、（宜野湾市宜野湾）
A U.S. military helicopter crashed into Okinawa International University
(Ginowan, Ginowan City)

② The U.S. military helicopter crash at Okinawa International University

Just after 2:00 p.m. on August 13, 2004, a large transport helicopter (CH-53) belonging to the Futenma Marine Corps Base lost control during a training exercise, crashed into Okinawa International University, and burst into flames. This was the first time since Okinawa's reversion to Japan in 1972 that a U.S. military helicopter crashed into a residential area, and the cause of the accident was a maintenance error on the aircraft. Fortunately, it was during the summer vacation period and no civilians, including students and staff, were injured, but three crew members on board were injured. As a result of the crash, the university's telephone and Internet lines were cut off, and parts of the helicopter fell on nearby houses, a gas station, and a daycare center. Immediately after the accident, the U.S. military cordoned off the site after the firefighting operations were completed, and no Japanese police, firefighters, government officials, or university staff were allowed to enter the site until the accident aircraft was removed. This accident caused an outcry from the people of the prefecture, as it was an incident that violated Japan's administrative authority and the autonomy of the university, and a protest rally was held on September 12 of the same year, attended by 30,000 people. In 2007, the Okinawa Prefectural Police referred four crew members, including a U.S. Marine sergeant, to prosecutors without identifying their names, but the Naha District Public Prosecutor's Office dropped the case against all of them, hampered by the Status of Forces Agreement. Today, a *Akagi* tree burned in the accident is preserved as a monument at the crash site.

（2）ナナサンマル（7・30 交通方法変更）

　沖縄の施政権返還にともない、1978 年（昭和 53）7 月 30 日を期して実施された交通方法の変更。変更日が 7 月 30 日なので「ナナサンマル」と呼ばれる。戦後の米軍占領に始まり、復帰後の 6 年を含めて 33 年間におよんだ「右走行」の交通は、この日から全国並みに「左走行」に変わった。「一国一方式」の国際条約や、本土―沖縄間の交流の増加による交通上の危険防止が変更の理由で、復帰処理事業の一つとして実施された。ナナサンマルでは、7 月 29 日午後 10 時に全県車両通行止めとなり、信号機など交通区分の切り替作業が行われた。翌 30 日午前 6 時を期して交通方法が変更されたが、混乱や交通事故続発のような大混乱を巻き起こした。特に那覇市を中心とした都市部では 19 日以上にわたってマヒ状態に陥った。車の流れが変わったことによる営業補償や交通渋滞による物流の悪化など間接的な被害も意外に大きく、県民の不満は絶えなかった。

ナナサンマル記念石碑（宮古島市）
Nana-san-maru Memorial Stone Monument
(Miyakojima City)

(2) *Nana-san-maru* (Change in traffic rules with the return of Okinawa's sovereignty)

With the return of Okinawa's sovereignty, the traffic rules were changed on July 30, 1978. It was called *Nana-san-maru* because the date of the change was July 30. Starting with the U.S. military occupation after the war, the right side of the road, which had lasted for 33 years including the six years after the return of the island to Japan, was changed to the left side of the road like the mainland after this day. The reason for the change was to prevent traffic hazards due to the international treaty of "One Country, One System" and the increased interaction between the mainland and Okinawa, and it was implemented as one of the reversion processing projects. In *Nana-san-maru*, the entire prefecture was closed to vehicular traffic simultaneously at 10 p.m. on July 29, and traffic signals and other traffic classifications were switched. The traffic rules were changed at 6:00 a.m. on the following day, July 30, but it caused a great deal of confusion and a series of traffic accidents. Traffic was paralyzed for more than 19 days, in urban areas, especially Naha City. The indirect damage, such as compensation for business due to the change in the flow of cars and the deterioration of logistics due to traffic congestion, was surprisingly large, and the people of the prefecture continued to complain.

（3）沖縄国際海洋博覧会（おきなわこくさいかいようはくらんかい）

　沖縄県の日本復帰記念事業として、1975 年 7 月から 1976 年 1 月までの会期で沖縄本島北部の本部町で行われた国際博覧会で、略称は「海洋博」、「沖縄海洋博」などである。「海—その望ましい未来」を統一テーマに、日本を含む 36 か国と 3 つの国際機関、7 つの民間企業が参加し、特別博としては当時、史上最大規模となった。海洋博開催によって、沖縄県の開発が劇的に進んだ。国道の拡幅・整備や大型ホテルなどの観光施設がこれに合わせて建設された。450 万人の目標に対し、最終的な来場者数は約 349 万人にとどまった。この結果は、海洋博を当て込んで様々な商売を目論んだ人たちを落胆させ、民宿経営者などからは「起爆剤ではなく、自爆剤になった」と不満が出た。海洋博の終了後、跡地は国営海洋博覧会記念公園となった。「海洋生物園」は現在では「沖縄美ら海水族館」と名称を変え、公園内の中核施設として営業を続けている。「未来の海上都市」をイメージとして建造され海洋博のシンボルであったアクアポリスは、2000 年 10 月、鉄屑として米企業へ売却処分された。

沖縄海洋博覧会のシンボル「アクアポリス」（沖縄タイムス社）
Aquapolis, the symbol of the Okinawa Maritime Expo

(3) Okinawa international Ocean Exposition

　The Okinawa Ocean Expo was an international exposition held in Motobu-*cho* in the northern part of Okinawa Island from July 1975 to January 1976 to commemorate the reversion of Okinawa Prefecture to Japan. The unified theme of the exposition was "The Ocean-Its Desirable Future," 36 countries, including Japan, three international organizations and seven private companies participated in the exposition, making it the largest special exposition in history at the time. The holding of the Ocean Expo led to a dramatic increase in the development of Okinawa Prefecture. National roads were widened and improved, and large hotels and other tourist facilities were built accordingly. The final number of visitors was only about 3.49 million against the target of 4.5 million. This result discouraged those who had planned various business activities in anticipation of the Ocean Expo, and innkeepers and others complained that it was not a catalyst, but a self-destruct mechanism. After the Expo, the site was turned into the National Ocean Expo Memorial Park. The "Marine Life Park" has now been renamed the "Okinawa *Churaumi* Aquarium" and continues to operate as the core facility in the park. Aqua-polis was built as an image of a "maritime city of the future" and was a symbol of the Ocean Expo, but in October 2000, it was sold as scrap metal to a U.S. company.

(4) SACO 合意

　SACO は、「Special Action Committee On Okinawa」の略で、1995 年 9 月に沖縄本島で起きた米海兵隊員らによる小学女児暴行事件を契機に設置された。沖縄における米軍基地の過重負担解消を協

議する特別委員会で、1996 年 12 月 2 日に最終報告が合意された。合意内容には、普天間飛行場を含む県内の米軍施設 11 カ所の返還、米軍機の騒音対策、日米地位協定の運用改善の推進などが盛り込まれた。しかし、その実態は米軍が使用していない土地の返還だけで、最大の懸案であった普天間飛行場は、合意から 25 年以上経っても返還のメドが立っていない。SACO 合意はもはや破綻しているという意見も多い。

普天間飛行場（2.700 m の滑走路を持ち、嘉手納飛行場と並んで沖縄におけるアメリカ軍の拠点である）
Futenma Airfield has a 2.700-meter runway and, along with Kadena Airfield, is the base for the U.S. military in Okinawa (surrounded by schools such as elementary, junior high, high school, and univercity, as well public facilities such as government offices)

（4）SACO agreement

SACO, which stands for "Special Action Committee On Okinawa," was established in response to the assault of an elementary school girl by U.S. Marines on the main island of Okinawa in September 1995. This was a special committee to discuss the elimination of the overburden of U.S. military bases in Okinawa, and its final report was agreed upon on December 2, 1996. The agreement included the return of 11 U.S. military facilities in the prefecture, including the Futenma Air Station, measures to reduce the noise level of U.S. military aircraft, and the promotion of operational improvements to the Status of Forces Agreement between Japan and the United States. However, the reality is that the only thing that has happened is the return of land that is no longer used by the U.S. military, and the Futenma Air Station, which was the biggest concern, has not been returned even more than 25 years after the agreement was reached. Many argue that the SACO agreement is no longer in order.

（5）辺野古新基地建設（へのこしんきちけんせつ）

1995 年に県内で発生した米海兵隊員らによる少女暴行事件を契機に、沖縄では米軍基地の撤去・整理縮小、普天間基地の返還や日米地位協定の見直しなどを要求する運動が燃え上がった。1996 年、日米両政府は、県内に別の飛行場を建設することを条件に、今後 5 ～ 7 年以内に普天間基地を返還することで合意した。普天間基地の移設先について様々な候補地が検討されたが、日本政府は 1998 年、名護市辺野古のキャンプ・シュワブ沿岸への新基地建設を閣議決定した。

普天間飛行場の周囲には住宅地や学校が密集しており、2003 年に上空から視察したラムズフェルド米国防長官（当時）は「世界一危険な飛行場」と表現した。2009 年の国政選挙で政権を取った鳩山由起夫首相は、普天間基地の移設について「最低でも県外に移設すべき」と述べ、普天間基地の撤去と米軍基地の縮小を求める県民の期待が高まった。しかし、県外移設に難色を示すアメリカ側の意向などもあり、鳩山首相は翌年 5 月、辺野古地区への飛行場建設に方針転換し多くの県民の期待は裏切られた。2012 年の国政選挙で、民主党が敗北し自民党が政権与党に復帰すると、辺野古移設計画が始動し 2018 年 12 月には埋め立て工事が始まった。

その後、建設予定地の海底に当初予想していなかった軟弱地盤が発見され、地盤改良工事が必要になった。さらに、埋め立て予定地に生息している貴重なサンゴ類の移植問題や県民の根強い反対などで工事は大幅に遅れている。時期の見通しは不透明だが、完成すると辺野古は 1800 メートルの V 字型滑走路 2 本を備えた巨大基地となる。

(5) Construction of a new base in Henoko

The 1995 assault of a young girl in Okinawa by U.S. Marines sparked a movement in Okinawa demanding the removal and downsizing of U.S. military bases, the return of the Futenma base, and a review of the Japan-U.S. Status of Forces Agreement. In 1996, the Japanese and U.S. governments agreed that the Futenma base would be returned within the next five to seven years, but with the condition that another airfield would be built in Okinawa Prefecture. Various candidate sites were considered for the relocation of Futenma Air Base, but in 1998, the Japanese government made a cabinet decision to build a new base along the coast of Camp Schwab in Henoko, Nago City.

The area surrounding Futenma Air Station is densely populated with residential areas and schools, and U.S. Secretary of Defense Rumsfeld, who inspected it from the air in 2003, described it as "the most dangerous airfield in the world". Prime Minister Hatoyama Yukio, who came to power in the 2009 national elections, stated that the Futenma base should be relocated "at least outside of the Okinawa prefecture," which raised the expectations of the people of the prefecture for the removal of the Futenma base and the reduction of U.S. military bases. However, in May of the following year, Prime Minister Hatoyama changed his policy to build an airfield in the Henoko area, partly due to the U.S.' reluctance to relocate the airfield outside of the prefecture, and the expectations of many prefectural residents were betrayed. After the Democratic Party of Japan (DPJ) was defeated and the Liberal Democratic Party (LDP) returned to power in the 2012 national election, the Henoko relocation plan was launched, and landfill construction began in December 2018.

Subsequently, soft ground was discovered on the seabed of the planned construction site, which had not been expected at the time, and ground improvement work became necessary. Furthermore, the construction work has been significantly delayed due to the problems of transplanting valuable corals inhabiting the planned landfill site and the deep-rooted opposition of Okinawans. The time frame is uncertain, but when completed, Henoko will be a huge base with two 1,800-meter V-shaped runways.

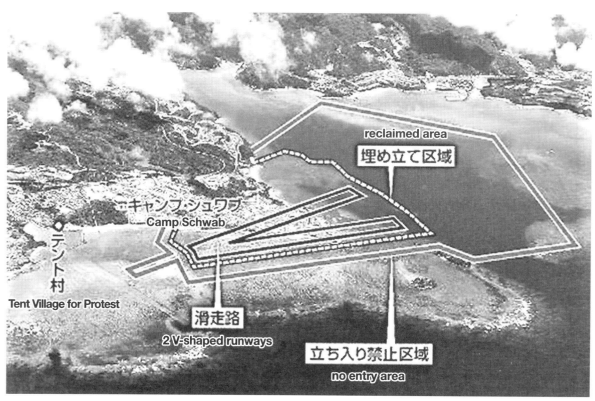

Ｖ字型滑走路 2 本が造られる予定の米軍辺野古新基地（名護市辺野古）
New U.S. military base at Henoko, where two V-shaped runways are to be built（Henoko, Nago City）

第9章　沖縄から世界へ

（1）ソテツ地獄（そてつじごく）

　大正末期から昭和初期にかけて起きた恐慌は、沖縄では「ソテツ地獄」と呼ばれた。当時の沖縄の人口は約60万人で、その7割が農民であった。しかも、その多くが零細農家でサトウキビを主作物とする農業を営んでおり、沖縄の出荷品の8割を砂糖が占めていた。第一次世界大戦後の国際的な砂糖価格の暴落によって沖縄の経済は深刻な影響を受けた。極度の不況のため、米はおろか芋さえも口にできず多くの農民が野生のソテツを食料にした。毒性を持つソテツは調理法を誤ると死の危険性があったが、その実や幹で飢えを凌ぐほど疲弊していた。さらに台風や干魃が追い打ちをかけたため県民の暮らしは文字通り地獄の様相を呈した。多額の借金を抱え、どうにもならない農家では、最後の手段として身売りが公然と行われた。男性は漁業に従事する糸満に、女性は遊女として辻の遊郭に売られた。それでも農民の生活が好転することはなく、海外移民や本土への出稼ぎとなって沖縄を出て行く人々も増えていった。

沖縄各地に自生する蘇鉄（左が雌株、右は雄株）
Female (left) and male (right) *sotetsu* plants growing wild in various parts of Okinawa

Chapter 9 From Okinawa to the World

（1）*Sotetsu-jigoku*（Hell of the Cycads）

　The depression that occurred from the end of the Taisho era (1912-1926) to the beginning of the Showa era (1926-1989) was called *Sotetsu-jigoku* in Okinawa. At that time, Okinawa had a population of about 600,000, 70% of which were farmers. Moreover, many of them were smallholder farmers, farming sugarcane as their main crop, and sugar accounted for 80% of Okinawa's shipments. Okinawa's economy was severely impacted by the international sugar price crash after World War I. Due to the extreme depression, many farmers were unable to eat rice or even sweet potatoes, so they turned to wild cycads for food. The toxic cycads were potentially deadly if cooked incorrectly, but they were so exhausted that they were able to survive their hunger with their fruits and trunks. In addition, typhoons and droughts followed, and the lives of the people of the prefecture literally went to hell. For farmers who were heavily in debt and unable to cope with the situation, selling themselves were openly practiced as a last resort. Boys were sold to fishermen in Itoman to engage in fishing while girls were sold in the entertainment quarters in Tsuji, Naha as prostitutes. Even so, the lives of the farmers did not improve, and more and more people left Okinawa to emigrate overseas or to work on the mainland.

（2）海外移民（かいがいいみん）

①日本の海外移民（にほんのかいがいいみん）

　1853 年のペリー提督の浦賀来航、1854 年の日米和親条約締結によって日本は長い鎖国政策が解かれた。1858 年に日米修好通商条約を調印した後、日本はオランダ・ロシア・イギリス・フランスとも同様の条約を締結した。その結果、外国人が日本に出入国できるようになり、1866 年（慶応 2 年）には日本人の商用と学業を目的とした海外渡航が認められた。捕鯨船の中継補給基地として繁栄したハワイ王国は、その後の国の経済を支える砂糖農園で必要な労働力を確保するため海外からの移民を受け入れた。ハワイから要請された江戸幕府は江戸と横浜で募集し、150 人ほど（女性 6 人含む）を選び新暦の 1868 年 5 月 17 日、英国籍の 3 本マストの帆船・サイオト号で横浜港を出港し、6 月 19 日にハワイに上陸した。奴隷のような過酷な条件下で、サトウキビ畑や製糖工場での労働に日本人は激しく抵抗し、度々ストライキを行った。アメリカのハワイ併合後の 1900 年（明治 33 年）には既存の労働契約が全て無効となり、厳しい労働条件が緩和された。1924 年の排日移民法成立までに約 22 万人がハワイへ渡っている。

　その後の本格的な海外移住は 1908 年（明治 41 年）、158 家族（781 人）を乗せて神戸港を出港した移民船「笠戸丸（かさとまる）」によるブラジル移民から始まる。ブラジルのコーヒー農園はアフリカ大陸からの奴隷によって運営されていたが、奴隷制度が廃止されたことにより労働力不足に陥った。一方、日本経済は 1904 年の日露戦争で悪化していた。日本人のブラジルへの大規模な移民は、日本とブラジル双方の思惑が一致した結果であった。笠戸丸はシンガポールや南アフリカのケープタウンを経由し、50 日間の旅を経て、6 月 18 日にブラジルのサントス港に到達した。6 月 18 日は「日本から海外各地に移住した人々の歴史や、国際社会への貢献などを振り返り、日本と移住先の国々との友好関係を促進するための日」と位置づけられ、1966 年、「海外移住の日」として制定された。

ブラジルのサントス港に入港した笠戸丸(1908 年)
The Kasato Maru in the port of Santos, Brazil, in 1908

(2) Overseas immigration

① Japanese Overseas Immigration

　Commodore Perry's arrival in Uraga in 1853 and the conclusion of the Treaty of Amity between Japan and the United States in 1854 broke Japan's long seclusion policy. After signing the Treaty of Amity and Commerce between Japan and the United States in 1858, Japan concluded similar treaties with the Netherlands, Russia, the United Kingdom, and France. As a result, not only were foreigners allowed to enter and leave Japan, but in 1866 (Keio 2), Japanese were allowed to travel abroad for business and academic purposes. The Kingdom of Hawaii, which prospered as a relay supply base for whalers, accepted immigrants from abroad to secure the labor force needed for the sugar plantations that would later support the nation's economy. At the request of Hawaii, the Edo shogunate recruited in Edo and Yokohama, and selected about 150 people (including six women) to leave Yokohama Harbor on May 17, 1868, the new calendar year, aboard the three-masted British-flagged sailing ship Scioto, and landed in Hawaii on June 19. Under slave-like harsh conditions, the Japanese violently resisted working in the sugar cane fields and sugar mills, and frequently went on strike. After the U.S. annexation of Hawaii, all existing labor contracts were nullified in 1900, and harsh working conditions were relaxed. About

220,000 people came to Hawaii until the passage of the Exclusion of Japanese Immigrants Act of 1924.

Subsequent full-scale emigration overseas began in 1908 (Meiji 41), when the emigrant ship "Kasato Maru" departed from Kobe Port with 158 families (781 people) to emigrate to Brazil. Brazilian coffee plantations were run by slaves from the African continent, but the abolition of slavery led to a labor shortage. Meanwhile, the Japanese economy was deteriorating due to the Russo-Japanese War of 1904. The large-scale Japanese immigration to Brazil was the result of a coincidence of intentions on the part of both Japan and Brazil. The Kasato Maru reached the port of Santos, Brazil, on June 18, after 50 days of travel via Singapore and Cape Town, South Africa. June 18 was designated as "Overseas Emigration Day" in 1966 to "reflect on the history of emigrants from Japan to other countries and their contributions to the international community, and to promote friendly relations between Japan and the countries to which they emigrated".

②元年者（がんねんもの）

1868 年にハワイに渡った約 150 人の一団は、日本から海外に集団で移り住んだ最初の人々となった。日本の元号が 1868 年 10 月に明治元年になったので、彼らは後に「元年者」（がんねんもの）と呼ばれるようになった。ハワイ上陸後の 2 週間後には、3 年契約でハワイ各島の砂糖農園へ移ったが、一部はオアフ島ホノルルに残り欧米人の従者として働いた。過酷な労働や差別によって約 40 人が契約期間満了を待たずに 1870 年 1 月に帰国したが、移民の多くが契約期間満了後もハワイに定着し、日系ハワイ人としてハワイ社会の基礎を作り上げていった。

② *Gan'nen-mono* (people who emigrated overseas in the first year of Meiji)

A group of about 150 people immigrated to Hawaii in 1868, becoming the first people from Japan to move overseas as a group. Because Japanese era name was changed to Meiji in October 1868, they were later called *Gan'nen-mono*. Two weeks after landing in Hawaii, they were transferred to sugar plantations on the Hawaiian islands under a three-year contract, but some remained in Honolulu, Oahu, to work as a squire for Westerners. Due to harsh labor and discrimination, about 40 of them returned to Japan in January1870 before their contracts expired, but many of the immigrants remained in Hawaii after their contracts expired and built the foundation of Hawaiian society as Japanese Hawaiians.

③沖縄県の海外移民（おきなわけんのかいがいいみん）

沖縄からの海外移民は、移民の父と呼ばれる當山久三の尽力によって 1899 年（明治 32 年）のハワイに上陸した 26 人から始まった。その後、1900 年頃から本格化し、戦前はハワイやフィリピンなどへの移住が多かったが、戦後はペルーやブラジル等、南米への移住が圧倒的に多くなった。その間に沖縄では「ソテツ地獄」に代表される経済危機が起きたが、その都度、移民した県系人からの経済援助が行われた。1929 年の世界恐慌時には、海外から沖縄への送金額が県歳入額の 66.4% に上った。海外移民の主な理由は、当時の沖縄が非常に貧しかったことだが、地割制が廃止され土地を自由に売買できるようになったことや、移民会社や移民指導者の存在、徴兵忌避など、当時の社会を取り巻く環境が海外への移住を後押しした。明治 32 年（1899 年）から昭和 13 年（1938 年）までの移民数は 72,134 人で、これは昭和 15 年（1940 年）当時の沖縄県人口の約 12% に相当するといわれる。都道府県別の移民数では、沖縄県は 2 位の東京

當山久三の銅像（金武町金武）
Bronze statue of Touyama Kyuzou
(Kin, Kin Town)

都よりも多く、沖縄県が「全国一の移民県」といわれる所以である。沖縄の海外移民を語る時に必ず紹介されるのが現在の金武町出身の當山久三。小学校の教員であった當山は、自由民権運動の指導者でもあり、後に沖縄県議会議員を務めたが、海外移住計画に熱心に取り組み、沖縄からハワイへの移民を実現させた。

③ Overseas immigration from Okinawa

Overseas immigration from Okinawa began with 26 people landing in Hawaii in 1899 through the efforts of Touyama Kyuzo, known as the father of immigration. After that, the migration started in earnest around 1900. Before the war, most of the immigrants went to Hawaii and the Philippines, but after the war, the overwhelming majority went to South America, including Peru and Brazil. In the meantime, Okinawa experienced economic hardships typified by the "cycad hell," but each time economic assistance was provided by immigrant prefectural residents. During the Great Depression of 1929, remittances from overseas to Okinawa amounted to 66.4% of the prefecture's revenue. The main reason for overseas immigration was the fact that Okinawa was very poor at the time, but the environment surrounding the society at the time, such as the abolition of the land division system and the ability to freely buy and sell land, the existence of immigration companies and immigration leaders, and escape from the draft, encouraged people to move overseas. The number of immigrants from 1899 to 1938 was 72,134, which is said to be about 12% of the population of Okinawa Prefecture in 1940. In terms of the number of immigrants by prefecture, Okinawa Prefecture ranks first in Japan, with more immigrants than Tokyo, which ranks second, which is why Okinawa Prefecture is called "the nation's largest immigrant prefecture". When talking about Okinawa's overseas immigrants, Touyama Kyuzo from present-day Kin Town is always introduced. As an elementary school teacher, Touyama was also a leader of the Civil Liberties Movement and later served as a member of the Okinawa Prefectural Assembly, but he worked diligently on the overseas migration program, and realized the immigration from Okinawa to Hawaii.

(3) 県民のハワイ移住（けんみんの はわいいじゅう）

　日本人のハワイ移民は 1868 年から開始されたが、沖縄からの移民は 1899 年が最初である。沖縄移民は 12 月 5 日に那覇港を出発し、横浜港で「チャイナ号」に乗船してハワイに向かい、翌 1900 年 1 月 8 日、ホノルル港に到着した。オアフ島のサトウキビ耕地で 26 人が契約移民として働き始めたが、1 日 10 時間労働で日当わずか 69 セントであった。厳しい監督者の監視の下、安い労賃と重労働で牛馬のように酷使された。1900 年 4 月、米国移民法がハワイにも適用され、ハワイでの契約移民は廃止となり、第 1 回の移民は 3 ヶ月で自由の身となった。1903 年には第 2 陣として 45 人の移民がハワイに送り出された。その後は徐々にハワイブームとなり大正期まで続いた。1924 年（大正 13）には米

ハワイ沖縄センター（オアフ島）。沖縄県人のハワイ移住 90 周年を記念して 1990 年 6 月に完成した沖縄県人会活動の拠点（沖縄タイムス社）
Hawaii Okinawa Center(Oahu Island). The base of Okinawan-*Kenjin* Association activities,completed in June 1990 to commemorate the 90th anniversary of the immigration of Okinawans to Hawaii.

国で「排日移民法」が制定され門戸が閉ざされたので、それ以後の移民先はペルーやボリビアなど南米諸国に移った。沖縄は日本人のハワイ移民としては後発であったが、戦後のハワイとの強固な関係などから、現在ではウチナーンチュがハワイの日系人の中で重要な位置を占めている。オアフ島・真珠湾の西側にある砂糖産業が盛んな「ワイピオ地区」が、沖縄からの最初の入植者が働いた場所であった。ワイピオには「ハワイオキナワセンター」が建てられており、イベント会場にも使用される大きな建物の琉球瓦の屋根にはシーサーが設置されている。敷地内には沖縄庭園や石敢當もあり、移民の父・當山久三の銅像が建てられている。

(3) Okinawan immigration to Hawaii

Japanese immigration to Hawaii was in 1868, and from Okinawa in 1899. The immigrants from Okinawa departed Naha Port on December 5, and boarded the "China" bound for Hawaii at Yokohama Port, arriving at Honolulu Port on January 8, 1900. Twenty-six people began working as contract immigrants in the sugar cane fields of Oahu, earning only 69 cents a day for a 10-hour day. Under the watchful eye of strict supervisors, they were abused like cattle and horses with cheap wages and hard labor. In April 1900, the U.S. Immigration Act was applied to Hawaii, abolishing contract immigrants in Hawaii, and the first immigrants were set free within three months. In 1903, the second batch of 45 immigrants were sent to Hawaii. After that, Hawaii gradually boomed and continued until the Taisho era. In 1924, the U.S. enacted the "Japan Exclusion and Immigration Act," which closed the door to immigrants, so, the immigrants moved to Peru, Bolivia and other South American countries. Okinawa was a latecomer to Hawaii as a Japanese immigrant, but *uchinanchu* now occupy an important position among Hawaii's *Nikkei*, mainly due to the strong relationship with Hawaii after the war. Located west of Pearl Harbor on the island of Oahu, the Waipio area, with its thriving sugar industry, was where the first settlers from Okinawa worked. "The Hawaii Okinawa Center" was built in Waipio, and there is a *shiisaa* on the Ryukyu tile roof of the large building that is also used as an event venue. There is also an Okinawan garden and an *ishigantou* on the premises, and a bronze statue of Touyama Kyuzo, the "father of immigrants," has been erected.

(4) 海から豚がやってきた
（うみからぶたがやってきた）

1945 年の沖縄戦（地上戦）で沖縄は壊滅的な被害を受け焦土と化した。惨状は、沖縄戦を直接体験した帰還兵たちによってハワイに伝えられた。郷里を憂えた沖縄県系人たちは募金集めに奔走し、豚 550 頭を購入して食糧難に苦しんでいた沖縄に送った。1948 年 8 月 31 日、7 人のウチナーンチュが船（オーウェン号）に乗り込んで出港したが、激しい暴風雨やまだ残っていた洋上に浮遊する機雷を避けながらの航行のため航路が長くなり、うるま市平敷屋のホワイトビーチに到着したのは約 1 ヶ月後であった。豚は広く公平に分配され、4 年後には 10 万頭まで増えた。沖縄県民とハワイのウチナーンチュの堅い絆を象徴するこ

オーウェン号内の豚（沖縄県公文書館所蔵）
Pigs being sent to Okinawa aboard the Owen

の逸話は、沖縄の代表的食文化の一つである豚肉文化を継続させ戦後復興に大きく貢献した。ハワイを中心に始まったこの運動は、やがてアメリカ本土や南米へ広がり、世界中のウチナーンチュからの暖かい支援が沖縄へ届いた。この史実を継承し、後世に歴史と意義を形として残したいという思いから記念碑建立実行委員会が発足。2016 年 3 月、うるま市民芸術劇場の敷地内に記念碑が建立された。

（4）Pigs came from the sea (*umi-kara-buta-ga-yattekita*)

　The Battle of Okinawa (ground war) in 1945 left Okinawa devastated and turned into a scorched earth. The devastation was conveyed to Hawaii by returning soldiers who had experienced the Battle of Okinawa firsthand. Concerned about their homeland, Hawaiian *Uchinanchu*, scrambled to raise funds and purchased 550 pigs to send to Okinawa, which was suffering from food shortages. On August 31, 1948, seven *uchinanchu* boarded a ship (the Owen) and set sail, but it took them about a month to arrive at White Beach in Heshikiya, Uruma City, due to a violent storm and the need to avoid the mines that were still floating in the ocean. The pigs were distributed widely and fairly, and after four years, the number of pigs had increased to 100,000. This anecdote, symbolizing the strong bond between Okinawans and Hawaiian *uchinanchu*, contributed greatly to the post-war reconstruction by continuing the pork culture, one of Okinawa's representative food cultures. This movement, which began in Hawaii, eventually spread to the U.S. mainland and South America, and warm support from *uchinanchu* around the world reached Okinawa. The committee for the erection of the monument was established with the hope of passing on this historical fact and leaving the history and significance of the event to future generations in a tangible form. In March 2016, a monument was erected on the grounds of the Uruma Civic Art Theater.

（5）世界のウチナーンチュ大会（せかいのうちなーんちゅたいかい）

　沖縄県は「移民県としての沖縄」の側面を持つ他に、歴史を紐解けば琉球王国が貿易国として繁栄していたことがあり、かつて首里城正殿に架けられていた「万国津梁の鐘」がまさしくその象徴であった。1899 年 12 月 5 日に那覇港を旅立った最初のハワイ移民者を皮切りに、小さな沖縄から広い世界へ雄飛したウチナーンチュたちがそれを実践したとも言える。先人たちは沖縄を遠く離れた国で新天地を開拓し、懸命な努力で困難を乗り越えた。各地で生活基盤を築き、異文化社会の中で根を下ろしながら、沖縄独自の伝統文化やアイデンティティを脈々と受け継いできた。

　世界のウチナーンチュ大会は、海外移民など沖縄にルーツをもつ沖縄県外の県系人を招待して沖縄県の主導で行われるイベント。ウチナーンチュの DNA を持つ多くの人々がさまざまな国の垣根を越え、言葉を超えて故郷・沖縄に戻り、交流を深める。1990 年 8 月 23 日 ～ 26 日、

第 1 回世界のウチナーンチュ大会（1990 年 8 月、沖縄コンベンションセンター）
The 1st Worldwide *Uchinanchu* Festival (August 1990, Okinawa Convention Center)

沖縄コンベンションセンターや宜野湾市立体育館などで行われた第1回大会では、海外19カ国から移民1世、2世を中心に約2,400人、入場者数約47万人が参加した。その後、ほぼ5年毎に継続的に開催され、県外に暮らす沖縄県系人が集うイベントとして定着している。

　同大会は、沖縄にゆかりのある人々が集い国際交流ネットワークを作り上げることを目的としている。海外に移住した沖縄県系人は今日、その子孫を含め約42万人が海外に居住していると推定されており、沖縄県の貴重な人的財産となっている。大会でのイベントでは、伝統的な琉球舞踊（琉舞）やエイサー、現代沖縄音楽、沖縄と海外の関係についての学術シンポジウム、海外の沖縄県系人の居住地の物産展など多岐にわたる。2022年の今年は沖縄の日本復帰50年目の節目にあたり、「第7回世界のウチナーンチュ大会」が10月30日の「世界のウチナーンチュの日」（前夜祭）から11月3日まで開催される。沖縄県主導による本大会の終了後は、参加者はそれぞれのルーツを持つ各自治体による歓迎会などのイベントにも引き続き参加する。その後も親戚宅などに長期滞在し、さらに交流を深める人も多い。

（5）The Worldwide *Uchinanchu* Festival

In addition to the aspect of "Okinawa as an immigrant prefecture," if you unravel the history of Okinawa, you will find that the Ryukyu Kingdom prospered as a trading nation, and the *Bankoku-Shinryo-no-Kane* (Bell of Bridging the Nations) once hung in the main hall of Shuri Castle was truly a symbol of this. It can be said that the first Hawaiian immigrants who left the port of Naha on December 5, 1899 were the first to do so, and the *uchinanchu* who soared from tiny Okinawa to the wider world put this into practice. Our predecessors overcame difficulties through their hard work and efforts to develop a new land in a country far away from Okinawa. While building their livelihood in various places and putting down roots in different cultural societies, they have inherited Okinawa's unique traditional culture and identity from generation to generation.

The Worldwide *Uchinanchu* Festival is an Okinawa Prefecture-led event held by inviting people of Okinawan descent from outside Okinawa who have roots in Okinawa, such as overseas immigrants from Okinawa. Many people with DNA of *uchinanchu* will return to their hometown Okinawa, transcending various national boundaries and languages to deepen exchanges. The first convention, held at the Okinawa Convention Center and Ginowan Municipal Gymnasium from August 23 to 26, 1990, attracted approximately 2,400 participants, mostly first-and second-generation immigrants from 19 foreign countries, and 470,000 visitors. Since then, the event has been held continuously almost every five years and has become an established event for Okinawans living outside of the prefecture to gather.

The purpose of the convention is to bring together people with connections to Okinawa to create an international exchange network. It is estimated that about 420,000 people of Okinawan descent who emigrated overseas are living abroad today, including their descendants, making them a valuable human asset for Okinawa Prefecture. Events at the convention include traditional Ryukyuan dance (*Ryubu*) and *Eisaa*, contemporary Okinawan music, an academic symposium on Okinawa's relationship with the rest of the world, and a product exhibition of Okinawan descent living abroad. This year, 2022, marks the 50th anniversary of Okinawa's reversion to Japan, and the "7th Worldwide *Uchinanchu* Festival" will be held from October 30, the "Worldwide *Uchinanchu* Day" (eve of the festival) through November 3. After the conclusion of the Okinawa Prefecture-led event, participants will continue to participate in welcoming parties and other events organized by the local governments of their respective roots. And many of them continue to stay at relatives' homes for extended periods of time afterward to further deepen exchanges.

（6）世界のウチナーンチュの日（せかいのうちなーんちゅのひ）

　2016年10月30日、第6回世界のウチナーンチュ大会の閉会式で、当時の翁長雄志知事より、海外の沖縄県人によるウチナーネットワークの継承と発展の願いを込め、毎年10月30日を「世界のウチナーンチュの日」に制定することが宣言され、沖縄県の記念日となった。世界のウチナーンチュ大会は5年に一度、開催されており、かつて沖縄から旅だった海外移民の子孫である県系人の方が多く参加する。参加者の中には、県系人ではないが「沖縄が大好き」という人も多く、ウチナーネットワークは世界中に広がっている。今日、世界には約42万人のウチナーンチュがいるといわれ、彼らは、戦前・戦後における困窮した沖縄経済を救ってくれた。最近でも、2019年10月31日に発生した首里城火災の後、直ちに各国の県人会で首里城再建のための募金活動が行われた。沖縄県では、「世界のウチナーンチュの日」の認知度を高めるため2017年から毎年10月30日にトークイベントを開催している。2022年の第7回世界のウチナーンチュ大会では、前夜祭パレードがその日に行われる。

（6）The World *Uchinanchu* Day（*Sekaino-Uchinanchu-no-hi*）

　On October 30, 2016, at the closing ceremony of the 6th Worldwide *Uchinanchu* Festival, then-Governor Onaga Takeshi proclaimed that October 30 of every year would be established as the "World *Uchinanchu* Day"

in the hope that Okinawans overseas would inherit and develop the *uchina* network, making it a commemorative day for Okinawa Prefecture. The Worldwide *Uchinanchu* Festival is held once every five years and is attended by many prefectural residents who are descendants of overseas immigrants who once traveled from Okinawa. Many of the participants, who are not prefectural residents but "love Okinawa," also participated in the event, and the *uchina* network is spreading throughout the world. Today, there are some 420,000 *Uchinanchu* in the world, and they helped save the impoverished Okinawan economy before and after World War II. Most recently, after a fire broke out at Shuri Castle on October 31, 2019, a fundraising drive for the reconstruction of Shuri Castle was immediately organized by prefectural associations from different countries. Since 2017, Okinawa Prefecture has held an annual talk event on October 30 to raise awareness of the "World *Uchinanchu* Day". The 7th Worldwide *Uchinanchu* Festival in 2022 will be held on October 30, with the pre-festival parade.

第6回世界のウチナーンチュ大会パレード
（2016年10月、那覇市国際通り）
The 6th Worldwide *Uchinanchu* Festival Parade
(Kokusai Street, Naha City, October 2016)

おわりに

　沖縄県は、1372年に察度王が琉球国王として明国皇帝から冊封を受けてから1879年（明治12年）の廃藩置県までの約500年間、独立した国（琉球王国）であった。その間、琉球王国は中国を宗主国として自らを臣下とし、国王が替わると中国皇帝の承認（冊封）を得て初めて正式な国王になれた。1609年に薩摩藩に侵略されて以降、その南海の王国は、270年の長きにわたり日中両大国に両属する独立国という特殊な歴史を歩み続けた。

　沖縄では祭祀儀礼にみられるように、はるか海の彼方に「ニライカナイ」と呼ばれる他界（楽土）の存在が古来より認識されてきた。豊穣や人間の幸福・生命はそこからもたらされるという「ニライカナイ思想」がそれである。それに基づき、外から来る人たちは「富をもたらす福の神」で、歓迎すべきお客さんという考えがウチナーンチュのホスピタリティの原点で、海を越えて外から来る人には実に親切なのである。沖縄の人たちはこの島を「蓬莱の島」と呼び、自らが世界を繋ぐ架け橋になろうとした。1458年に鋳造され首里城に架けられた「万国津梁の鐘」にその決意を内外に高らかに宣言している。

　大交易時代の15世紀には、中国・日本・朝鮮・東南アジア各地の貿易船が那覇港に入港し、東アジアでも有数の中継貿易港として賑わった。一方で、当時の那覇には「漂流民」や「倭寇」にさらわれ転売された人々の姿もあった。倭寇にとって、東アジアにおける重要な「奴隷市場」であり、海港都市・那覇には光と影の二つの顔があったといわれる。1512年からしばらくマラッカ商館に勤めたポルトガル人が琉球人（レキオ）の性格について記録を残している。それによると、「レキオ人は正直な人間で、奴隷を買わないし、たとえ全世界との引き替えでも自分たちの同胞を売ることはしない。彼らはこれについては死を賭ける」。当時、東南アジアの人々の間で「正直な人間」として知られていた琉球人の活躍を示す記録である。

　首里城の城郭内へ入る第一の正門は「歓会門」（かんかいもん）と呼ばれる。歓会とは「歓迎する」という意味で、王朝時代に中国皇帝の命を受けた使者「冊封使」たちを歓迎するという意図からこの名称がつけられた。この門は「あまえ御門」（あまんじょう）という別名を持つが、「あまえ」とは『おもろさうし』にも出ている琉球古語で、「神と人間が一体となって歓喜すること」を意味する。さらに、首里城跡の入り口西方にある門は尚清王時代（1527～55）に創建され、当初は「待賢門」（たいけんもん）と呼ばれていた。「賢い人を待つ門」という意味で、賢い人とは中国皇帝の名代である冊封使一行を指す。後に「首里」の文字を掲げ「首里門」と俗称されたが、尚育王時代の1664年から「守禮之邦」という扁額が常に掲げられ、「守礼門」と称するようになった。この門によって「琉球は礼節を守り、文化の進んだ国」であることを彼らに示したのである。首里城はじめ沖縄の各城の城壁は曲線や曲面で出来ている。その構造は防御面だけでなく、来訪者に威圧感を与えず、ゆるさ・優しさを醸し出す効果もあるといわれる。それに対して中国側は、歴代冊封使の正・副使に科挙のトップ合格者などの超エリートたちを採用し、決して琉球を見下すようなことはなかった。本書では表紙に首里城正門の「歓会門」を、裏表紙に「万国津梁の鐘」の写真を使用した。激動する国際社会の中で、かつてナポレオン皇帝をも驚嘆させた「琉球王国の誇りと心の豊かさ」を感じるのである。

　チャンプルー料理のみならず、沖縄版オペラ・組踊や首里城・勝連城跡などの世界遺産は「中国にも日本にもない沖縄独自の産物」である。沖縄という小さな島は、黒潮という大きな流れとともにやって来る異国の珍しい漂着物を独自にうまく取り入れ、世界に認められるチャンプルー文化を開花させた。異文化に接する際、ウチナーンチュは「これはいいが、あれはダメだ」という排他的な考えはなく、「これもいいし、あれもいい」と迎え入れた。チャンプルー文化は小国が諸国との争いを避け、生き延びる知恵でもある。

　琉球王国はアジアの交差点に位置し、20世紀に入っても大国からの攻撃に晒される地理的環境下にあった。絶えず列強諸国に翻弄されながらも、沖縄は注意深く相手国を見つめて考え、懸命に、そして賢明に生き抜いた王国だった。明治政府による強引な琉球処分によって王国が解体されても、沖縄戦後の米軍統治下においても自らのアイデンティティを失うことなく沖縄であり続けた理由がそこにある。

　今や世界中に約42万人いると言われる琉球王国にルーツを持つウチナーンチュたち。琉球・沖縄の長くて特異な歴史や、世界で活躍するウチナーンチュを見ると、小さな「琉球王国」が実は「琉球大国（おうごく）」であったように思える。読者にもそのことを感じとってほしい。

　最後になりましたが、本書が読者諸氏の沖縄学習に少しでもお役に立てれば、著者としてこれ以上の喜びはありません。

2022年10月30日（世界のウチナーンチュの日）　宮城信夫

Afterword

Okinawa Prefecture was an independent country (Kingdom of Ryukyu) for about 500 years, from the time King Satto received the title from the Ming Emperor as King of Ryukyu in 1372 until the abolition of the prefecture in 1879. During that time, the Ryukyu Kingdom had become a vassal state of China, the suzerain nation, and when the king was replaced, he could only become the official king with the approval of the Chinese emperor. After the invasion by the Satsuma Domain in 1609, the kingdom in the South Sea had a unique history of being as an independent country that belonged to both Japan and China for 270 years.

In Okinawa, the existence of another world (paradise) called *Niraikanai* far beyond the sea has been recognized since ancient times, as seen in rituals. The *Niraikanai* philosophy is that fertility, human happiness, and life are brought from there. Based on this concept, the origin of *uchinanchu* hospitality is the idea that people from outside are "gods of good fortune" who bring wealth and should be welcomed as guests, and they are very kind to people who come from beyond the sea. The Okinawans called this island *Horai-no-shima* and tried to become a bridge between the world themselves. This determination is proclaimed to the world in the *Bankoku-shinryo-no-kane* cast in 1458 and hung on Shuri Castle.

During the 15th century of the great trading period, trading ships from China, Japan, Korea, and Southeast Asia arrived at Naha Port which was one of the busiest transit trading ports in East Asia. On the other hand, there were also drifters and people kidnapped and resold by *wakou* (Japanese pirates) in Naha at that time. It is said that the seaport city of Naha, an important slave market in East Asia for Japanese pirates, had two faces: light and shadow. The Portuguese, who served in the Malacca trading post for some time from 1512, left a record of the character of the Ryukyuans (*Lequio*). According to the record, "The people of *Lequio* are honest people and will not buy slaves, nor will they sell their own people, even in exchange for the whole world, they will risk death for this. It is a record of the activities of Ryukyuans, who were known as "honest people" among the people of Southeast Asia at the time.

The first main gate to enter the Shuri Castle is called *Kankai-mon*. The word *Kankai* means welcome, and the name was given in order to welcome the *sappuu-shi*, which are envoys of the Chinese emperor during the dynastic period. This gate is also known as *Aman-jou* (*Amae-mon*), *amae* is an ancient Ryukyuan word that appears in *Omoro-soushi* (the songbook of God) and means "to rejoice in the union of gods and humans. In addition, the gate at the west of the entrance to the Shuri Castle was built during the reign of King Sho Sei

(1527-55), and was first called *Taiken-mon*. It means "the gate to wait for wise men," and the wise men is a delegation of envoys from the Chinese emperor. Later, it was commonly called *Shuri-mon* with the word Shuri on it, since 1664, during the reign of King Sho Iku, the gate has been called the *Shurei-mon* because it was always marked with a plaque that read *Shurei-no-kuni*. The plaque on the *Shurei-mon* showed them that Ryukyu is a country with advanced culture and respect for civility. The walls of Shuri Castle and other castles in Okinawa are made of curves and curved surfaces. It is said that the structure of the wall is not only defensive, but also has the effect of creating a sense of looseness and gentleness without intimidating visitors. China, on the other hand, never looked down on Ryukyu, assigning super elites such as those who had passed Chinese Imperial examination at the top of their class as regular and deputy envoys of successive generations of envoys. This book uses a photograph of the main gate of Shuri Castle, the *Kankai-mon*, on the front cover and the *Bankoku-Shinryo-no-Kane* on the back cover. This is because in the midst of the turbulent international society, I feel the "proud and richness of heart" of the Ryukyu Kingdom, which once astonished even Emperor Napoleon.

In addition to *champuruu* cuisine, Okinawa's version of opera, *kumi-odori*, and world heritage sites such as the ruins of Shuri Castle and Katsuren Castle are "unique products of Okinawa, not found in China or Japan". The small island of Okinawa has successfully and uniquely incorporated the exotic and rare flotsam that comes with the great Kuroshio Current, and has blossomed into a "*Champuruu* culture" recognized around the world. When dealing with other cultures, *uchinanchu* did not have an exclusive mindset of "this is good, but that is not good," but welcomed them with "this is good, and that is good". *Champuruu* culture is the wisdom of a small country to survive and avoid conflicts with other countries.

The Kingdom of Ryukyu was located at the crossroads of Asia, in a geographical environment that was exposed to attacks from major powers even in the 20th century. While constantly at the mercy of the powerful nations, Okinawa was a kingdom that carefully looked and thought about its opponents, and survived hard and wisely. This is the reason why even after the Meiji government forcibly dismantled the Kingdom of Ryukyu, and even under the U.S. military rule after the Battle of Okinawa, Okinawa continued to be Okinawa without losing its identity.

It is said that there are now about 420,000 *uchinanchu* around the world who have their roots in the Ryukyu Kingdom. Looking at the long and unique history of Ryukyu/Okinawa and the *uchinanchu* who are active in the world, I feel that the "Small Ryukyu Kingdom" was actually the "Great Ryukyu Kingdom," and I hope readers can feel that as well.

Finally, it would be my great pleasure as an author if this book could be of some help to readers in learning about Okinawa.

October 30, 2022 (The World *Uchinanchu* Day)　MIYAGI Nobuo

年 表

西 暦	琉 球 王	記　　　事
	旧石器時代	山下洞人（32,000年前）、港川人（22,000年前）
1157	天孫氏王朝	源為朝、伊豆大島に流罪
1165	二十五世王	源為朝、沖縄の運天港に漂着（伝説）
1166		源為朝、大里按司の妹を娶り尊敦が生まれる（伝説）
1185		壇ノ浦の戦いで平家が滅亡する
1186		平家軍3,000騎、南海に逃走（南走平家）
		天孫氏25世・大里思兼松金、逆臣・利勇に滅ぼされる
1187	舜天	舜天が利勇を討って王位に就く
1238	舜馬順熙	基益美王子が、舜馬順熙王として即位する
1249	義本	玉城王子が、義本王として即位する
1250		大飢饉と干魃で、島民の約半数が死亡する
1260	英祖	義本王が、英祖に王位を禅譲し身を隠す（この頃の沖縄の人口は約40,000人）
1266		奄美大島などが英祖王に入貢し、泊御殿を建設する
1292		元軍が6,000の兵で瑠求国（台湾か?）を攻める
1296		元軍が瑠求国を攻めて、130人を捕虜にする
1300	大成（大城）	英祖王の三男・中城王子が、大成王として即位する
1309	恵慈	大成王の次男・八重瀬王子が恵慈王として即位する
1314	玉城	恵慈王の四男・玉城王子が、玉城王として即位する。この頃、三山に分立する
		大里按司が与座按司を滅ぼして南山王を自称する
1322		本部大主が「仲北山」の今帰仁按司を滅ぼす
1337	西威	玉城王の四男・大城王子が、西威王として即位する
1340		丘春が今帰仁城を取り戻す
1350	察度	浦添按司・察度が、推されて中山王に即位する
1355		この頃、宮古島で与那覇原軍（1,000人）が暴動を起こす
1372		明国の太祖帝が、使者・楊裁を琉球へ派遣する
		察度王が、明王朝へ進貢を開始する
1380		南山王・承察度が、師惹を明に遣わし進貢を開始する
1383		北山王・伯尼芝が、模結習を明に遣わし進貢を開始する
1388		南山王叔・汪英紫が、明に進貢を開始する
		元国の王子・地保奴発が、琉球に流罪
1390		宮古・八重山が、中山に入貢する
1392		久米三十六性の帰化が始まる
		豊見城按司（汪応祖）が、漫湖でハーリー競漕を始める
1398	武寧	察度王の次男・宜野湾王子が武寧王として即位する
1402		尚巴志が、島添大里城を滅ぼす
1405		尚巴志が、中山・武寧王を追放する
1406	尚思紹	尚巴志の父・尚思紹が中山王に即位する
1415		南山の諸按司が達渤期を討って、他魯毎が南山王に即位する
1416		尚巴志が今帰仁城を攻め、攀安知王が滅ぶ

西　暦	琉球王 （県知事等）	記　　事
1422	尚巴志	父の死後、尚巴志が中山王に即位し、尚巴志の次男・尚忠が北山監守になる
1429		尚巴志王が、南山・他魯毎王を滅ぼして三山統一を成し遂げる
1439		尚巴志王が死去。金丸は伊是名島を出て国頭に渡る
1440	尚忠	北山監守・尚忠が即位。座喜味城主・護佐丸は中城城へ移封される
1451	尚金福	那覇浮島から安里の崇元寺まで長虹堤を築く
1453		尚志魯と尚布里が王位を争い、首里城が焼失（布里・志魯の乱）
1454	尚泰久	尚巴志の七男・越来王子が即位
1458		中城按司（護佐丸）が勝連按司（阿麻和利）に滅ぼされ、 阿麻和利は鬼大城に滅ぼされる（護佐丸・阿麻和利の乱）
1470	尚円	金丸がクーデターにより尚円王として即位する。（第二尚氏王統の始まり） 尚徳王は喜界島へ逃亡
1477	尚真	尚円王の世子・久米中城王子が 13 歳で即位し、尚真王を名乗る
1488		各地の城主を首里に移住開始（1526 年に完了）
1500		首里王府軍が八重山のオヤケアカハチを成敗
1600	尚寧	関ヶ原の戦い（日本）
1609		薩摩藩の侵略。以降、実質的な島津の支配下に置かれる
1771	尚穆	八重山で大津波（明和の大津波）による大被害、最大波高 85m
1853	尚泰	ペリー提督の来航（5 月）
1879	鍋島直彬	明治政府、「琉球処分」を敢行し沖縄県を設置する
1899	奈良原繁	最初の海外移民がハワイに向けて出港
1903		宮古・八重山の人頭税廃止
1914	大味久五郎	第一次世界大戦の勃発（〜 1918）
1944	泉守紀	学童疎開船「対馬丸」の沈没。10・10 空襲
1945	島田叡	3 月 26 日、沖縄の地上戦始まる。6 月 23 日、第 32 軍司令官・牛島満の自決 により組織的抵抗が終了
1951	比嘉秀平	サンフランシスコ講和条約・日米安全保障条約調印（52 年発効）
1953		第 1 回祖国復帰総決起大会の開催。奄美群島が日本復帰
1956	当間重鋼	米軍の強権的な土地使用に反対する「島ぐるみ闘争」起こる
1959		宮森小学校に米軍機墜落（死者 17 人、負傷者 121 人）
1960	大田政作	沖縄県祖国復帰協議会の結成。アイゼンハワー米大統領の沖縄訪問
1965	松岡政保	佐藤首相来沖「沖縄が復帰しない限り日本の戦後は終わらない」と声明。 イリオモテヤマネコ発見
1968	屋良朝苗	初の主席公選に屋良朝苗氏が当選。B52 が墜落、炎上
1969		佐藤・ニクソン会談で沖縄の 72 年返還が決まる
1970		戦後初の国会議員選挙の実施。コザで反米騒動（コザ事件）
1972		施政権が日本に返還され、沖縄県が誕生
1975	平良幸市	国際海洋博覧会開催（7 月 20 日〜 1976 年 1 月 18 日）
1978	野島武盛（副知事）	交通方法の変更（ナナサンマル）
1990	西銘順治	第 1 回世界のウチナーンチュ大会開催
1995	大田昌秀	米兵の少女暴行事件に抗議する県民総決起大会
1996		「象のオリ」、国による不法占拠状態となる。普天間飛行場の全面返還合意
2019	玉城デニー	首里城焼失
2022		第 7 回世界のウチナーンチュ大会開催。復帰 50 周年

Chronology of historical events

Western calendar	Ryukyu King's Name	Articles
Paleolithic Period		Yamashitadou-*jin* (3,2000 years ago), Minatogawa-*jin*(2,2000 years ago)
1157	Tenson Dynasty	Minamoto-no Tametomo was exiled to Izu Oshima
1165	The 25th King	Minamoto-no Tametomo washed ashore at Unten Port in Okinawa (legend)
1166		Tametomo married Ozato-*aji's* younger sister, and Sonton was born
1183		The Heike clan has fallen from the capital
1184		The Heike army was defeated by Minamoto-no Yoshitsune's army at Ichinotani
1185		The Heike was defeated by the Genji in decisive battle at Dan'noura
1186		The Heike army, with 3,000 cavalry, escaped from Yashima to the South Sea (Nanso Heike)
		Tenson 25th, King Ozato-Umikani-machigani, destroyed by his adversary, Riyu
1187	Shunten	Shunten defeated Riyu and ascended to the throne
1202		The Heike moved Emperor Antoku to the Jana Coutry
1205		Taira-no Sukemori, Taira-no Arimori, and Taira-no Yukimori moved to Amami Oshima
1238	Shumba Junki	Prince Kiyami was crowned King Shumba Junki
1249	Gihun	Prince Tamagusuku was crowned King Gihun
1250		The famine and drought killed about half of the islanders
1255		Eiso took over as *shisshii*, and the country was governed
1260	Eiso	King Gihun ceded the throne to Eiso and went into hiding (Okinawa's population about 40,000)
1266		Amami Island and other islands paid tribute to King Eiso and Tomari-*udun* was built
1292		6,000 Yuan soldiers invade Ryukyu Country (Taiwan?)
1296		Yuan forces invaded Ryukyu Country and captured 130 people
1300	Taisei	Prince Nakagusuku, the third son of King Eiso, was crowned King Taisei
1309	Eiji	Prince Eiji, the second son of King Taisei, was crowned King Eiji
1314	Tamagusuku	Prince Tamagusuku, the fourth son of King Eiji, was crowned King Tamagusuku
		Around this time, Ryukyu was divided into three kingdoms (Sanzan)
		Ozato-*aji* destroyed Yoza-*aji* and claimed to be King Nanzan
1322		Mutubu-*uhunushi* destroyed the Nakijin-*aji* of "Naka-Hokuzan"
1337	Irii	Prince Irii-uhugusuku, the fourth son of King Tamagusuku,was crowned King Irii
1340		Okaharu has recaptured Nakijin Castle
1350	Satto	Urasoe-*aji*, Satto,was recommended and enthroned as King of Chuzan
1355		Around this time, the Yonahabara army (1,000 men) came on the rampage on Miyako Island
1372		Emperor Taiso sent a messenger, Yousai, to Ryukyu
		King Satto(Chuzan Kingdom) began to send tributes to Ming Country(China)
1380		King Uzatu(Nanzan Kingdom) began to send tributes to Ming Country
1383		King Haniji(Hokuzan Kingdom) began to send tributes to Ming Country
1388		Eiji-*aji*(younger brother of King Uzatu) began to send tributes to Ming Country
		Chibonuhatsu, a prince of the Yuan, came to Ryukyu in exile
1390		Miyako and Yaeyama sent tributes to Chuzan
1392		The naturalization of Kume-*sanjuroku*-Sei into Ryukyu began
1392		Tomigusuku-*aji* (Yahusu) started a *haarii* race at Lake Manko
1406		Sho Hashi's father, Sho Shisyou, ascends to the throne as King of Chuzan

Western calendar	Ryukyu King/ PrefecturalGovernor	Articles
1416	Sho Shisyo	Sho Hashi attacked Nakijin Castle and King Han Anchi was destroyed
1429	Sho Hashi	King Sho Hashi destroyed the Nanzan and unified the three kingdoms
1453	Sho Taikyu	Sho Shiro and Sho Furi fought for the throne and Shuri Castle was burned down (Furi/ Shiro Rebellion)
1458		Nakagusuku-*aji*(Gosamaru) was destroyed by Katsuren-*aji*(Amawari), and Amawari was defeated by *Uni*-Uhugusuku.(Gosamaru/Amarari Rebellion)
1469	Sho Toku	Kanamaru asceded to the throne by *coup d'etat* and took the name of King Sho En,
1470	Sho En	(beginning of the Second Sho Dynasty), and King Sho Toku fled to Kikai Island
1477	Sho Shin	Prince Kume-Nakagusuku, a son of King Sho En's successor, ascended to the throne at the age of 13 and took the name of King Sho Shin
1488		Lords of castles from all over region began to move to Shuri(completed in 1526)
1500		Shuri royal army defeated Oyake Akahachi on Yaeyama
1600	Sho Nei	Battle of Sekigahara(Japan)
1609		Invasion of Satsuma and subsequent real domination of the Ryukyu Kingdom by Shimazu
1771	Sho Boku	Heavy damage from the Great Meiwa Tsunami in Yaeyama, maximum wave height 85m
1853	Sho Tai	Perry visited the Ryukyu Kingdom (May)
1879	Nabeshima.N	Abolished Kingdom; established *Ken*(Prefecture) "Disposal of the Ryukyu Kingdom"
1899	Narahara.S	The first emigrants left for Hawaii
1903		*Nintou-jei*(poll taxation) in Miyako & Yaeyama Islands abolished
1914	Omi.K	Outbreak of World War I (until 1918)
1944	Izumi.S	The Tsushima Maru, a ship for evacuation of school children, sunk; Oct.10 Air Raids
1945	Shimada.A	Battle of Okinawa began March 26; organized resistance ended (June 23 by the suicide of Ushijima Mitsuru , commander of the 32nd Army)
1951	Higa.S	San Francisco Peace Pact/U.S.-Japan Security Treaty signed(entered into force in 1952)
1953		First prefectual rally for reversion of Okinawa held; the Amami Islands reverted to Japan
1956	Toma.J	"All-Island Struggle" against compulsory land use by U.S. military forces
1959		A U.S. jet fighter crashed into Miyamori Elementary School(17 dead, 121 wounded)
1960	Ota.S	Council for Okinawan reversion to Japan organized; Pres. Eisenhower visited Okinawa
1965	Matsuoka.S	Prime Minisrer Sato visiting Okinawa stated "Japan's postwar will not end unless Okinawa is returned to Japan"; Iriomote *yamaneko* (wildcat)discovered
1968	Yara.C	Yara Chobyo became the first publicy elected governor; B52 crashed in flames
1969		1972 reversion of Okinawa was agreed upon by Sato-Nixon Conference
1970		First post-war Diet members election held; The Koza Anti-American riots broke out
1972		Administrative rights over Okinawa returned to Japan; Okinawa Prefecture established
1975	Taira.K	Okinawa International Ocean Expo held(July 20-January 18, 1976)
1978	Nojima.T	Traffic Regulations altered(*Nana-san-maru*)
1990	Nishime.J	The 1st Worldwide *Uchinanchu* Festival held
1995	Ota.M	Prefectural Citizens Rally to protest U.S. soldier's raping of an Okinawan young girl
1996		An antenna site called "Elephant Cage" in Yomitan was "illegally occupied" by the state
		An agreement reached on total return of Futenma Air Station
2019	Tamaki.D	Shuri castle burns down
2022		The 7th Worldwide *Uchinanchu* Festival held; 50th anniversary of the return to Japan

沖縄文化への招待（参考・引用文献）

著　名	発行年	発行所
日本最期の戦い（沖縄戦記録写真集）	1977 年	月刊沖縄社
沖縄大百科事典（上巻）	1983 年	沖縄タイムス社
沖縄大百科事典（中巻）	1983 年	沖縄タイムス社
沖縄大百科事典（下巻）	1983 年	沖縄タイムス社
（写真集）首里城今・昔	1987 年	那覇出版社
アジアのなかの琉球王国	1998 年	吉川弘文館
沖縄の素顔	2000 年	（株）テクノマーケティングセンター
琉球王国の真実	2013 年	琉球歴史伝承研究所
南城市のグスク	2017 年	南城市教育委員会
南城市の御嶽	2018 年	南城市教育委員会
母と娘が伝える琉球料理と食文化	2020 年	琉球新報社

著者略歴

宮城　信夫（みやぎ　のぶお）

1951 年（昭和 26）　南風原村山川（現・沖縄県南風原町山川）に生まれる
1967 年（昭和 42）　南風原村立南風原中学校卒業
1970 年（昭和 45）　知念高等学校卒業
1975 年（昭和 50）　琉球大学理工学部物理学科卒業
1976 年（昭和 51）　運輸省（現・国土交通省）に航空管制官として入省
2017 年（平成 29）　国土交通省定年退職
2017 年（平成 29）　南山歴史研究会会員
2019 年（令和　1）　南風原町観光協会ガイド
2020 年（令和　2）　『南風原町の歴史散歩』初版出版

MIYAGI Nobuo

1951 Born in Yamakawa, Haebaru Town, Okinawa Prefecture
1967 Graduated from Haebaru Junior High School in Haebaru Village
1970 Graduated from Chinen High School
1975 Graduated from the University of the Ryukyus, Faculty of Science and Engineering, Department of Physics
1976 Joined the Ministry of Transport (currently the Ministry of Land, Infrastructure, Transport and Tourism) as an air traffic controller
2017 Ministry of Land, Infrastructure, Transport and Tourism retired
2017 A member of the "Nanzan History Study Group"
2019 A guide for the "Haebaru Town Tourist Association"
2020 "A Historical Walk in Haebaru Town：Revealing the Legends of the Hometown" first edition published

沖縄文化への招待　Sketches of Okinawa World

ISBN 978-4-89805-243-3 C0020

2022 年 12 月 24 日　印刷
2022 年 12 月 27 日　発行

著　者　宮　城　信　夫
発行者　武　石　和　実
発行所　榕　樹　書　林

〒 901-2211　沖縄県宜野湾市宜野湾 3-2-2
TEL.098-893-4076　FAX.098-893-6708
E-mail:gajumaru@chive.ocn.ne.jp

印刷・製本　（有）でいご印刷　〒 901-0152 那覇市小禄 878-5　TEL 098-858-7895